Alexander to Constantine

The Anchor Yale Bible Reference Library is a project of international and interfaith scope in which Protestant, Catholic, and Jewish scholars from many countries contribute individual volumes. The project is not sponsored by any ecclesiastical organization and is not intended to reflect any particular theological doctrine.

The series is committed to producing volumes in the tradition established half a century ago by the founders of the Anchor Bible, William Foxwell Albright and David Noel Freedman. It aims to present the best contemporary scholarship in a way that is accessible not only to scholars but also to the educated nonspecialist. It is committed to work of sound philological and historical scholarship, supplemented by insight from modern methods, such as sociological and literary criticism.

JOHN J. COLLINS
General Editor

The Anchor Yale Bible Reference Library

Alexander to Constantine

Archaeology of the Land of the Bible

VOLUME 3

Eric M. Meyers Mark A. Chancey

Yale UNIVERSITY PRESS
AYBRL   New Haven and London

Published with assistance from the foundation established in memory of Calvin Chapin of the Class of 1788, Yale College.

Designed by Sonia Shannon.
Set in Garamond type by BW&A Books, Inc., Durham, North Carolina.
Printed in the United States of America.

Library of Congress Cataloging-in-Publication Data
Meyers, Eric M., and Mark A. Chancey
Alexander to Constantine : archaeology of the land of the Bible, volume 3 / Eric M. Meyers and Mark A. Chancey.
    p.   cm. — (The Anchor Yale Bible Reference Library)
   Includes bibliographical references and index.
   ISBN 978-0-300-14179-5 (alk. paper)
   1. Bible—Antiquities. 2. Palestine—Antiquities. I. Title. II. Series.
BS621.M39   1990
220.9'3—dc20   88030999

A catalogue record for this book is available from the British Library.

This paper meets the requirements of ANSI/NISO Z39.48–1992 (Permanence of Paper).

10 9 8 7 6 5 4 3 2 1

In memory of David Noel Freedman, biblical scholar par excellence, who conceived the idea of the Anchor Reference Series and this volume, and

In honor of Mark's brothers David, Keith, and Andy

Contents

Preface

This volume has a bit of history behind it. The idea originated when David Noel Freedman was editor in chief of the Anchor Bible Commentary and Reference Library. Freedman wanted to have a third volume in the Reference Library following the highly regarded initial volumes in the series on biblical archaeology, the first by Amihai Mazar and the second by Ephraim Stern. Although Stern's volume ends with the Hellenistic period and the conquest of Alexander the Great (332 B.C.E.), our volume offers a very short review of the material from the Persian period, which in recent years has seen much new work and consequently its importance for the study of the Bible and the Second Temple in particular has greatly increased. This book in truth takes off where Stern's ends and focuses on the advent of Hellenism introduced by Alexander the Great as the unifying factor that bridges his era with the time of Constantine at the beginning of the fourth century C.E. With the introduction of Greek culture into Near Eastern society, Hellenism became the vehicle that allowed many different cultures in that region and in other regions as well to express themselves in a more universal way. While we lean heavily on material culture throughout our treatment, we give no less attention to the tumultuous intellectual and religious changes that affected world history at key moments in the time periods covered.

For this reason our book is a collaborative one between two scholars with extensive expertise and field experience in archaeology, one trained in Hebrew Bible and Jewish history and the other in New Testament and early Christianity. The transformation of the ancient Near East under the influence first of the Greeks and then of the Romans led to foundational changes in both the material and intellectual worlds of the Levant. In the case of the "lands of the Bible," Hellenism and its stepchild Greco-Roman culture contributed to the ultimate shape and character of the two main religions that emerged from ancient Palestine, Judaism and Christianity; and it was the world of the Bible that took shape in the Second Temple period that definitively enabled early Judaism and Christianity to evolve in the distinctive ways they did, both in the land of the Bible and beyond.

Let us say up front that even though we pay attention to the many varied literary sources at our disposal we have in no way undertaken any systematic treatment of them—the intertestamental writings, all the biblical books, or the Dead Sea Scrolls. In considering this wealth of material we have only been able to point to some of the main ways that they contribute to our understanding of the periods under consideration. In the same manner we have not attempted to gather all the archaeological data that might inform some aspects of the subjects in our study but have instead highlighted what we believe are the most significant or representative aspects of the material corpus of data for discussion and elucidation, especially those that enhance the historical narrative that we may infer from the major literary sources. To maintain the accessibility of the text for a broad audience, we have tried to keep bibliographical detail to a minimum. Additional information about individual sites and the contributions of specific excavations is readily available in reference works such as *The New Encyclopedia of Archaeological Excavations in the Holy Land,* for which an updated volume appeared in 2008, and *The Oxford Encyclopedia of Archaeology in the Near East.* We have avoided the organizational templates of the volumes by Mazar and Stern, which had technical sections and chapters devoted to particular categories of artifacts (pottery, metal and stone artifacts, seals and seal impressions, and so on), opting instead for a chronological and thematic structure. Geographically, our focus is on ancient Palestine although we occasionally incorporate material from nearby areas.

It is clear that already in the Persian period Greek culture was interacting with Jewish and other local cultures in the land of the Bible. At the level of material culture, Hellenism affected the aesthetics of city building and artistic decoration with sculpture, painted pottery, and other objets d'art. In literature and language it meant that Greek would become the new lingua franca of the Near East and that Semitic writers would adapt new writing styles in history and entertainment literature, with some, like the author of the Book of Ecclesiastes (Qoheleth), reacting to the Hellenistic world. Similarly, in the recounting of the Books of Maccabees we may observe the head-on culture clash between those who embraced the new Hellenized world and those who rejected it.

Dealing briefly with such matters from a literary and historical perspective allows us to place the successive developments in the larger context of what was happening in the greater Near East. Indeed, the rise of Hellenism and its later adoption and adaptation by the Romans imposed a kind of global feature and overlay to ancient civilization that lasted all the way to the early medieval period. We believe that this aspect of the period is what makes it different from both earlier biblical history and later antiquity. It is also why we have blended together in a single narrative the two strains of civilization, the material and literary-intellectual, because they are so inextricably tied one to the other.

As most readers know, the Dead Sea Scrolls and the excavation of the site of Khirbet Qumran and the surrounding caves have provided some of the most important new information concerning the periods under observation here. Not only have many of the Scrolls provided unfiltered testimonies to the socio-religious situation on the ground in Judea in late Second Temple times but they have also provided scholars with an entirely new view of the emergence of Scripture at that time as well as the special role that sacred writing played in society. Moreover, the excavation of Qumran and other nearby sites has produced all manner of new evidence that helps us to better understand the complex circumstances of Roman rule from the last decades before 70 C.E. until the Second War with Rome, the Bar Kokhba Revolt (132–135 C.E.). It is impossible to understand adequately the dramatic events before and after the destruction of the Jerusalem Temple in 70 C.E. without recourse to much of this material. We add too a note on the ongoing excavations in Jerusalem, which are shedding new and unprecedented light on the last days of the Second Temple period. We have introduced some of this new data into our discussion as appropriate, but since the bulk of it is not yet published we have done so somewhat sparingly. In the main we have consulted scientifically published material for our presentation.

In turning to the later periods we have relied considerably on the material from Sepphoris for good reason. First, we both have worked together there for years, and many of the rights to images and drawings are the intellectual property of Eric and Carol Meyers. We do believe, however, that Sepphoris in Galilee presents a paradigmatic example of how a major Jewish urban center adjusted to Roman rule and accommodated to Greco-Roman culture in both the short term and the long term. Its evolution as a center of Jewish learning where the Mishnah took shape and where sages for centuries taught their students is proof positive of how comfortable Jews in the Talmudic period were in the complex cultural milieu of Roman-period Galilee. Similarly, the work of the Meyerses has been used in elucidating the history of the ancient synagogue, which in our reckoning began emerging in architecturally distinctive forms at the very same time that the rabbinic writings were being collected and edited at Sepphoris.

Constantine's reign inaugurated a systematic effort to reclaim many of the holy places of the two testaments through the construction of churches, chapels, and monasteries. As any visitor to the land of the Bible knows, evidence of this effort is still abundantly visible. Identifying archaeological evidence of Christianity from earlier centuries, however, remains difficult. Places that have figured prominently in discussions of this topic, such as Capernaum and Nazareth, are addressed critically in our text, as are recent attempts to link inscribed ossuaries with key figures in the Jesus movement, a development that recalls an earlier period when ossuary inscriptions first attracted scholarly attention. To a considerable degree, however, Christianity seems to have faltered in Palestine in the period between the first Jewish revolt and the accession of Constantine, although this observation should not blind us to its flourishing elsewhere in the Semitic Near East or its growth among Gentiles in the larger Mediterranean world.

This work is aimed at a broad audience that includes scholars, students, and the general public. In attempting to keep the text accessible to the general public we have refrained from using diacritical marks and have preferred the more popular spellings of place names. Although we have strived to be attentive to the concerns of readers with interests and expertise in the broader fields of Syro-Palestinian archaeology and classical studies, it is only appropriate, given the volume's place in the Anchor Bible Reference Library, that we foreground implications of the material for understanding Judaism and Christianity. We hope that our collaboration has resulted in a new perspective on the overlapping nature of the evolution of those two traditions and insight into how they eventually went their separate ways.

Acknowledgments

The encouragement of David Noel Freedman, both before and after Mark joined me as co-author, is a major reason for the book's completion. Noel's indefatigable work in behalf of biblical studies and archaeology of the land of the Bible is reflected in the Anchor Bible Commentary, Dictionary, and Reference Series. We are delighted to be part of the continuation of this important publication project with Yale University Press. It was Jennifer Banks at Yale who guided the two of us in the time between Noel Freedman's death and the appointment of John J. Collins as his successor to the editorship. John's involvement with us has been most welcome and we have been greatly aided by his careful reading of the manuscript and his numerous constructive suggestions. The volume is all the better for it and we are most grateful to him for his insights and suggestions. At Yale University Press we also offer thanks to Piyali Bhattacharya, who has assisted us in final preparation of the manuscript and in many technical matters. We also extend our deep gratitude to Phillip King at Yale University Press who has offered many helpful editorial suggestions and helped to oversee the manuscript to final production.

One of the major challenges for us in preparing this volume has been getting appropriate images and permissions. We are grateful to the numerous providers who have allowed us to publish materials and images that illustrate much of what we write about in the book. Among them are the Israel Exploration Society, the Israel Antiquities Authority, the Israel Museum, and the archives of the American Schools of Oriental Research. Carta, Jerusalem, provided our maps, which sometimes use alternative spellings for place names mentioned in the text. In addition we would like to thank Leen Ritmeyer, Balage Balogh, David Hendin, Sharon Herbert, Jonathan Reed and John Dominic Crossan, Mordechai Aviam, Boaz Zissu, Oded Lipschits, J. Andrew Overman, James Tabor, Lori Woodall, Uzi Leibner, Sean Burrus, and Todd Bolen of BiblePlaces.com. Sean Burrus has also kindly assisted with preparing various illustrations.

At Duke University, Mark and I are grateful to Ben Gordon, a graduate student, for his careful reading and comments on an early version of the manuscript and his continuing interest in the book. Another graduate student at Duke, Bradley Erickson, has assisted with organizing and converting all the images and illustrations to digital format. His good cheer in doing a lot of scanning and other related tasks is deeply appreciated and his technical assistance has been invaluable.

Working with Mark has been a genuine pleasure. We have read each other's drafts carefully and shared editorial suggestions easily and peacefully. Our collaboration has been both productive and mutually rewarding.

EMM

My own work on this book would not have been possible without the support of others. I would like to thank the Southern Methodist University Research Council for a grant that helped cover the costs for many of the book's images. Funds for research trips to Israel were provided by another University Research Grant and by a generous Sam Taylor Fellowship from the United Methodist Church's General Board of Higher Education and Ministry. My colleagues in the SMU Department of Religious Studies have been an unfailing source of encouragement and good humor.

It is difficult to describe the excitement I felt when Eric invited me to join him on this project. Eric is one of the formative influences on my academic career. He has always been an excellent teacher and mentor, first as my professor and now as my colleague. I count myself lucky to have him as not only a collaborator but also a friend.

The beginning of my work on this book coincided with the birth of my first child, Gabriel, who has since been joined by a sister, Sally. For the entirety of their young lives, Gabriel and Sally have had to teach this typical academic how to shift gears from the deep mental absorption of doing research to the equally absorbing but far more important (and rewarding) role of parenting. They have tolerated their father's occasional distractedness with good cheer and provided encouragement in ways they could not possibly understand. My wife Tracy Anne has been incredibly supportive, listening to my reports of research findings, acing solo parenthood while I traveled, and helping me maintain a sense of priorities. I realize how fortunate I am to have such a family.

My parents, Gladys and the late Gene Chancey, first exposed me to the riches of the Bible, and my three older brothers David, Keith, and Andy provided models for its serious study. Keith and Andy, in different ways, helped cultivate within me a love for history that I hope comes through in the following chapters. The highlight of my work on this book was when David joined me on a research trip to Israel in 2008. It was the most time he and I had spent together in thirty years, and we learned as much about each other as we did about the archaeology of Israel. I could not have asked for a more fun and rewarding experience. His trip was made possible by the extraordinary generosity of McDonough Road Baptist Church in Fayetteville, Georgia. Dedicating this book to my brothers is but a small way to honor them for all the ways they have taught and shaped me.

MAC

CHAPTER I

The Persian Period and the Transition to Hellenism

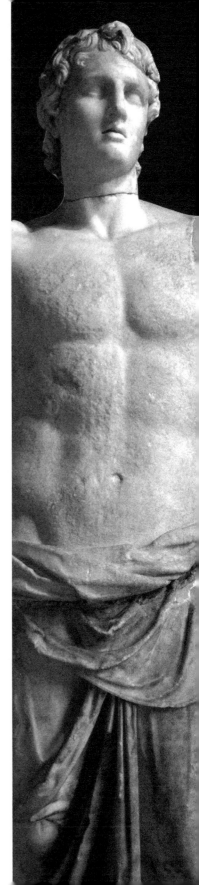

Since the completion of Ephraim Stern's significant volume in 2001 on the archaeology of the land of the Bible, ending with the Persian period, there has been a serious reengagement with the material culture of that period and a renewed interest in its history. The events that are assigned to these years had a major influence on the development of Second Temple Judaism as it was to emerge. Among those are the loss of Judean independence; the return of many Judeans from Exile to the homeland; the rebuilding of the Temple; and the writing, editing, and promulgation of large portions of the Hebrew Bible, all under the oversight of a small, elite community of priests and leaders in the city of Jerusalem.

One of the major new developments since Stern's work has been the interest in and focus on demographics and in particular the size of the Persian province of Yehud and the size and population of Jerusalem. While some of this work had been done earlier and was available to Stern, more recent studies have shown that both the size and population numbers are much smaller than previously thought. Most of the new evidence has been arrived at from new archaeological surveys and excavations, utilizing standard norms of measurement derived from allied fields of research, especially anthropology. Estimates from the 1970s in respect to the population of Jerusalem already had begun to drop by at least half of previous ones. The lower population numbers were found also to carry over into the early Hellenistic period when the city was occupied only on the Southeastern Hill where the so-called City of David is located.[1] The older view adhered to by many scholars held that Jerusalem had approximately 15,000 inhabitants after the return from Exile, whereas from the late 1990s that figure had dropped by one estimate to as low as circa 750 in the time of Nehemiah (fig. 1.1).[2] The majority of scholars until that time, however, still

Fig. 1.1. Jerusalem in the time
of Nehemiah, fifth century
B.C.E. (Reconstruction by
Leen Ritmeyer)

adhered to a figure around 5,000–7,000.[3] In the light of recent excavations in Jerusalem and new survey methods, however, Israel Finkelstein has estimated the population of Jerusalem in the time of Nehemiah (fifth century B.C.E.) to be only about 400 people, including
women and children, and just 100 men.[4] In arriving at this estimate,
Finkelstein assesses the size of the Southeastern Hill at 20–25 dunams
(one dunam equals 1,000 square meters, or a quarter acre). He estimates the entire population of Yehud in the Persian period at around
12,000 people, growing to about 40,000 in the early Hellenistic period, in the 160s B.C.E.; he argues that the population explosion of Judea came only after the Maccabean Revolt, especially in the 140s, by
which time the population had doubled.[5] Even Oded Lipschits's more
moderate view of the size and population of Jerusalem, 20–30 dunams
in the City of David and 20 dunams on the Ophel, and using a population coefficient of either 20 or 25 people per built-up area, brings the
population of Jerusalem in the Persian period only to either 1,000 or
1,250, a factor of two or three times higher than Finkelstein.[6]

The implications of this kind of research are far reaching despite the kind of differences in the estimates. In view of the fact that
so much literary activity—the Deuteronomic history, the last of the

prophets, Ezra-Nehemiah, Chronicles, and so on—is attributed to the Judean leadership at this time, the material data suggest that we need to think more about how so few could do so much even though we know that the leadership was drawn from elite groups of individuals such as priests, scribes, and the like. Moreover, the smaller population numbers that carry over into the early Hellenistic period by all accounts allow us to assess better the accomplishments of the Maccabean rebellion and of the post-Hasmonean era and Roman period when an entirely different demographic took hold and a major population expansion occurred. However, even for the later periods, the kind of research described here has had a major impact on population estimates, and the new, low estimates of the size and population of Jerusalem in the time of Jesus, for example, call into question much of the older research into the matter (discussed in more detail in Chapter 5).

Material Culture

One of the more surprising features of the Persian period that is reported fully by Stern but which bears repeating is that despite the more than two centuries of Persian oversight and control of the Levant and Yehud in particular, and the devastating wars between Greece and Persia in the fifth century, Greek cultural influence rose steadily at the same time, as reflected in the import of Greek Attic pottery. W. F. Albright noted this many years ago and attributed it to the establishment of Greek trading emporia along the coasts of Egypt, Palestine, and Phoenicia in the sixth century. Albright put it this way in his revised edition of *The Archaeology of Palestine* in 1961 (originally published in 1949): "Excavations at these sites have brought quantities of Ionian and Attic black-figured pottery to light. . . . After the beginning of the fifth century Attic red-figured ware replaced Ionian and black-figured ware and soon became one of the most popular imports into the country; vases and sherds turn up in every excavated site of this period. . . . Attic currency . . . became the standard medium of exchange in Palestine more than a century and a quarter before the Macedonian conquest."[7] So popular were these imports from the west that it did not take long for local potters to imitate those fine wares, though they could not duplicate the high quality of manufac-

Fig. 1.2. Persian-period drinking vessel, or rhyton, from Sepphoris (Drawing courtesy of the American Schools of Oriental Research [ASOR], *Biblical Archaeologist*)

ture for which the Greeks were known, mainly the products from eastern Greece, Rhodes, Cyprus, and Athens.[8] Others have also pointed out that although the Persians controlled Palestine there were numerous Greek traders in the area who had probably arrived, as argued, as early as the sixth century, when we first begin to note the presence of Attic black ware at numerous archaeological sites.

Several archaeologists have been successful in identifying and locating Greek trading posts within the Phoenician cities. Even in inland Galilee at Sepphoris, located less than twenty kilometers from the coastal port of Akko, later Ptolemais, we have discovered significant finds from the Persian period where we believe there was a Greek lookout post presumably related to the activities of Greek traders.[9] Given the site's location just south of a major east–west road, an alternative interpretation is that a Persian garrison was stationed there to control the highway. Such troops could well have included soldiers from a variety of ethnicities, including Greek mercenaries. Among the finds from Sepphoris were an Attic black-ware *rhyton,* or drinking or pouring goblet, dated to the late fifth century B.C.E., a jar fragment with an Achaemenid royal inscription in four languages, a small group of limestone-footed incense altars, and hundreds of Attic sherds, all from the fifth to the fourth century B.C.E. (fig. 1.2). From a purely contemporary point of view we find it curious to say the least that at the height of the Persian period at Sepphoris the use and sale of luxury items of Greek manufacture and style are attested at a time when the Greeks and the Persians were at war. Despite these hostilities, the overall impression from the country and indeed the Levant at this time is of the growing influence of Greek culture. We need only point to Tel Dor on the coast to find the best example of a city built on the Hippodamian plan whose closest parallel is Olynthus in Macedonia, which Stern calls a "Phoenician-Greek polis" in the Hellenistic period.[10] The Hippodamian plan divides the residential areas into symmetrical blocks separated by streets that cross one another at right angles. Recently, however, a few scholars have challenged the view that the Greeks were the first to organize the urban layout in such a manner, suggesting that it could even have been a Persian innovation.[11]

Both Phoenicians and Greeks carried out trade in Attic ware imports simultaneously from the beginning. The first Athenian imports to be identified included perfumed oil flasks, *lekythoi* and *am-*

phoriskoi, drinking vessels such as *skyphoi* and the rhyton mentioned above, and kraters for mixing wine. An excavation at Akko, for example, has uncovered a large assemblage of Greek imported pottery that its excavator has associated with part of a merchant's quarter occupied by Greeks in an otherwise Semitic, probably Phoenician environment. The same is true for Jaffa, where a large group of red-figured ware has been found and interpreted as coming from a Greek merchant warehouse. In addition we may point to Greek settlements at Al-Mina, Tel Sukas, and Ras el-Basit in Phoenicia and Tel Dor, Mezad Hashavyahu, and Migdol in Palestine, all of which no doubt served as merchant outposts. Greek tombs have been found at Tel el-Hesi and Atlit. These discoveries, however, only demonstrate the fact that there were Greek traders living in mixed population centers, none of which can be identified as being Jewish in this period, though we have every reason to believe that there were Jews in some of these places.[12]

Fig. 1.3. Classic silver tetradrachm of Athens, 449–413 B.C.E., with a head of Athena on the obverse and an owl on the reverse (Copyright David Hendin, used by permission)

The adoption of the Athenian owl on coins of the province of Yehud from the early Persian period, along with other symbols or motifs familiar from Athenian coins, indicates the orientation of the Jewish leadership on the eve of the Hellenistic period (fig. 1.3). Dated by consensus to the fourth century B.C.E., the tiny coins that have been discovered so far come mainly from the Jerusalem area and Jericho and were clearly minted in Yehud. In recent years, however, many more coins of this type have turned up in the market and at the site of Khirbet Qeiyafa in the Shefelah between Socho and Azekah. The word *yhd* is stamped in paleo-Hebrew and had the secondary meaning of Jerusalem (see 2 Chr 2:26, 28).[13] Other symbols include bearded men's heads with helmets, crowns, or turbans; women's heads; falcons; the lily; and the "god's ear" (fig. 1.4).[14] A smaller group of coins with the *yehud* stamp on them in Aramaic along with the title of "governor," or *peha,* and the personal name of *yhzqyh* (Ezekias) often have the owl on one side and the Greek goddess Athena on the other side. In addition, many coins have been found with motifs of various griffin heads, and the head of a young man with or without a crown. This corpus of coins is dated to the end of the Persian period as well. Also, several coins of Yehud with the names of priests on them have been found, such as *yehohanan hakohen,* or "Yochanan the priest." One very large Yehud coin has been understood to come from the Persian satrap Bagoas, and is dated to the mid–fourth century, the only Yehud

Fig. 1.4. Silver Yehud coins struck before 333 B.C.E. The two coins on the left are local copies of Athenian coins; other coins from this region copy heads of the Persian king or his satrap. The coins at right depict the lily, an ancient symbol of Jerusalem. (Copyright David Hendin, used by permission)

coin thus far known to be minted from an authority higher than the local governor. The numismatic evidence from the late Persian period thus accords with the familiar picture, namely, of a province administered by governor and priest and reporting to a higher authority—in the case of this last coin, the satrap of the province of Beyond the River. The introduction of the Attic standard and the Athenian owl along with the image of Athena attests to the growing appeal and influence of Greek culture, which as we have noted was the case also in architectural planning and in imported pottery.[15]

To the corpus of Yehud coins we may add the growing array of Yehud seals and bullae that have been identified and dated to the Persian period (fig. 1.5). We mention the archive published by Nahman Avigad, which has helped greatly to resolve the debate over the so-called governor gap after Zerubbabel. Among those seals was the important black scaraboid one mentioning Shelomit, *amah* or "maidservant" or official of Elnathan, governor circa 510–490 B.C.E. Shelomit is apparently the last of the Davidic descendants to serve in a high-ranking office and was probably the daughter of Zerubbabel (1 Chr 3:19).[16] Most of the corpus of seals has been discovered from sites in Judah and Benjamin and is supplemented from Avigad's postexilic hoard, presumably from Judah.[17] All have Aramaic on them and mention either "governor" or a personal name along with the name of the province, *yhwd*. However, there has been and continues to be a debate over the date and sequence of many of these items, with a number of scholars suggesting to lower the dating of some items to as late as the second century B.C.E. Hopefully, the publication of the recent excavations at Ramat Rahel by Oded Lipschits will shed further light on these items and settle some of the paleographical issues.[18] We already

know that the excavation produced 302 new Yehud stamps dated to the Persian period, and we may infer from the expansion of the site at that time that Ramat Rahel functioned as an administrative center especially for the collection of taxes.[19]

On the Eve of the Hellenistic Period

The last years of Persian rule in Palestine and in the provinces were as chaotic as ever. The fourth century was dominated by the reign of Artaxerxes II Memnon (404–358 B.C.E.), during whose tenure in office the Persian Empire began its final decline. First Artaxerxes fought with his younger brother, Cyrus, over the succession, the war being described in Xenophon's *Anabasis*. During this time the Egyptians rebelled and sent an expeditionary force to Palestine to pursue the Persians, taking control of the northern part of the coastal plain and for a short time part of the Phoenician coast including Akko and Sidon as well. By 397 B.C.E. the Egyptians were no longer part of the Persian Empire, but by 385 B.C.E. the Persians had repelled their forces and expelled them from these coastal areas along with their allies from Cyprus. From 366 to 360 B.C.E., however, another rebellion, called "the revolt of the satraps," had broken out, which brought back the Egyptians to Palestine along with many Greek mercenaries. Artaxerxes III Ochus (358–336 B.C.E.) had helped to put down the satrapal revolt but soon was faced with another rebellion led by Tennes, king of Sidon, who was allied with Pharaoh Nectanebo (359–341 B.C.E.). Artaxerxes III's failure to win back Egypt led him to pursue Tennes with all the strength he had, and subsequently he marched to Sidon with a large army in 345 B.C.E. Sidon was ultimately razed to the ground; subsequently the Persians led by Bagoas marched to Egypt and recovered it in 343 B.C.E. However, Persian hegemony came to an end only eleven

Fig. 1.5. Seals from Yehud. The seal at left, which reads "Belonging to Ahîâb, the Governor," is one of sixteen known examples of the type found from the City of David, Ramat Rahel, and Nebi Samwil. Paleographic considerations date this type to the sixth or the first half of the fifth century B.C.E., early in the Persian period. Middle, an example of a very common type of Yehud stamp, using only the toponym yhwd. Forty-two examples of this type were found from Ramat Rahel, the City of David, Ein Gedi, Rogem Gannim, and Gezer. This type belongs to the Persian period. At right, the text says, "Yehud, Yehoezer, the governor." Six examples of this type are known from Ramat Rahel, the City of David, and Tel Harasim; this is the only one that contains the toponym yhwd, a personal name, and a title. Paleographic considerations suggest a date sometime in the fifth century B.C.E. (Drawing and caption courtesy of Oded Lipschits)

Fig. 1.6. Statue of Alexander the Great, Istanbul Museum, mid–third century B.C.E. (Photo courtesy of Todd Bolen/BiblePlaces.com)

years later, when Alexander the Great conquered the region in 332 B.C.E. (fig. 1.6).

The main question for our readers now is did Judah take part in the Tennes Rebellion along with the Phoenician cities? Supporting an answer of yes, the Jews did participate in the revolt, are Ephraim Stern and Dan Barag, who note ancient allusions to a revolt in the time of Artaxerxes III and the punitive expulsion of a certain number of Jews to the Caspian Sea.[20] Who these Jews were and if the report is true we cannot say. Whatever the reliability of such claims, it is clear that Alexander met strong resistance to his armies only at Tyre and Gaza, though in 332 B.C.E. he met very limited resistance in the form of a revolt by the Samaritans, traces of which have been found in caves in the Wadi ed-Daliyeh where fleeing rebels took refuge and died. Papyri found in the caves indicate that the Samaritans were indeed a very mixed population, with numerous foreign deities included in the names mentioned.[21] Samaria proper, however, along with Judea/Yehud shows no evidence of destruction, giving some credence to the legend that Alexander was welcomed with open arms into Jerusalem without a struggle of any sort. The highly embellished account in Josephus (*Jewish Antiquities,* cited here as *Ant.,* 11.329–39) adds that Alexander prostrated himself before the High Priest (333) and even sacrificed at the Jerusalem Temple (336). These exaggerations of Alexander's actions led later generations of rabbis to accord him a place of special recognition in their literature.[22] A Greek version of Alexander's legendary pursuits coalesced into what is known as the *Alexander Romance,* attributed to Pseudo-Callisthenes (2.24), in the third century C.E., which formed the basis of the medieval version. The Greek version was most likely based on more ancient accounts of Alexandrian Jews who wished to bolster their standing in the Hellenistic city.[23]

We should also note that it was on the eve of Alexander's entry to Palestine that the Samaritan Temple on Mount Gerizim was built, around 332 B.C.E., apparently by Sanballat III, grandson of the Sanballat who had opposed Nehemiah's rebuilding of Jerusalem.[24] Though modeled on the Temple in Jerusalem, it was nonetheless an expression of the Samaritans' own national identity. It was undertaken partly as a result of difficulties in getting along with their Judean neighbors, difficulties that eventually led to a final break when

Fig. 1.7. Hellenistic round
tower from Samaria (Photo
courtesy of the ASOR
Archive)

the Hasmonean ruler John Hyrcanus (134–104 B.C.E.) destroyed the
temple in 128 B.C.E. Alexander is reported to have settled Macedonians in Samaria as a result of their opposition to him. The rebuilding
of Shechem just a few kilometers from Mount Gerizim at this time after a long abandonment and the construction of the Hellenistic round
towers at Samaria around this time also may well be related to these
tumultuous events and lend further credence to the ancient reports of
Macedonian settlers being introduced to shore up support for Alexander after his experience with the Samaritan rebels (fig. 1.7).[25]

The Advent of Hellenism Under the Greek Kingdoms and the Hasmoneans (332–37 B.C.E.)

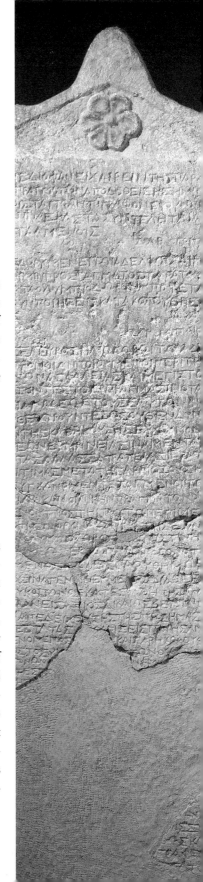

Alexander the Great's conquest of the ancient Near East could not have happened had the Greeks not prevailed over the Persians in the years of turmoil that followed the Greco-Persian wars. The fate of the West would have been quite different had the Persians defeated the Greeks and moved to extend their rule into Europe. The Greek trage-dian Aeschylus captures the significance of these events in his play *The Persians,* which records the momentousness of the times:

> Nations wail their native sons,
> Who by Xerxes stuffed up Hell;
> Many heroes, Persia's bloom,
> Archers, thick array of men,
> Myriads have perished. Woe O King of noble strength
> Cruel! Cruel! Asia kneels.[1]

In a very real sense, the conquests of Alexander the Great rank among the most important events in world history. Tutored by Aris-totle, Alexander was motivated by the idea of pan-Hellenism, which he saw as a way of uniting the world under a common culture, a blend-ing of East and West under the umbrella of what we call Hellenism. In the Jewish people, Alexander encountered a Semitic nation deeply rooted in its ancient customs and beliefs that focused on a group of sacred writings that summarized its heritage from a variety of points of view. Many would like to understand this encounter between Ath-ens and Jerusalem solely as a clash of civilizations; we would like to propose that another way to understand what occurred over the next six hundred years or so is a kind of confluence or convergence of cul-tures that often allowed the conquered people to develop in new ways and to absorb aspects of Greek culture without sacrificing its indepen-

dence of thinking and beliefs. For Jewish civilization Hellenism became a vehicle by which Jewish culture could effectively express itself
and preserve its ways. The degrees to which the Jewish community in
various places and at various times accomplished this sort of accommodation is the focus of much of the rest of this volume.

One of the reasons it is so complicated to assess the degree of
Jewish acculturation to Hellenism is that the precise nature of Greek
culture varied from place to place and from time to time. So the kind
of Hellenism one encountered in the Phoenician cities in the third
century B.C.E., for example, was different from what one found in
Alexandria in the first century C.E. or in Antioch, or Ephesus even
later still, where one might find what Erich S. Gruen has called a
kind of hybrid version of Greek culture. In the Near East, then, the
term "Hellenistic" conveys the "complex amalgamations . . . in which
the Greek ingredient was a conspicuous presence rather than a mo-
nopoly."[2] According to Josephus's legendary account from four centuries later, however, the Jews welcomed Alexander and all that he
signified and in his honor named their firstborn males Alexander
(*Ant.* 11.329–39).

In earlier scholarship "Hellenistic Judaism" was usually associated with Diaspora Jewish life where the language of daily communi-
cation was Greek. With the publication of Martin Hengel's influential
Judaism and Hellenism in German in 1969 and in English in 1974, however, many scholars have wanted to characterize the Judaism of both
Palestine and the Diaspora after Alexander as "Hellenistic." While this
works to a certain extent if we understand the term "Hellenistic" as
a kind of blending of Semitic and Greek cultures, we will endeavor
to refine this terminology somewhat in the hopes of identifying the
most salient features of Palestinian Jewish culture, or what was most
distinctive or common about Judaism and Jewish culture in the homeland. To be sure, it was Greek language and culture that enabled the
Bible to be exported to new lands in the form of the Septuagint and
Jewish ideas and beliefs to be understood in terms of Greek philoso-
phy in the works of Philo of Alexandria, not to mention Jewish history from the point of view of Josephus. But the distinctiveness of Judaism is best understood first in terms of its own Semitic, local, and
indigenous environment and context, and it is only then that we can
better understand its true nature and identify the accretions that come

from without and often strengthen those Semitic beliefs and practices. For the time being we will maintain a verbal distinction between Judaism in the homeland—that is, in Eretz Israel, the Land of Israel—and Judaism in the Diaspora.

The Greek Cities: The Ptolemies and the Seleucids

The most effective means of introducing the new culture into what was then known as Coele-Syria was through the founding of new cities or refounding of existing ones as Greek *poleis*. As might be expected, many of the resettled cities had long and distinguished prehistories. In the case of Beth Shean, for example, which had served as a major Egyptian stronghold in the Bronze Age (sixteenth to twelfth centuries B.C.E.), it was resettled along the flat plain and stream below the tel in the Hellenistic period when it became known as Scythopolis (fig. 2.1). In some cases, such as with the Macedonians in Samaria, the imposition of foreign settlers was designed as a strategy for changing

Fig. 2.1. Aerial photograph of Beth Shean, showing Roman-Byzantine city (Photo courtesy of Todd Bolen/ BiblePlaces.com)

the character of a city and controlling it. A Greek legislative council or *boule* with up to several hundred members would have been established to rule the city, and Greek deities would have been introduced into the religion of the city along with appropriate entertainment and educational institutions. For many cities these would have included a stadium for races, a theater for performances, and a gymnasium for the training of youth in mind and body into an ephebate, although for cities in Palestine, evidence for these features is often lacking. The *polis* usually had a walled area in the center with smaller satellite settlements nearby that provided food and other necessaries to the city. Although the establishment of these cities began soon after Alexander's conquest, the process of urbanization took a considerable amount of time over the next century to complete, and in view of what we have said about the nature of Hellenism each of the cities managed to maintain a bit of its own distinctive character. Among the most prominent of these cities were Samaria, later known as Sebaste; Beth Shean, later renamed Scythopolis; Banias (Paneas), later known in the first century as Caesarea Philippi; Antiochia; Seleucia; Arbila; Akko, renamed later as Ptolemais; Dor; Strato's Tower, later known as Caesarea Maritima; Gaza; Mareshah/Marissa or later Eleutheropolis; Tyre; and Sidon. In addition, this network of Greek cities enabled them as a whole to reinforce the work of one another in the commercial and cultural realms, which had the effect of spreading the new forms of culture that were taking shape.

After Alexander's conquest of Egypt in 332/1 B.C.E. and mild resistance he met in Samaria en route to the east, he continued on to India where his troops would go no further (fig. 2.2). He died in Babylon as he reversed directions in 323 B.C.E. As a result his generals moved forward to make rival claims for much of his conquered territories; this troubled period is known as the period of the Diadochi or "successors" (321–301 B.C.E.). Palestine or Coele-Syria became a major bone of contention between the two main rival factions since it was the land bridge between Asia and Africa and hence a key strategic location in the Fertile Crescent with its excellent harbors and port cities; and it had been traditionally viewed as a major political objective of various conquering peoples. The most powerful of Alexander's generals was Antigonus, but Ptolemy challenged him for control of Coele-Syria; Antigonus was finally defeated and killed at the Battle of

Fig. 2.2. A silver tetradrachm showing Herakles and Zeus, with the name Alexander under an eagle, and the mint Akko, from 315/314 B.C.E.; at right, a gold stater featuring a bust of Athena wearing a helmet on the obverse, and winged victory with the name Alexander on the reverse, from 317/316 B.C.E. (Copyright David Hendin, used by permission)

Ipsus in 301 B.C.E. A tentative agreement between Ptolemy and Seleucus reached some years earlier about the status of Coele-Syria was not honored, and the next century was punctuated by the five Syrian Wars in which the Seleucids challenged Ptolemaic control of the region. Huge destruction levels at Ashkelon and Dor provide vivid testimony to such a reality.

In the main, however, the Ptolemies took control of Palestine and south-central Phoenicia, and the Seleucids controlled northern Phoenicia and Syria. This began a phase of urbanization and urban transformation that was to continue through the Roman period. As a result, the Ptolemaic authority sent a number of soldiers, merchants, and other officials to Palestine to exercise control of the area and collect taxes, but in the main the number of foreign individuals remained somewhat low in relation to the indigenous population (fig. 2.3).[3] Any number of new cities and sites were developed, and although there was not a dramatic increase in population in Palestine till the Hasmonean period, a gradual increase may be noted for the third century. Chief among the sites that were developed and fortified to some degree, though all existed in various earlier periods, were Akko (Ptolemais, the tel and lower city), Samaria, Shechem, Mount Gerizim (temple and lower city), Gezer, Jaffa, Mareshah (the tel), and Gaza.[4] In many ways the new infrastructure that was imposed from the outside contributed more than anything else in promoting a new world order and Hellenistic way of life. This seems to contrast with the experi-

Fig. 2.3. Three Ptolemaic coins struck in port cities of Israel. At left, a silver tetradrachm of Ptolemy II, minted at Gaza, with a portrait of Ptolemy I on the obverse. Center, a gold octodrachm of Ptolemy III, minted at Joppa, with a depiction of Arsinoe II (mother of Ptolemy II) on the obverse. At right, a silver tetradrachm of Ptolemy V (204–180 B.C.E.), minted at Dor. (Copyright David Hendin, used by permission)

ence during the Persian period, when Persian officials kept a safe distance from the local population and in no way tried to impose their language or culture. Most affected by this change in the style of occupation was the leadership in Judea and Jerusalem. Nonetheless, evidence from coins and jar inscriptions indicates that the role of the high priest was maintained if not strengthened.

Despite the high tension between the rival factions for control of Palestine, the third century may be viewed as a time of relative prosperity and quiet. Extensive commercial activities were resumed and local products from Palestine such as oil, wheat, and wine were highly valued and taxed, and we have extensive documentation of these matters in the form of the Zenon papyri that date to midcentury.[5] Zenon was the private agent of Apollonius, the finance minister of Ptolemy II (285–246 B.C.E.). One of the Zenon papyri, an anonymous letter to Zenon written circa 256–255, reads in part:

> to Zenon greeting. You do well if you keep your health. I too am well. You know that you left me in Syria with Krotos and I did every thing that was ordered in respect to the camels and was blameless toward you. When you sent an order to give me pay, he gave me nothing of what you ordered. When I asked repeatedly that he give me what you ordered and Krotos gave me nothing, but kept telling me to remove myself, I held out a long time waiting

for you; but when I was in want of necessities and...get
nothing anywhere, I was compelled to run away into Syria
so that I might not perish of hunger. So I wrote you that
you might know that Krotos was the cause of it. When
you sent me again to Philadelphia to Jason, though I do
everything that is ordered, for nine months now he gives
nothing of what you ordered me to have, neither oil nor
grain, except at two month periods when he also pays the
clothing (allowances). And I am in difficulty both summer
and winter. And he orders me to accept ordinary wine for
salary. Well, they have treated me with scorn because I am
a "barbarian." I beg you therefore, if it seems good to you,
to give them orders that I am to obtain what is owing and
that in future they pay me in full, in order that I may not
perish of hunger because I do not know how to act the
Hellene. You, therefore, kindly cause a change in attitude
toward me. I pray to all the gods and to the guardian
divinity of the King that you remain well and come to us
soon so that you may yourself see that I am blameless.[6]

Additional products that were exported from Palestine included
smoked fish, cheese, various meats, dried figs, fruits, honey, and
dates. Ptolemy I (323–285 B.C.E.) had already in his day established
a tax supervisor for revenues from Syria and Phoenicia. The new tax
system, however, had no apparent negative effect on the coastal economy, which appears to have thrived during this period. Beginning
with Ptolemy II, coins were minted at seven coastal cities: Berytus
(Beirut), Tyre, Sidon, Akko (Ptolemais), Jaffa, Ashkelon, and Gaza
but at no inland city. Even in Jerusalem huge quantities of Rhodian jar
handles have been discovered in excavations, most dating to the mid–
third to second centuries B.C.E. Since these jars were used for the import of wine from the island of Rhodes it raises the question to what
degree the Jewish population at this time was sensitive to the matter of
associating Gentile wine with idolatrous practices, a concern reflected
in the later prohibition against drinking Gentile wine.[7] It is unlikely
that a garrison in the Acra of Jerusalem would have consumed all this
wine. This sort of consumption as well as the general picture we are
able to reconstruct of the time indicates that Judea and the coastal

areas were increasingly Hellenized, though we could not say the same for Galilee, where there was no urban center till much later and the repopulation of the area had not yet begun.[8]

From this brief description of some of the commercial activities of the times it is easy to understand how the southern areas and coastal cities especially were the real prize as far as the battling dynasties were concerned. The first three wars between the Ptolemies and the Seleucids did little to change the status quo, but by midcentury, after the death of Ptolemy II Philadelphus in 246 B.C.E. and during the Third Syrian War, the Jewish high priest in Jerusalem, Onias II, who had been accustomed to a good deal of power and control over both religious and fiscal matters including tax collecting for the Ptolemies, refused to pay taxes to Ptolemy III (246–221 B.C.E.). The clear motivation for such a dramatic action was to become more independent and wealthier, but in doing so he sided with the Seleucids in the Third Syrian War (254–241 B.C.E.), which tilted the balance in their favor. As a consequence of this action Joseph, the son of Tobias and the nephew of Onias, was dispatched to Ptolemy by the Jerusalemites in hopes that he could persuade Ptolemy not to take retributive action against them. Joseph, with his winning ways and humor, succeeded and, according to Josephus's narrative, became the chief tax farmer for the Ptolemaic government for all Coele-Syria, Phoenicia, Judea, and Samaria (*Ant.* 12.169, 175).

The consequence of all this was that the rivalry between the two families, the Oniads and the Tobiads, only intensified. The Tobiad family had a long and distinguished pedigree that went back to pre-exilic times.[9] During the restoration period, the Tobiads may even have played a special role in guarding the "crowns" in the Temple (Zech 6:14). The family is also known from the Persian period at Iraq el-Emir in Transjordan where there is a well-known Aramaic inscription with their name in a cave near the site that has been authenticated, most likely pointing to their burial place.[10] Tobias and his son Joseph the Tobiad accumulated his great wealth there during the third century as chief financial officers of the Egyptian Ptolemies. Although much of the site of Iraq el-Emir dates to the second century B.C.E., it was probably occupied in the previous century when the family controlled a large stretch of farmland nearby. Also from the first quarter of the second century at the same site a large trading em-

Fig. 2.4. Qasr el-Abd, Tobiad palace built circa 169 B.C.E. Josephus describes the palace as a "mighty manor" akin to a fortified residence. The northern facade (shown here) features a monumental entrance distyle in antis, and there is another on the southern facade. (Photo courtesy of the ASOR Archive)

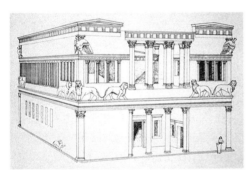

Fig. 2.5. Reconstruction drawing of the Qasr el-Abd Tobiad palace. Its twenty-one fluted Corinthian columns on the east and west sides amply demonstrate its Hellenistic character. (Drawing courtesy of the Department of Classical and Near Eastern Studies, University of Minnesota)

porium or fortress, the Qasr el-Abd, has been associated with the family, its high-relief felines decorating the four corners of the structure (figs. 2.4, 2.5). The site of Iraq el-Emir was discovered in the nineteenth century by the British and the Germans, and Paul Lapp was the first American to excavate there on behalf of the American Schools of Oriental Research (ASOR); Charles Butler was the first to publish a reconstruction of the Qasr el-Abd.[11] Josephus describes the estate, which the last of Joseph's sons, Hyrcanus, built with the wealth that he inherited from his father: "[Hyrcanus] built a strong fortress, which he constructed entirely of white marble up to the very roof, and had beasts of gigantic size carved on it, and enclosed it with a wide and deep moat. He introduced also a vast quantity of waters which ran along it, and which were very delightful and ornamental in the court.

He also made caves of many furlongs in length . . . and then he made large rooms in it, some for feasting, and some for sleeping and living in. But still he made the entrances at the mouth of the cave so narrow that no more than one person could enter by them at once. . . . Moreover, he built courts of greater magnitude than ordinary, which he adorned with vastly large gardens" (*Ant.* 12.230–33).

The congruence of Josephus's text with the actual site at Iraq el-Emir, especially the Qasr el-Abd, makes the identification with the Tobiad family estate absolutely certain. The much embellished account in Josephus (*Ant.* 12.154–236) has been called the "Tobiad Romance," taking its inspiration no doubt from the story of Joseph in Genesis (39–47), who like Joseph the Tobiad had risen to the highest echelons of society where he enjoyed much political clout in the Egyptian court. While there are many nuggets of history in the tale of the Tobiads, only when read alongside other documents and with the archaeology in mind can we infer any reliable information from the Josephan narrative.

Most notable of the achievements of this era is the translation of the Hebrew Bible into Greek during the reign of Ptolemy II Philadelphus.[12] The translation is traditionally ascribed to the work of seventy-two sages who knew the Torah and who were fluent in Greek and who were brought to Alexandria from Jerusalem to do the work. The account of the translation is conveyed in the Letter of Aristeas, and the term "Septuagint" is taken from the Latin for seventy, referring to the seventy-two sages. Whatever the degree of accuracy in this account the point to emphasize is the extent to which Greek language had penetrated Jewish life in Egypt at this time or by the third century B.C.E. The fact is that the first Greek translation of the Torah at this time made it possible for Jewish thought to be read and understood in the Diaspora where Hebrew was not the lingua franca.[13] By the second century B.C.E. other major Jewish works had to be translated into Greek as well, most probably for the Egyptian Jewish community. The most famous of them is the Wisdom of Jesus Son of Sirach, also known as the Wisdom of Ben Sira, indicating that the spread of Greek in Egypt at this time had greatly accelerated. About two-thirds of the book has survived in Hebrew. It was translated around the year 132 B.C.E. by the author's grandson, who writes in the prologue that even with all his good efforts once the Hebrew is rendered into Greek it loses quite a bit: "You are invited therefore to read it with goodwill and attention, and to be indulgent in cases where, despite our diligent labor in translating, we may seem to have rendered some phrases imperfectly. For what was originally expressed in Hebrew does not have exactly the same sense when translated into another language. Not only this book, but even the Law itself, the Prophecies, and the rest of the books differ not a little when read in the original."[14] A fragmentary copy in Hebrew found at Masada in 1964 suggests that the book was being read in Hebrew in Palestine in late Second Temple times.

The Yehud Coins and Jar Handles

The Hellenistic Yehud coins appear in the early part of the third century and continue well into the Ptolemaic era, being attested through the reign of Ptolemy II. Although only a small number have been found in controlled excavations it is fairly certain that the Yehud issues were minted in Jerusalem or its environs. As we have already seen, the earlier coins and bullae from the Persian period refer to the governor, whose name and title (*peha*) disappear from the Yehud series in the Hellenistic period. The reason for this development is not entirely clear, but with the rapidly changing social and economic scene in the third century and the growing politicization of the temple establishment, especially the high priesthood, we may understand this new pattern to reflect the new political realities and changed conditions of the third century B.C.E. The regular design of the coins in the time of Ptolemy I, which bear either his image or that of his consort Bernice, and the Ptolemaic eagle, point to the strong influence of the Egyptian Ptolemies, who had direct responsibility for administering Coele-Syria; the Hebrew inscriptions on them appear to be of secondary importance. The denominations are very small and the tiny silver coins were intended to serve a constituency that was limited in size and wealth. If this is the case then, and given the absence of the term for governor on any examples, we may suggest that authority had shifted to the high priesthood, a likely scenario in view of the subsequent further politicization of the office at the end of the century and beginning of the next.[15]

The fact that the Ptolemies took control over the Yehud coins early in their rule, within decades of their conquest of Palestine, and that the coins were nearly standardized, indicates the degree to which they were interested in the minutest details of the administration of Yehud from Alexandria. The minting of local coins, however, in no way suggests that Yehud during this time had any higher degree of independence or even administrative autonomy than before. Moreover, the coinage ends in the reign of Ptolemy II. In addition, the very small denominations show that they were intended for only minimal exchanges. Together with the Zenon papyri and the Tobiad estate, the Ptolemaic coins illustrate the degree to which the southern Levant and Transjordan were integrated into the Ptolemaic kingdom and how the rulers exploited the local populations in the third century. Whether one can consider this corpus of numismatic material as supporting a case for rapid Hellenization, as some do, is not clear. At the very least the coins suggest that Judean traditions remained very strong and utilized Hellenistic symbols and conventions to promote their own political and religious agenda.

The discovery of the bilingual (Greek and Aramaic) ostracon, from Khirbet el-Kom, located between Hebron and Lachish, in 1971 along with four other ostraca in Aramaic and one in Greek, indicates how even as far south as Idumea the Greek world of commerce had penetrated.[16] Dated to the "year 6" of the reign of Ptolemy II, or 277 B.C.E. by the excavator, the text included a Semitic transliteration of the Greek term *kapelos,* probably "moneylender," referring to someone named Qos-yada who had lent thirty-two drachmas to a Greek by the name of Nikeratos. The text suggests that the Idumeans, like the Jews in other parts of Coele-Syria, were deeply affected by the growing monetization of the local economy and that parts of the population were already multilingual. But the use of Greek in these instances may only provide evidence that those individuals inhabiting the military installation at Khirbet el-Kom were capable of engaging in financial interactions with the Greek-speaking world.

Another group of artifacts, some of which date to the third century, may assist us in the task of reconstructing the world of that century. These inscribed stamps with YHD on them or a shortened form have turned up in large numbers of late, with most coming from the recent excavations at Ramat Rahel (fig. 2.6).[17] Oded Lipschits and David Vanderhooft have identified a "middle type" that does not bear

Fig. 2.6. Inscribed stamps from Yehud. The first is an extremely popular form, with more than 96 examples across 9 subtypes. This type contains only the toponym yhd and lacks the waw. Dates paleographically to the fourth century B.C.E. At middle is one of two subtypes of the most common from of Yehud stamp impression, counting 175 examples. These impressions read yh, dropping the daled. Paleographic and stratigraphic considerations indicate a date in the later half of the fourth century B.C.E. The bottom example, known only from Ramat Rahel, has been read by Lipschits and Vanderhooft as an overlapping yod and he, a variation on the preceding example, and perhaps a transitional type between earlier yh stamp impressions and later types. Only a general date of the fourth to third century C.E. can be suggested. (Drawing and caption courtesy of Oded Lipschits)

any personal names as the earlier ones from the Persian period do, and they date the later ones to the fourth–third century B.C.E. Yehud coins from the same period have been most helpful in establishing a chronology using paleographical analysis. The corpus points to an administrative continuity between the Persian and Macedonian through the Ptolemaic period, possibly down to the Seleucid period. The next change in this artifact class occurs in the second century B.C.E., during the Hasmonean period. The distribution of the Yehud stamp impressions in the Hellenistic period before the Hasmoneans shows the increasing importance of Ramat Rahel as an administrative center for the collection of taxes in kind and trade. While numerous subtypes from this period have been identified, their similarity indicates an increasing consolidation and centralization of provincial power in the Jerusalem area, with Ramat Rahel the major administrative center and Nebi Samwil and Tel en-Nasbeh serving as lesser administrative centers.

The Initial Impact of Hellenization

What can we say about the nature of evidence for the Hellenization of Palestine at this time? To be sure we have observed increasing signs of Greek culture reflected in language, symbols, coins, and the socio-economic world that was enveloping the region and dominated by the Egyptian Ptolemies. Palestine and the various ethnic groups within it to differing degrees began to absorb the new international culture in architecture as well as internal affairs (fig. 2.7). But as we have said

Fig. 2.7. Hellenistic tomb of a Sidonian at Mareshah, in use from the third to the first century B.C.E. The painted tomb with arcosolia provides striking evidence of the early traces of Greek influence in Palestine. (Photo courtesy of Todd Bolen/BiblePlaces.com)

already, the greatness of Hellenism was that it did not require of its newly conquered peoples that they give up their indigenous ways; rather, it often allowed them to express themselves within the new culture in ways that were true to their own tradition. At another level, however, the speed with which Greek culture spread did not pick up significantly till the second century B.C.E., when we have increasing evidence for Greek monuments and architecture. Judea, as before in the Persian period, remained more or less encircled by Hellenistic settlements and the military in the west on the coastal plain, in Idumea to the south, Samaria to the north, and Transjordan to the east. This is not to say that Greek ideas could not have penetrated by this time, and indeed the author of the Book of Ecclesiastes reflects the changing world about him and the new and acquisitive age that was dawning before his very eyes.[18] At a time when there was not yet a true belief in eternal life in Jewish society, the author writes of "futility" (1:1) and that all humanity will meet the same end (9:3–6) regardless of actions taken on earth. No doubt also influenced by the changing social and economic scene, Ecclesiastes is surely reacting to the effects of the Ptolemaic domination of the local economy, which affected the class structure in Palestine in a definitive way. The rise of a new middle class was among the most significant developments. By the Seleucid period and the Hasmonean Revolt, however, the Book of Daniel embraces a view of eternal life and resurrection (12:2–3), partially the result of the debilitating wars with the Seleucid rulers, in which the author of chapters 7–12 accepts passive resistance and martyrdom as the way to fight evil.[19]

One of the ways in which the introduction of the concept of an afterlife affected burial customs is that in the Hellenistic period a key change from the Iron Age and Persian periods occurred, namely, the introduction of the coffin or individual burial receptacle. Notwithstanding that Jews continued to bury in subterranean chambers, the inauguration of the separate burial container corresponded to growing notions of individual identity in death. This contrasted strongly with the Iron Age custom of gathering the bones of the dead and placing them in pits or benches in underground tombs, reflected in the biblical expressions "to sleep or be gathered to one's ancestors." In the Hellenistic and Roman periods the containers of the bodies or bones of the dead were often inscribed with the names of the deceased.[20]

Indeed, the cumulative impact of the growing Hellenization of Palestine during the Persian and early Hellenistic periods is reflected in the events that led to the Maccabean uprising and the complex interactions of the temple leadership with the various powers that were vying for control over their lives as well as the Temple and its treasury. This is the story of the second century B.C.E., when important elements of the priestly establishment and allied elements of the population became embroiled in serious and misguided attempts to change the character of the holy city of Jerusalem and of the high priesthood itself. It is to that story we now turn.

The Maccabean Revolt

The struggles between the Ptolemies and the Seleucids for possession of Syria, Palestine, and nearby territories continued for well over a century after Alexander's death. The issue was not settled until the Fifth Syrian War, when the Seleucid king Antiochus III triumphed over Ptolemaic forces at the Battle of Paneas (Banias) and gained control of the region circa 200 C.E. The Seleucids soon faced challenges from a new direction, however, as Rome began its ascent as a major power. The Romans defeated the Seleucid army at the Battle of Magnesia in western Asia Minor in 190 B.C.E., stopping Seleucid expansion westward, and the Peace of Apamea two years later required large indemnity payments by the Seleucids to Rome. When the Seleucid ruler Antiochus IV attempted to conquer Egypt in 168 B.C.E., the Romans forced him to withdraw.

As it entered the second century B.C.E., Palestine thus found itself in a political environment characterized by shifting power dynamics. Such developments, however, did not hinder the ongoing diffusion of Hellenistic culture. We have noted that conquered societies sometimes absorbed aspects of Hellenistic culture, using it to find new ways to create and express their own cultural identities. On other occasions, subject peoples constructed their identities by resisting Hellenistic ways. The processes of interaction between Hellenistic and local cultures were complex and variegated, and individual societies experienced conflict over which aspects of Hellenism to adopt or adapt and which ones to reject. Such tensions were clearly evident in Seleucid Jerusalem as factions competed for political power and for the priesthood, and the introduction of Hellenistic customs resulted in fissures in the Jewish community.

The weakening of Seleucid rule allowed these intra-Jewish debates to play out in a new political context of growing autonomy. The Maccabees emerged as leaders, launching a successful revolt against the Seleucids in 167 B.C.E. that resulted in the establishment of the Hasmonean dynasty. Although the Hasmoneans remained under the Seleucid shadow for decades, their rule marked a level of independence that Jews in Palestine would not experience again until 1948. Over the next century, the Hasmoneans increased the territory under Jewish control to an extent that rivaled biblical descriptions of the kingdoms of David and Solomon. Their conquests resulted in demographic shifts in parts of Palestine as some Gentiles left to escape Hasmonean rule, others apparently adopted Jewish ways, and Jewish colonists established new communities. The Hasmoneans and their subjects readily embraced some dimensions of Hellenistic culture while spurning others, and archaeological remains attest to the new ways that Jews and other peoples found to construct and express local and ethnic identities.

Tensions between the Seleucids and their Jewish subjects often centered on Jerusalem. Second Maccabees 3 reflects discomfort with Seleucid interaction with the Temple, preserving a legend in which only the appearance of heavenly defenders prevented the Seleucid official Heliodorus, acting on orders from the king, from taking money from the Temple treasury. A stele from 178 B.C.E. provides context for this story, recording that Seleucus IV had appointed an individual named Heliodorus as the overseer of temples throughout Coele-Syria and Phoenicia (fig. 2.8). This Heliodorus is likely the same individual referred to in 2 Maccabees 3.[21]

Seleucid officials were not the only objects of distrust in the intrigue that surrounded the Temple, as Jewish figures competed for the powerful position of high priest. The rivalry between two contenders for the position, Jason and Menelaus, led to civil war circa 170/169 B.C.E., and Antiochus IV responded to the instability by invading Judea, plundering the Temple, and constructing the Akra fortress to house a garrison to keep watch over Jerusalem. Because no archaeological evidence from the fortress has yet been discovered, its location is unknown.

Seleucid suppression of Jewish unrest included prohibition of Jewish traditions like circumcision, Sabbath observance, and the sacrificial cult and even the defiling of the Temple with pagan sacrifices. Harsh measures prompted the Maccabean Revolt in 167

Fig. 2.8. The Heliodorus Stele (178 B.C.E.) documents in Greek Seleucus IV's (187–175 B.C.E.) intention to oversee temples in Coele-Syria and Phoenicia (Photo courtesy of the Israel Museum)

Table 2.1. The Maccabees and Hasmoneans

Judah	164–161 B.C.E.
Jonathan	161–143 B.C.E.
Simon	143–135 B.C.E.
John Hyrcanus I	135–104 B.C.E.
Aristobulus I	104–103 B.C.E.
Alexander Jannaeus	103–76 B.C.E.
Alexandra Salome	76–67 B.C.E.
Hyrcanus II and Aristobulus II	67–63 B.C.E.

B.C.E. Jewish forces led by Judah and his brothers, sons of the priest Mattathias, succeeded in retaking Jerusalem and rededicating the Temple, although conflicts with Seleucid forces continued for decades. Eventually, the new Jewish state achieved sufficient stability and security to enjoy genuine autonomy, led by the Hasmonean dynasty, so named for the priestly ancestor Asamonaios (in Hebrew, *Hashman*) of Judah and his brothers (*Ant.* 12.265).

The Expansion of Jewish Territory

Maccabean struggles with the Seleucids were not limited to Judea proper, and Jewish forces often made major incursions into surrounding areas to the north, east, and west (fig. 2.9). Judah attacked Mareshah and Hebron in Idumea, Azotus near the coast, and Gilead and elsewhere in the Transjordan (1 Macc 5:1–8, 24–44, 65–68); his brother Simon campaigned in Galilee (1 Macc 5:9–23). After the death of Judah, his brothers succeeded in capturing the important coastal sites of Jaffa, Ashkelon, and Gaza. Jonathan ventured into Galilee and beyond, reportedly going as far northwest as the Tyrian village of Kedesh and as far northeast as Damascus (1 Macc 11:60–74, 12:24–53). These battles are usually not discernible in the archaeological record, though the timing of the temporary abandonment in the mid-140s B.C.E. of a large administrative building at Kedesh corresponds nicely with reports of Jonathan's northern activities in 1 Maccabees 11:60–64 and 12:24–53. Over two thousand clay sealings show that the building was a government archive; the reoccupied archive was later burned, though by whom is unclear.[22]

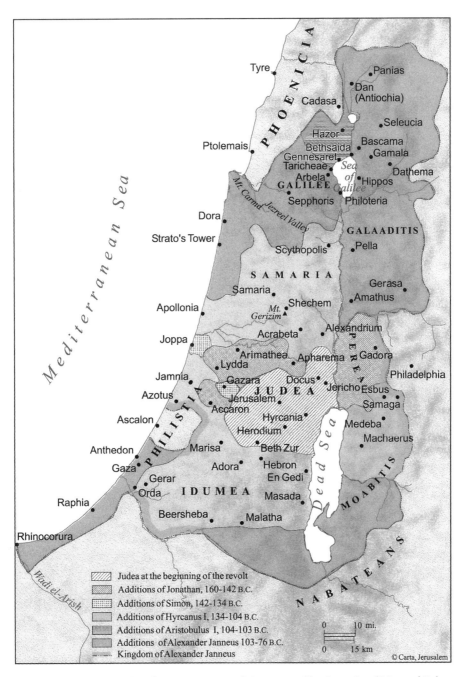

Fig. 2.9. The Hasmonean kingdom, 143–63 B.C.E. (Map prepared by Carta, Israel Map and Publishing Company, Ltd.)

The Maccabees' rise to power led to significant changes in the administration of the Temple. High priests had traditionally been from the lineage of the ancient priest Zadok (2 Sam 20:25; 1 Kgs 4:2, 4), but around 153/152 B.C.E., Alexander Balas, a claimant to the Seleucid throne, appointed Judas's brother Jonathan to the position (1 Macc 10:18–44). After Jonathan's death, his brother Simon succeeded him; a sympathetic account (1 Macc 14:41–47) claims that a stele erected circa 140 B.C.E. proclaimed Simon commander and ethnarch as well as "leader and high priest forever until a trustworthy prophet should arise." Later Hasmonean coins show that members of the dynasty often proudly placed the title of "high priest" on their currency; contemporary Iturean coins with similar inscriptions demonstrate that the combination of ruler and priest was not uncommon in the region.[23] No doubt the usurpation of the temple leadership contributed to the divisiveness in Jewish society during the early Hasmonean period, and some scholars have identified it as a cause for the foundation of the communal site at Khirbet Qumran and the emergence of the sectarians alluded to in several of the Dead Sea Scrolls. The fact that the settlement there cannot be dated before 100 B.C.E., however, suggests a much more complex set of circumstances behind the establishment of that community.[24] Regardless of any public opposition they encountered, Hasmonean rulers had the prestige, power, and authority of the position of high priest for over a century. They held it until the time of Herod, who in around 36 B.C.E. had the last Hasmonean priest, Aristobulus III, drowned in his swimming pool at Jericho (*Ant.* 15.50–56) and began appointing priests of his own choosing.

Simon expelled the last of the foreign garrison from the Akra fortress circa 142 B.C.E., leveling it to the ground, and achieved a new level of independence from the Seleucids (1 Macc 13:41–53; *Ant.* 13.217; Josephus, *The Jewish War,* cited here as *War,* 5.139). The removal of the threat posed by the Akra in the heart of Jewish territory allowed the Hasmoneans to focus on the conquest of new areas, a development that in turn led to a sizable increase in the number of their subjects as well as the strengthening of the agricultural and economic base. Simon first turned his attention westward, conquering Gezer and Beth-Zur (1 Macc 13:43–48, 14:6–7).[25] How Beth-Zur fared under Simon is not entirely clear, though archaeological evidence suggests the site was abandoned circa 100 B.C.E., several decades after its reported capture. Changes at Gezer are much easier to discern.[26] First Maccabees says that Simon "removed the uncleanness" from the city (14:7) and settled in it "those who observed the law" (13:48)—that is, he drove out the Gentile inhabitants and replaced them with Jews. A late Hellenistic destruction layer seems to reflect Simon's siege of the city, and a Greek inscription records the ill will of one of its inhabitants for the Hasmonean ruler: "Pamparas [wishes] that fire should fall on Simon's palace."[27]

The city was rebuilt with new walls and a new gate, and archaeological finds confirm that its new residents were Jews. Several of the houses built in the late second or early first century B.C.E. were equipped with small stepped pools cut into bedrock, installations that most archaeologists regard as Jewish ritual baths (*miqvaot*) on the basis of their general similarity to those described in later rabbinic sources. The practice of removing impurity through ritual immersion was prescribed in the Torah;[28] Jewish literature from the late Second Temple period records the use of the practice to help remove impurity caused by a variety of factors such as childbirth, menstruation, genital discharges, and corpses.[29] The appearance of specially constructed pools devoted to the purpose appears to be a new phenomenon of the late Hellenistic period. The oldest ritual baths in Judea date to the second half of the second century B.C.E. "From that period on, the ritual baths have been found at every farm, estate, or village" in Judea.[30] When the Hasmoneans expanded into Galilee around 100 B.C.E., the custom spread there, too, as late-Hellenistic-period baths at Sepphoris attest.[31] These baths reflected the importance of ritual purity in early Judaism, an emphasis that would be seen in both rabbinic and New Testament literature.

Bilingual stone markers established the city's limits: Hebrew inscriptions read "boundary of Gezer," while Greek inscriptions read "belonging to Alkios," apparently referring to an otherwise unknown owner of adjacent land. The stones were placed so that the Greek inscriptions faced away from Gezer and the Hebrew inscriptions faced inward. Thus, they not only demarcated the city's physical territory but also symbolically separated a community for whom Hebrew was the preferred epigraphic language from neighbors for whom that language was Greek. The markers may have indicated the Sabbath limit beyond which one could not carry items as is explained in the much later Mishnaic tractate of *Erubin*.

Simon's refusal to pay tribute to the Seleucid king Antiochus Sidetes VII prompted the latter to invade. Antiochus's forces waged war not only on the Hasmoneans but also on the Seleucid rival Tryphon (1 Macc 15:10–14, 25, 40ff). Lead sling bullets attest to the battle for Dor between the Seleucid factions, bearing inscriptions that hope "for the victory of Tryphon."[32] When Simon died, around 135 B.C.E., his son John Hyrcanus inherited a tense situation. Antiochus's forces eventually besieged Jerusalem (*Ant.* 13.236), and Hyrcanus preserved the city only by reinstituting the payment of tribute, becoming a Seleucid client ruler until the death of Antiochus, circa 129 B.C.E. Numerous ballista stones, bronze arrowheads, and lead sling bullets recovered in excavations at the fortifications adjacent to the modern Jaffa Gate likely originated from this battle.[33]

With the decrease of the Seleucid threat at Antiochus's demise, Hyrcanus initiated a series of campaigns to increase his territory. Josephus provides a long list of conquered cities and regions: Madaba across the Jordan; Mareshah and Adora in Idumea; Scythopolis (Beth Shean) on the southern border of Galilee; Mount Gerizim, Shechem, and the city of Samaria (*Ant.* 13.254–58, 275–80; *War* 1.63–65). The archaeological record corroborates Josephus's claims in some cases. At Beth Shean, the substantial settlement on Tel Istabah suffered a major fire at the end of the second century B.C.E., though amphora handles bear dates as late as circa 80 B.C.E., making the picture there complex; the more modest occupation atop Tel Beth Shean itself continued. On the coast, a destruction layer and subsequent new phase of occupation at Ashdod might reflect Hyrcanus's conquest, and at Shiqmona, an amphora with an inscription naming a market official dates the destruction of a fortress to 132 B.C.E., squarely in the reign of Hyrcanus. At Mareshah, the damage and abandonment of the lower city soon after 112 B.C.E. should probably be attributed to the Hasmoneans. Josephus reports that after Hyrcanus's conquest, the Idumeans adopted Jewish ways (*Ant.* 13.258), and later strata from the Roman period provide evidence of a Jewish presence in Idumean territory in the form of limestone vessels, which reflect purity concerns (discussed in Chapter 7).[34]

The most vivid archaeological evidence of Hyrcanus's conquests comes from the region of Samaria. The temple and the settlement

Fig. 2.10. A coin of Judah Aristobulus (104 B.C.E.). On the obverse is the legend "Yehudah the high priest in community of the Jews" surrounded by a laurel wreath; the reverse shows a pomegranate between double cornucopia. At right is a schematic view of the coin. (Copyright David Hendin, used by permission)

overlooking Shechem on Mount Gerizim dating back to the Persian period were completely destroyed and buried under a massive layer of ash. Attempts to strengthen the city's defenses by blocking windows, doors, and streets, constructing additional walls, and stockpiling food and supplies left their marks in the archaeological record but were insufficient to ward off the Hasmoneans. Seleucid coins date the conflagration to 112–111 B.C.E. or shortly thereafter, demonstrating the inaccuracy of Josephus's dating of the destruction to 128 B.C.E. (*Ant.* 13.255–57).[35] Shechem itself fell a few years later; the latest coin in the destruction layer there dates to 107 B.C.E. By then, the city of Samaria had also fallen; though no massive destruction layer has been found, damage to the upper city's wall may be associated with the battle, and it is often thought that a temple to Serapis-Isis went out of use at approximately this time.[36] Elsewhere in the region, the Hasmonean conquest was probably responsible for the destruction of a farm at Tirat Yehuda and the abandonment of several others. New settlements began appearing, perhaps due to the arrival of Hasmonean colonists. The subsequent population would be a diverse mixture of Samaritans, Jews, and pagans.[37]

When Hyrcanus's son Aristobulus rose to the throne, he "took the diadem" (*Ant.* 13.318), becoming the first Hasmonean to claim the title of king. Another title he took fully illustrated his affinity for the trappings of the Hellenistic monarch: Philhellene, "friend of the Greeks" (*Ant.* 13.301; *War* 1.70); Aretas, king of the neighboring Nabateans, would later also employ the title.[38] Aside from coins, his one-year reign left few archaeological remains (fig. 2.10). Although Josephus claims that Aristobulus conquered the territory of the Itureans, an Arab tribe dwelling in the vicinity of Mount Hermon, Mount Lebanon, and Anti-Lebanon, excavations in those areas have found no hint of conflict or cultural change. To the contrary, Iturean habitation appears to have continued steadily and within a few decades Iturean coinage appeared. Although Aristobulus's Iturean campaign has sometimes been associated with the Hasmonean annexation of Galilee, this linkage now appears questionable. Pottery finds suggest that any penetration of Galilee by the Itureans was minimal, so the region would not have been the primary focus for an expedition against them, though any forces traveling from Judea to Iturean territory would have passed through or near it.

Under Alexander Jannaeus, Hasmonean territory reached its maximum extent (*Ant.* 13.324–97, 14.18; *War* 1.86–87, 104–5). Josephus claims that Jannaeus took the coastal cities of Raphia, Gaza, Anthedon, and Strato's Tower, although efforts to seize Akko (Ptolemais) and Ashkelon failed (*Ant.* 13.395–97). East of the Jordan, he attacked Jerash, Gadara, Amathus, Pella, Dium, and perhaps Hippos and campaigned against the Nabateans. To the north, his forces moved into Gaulanitis and took Seleucia and Gamla. Patches of destruction and the remains of a burned house at Pella may reflect Jannaeus's conquests, but activities in other cities are not easy to corroborate.[39] The general portrayal of territorial expansion finds strong support, however, particularly north of Judea, with evidence falling into three main categories: the abandonment of older sites, the establishment of new ones with subsequent Roman-period strata attesting to Jewish inhabitants, and the widespread appearance of Hasmonean coinage.[40] Despite his military successes, Jannaeus still faced a worrisome Seleucid threat and had to deter an incursion by Antiochus XII Dionysos circa 86 B.C.E. A line of fortifications and towers found along the southern bank of the Yarkon River may be related to the wall stretching from Antipatris to Jaffa that Josephus reports Jannaeus built for defense (*Ant.* 13.390–91).[41]

If evidence for Aristobulus's conquest of Galilee is lacking, evidence that the region was in Jewish hands by the end of Jannaeus's reign is abundant, and the predominantly Jewish population of the Roman period has its primary historical roots in Hasmonean colonization in the early and mid–first century B.C.E.[42] Throughout the region, some sites went out of use, others appear to have had a change of occupants, and new settlements appeared. Hasmonean coins at Khirbet esh-Shuhara in eastern Upper Galilee show that it was resettled after having been destroyed a few decades earlier.[43] Numismatic finds at Jotapata and Meiron provide striking testimony of change: the influx of Seleucid coins ceased and that of Hasmonean coins began. The fortifications at Shaar ha-Amaqim were abandoned, those at Jotapata were renovated, and new ones were constructed at Khirbet el-Tufaniyeh.[44]

Especially in Upper Galilee, the changing ceramic profile illustrates shifts in settlement patterns. In the western part of the region, users of Phoenician jars began slowly retreating toward the coast, leaving behind their inland sites. Toward the east, Galilean Coarse Ware, a pinkish-gray pottery with white grits that had been common around Mount Meiron, began to disappear, and many of the sites that had used it were abandoned. It was replaced in later decades by the new pottery from Kefar Hananyah that was favored by Jewish communities.[45]

At some Upper Galilean sites, cultic objects were destroyed. The temple dating back to the Persian era at Mizpeh Yamim—the only pagan temple found in the interior of Galilee from the Second Temple period—went out of use in the early first century B.C.E., despite having been renovated only a few decades earlier, and figurines there were broken. Three pagan figurines were likewise damaged at Beersheba of Galilee.[46]

The evidence for Hasmonean expansion beyond Galilee to the north and northeast is mixed. Support is strongest at nearby Gamla, where pottery forms akin to those used in Judea appeared, along with Hasmonean coins and a building that included a miqveh. Farther north, however, Iturean settlement around Mount Hermon continued unabated. The cultic center at Banias continued to thrive, and the large quantity of cooking and dining dishes left behind as offerings suggests that the number of worshipers increased.[47] In contrast, the settlement at Tel Anafa, located in the Huleh Valley 9.5 kilometers south of Banias, was abandoned, presumably in response to the expansion of Hasmonean influence. A community had flourished there around 125–80 B.C.E. The exact identity of its inhabitants is unknown, but the presence of several figurines demonstrates that they were pagans. Among their several buildings was a large residence (38 square meters) that strongly resembled Greek peristyle houses. Constructed using Phoenician-style techniques, its walls were painted and stuc-

Fig. 2.11. Three coins of Alexander Jannaeus, "Yehonatan" (103–76 B.C.E.). At left, a palm branch with "Yehonatan the king" in paleo-Hebrew, and a lily on the reverse. At center, the only Hasmonean coin with a date, reading "King Alexander, Year 25"; on the reverse is an inverted anchor. At right, the same as coin overstruck on an earlier coin. (Copyright David Hendin, used by permission)

coed, often with geometric designs, and its architectural fragments bear Corinthian, Doric, and Ionic motifs. Adjacent to it was a three-room bathing complex with a black and white mosaic and other decorations. The site was thus among the most Hellenized in northern Palestine, and bowls, red-slipped pottery, lamps, imported wines from Rhodes and other Aegean isles, and a cache of garnets and amethysts attest to the wealth of its inhabitants. By about 75 B.C.E., however, it had been completely abandoned.[48]

Archaeological evidence to the south of Jannaeus's territory also shows the limits of his influence (fig. 2.11). He was unable to substantially deter the activity of the Nabateans, and their coins, architectural fragments, and distinctive painted pottery show that their area of settlement and movement expanded from the Transjordan into the Negev and the Sinai, particularly along the northern coastal route. By the end of the first century B.C.E., they had developed an extensive network throughout those areas of caravan routes, trade stations, fortifications, and settlements with temples and other public buildings.[49]

Within the newly enlarged Hasmonean territory, significant changes were occurring in trade networks and pottery usage, a point that Andrea M. Berlin has insightfully demonstrated.[50] Earlier in the second century B.C.E., inhabitants at many sites had imported wine from Rhodes and other Aegean islands, red-slipped pottery such as Eastern Sigillata A from Phoenician cities, and round lamps and various luxury goods. Now, these products began disappearing, their place taken by locally manufactured wares. Around 100 B.C.E., a new large square-rimmed jar replaced earlier forms, and the boundaries of its usage conform closely to those of the Hasmonean kingdom. Such jars were intended to hold liquids, and Berlin suggests that they were probably used for olive oil and wine. Their appearance corresponds to that of an increasing number of olive and wine presses, suggesting

Fig 2.12. Coins of John Hyrcanus, "Yehohanan," (132–104 B.C.E.), with legend "Yehohanan the high priest and community of the Jews." Each coin has a Greek monogram signifying a Hasmonean relationship with the Seleucid kings Antiochus VII (138–129 B.C.E.) and Zebina (128–123 B.C.E.). (Copyright David Hendin, used by permission)

a growing demand for products made within Jewish contexts, rather than imports. Taken together, these trends indicate an increasing economic isolation under the Hasmoneans and perhaps a heightened desire for locally made goods produced by Jewish artisans, craftspeople, and farmers. If the latter suggestion is correct, these patterns correlate to the ongoing work to construct and display Jewish identity in the new political, social, and economic circumstances created by the Hasmonean rise to power.

Jerusalem Under the Hasmoneans

Jerusalem flourished as the center of power for the new Jewish state (fig. 2.12). At the time of the Maccabean Revolt, it consisted primarily of the Temple complex and the eastern hill, where settlement extended down the slope in the so-called City of David area. Literary sources report that the eastern walls of the city and Temple underwent a cycle of destruction, reconstruction, and renovation that lasted for decades as the Seleucids sought to weaken the city's defenses (1 Macc 1:31, 6:62, 10:11; *Ant.* 12.383, 13.41, 13.247), aided on one occasion by an earthquake (1 Macc 12:35–38; *Ant.* 13.181–83), and Jewish leaders seized opportunities to strengthen them (1 Macc 4:36–61, 10:11, 12:35–38, 13:10; *Ant.* 13.41, 13.181–83). For the most part, few archaeological signs of Hasmonean-era work remain, though ashlars in the Temple complex's eastern wall have crude bosses akin to Hasmonean masonry, suggesting that the dynasty extended the platform southward. The Hasmoneans also erected a new fortress north of the Temple that they named the Baris (*Ant.* 15.403). It is often thought to have stood at the site of the later Herodian Antonia Fortress, where Josephus locates a Hasmonean palace (*Ant.* 18.91).[51]

The city expanded considerably toward the west, stretching

across the Tyropoeon Valley into what became known as the "Upper City" and beyond that as far as modern Mount Zion.[52] Defensive towers appeared in the area just inside the present-day Jaffa Gate. Remains of two such towers are visible, and it is likely that a third stood where the so-called Citadel of David, a Herodian foundation with substantial later additions, stands. At some point—estimates range from the reign of Jonathan to that of John Hyrcanus—the Hasmoneans more fully enclosed the city's new territory with a major defensive wall equipped with additional towers. A 200-meter stretch of this wall made of ashlars and fieldstones ran roughly along the line of later Ottoman defenses from the Citadel of David toward the southwest corner of the modern Old City, with segments still visible in the lower courses of the Ottoman wall. An east–west segment of this wall has been discovered in the Jewish Quarter south of David Street, and other parts have been found on the southern slope of Mount Zion. This wall was strengthened several times by later additions and renovations, and given its route it is no doubt the "First Wall" described in detail by Josephus (fig. 2.13). Though Josephus's attribution of it to David and Solomon is obviously mistaken (*War* 5.142–45), the wall does follow earlier Iron Age defenses in places, suggesting that its builders may have been attempting to demonstrate continuity with earlier Israelite history. Lee I. Levine has estimated that the total area encompassed within the First Wall was approximately 160 acres, a size that could have supported a population of 30,000, but other estimates vary considerably. Hillel Geva, for example, has placed the population of Hasmonean Jerusalem as low as 8,000. Israel Finkelstein suggests that the population of all Judea grew from only 42,000 in the 160s B.C.E. to perhaps over 100,000 in the days of Simon (d. 135 B.C.E.), numbers so small as to require a fairly low estimate for the city of Jerusalem itself.[53] The Hasmoneans may also be responsible for what Josephus calls the "Second Wall" (*War* 5.146), though others attribute it to Herod. Josephus briefly refers to this wall (*War* 5.416, 158), but little evidence of it has yet been found.

Despite the Hasmoneans' openness to important aspects of Hellenism, they apparently did not construct typical examples of Greek civic architecture such as a theater or stadium. The gymnasium denounced in 1 Maccabees 1:14–15 and 2 Maccabees 4:12–17 appears to

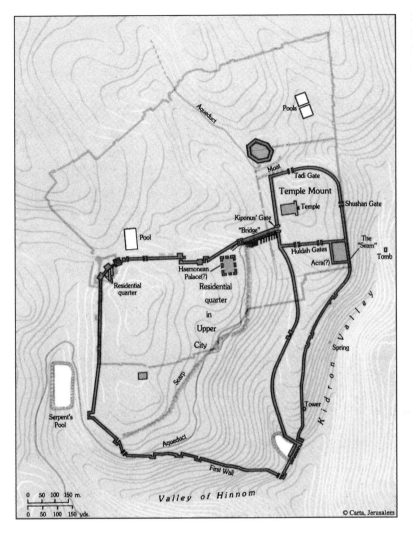

Fig. 2.13. Hasmonean Jerusalem (Map prepared by Carta, Israel Map and Publishing Company, Ltd.)

have completely disappeared, unless the later xystus mentioned by Josephus was somehow associated with it (*War* 6.325, 8.377; *Ant.* 20.189). Little is known of the Hasmonean street plan, but nothing suggests that it was organized on an orthogonal grid. Nor is there much evidence for a new proliferation of inscriptions, public or private.

Another development, however, illustrates a way in which Jerusalem elites adopted a Hellenistic custom to display their status and wealth: the construction of prominent, publicly visible monumental

Fig. 2.14. Tomb of Benei
Hezir, at left (second century B.C.E.), in the Kidron
Valley, Jerusalem, along-
side the Tomb of Zechariah
(first century B.C.E.), both
demonstrating the extent to
which classical architectural
styles influenced tombs in
the heart of Judea at an early
date (Photo courtesy of Sean
Burrus)

tombs outside the city walls. These tombs followed the example of
the Maccabean Simon, who had constructed a monument at Modiin
over the tomb of Jonathan to honor his brothers and parents (1 Macc
13:25–29). Seven pyramids, columns, carvings of ships, and a trophy of
armor decorated it. First Maccabees claimed that it was large enough
to be seen from the Mediterranean Sea, a bit of obvious rhetorical excess. With its close resemblance to monumental tombs elsewhere in
the Hellenistic world, Jonathan's tomb functioned as more than a memorial; it demonstrated the political power, independence, authority,
and abundant resources possessed by Simon.

Jerusalem's examples of early monumental sepulchers included
the Tomb of Benei Hezir, which stood just outside the eastern walls
of the city (fig. 2.14). The tomb was built in the second half of the second century B.C.E., and its name is drawn from a red-painted Hebrew
inscription that associates it with "priests of the sons of Hezir," a family mentioned in 1 Chronicles 24:15 and Nehemiah 10:21. Its interior
chambers had loculi and arcosolia, the types of burial slots that would
be typical of Jewish burials for centuries, while its exterior was decorated with a Doric facade with a frieze, two Doric columns, and a pyramid. Another impressive burial, Jason's Tomb, stood west of the ancient city in what is now the neighborhood of Rehavia (fig. 2.15). Built
in the early first century B.C.E., its use extended well into the first cen-

tury C.E. A pyramid marked its top as well, and three successive courts led up to a porch decorated with a Doric architrave and a Doric-style column flanked by two pilasters. The walls of the porch bore two inscriptions: an Aramaic one names one of the interred as Jason, calls for visitors to lament, and includes the traditional Jewish consolation "Shalom," while a Greek one seems to urge the living to rejoice in the present life. An intriguing combination of charcoal drawings adorned the porch walls: three crudely drawn ships may hint that one of the interred had maritime interests, a palm branch is an early example of a symbol that typifies ancient Jewish art, and five menorot are among the earliest images of the Temple candelabrum. In addition, a drawing of a stag shows that not all Jews shied away from figural representations of living things, suggesting that modern notions of strict ancient Jewish aniconism are incorrect. For some Jews, at least, images were acceptable as long as they were not functioning as idols, a perspective that Steven Fine has labeled anti-idolic. The porch provided access to two chambers, one with kokhim for individual burials, the other with a common bone depository.[54]

The tombs of Benei Hezir and Jason were hardly alone. Josephus's frequent references to the tomb of the "High Priest John" sug-

Fig. 2.15. Jason's Tomb, first century B.C.E., the vault of a wealthy family in Jerusalem built in the classical mode (Photo courtesy of Todd Bolen/BiblePlaces.com)

Fig. 2.16. Monument of
Absalom in the Kidron
Valley, Jerusalem (first
century c.e.), in the shape
of a dome or nephesh on
top, blending east and west
(Photo courtesy of Sean
Burrus)

gest that the tomb of John Hyrcanus was a well-known landmark as
late as the Great Revolt, though its location is no longer known (*War*
5.259, 304, 356, 468, and 6.169). Funerary structures like these are fore-
runners of later monuments such as the recently discovered tomb at
Herodium that likely served as the burial spot of King Herod, the
Tomb of the Kings north of the Damascus Gate, and the Tomb of Absalom and Tomb of Zechariah in the Kidron Valley (fig. 2.16).

The Hasmonean Palace-Fortresses

Although the Hasmoneans possessed a number of palaces in Jerusalem (1 Macc 13:52; *War* 2.344; *Ant.* 18.91), later construction has hidden whatever remains of them. By comparison, the remnants of their desert palaces are much better preserved.[55] The locations of these palaces made them ideal for resorts and places of refuge, and some doubled as fortresses. The buildings made ample use of Hellenistic elements such as Doric and Corinthian columns, bathing facilities, and frescoes and mosaics. They also sometimes included a distinctively Jewish feature, miqvaot, revealing attention to Jewish purity concerns. Architectural fragments from them appear at several sites, such as Kypros, Alexandrium, and Machaerus, and some of the cisterns at Masada may have Hasmonean origins.

The Hasmonean palace from which archaeologists have recovered the most information stood at the oasis of Jericho. Only sixteen miles from Jerusalem, Jericho provided a temperate climate and springs with water abundant enough for the cultivation of dates, balsam, and other crops as well as for luxury use in numerous domestic installations. The earliest mansion there, dubbed the "Winter Palace" by its excavator the late Ehud Netzer, appears to have been constructed during the reign of John Hyrcanus. Built primarily of mud bricks, as was typical of the locale, the structure consisted of at least three wings, and portions of it probably had two stories. A well-designed system of channels connected it to the nearby Wadi Qelt and assured that sufficient water would be available for its various needs. Its northern wing had forty to fifty rooms, including a large courtyard (twenty-five by eighteen meters), a room decorated with stucco panels, a bathing complex with a tub and heating apparatus, and a stepped pool connected by a pipe to another pool, an installation that appears to be a ritual bath with a storage tank (*otsar*). The building's eastern and southern wings have been less extensively excavated, but the latter included a frescoed room that may have been used for dining. West of the complex stood two swimming pools, features that in a desert climate accentuated the palace's lavish nature.

The complex underwent frequent renovation by subsequent rulers. Alexander Jannaeus almost completely rebuilt it, covering it with a mound of earth, constructing a new fortified palace atop it, and digging a new pool to replace one that he had filled in. Two additional swimming pools provided the architectural focus of a new structure to the northeast, each surrounded by a large paved plaza and a colonnaded garden, with additional gardens to their east and west. Alexandra Salome may have been responsible for the construction of two more buildings that the excavator has called the "Twin Palaces" because of their similarity in design and size (25.5 by 22.5 meters). Each had an internal courtyard accompanied by a rectangular room decorated with frescoes and black and red stucco as well as pooled gardens, a plastered bathtub, and a miqveh. New structures with pools and miqvaot appeared in later decades, one of which included Hellenistic-style bathing facilities. An earthquake that struck the region in 31 B.C.E. appears to have leveled the entire complex, allowing Herod the Great to fashion a new palace according to his own tastes.

The Minting of Hasmonean Coinage

The mints of the Hellenistic kingdoms had increased the amount of coinage throughout the eastern Mediterranean, but as the power of the Ptolemies and Seleucids waned, cities and local monarchs themselves increasingly began striking currency. By the late second and early first centuries B.C.E., coastal cities in the southern Levant that had previously served as royal mints, such as Tyre, Sidon, Ptolemais, Gaza, and Ashkelon, were issuing their own coins. The Nabateans minted coins perhaps as early as the late second century B.C.E., and the Itureans began five decades of minting activity in 73/72 B.C.E. Most of these new mints issued only bronze, though the Nabateans and a few cities (such as Ashkelon, Ptolemais, Tyre, Sidon) also struck silver coins.[56]

When the Hasmonean rulers struck their first coins in the final decades of the second century, they were conforming to this larger regional pattern. Exactly when they began to do so is unclear. According to 1 Maccabees 15:6, Antiochus VII gave Simon the right to mint coins circa 139 B.C.E., but any minting he did must have been minimal, as no coins associated with him have yet been found. Coins have been identified with the reigns of John Hyrcanus I, Aristobulus (probably I), Alexander Jannaeus, Mattathias Antigonus, and perhaps Hyrcanus II, with those of Jannaeus being particularly numerous and widespread. Aside from a few lead coins minted by Jannaeus, all Hasmonean coins were bronze. For silver, the Hasmoneans relied on Tyr-

Fig. 2.17. Coins of Mattathias Antigonus (40–37 B.C.E.), the last Hasmonean king. The coin at right is extremely rare; the obverse depicts a Temple showbread table with the legend "Mattatayah the high priest," and the reverse has a seven-branched menorah surrounded by "Of king Antigonus" in Greek. This is the only depiction of a menorah on an ancient Jewish coin. (Copyright David Hendin, used by permission)

ian and to a much lesser extent Sidonian shekels and half-shekels. The sizes and weights of Hasmonean pieces vary considerably, making it difficult at times to identify their denominations, though the smaller ones are generally associated with the *prutah* system mentioned in later rabbinic literature. In general, the coins seem closer to the Attic standard used by the Seleucids than to the Phoenician standard.[57]

Most Levantine coinage bore images of royalty, deities, mythological figures, and animals. Nabatean coins, for example, bore busts of the monarch as well as images of deities such as Tyche and Nike, while Tyrian shekels depicted an eagle on one side and Herakles-Melqart, patron deity of the city, on the other.[58] In contrast, Hasmonean coins avoided anthropomorphic and zoomorphic imagery. They displayed a variety of symbols, such as a lily, palm branch, helmet, anchor, wreath, double cornucopiae, and what appears to be a star and diadem. Such symbols were hardly unique; cornucopiae, for example, had appeared elsewhere on Mediterranean coinage, and a lily and anchor had appeared on Seleucid coinage. In drawing images from the standard repertoire, the Hasmoneans were participating in the numismatic culture of the larger Hellenistic world. At the same time, these images differentiated Jewish coins from those with figural representations. Only coins from the last Hasmonean ruler, Mattathias Antigonus, bore what might be described as uniquely Jewish symbols: some depicted a menorah, and others portrayed what may be the showbread table from the Temple (fig. 2.17). In using designs that linked himself to the Temple, Antigonus perhaps sought to legitimize his political stature.

This range of images shows how the Hasmoneans used coins to construct Jewish identity. Subordination to the Seleucids, the memory of subordination to the Ptolemies before that, and the increased contact with neighboring peoples brought about by their own expansion may have heightened the Hasmoneans' desire to distinguish themselves from other authorities with their coins, the most widely circulating medium for advertising their political power among their subjects. Coins of other peoples might depict living things, but their own did not. Nonetheless, the presence of anthropomorphic and zoomorphic imagery on foreign coins did not disqualify them from usage in Jewish territory, suggesting that the Hasmoneans and the inhabitants of their territories were not as aniconic as they are often thought to be.[59] Not only did the Hasmoneans rely on Tyre's mint for silver, they also seem to have instituted the half-shekel tax that brought that city's image-bearing coins into the heart of the Jewish Temple.[60]

Hasmonean coins also differed from others in the region in their less prominent use of Greek. Only a few Greek characters and monograms appeared on coins of Hyrcanus I, which had primarily Hebrew inscriptions written in archaic characters, not the Aramaic script that had been the norm since the Persian period. Subsequent Hasmonean coins continued to employ this ancient script, which symbolically connected the dynasty to earlier eras of Jewish history. The coins of Alexander Jannaeus and Mattathias Antigonus sometimes had only Hebrew inscriptions, although at other times they included both Semitic and Greek inscriptions. Such coins reflected an attempt to combine a distinctive aspect of local and ethnic culture, the use of a Semitic language, with the region's standard numismatic convention of Greek.

The names and titles inscribed on Hasmonean coins also show how Jewish and broader Hellenistic culture interplayed. Although the Hasmonean rulers took Greek names, those names did not always appear on their coins. Coins of John Hyrcanus, for example, bear only the name Yehohanan and those of Judah Aristobulus only Yehudah, while Alexander Jannaeus and Mattathias Antigonus placed both their Semitic and Greek names on theirs. The title of "king" did not appear until the coins of Alexander Jannaeus, but the title of "high priest" appeared throughout the Hasmonean era, and claims to be the "head of the council of the Jews" marked the currency of some rulers.

Sectarian Judaism and Common Judaism

Literary sources attest to the emergence in the Hasmonean period of new sects with contesting ideas of how to be Jewish. Josephus first mentions the Pharisees, Sadducees, and Essenes in his discussion of Hyrcanus (*Ant.* 13.171–73, 288–99), and it is clear that the first two groups in particular competed for favor and power for the rest of the Hasmonean era. The Essenes seem to have been less politically prominent, though Josephus and Philo describe them as numerous (*War* 2.124; Philo, *That Every Good Person Is Free*, 12.75). Evidence for an Essene Gate and Quarter in Jerusalem may be dated to the Herodian period and probably to the first century C.E., though more recent excavations there by Shimon Gibson are not yet published.[61] At least one other scholar has tried to relate Jewish villages or "poorhouses" in the Judean heartland to Essene settlements, but these are dated to the first century C.E. also and the evidence is far from conclusive.[62] The extent to which the Dead Sea Scrolls should be associated with such groups in Jerusalem or in greater Judea, or with any other sect let alone with the earliest remains at Qumran, is still a matter of vigorous debate, though the majority of scholars today favor an association between the scrolls found in the caves at Qumran and the community at the site, which does not negate any possible connection with other groups described in the scrolls who might have lived elsewhere (as discussed in Chapter 4). All the sects differed in matters of theology, halakha, and sociological composition, although the lines between them were not always sharply defined. Thus, although the Sadducees are often associated with the Temple on the basis of references in Acts (4:1, 5:17) and Josephus (*Ant.* 13.297 and 20.17, where he characterizes them as aristocratic), Pharisees could be priests, too, and one need look no further for an example than Josephus himself. The Sadducees are usually assumed to have taken their name from the traditional Zadokite priesthood, but some Dead Sea Scrolls also show interests in the line of Zadok.

   All of these groups were concerned with ritual purity, and their appearance dovetails with that of miqvaot at the Hasmonean palaces, Jerusalem, Gamla, Gezer, and Qumran. Indeed, the number of pools and their great size at Qumran is nothing less than remarkable, with ten serving a population that probably numbered only around 150.

The increase in the number of miqvaot throughout Jewish parts of Palestine in the decades following the Hasmonean period shows that many Jews (sectarian or not) shared the fundamental premise that some level of purity was desirable (though not necessarily required) and were open to new practices such as bathing in a specially created pool to help them achieve that status. In addition to the discovery of many ritual baths in the urban context in late Hellenistic times, Boaz Zissu and David Amit report that one to seven ritual baths have been found in rural settlements; the wide variety in the number of ritual baths per site, however, may or may not reflect demographic factors.[63] Ritual baths from the late Second Temple period have also been found near major roadways, probably intended for pilgrims headed to Jerusalem; inside wine and oil presses, so that wine and oil could be prepared in a way that accorded with purity rules; near cemeteries, so that individuals who attended funerals and contacted secondary impurity could purify themselves before going home.[64]

Ritual baths have also been found at the royal desert fortresses built and maintained first by the Hasmoneans and later by Herod the Great. Zissu and Amit conclude that the attestation of these extensive remains of ritual baths in the Hasmonean and Herodian periods strongly support the view of E. P. Sanders that "ritual purity was a central feature of common Judaism."[65] Although we do not have precise numbers on how many miqvaot there are from these periods, we may simply say that they are extensive. Extracting specific data on which Zissu and Amit base their work, ritual baths existed (in domestic contexts in Judea) at Jerusalem (Upper City), Jericho (Hasmonean palaces), Masada (Western Palace, near storerooms), lower Kypros, upper and lower Herodium, Gezer, Horvat Ethri, Kiryat Sefer, Nahal Yarmut, Horvat Burnat, and Qalandia. They also mention that at Horvat Ethri in the Shefelah and at Horvat Rimmon in the Judean desert the ones in domestic contexts were in general "small," able to accommodate individuals in single family units, while there were larger units at locations where rain and groundwater from drainage could be more easily collected in dry seasons and used for community emergencies.[66] They are quick to comment that these do not compare to the "exceptional" size and nature of the ones at Qumran, which could accommodate many individuals on a regular basis in the dry climate of the Dead Sea area. The best known ritual baths associated with synagogues are at Gamla, Masada, and Herodium, with examples also known from Horvat Ethri and Khirbet Umm el-Amdan. Explanations for their special location alongside synagogues vary but once again focus on purity concerns, including ritual hand and foot washing or accommodating special guests who would need to go to a ritual bath.[67]

Despite the emphasis ancient texts and modern scholars have placed on the sects, most Jews may not have identified with any particular group, and too much attention to their differences may obscure what they held in common: an identification with the biblical people of Israel, fidelity to the Torah, and the maintenance of distinctive customs such as Sabbath observance, following biblical dietary laws, and circumcision. E. P. Sanders's notion of a "common Judaism" practiced by priests and laypeople alike finds support in the increasing similarity displayed in the material culture of Jewish sites throughout Palestine from the late Hasmonean era onward, embracing more features than ritual baths.[68] Such features include stone vessels, evidence of special dietary habits, and distinctive burial customs.

The beginning of the end of the Hasmonean era began with the death of Alexandra Salome in 67 B.C.E. Civil war quickly broke out between her sons Hyrcanus II and Aristobulus II as each sought the titles of high priest and king. Aristobulus received considerable aid from his sons Alexander and Antigonus, but Hyrcanus had weightier allies: the Nabateans, the influential Idumean Antipater, and, most important, the Romans, who were emerging as the superpower of the Mediterranean. Rome's looming entry into the region on his behalf meant that inhabitants of Palestine would soon be subject once again to a foreign empire.

CHAPTER 3

Herod the Great and the Introduction of Roman Architecture

Roman troops entered Palestine in 63 B.C.E., marching south from Syria under the leadership of the general Pompey, whose adventures in the eastern Mediterranean dramatically expanded Rome's territory. When Pompey arrived, the Hasmonean kingdom was in disarray as the brothers Aristobulus II and Hyrcanus II vied for power. Pompey settled their dispute by imprisoning Aristobulus and leaving Hyrcanus nominally in charge. Hyrcanus held the titles of high priest, ethnarch, and "Ally and Friend of the Roman People," but it was the newly appointed Roman governor in Syria who wielded true authority over the region. Hasmonean influence quickly declined. The Romans annexed many of the non-Jewish cities conquered by the Hasmoneans to the province of Syria (*War* 1.156; *Ant.* 14.75–76), and they empowered a non-Hasmonean from Idumea, Antipater, as the overseer of Palestine. Antipater in turn delegated responsibility to his sons Phasael and Herod, whom history has remembered as Herod the Great. Herod served as governor of Galilee, then governor of Syria, and then cotetrarch of Judea with Phasael until 40 B.C.E., when Phasael died and Herod himself fled in the face of the Parthian invasion. Herod journeyed to Rome, where the Senate appointed him king of Judea before sending him back the following year at the head of a Roman army to seize Palestine from the Parthians and their Hasmonean allies. By 37 B.C.E., Herod was fully in charge of the area. For the next thirty-three years, he was one of Rome's most loyal client kings and an influential sponsor of Roman architecture throughout the Levant (fig. 3.1).[1]

Herod's trip to Rome in 40 B.C.E. was not his only visit to the city; he returned sometime between 19 and 16 B.C.E. and again in 12 B.C.E. He experienced Rome in a time of architectural transformation, as Augustus famously turned it from a city of bricks to a city of marble. The last decades of the first century B.C.E. saw the construc-

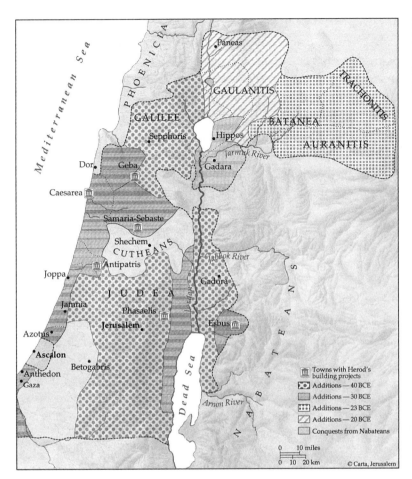

Fig. 3.1. The growth of
Herod's kingdom, 40–4
B.C.E. (Map prepared by
Carta, Israel Map and Pub-
lishing Company, Ltd.)

tion and renovation of numerous basilicas, rectangular buildings with
colonnaded aisles often used for municipal functions; forums, plazas
surrounded by a variety of public buildings, monuments, and busi-
nesses; and temples. The city's first permanent theater, made of stone
rather than wood, had been erected by Pompey only a few years earlier
in the 50s B.C.E.[2]

Herod was clearly impressed by such monumental displays of
Roman culture, wealth, and power, both on his own visits to Rome
and by reports from there that no doubt reached him over the years. He
embraced newer Roman architectural styles as well as older Hellenistic
ones. In his own territory, he sponsored the construction of a variety

of monumental buildings, sports facilities, and other public and private structures that blended Roman, Hellenistic, and local elements. Some structures employed such distinctively Roman techniques as *opus reticulatum,* in which walls were faced with diamond-shaped blocks. Opus reticulatum was a recent innovation that never gained wide usage outside parts of the Italian peninsula, making Herod's limited introduction of it to the Levant all the more notable. His palaces had rooms with floors with the Roman decoration of *opus sectile,* in which inlaid multi-shaped and multi-colored stone tiles made vivid patterns, and Roman-style mosaics with geometric and floral motifs, usually with the principal elements in black but sometimes in other hues. Roman-style painted walls also decorated his palace, with colored panels, stripes, dots, and patterns that resembled the frescoes of Pompeii. Greek-style bathing facilities had been present in Palestine in the Hellenistic era, but Herod introduced the Roman bath with its multiple chambers devoted to different temperatures and the use of hypocaust technology for warming. Outside his territory, he donated theaters, stadiums, baths, fountains, stoas, temples, gymnasia, and agoras to cities along the eastern Mediterranean coast and as far away as Greece (*War* 1.422–25; *Ant.* 16.146–48). Taking into consideration the geographical breadth of Herod's construction projects and the range of Roman elements he used, it is fair to say that he did more to introduce Roman architecture to the Near East than any other single figure.[3]

The economic impact of Herod's building program has long been a matter of scholarly discussion. It has often been assumed that it required excessive taxation, a policy that Herod's sons continued after him.[4] The picture is not so clear, however, and Peter Richardson has pointed out that Herod's tax policies were more lenient than has often been thought, noting that Herod, following sabbatical law practices, remitted taxes on several occasions.[5] Fabian E. Udoh, who has written the definitive treatment of the topic, interprets the common notion that taxes were very high from Herod's reign through the first century C.E. more as a result of New Testament scholars' desire to amplify Jesus' role in helping the poor and downtrodden than as an obvious reading of the available evidence.[6] Whatever the case may be in regard to the degree to which taxes contributed to social unrest in the Herodian era and first century C.E., neither Herod nor Rome had any tolerance for opposition.

The Jerusalem Temple

By far the most impressive of Herod's building projects, and the one
history has most remembered him for, was his extensive renovation
of the Jewish Temple and the platform on which it stood (fig. 3.2).
The Jewish and Christian traditions know that platform as the Temple
Mount, a name drawn from the rabbinic *Har ha-Bayit.* Muslims call it
by its Arabic name, *Haram esh-Sharif,* and it now houses two Islamic
holy places, the Dome of the Rock (completed in 691 C.E.) and Al-
Aqsa Mosque (originally built in the eighth century C.E.). (See plates 1
and 2 in the color gallery.) Though European and American explorers
made a number of significant discoveries regarding the Temple Mount
in the 1800s, and Israeli excavations have uncovered adjacent areas to
its south and west since 1967, much of the Temple Mount and its en-

Fig. 3.2. Aerial photograph of
the Temple Mount, Jerusa-
lem (Photo courtesy of Todd
Bolen/BiblePlaces.com)

virons remain unexcavated. A number of factors complicate its archaeological investigation: the thoroughness of its destruction by the Romans in 70 C.E., centuries worth of subsequent construction, the sacredness of the space in both Judaism and Islam, attendance of its holy sites by contemporary worshipers, the presence of adjacent modern neighborhoods, and the region's ever volatile political climate. Ancient literary sources such as Josephus, the rabbis, the New Testament, and Philo provide a wealth of information about the Temple and its courtyards, though these texts often contain irreconcilable discrepancies. The complexity of the data leaves many questions disputed, such as the exact sizes of the various courts, the number and locations of gates, the precise location of the Temple building itself, and the relationship of that building to the stone now highlighted in the Dome of the Rock.[7]

Herod's earliest work in the vicinity was the construction of a fortress on the rock scarp that came to delimit the Temple Mount's northern boundary (*War* 5.238–46; *Ant.* 15.403–9). The fact that Herod named this fortress Antonia after his patron Mark Antony strongly suggests that he built it before Antony's defeat at the Battle of Actium in 31 B.C.E. Josephus claims that the Antonia Fortress stood on the site of the earlier Baris fortress (*Ant.* 13.307), though he does not make clear the exact relationship between the old and new fortifications. The Antonia Fortress provided an elevated view of the Temple platform and quick access to it, and in the procuratorial period it would host much of Jerusalem's Roman garrison. One of its walls has been incorporated into the modern Umariyya School.

Within a few years of constructing the Antonia Fortress, Herod turned his attention to the *temenos* (the sacred precinct in which the Temple building itself stood). His engineers began expanding the Temple Mount northward to the Antonia Fortress, westward, extending over the easternmost part of the Tyropoeon Valley, and southward. Although it has traditionally been believed that Herod's workers completed this expansion, recent discoveries suggest otherwise. Bronze coins found in a ritual bath at the wall's base date to 17/18 C.E., proving that work in the area continued for at least two decades after the king's death.[8] Evidence of the southern extension is still visible in the eastern retaining wall, where a vertical "seam" separates Herodian ashlars from earlier ones. Only the eastern boundary of the temenos remained largely unchanged, defined by the steep decline into the Kidron Valley. The Hasmonean-period Temple Mount had measured approximately 250 by 300 meters. Judging from the dimensions of the modern Temple Mount, the new platform measured approximately 315 meters on the north, 280 meters on the south, 488 meters on the west, and 470 meters on the east, encompassing an area of approximately 14.4 hectares.[9] Josephus's comment that Herod had doubled the platform's size was thus roughly accurate (*War* 1.401). (See plate 3.)

Expanding this platform required considerable amounts of fill, particularly for areas at lower elevations. To support the surface level in the southeastern corner, for example, workers constructed a vaulted substructure. Rabbinic tradition later offered a non-architectural explanation for this underground space: "The ground beneath the Temple Mount courts was hollow, because of deep-lying graves" (*m. Parah* 3:3). Remodeled in the medieval period, the chamber came to be known as Solomon's Stables.

Such an enormous platform necessitated equally massive retaining walls. Josephus called the surrounding enclosure "the greatest ever heard of" (*Ant.* 15.396). Stonemasons cut huge limestone ashlars, some near the vicinity of the Temple, others probably at quarries just north of the city. Rolling stones, logs, and cranes would have been required to put the huge blocks into place. The ashlars typically weighed several tons apiece, measuring approximately a meter and a half high and ranging from one to four meters long. Unusually large ones can be seen at the southwest corner of the Temple Mount, where some stretch twelve meters long and weigh tens of tons. A single ashlar in a tunnel running along the Western Wall is nearly fourteen meters long and over four meters high. By one estimate, it weighs approximately six hundred tons, although other proposals are smaller but still impressive.[10]

The lower courses elsewhere in the retention walls also preserve typical Herodian ashlars and sometimes even earlier blocks. Workers building the walls set each course of stones slightly back from the one below; this technique, combined with the sheer weight of the stones, obviated the need for mortar. The walls penetrated below street level to bedrock. Pilasters, probably similar to the engaged columns still visible on the Tomb of the Patriarchs at Hebron, decorated at least

Fig. 3.3. A ritual bath for
pilgrims, south of the Temple
Mount (Photo courtesy of
Todd Bolen/BiblePlaces.com)

portions of it. A special station stood on top of the wall at the south-
western corner for the blowing of the shofar to announce the arrival
and conclusion of the Sabbath (cf. *War* 4.582–83).[11]

Literary sources refer to several different gates leading into the
Temple Mount. Though the remains of some of these have long van-
ished, archaeologists have verified the existence of others. The primary public points of entry were the Huldah Gates, perhaps named
after the biblical prophetess (2 Kgs 22:13–20; 2 Chr 34:22–28). Located
in the southern wall, they consisted of a western double gate and an
eastern triple gate. Huge staircases led up to them from the surrounding city, and a Hebrew inscription found nearby has been interpreted
as a reference to the "elders" that rabbinic sources say met on the
Temple steps. Nearby ritual baths offered worshipers one last chance
to purify themselves before ascending to the sacred precinct (fig. 3.3).
According to *m. Middot* 2:2, worshipers entered through the eastern
gates and exited through the western ones, an observation that archaeology seems to bear out. The western gate is the wider of the two,
presumably because a larger space would be needed for the simulta-
neous exit of crowds after an assembly than for their sporadic arrival.
Tunnels, impressive in their own right, led up from these gates onto
the temenos. The Huldah Gates were later renovated and eventually

filled in, but their outlines (particularly that of the eastern set) remain. The tunnel from the western one is well preserved, with a ceiling supported by columns and decorated with carved domes, two of which display unusually intricate geometric and floral designs.

Josephus referred to four gates in the Western Wall of the Temple Mount, and archaeologists have confirmed his description (*Ant.* 15.410–11). The gates are now known for European and American explorers who first reported their discovery to the western world. Robinson's Arch, a small fragment of which juts out from the Western Wall, marks the location of the southernmost gate. Once believed to be the remnants of a bridge over the Tyropoeon Valley, the arch is now thought to have supported a monumental stairwell leading from the temenos down to the valley floor. Farther north, Wilson's Arch supported a bridge connecting the Temple Mount and the Upper City. Because the gate there would have opened up near the *naos* (the Temple building at the symbolic center of the sacred precinct), it was likely used primarily by priests. On either side of Wilson's Arch were Barclay's Gate and Warren's Gate, providing additional access to the Temple from the ancient street at the base of the Western Wall. (See plate 4.)

Porticoes lined all four sides of the temenos, their existence reflected in the numerous column capitals and fragments recovered from the debris of the Great Revolt and from the rectangular holes in the northern scarp below the Umariyya School, which presumably were sockets for roof beams. Josephus (*Ant.* 20.221–22) refers to the eastern portico as the Portico of Solomon (cf. John 10:23); the attribution of the building to Solomon is obviously erroneous but suggests that it was already quite old and thus predated Herod's renovations. The porticoes on the other sides of the complex were all apparently Herodian. The most notable of these was the Royal Portico, which ran along the southern wall. According to Josephus, it consisted of 162 Corinthian columns in four rows, which would have made it one of the largest basilical structures in the Roman East (*Ant.* 15.411–17). Like the rest of the Temple complex, its columns appear to have been made primarily of limestone, not marble as reported by Josephus, as marble remained uncommon in Palestine until the second century.[12] The Royal Portico's size and location near the main entrances from the Huldah Gates and the gate supported by Robinson's Arch make it the most likely location for the booths of the animal sellers and money-changers whose work was essential for the sacrificial cult.

Herod's expansion of the Temple Mount included a reorganization of its courts (*Ant.* 15.420), the names of which are preserved in various texts. The Mishnah interpreted the different courts as concentric zones of holiness in which the degree of sacredness increased as one drew nearer the naos (*m. Kelim* 1:6–9), and such an idea is implicit in Herod's design. Entering each court or zone required walking up stairs, so that approach to the Temple was always characterized by ascent.

The outermost was the Court of the Gentiles. Taking up most of the platform, it was open to Jews and Gentiles alike, excluding only women in a state of ritual impurity (*Against Apion* 2.102–5). It must have served as the primary assembly point for crowds gathering for worship or to hear political addresses (*War* 2.1–7; *Ant.* 16.132–35, 17.200–209). A 1.5-meter-high wall, known as the *soreg* in Semitic sources, marked the limits beyond which Gentiles could not go. Josephus writes that warnings in both Greek and Latin were posted along this wall (*War* 5.194). Remains from two of the Greek inscriptions have been recovered, reading: "No foreigner is to enter within the forecourt and the balustrade around the sanctuary. Whoever is caught will have himself to blame for his subsequent death" (fig. 3.4).[13] Acts implies that the apostle Paul was arrested because of accusations that he had taken a Gentile companion beyond this point (21:26–41).

Fig. 3.4. Inscription banning Gentiles from the Temple Mount, discovered by Charles Clermont-Ganneau in 1871, from Istanbul Museum. The text forbids Gentiles to enter the enclosure around the Temple, and warns that death will result for any who fail to heed the warning. (Photo courtesy of Todd Bolen/ BiblePlaces.com)

The next area was the Court of Women, which was open to Jews of both genders. (See plate 5.) Literary sources attest to the presence of Jewish females in the Temple complex before this time, but the explicit demarcation of an area specifically inclusive of women was apparently a Herodian innovation. While it is true that the court limited the participation of women in the sacrificial cult by prohibiting them from proceeding any closer to the naos, at the same time it provided unprecedented formal recognition of the importance of female worshipers.[14] Rabbinic sources note the presence (whether occasional or permanent is unclear) of a women's gallery where women could ascend to peer down upon the sacrifices conducted in the Court of the Priests (*m. Middot* 2:5).

Jewish males could go through the Court of Women into the relatively small Court of the Israelites. Ten gates gave access to it, nine plated with gold and silver and the tenth with bronze, according to literary sources. This latter gate is likely the bronze gate that *m. Middot* 2:3 refers to as Nicanor's Gate. It is tempting to associate this gate with the Nicanor whose ossuary was discovered in the early twentieth century on the Mount of Olives. A Greek inscription identifies the ossuary's contents as the "bones of Nicanor of Alexandria, who built the doors," while a Semitic one reads simply "Nicanor the Alexandrian."[15]

Priests could go beyond the Court of the Israelites into the Court of the Priests. These two courts were divided by a half-meter wall, over which worshipers could easily hand their sacrificial animals (*War* 5.226). The Court of the Priests was lined with chambers and contained the altar and a sizable basin for ablutions, as well as the naos itself, which faced east.

Remains of the naos have not been found, but approximate details are known. According to Josephus, it rose roughly forty-four meters into the sky. Its front facade measured the same distance horizontally, though behind it the width of the building narrowed to approximately twenty-five meters (*War* 5.207, 209, 221). Silver tetradrachms from the Bar Kokhba Revolt depict the Temple facade as having four columns and a cornice, an image that is likely historically accurate (fig. 3.5).[16] The naos consisted of a porch and two chambers. The outer room contained the golden menorah, an incense altar, and the showbread table. The inner one, the Holy of Holies, was entered only by the High Priest and only on Yom Kippur. Because Judaism prohibited cult images, the Holy of Holies contained no statues, a fact that differentiated it from pagan temples and startled Pompey when he transgressed it in 63 B.C.E. (*Ant.* 14.72).

Herod's rebuilt Temple complex exhibited a combination of Jewish, Near Eastern, Hellenistic, and Roman influences.[17] The spatial organization of the naos itself reflected priestly descriptions of the Tabernacle (Exod 25–30, 35–39). The placement of a sanctuary within a temenos was typical of temples in the Hellenized East, though not

Fig. 3.5. A coin of Bar Kokhba (132–135 C.E.). The obverse shows the Jerusalem Temple facade surrounded by "Jerusalem" in paleo-Hebrew; the reverse depicts a lulav bunch (palm, myrtle, willow) and an ethrog with inscription reading "Year one of the redemption of Israel" (132/133 C.E.). (Copyright David Hendin, used by permission)

the Roman West, but the sheer size of the Herodian temenos separated it from other contemporary examples. The massive complex was the largest in the Roman Empire and one of the biggest anywhere in the ancient world.[18] Its extensive use of columns reflected a Roman appropriation of an earlier Hellenistic architectural motif, with a distinctively Roman influence most strikingly apparent in the basilical shape of the Royal Portico. Thus, while the newly renovated Temple remained an expression of local Jewish culture, it also brought Rome right to the center of Jerusalem.[19] The most sacred site in Judaism was now decorated with Roman architecture.

What motives lay behind such a huge expenditure of time, effort, and resources? Josephus attributes a speech to Herod in which the king deems his renovation an act of piety (*Ant.* 15.382–87). Genuine religious sentiment might partly explain the undertaking, but other factors must also be taken into consideration. Herod's architectural enhancements of the Temple far outshone anything his predecessors had done. Herod had refrained from building a naos larger than that of Solomon (*Ant.* 15.386), but his complex as a whole was much bigger than that of the First Temple. More important politically, perhaps, he had outdone his immediate predecessors, the Hasmoneans, to whom some of his subjects held lingering loyalties. The Hasmoneans had rededicated the Temple after its defilement and had assumed the high priesthood. Herod could not be high priest, but he could demonstrate his fealty to Judaism by making the embellishment of the Temple one of his signature projects. He no doubt won over many opponents simply by providing employment to the numerous workmen needed for his construction program.

The effort also imitated the actions of his patron Augustus. Augustus had prioritized the repair, renovation, and construction of temples in the Forum Romanum, the Forum Augustum, and elsewhere in Rome. By his own count, he had restored eighty-two temples even before becoming emperor (*Res Gestae,* 20). His actions demonstrated respect for Roman tradition while simultaneously symbolizing the beginning of a new era. Herod's work should be understood similarly; it was not only a physical expression of respect for the ancient Jewish cult but also a bold architectural statement that the people of Israel, too, had entered a new era, one in which they would be ruled by a nearby king and a distant emperor.

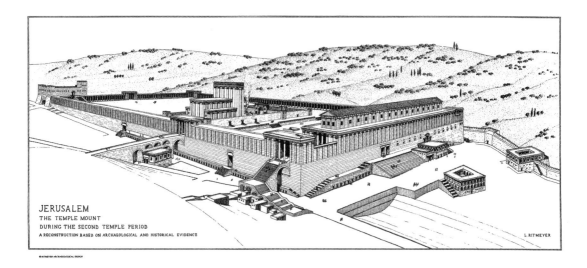

JERUSALEM
THE TEMPLE MOUNT
DURING THE SECOND TEMPLE PERIOD
A RECONSTRUCTION BASED ON ARCHAEOLOGICAL AND HISTORICAL EVIDENCE

L. RITMEYER

Herod's expansion of the Temple Mount created significantly more space to hold crowds, a development that made the Temple accessible to more worshipers (fig. 3.6). The devotion of so much of that space to the Court of the Gentiles had the further effect of encouraging non-Jews from near and far to come and visit the magnificent Temple of the Jews. Increased Jewish pilgrimage and Gentile tourism would profit the city of Jerusalem, the politically influential priesthood, and Herod himself. Opening up an area around the Temple specifically for Gentile visitors also would have reminded Jewish worshipers of the larger, Gentile-run political order they were now a part of, the emerging Roman Empire.[20]

Work on the Temple continued long after Herod himself had passed away. The Gospel of John comments on ongoing construction for forty-six years (2:20), and according to Josephus it did not end until around 64 C.E., when new employment had to be found for the thousands of affected laborers (*Ant.* 20.219–23). Even then, features were left incomplete; archaeologists excavating the tunnel along the Western Wall discovered an unfinished segment of an adjacent ancient street. The grandeur of Herod's Temple was remembered centuries later. One rabbinic tradition looked back longingly, reflecting that "he who has not seen the Temple has not seen a beautiful building" (*b. Sukkah* 51b).

Fig. 3.6. Reconstruction drawing of the Temple Mount before its destruction in 70 C.E. The drawing features the pilgrim steps on the south wall (facing right), the stairwell entrance at the southwest corner, and the arched overpass entrance on the Western Wall beneath the Holy of Holies, which rises above it. The Antonia Fortress is at extreme left. (Drawing courtesy of Leen Ritmeyer)

Other Jerusalem Building Projects

If the renovation of the Temple reflected the fusion of traditional Jewish and newer Greco-Roman elements, other buildings Herod built in Jerusalem symbolized an enthusiastic embrace of Greco-Roman architectural forms. According to Josephus, Herod erected a theater in the city and an amphitheater "on the plain" (*Ant.* 15.268), characterizing them and their associated activities as "spectacularly lavish but foreign to Jewish custom." Neither building has yet been found, though an indentation south of the Hinnom Valley is a possible site for the theater. Because terminology for sports architecture was not yet firmly defined when Josephus wrote, the "amphitheater" he refers to may not have been the round or oval structure the term usually denotes but could have been some other form of entertainment or sports architecture.[21] The passage has generally been interpreted to mean that Herod placed the "amphitheater" in or near the city proper, although the exact location has long been a source of speculation.[22] Alternatively, the term "plain" could suggest an area outside the city where space was more plentiful, such as the coastal plain.[23] At the time of the Great Revolt, Jerusalem had a "hippodrome," a term that might refer to the aforementioned amphitheater or could refer to a different structure (*War* 2.44; *Ant.* 17.254–55). If the latter, then whether Herod himself or one of his successors built it remains a mystery. A dozen flat inscribed stones that were reused first in a Roman latrine and later in the Umayyad palace south of the Temple Mount may have originally been seats in one of these structures or some other public building.[24]

Herod also strengthened Jerusalem's fortifications. The lower courses of the present-day "Citadel of David" at the Jaffa Gate are actually remnants of one of the three towers he built there (*War* 5.161–75). The walls visible in the courtyard of the Citadel of David museum include other Herodian remains, and portions of the supporting platform for the king's palace run toward the south under the present-day Armenian Garden.[25]

Caesarea Maritima

The Jerusalem Temple was hardly the only one of Herod's construction projects reflecting fealty to a deity. An even larger project indicated devotion to the divine figure Herod was more immediately sub-

ject to, the Roman emperor. In 22 B.C.E., Herod began work on a new city at the site of the older settlement of Strato's or Straton's Tower (*War* 1.408–14; *Ant.* 15.331–41, 16.136–41). For the next twelve years, his engineers constructed a citywide monument to Roman imperial culture. The name Herod chose for his new city was unambiguously honorific: Caesarea Maritima, or Caesarea by the Sea (fig. 3.7). It was also propagandistic: anyone who saw this city from sea or land would associate it with Caesar and witness the visual grandeur of the Roman Empire as well as the loyalty of one of its most prominent client kings.[26]

Caesarea Maritima was bounded on the west by the sea and on the east by a semicircular wall that probably functioned more as a symbol of Caesarea's status as a city than as a defensive measure (fig. 3.8). Herodian courses from that wall have been found, particularly in the northern sector of the city. Two towers flanked the wall's northern gate, and towers may also have accompanied each of several other gates. The streets leading inward from the gates were designed according to an orthogonal plan, intersecting at right angles. Though the streets visible in the modern archaeological park are from later

Fig. 3.7. Aerial photograph of Caesarea Maritima (Photo courtesy of Todd Bolen/ BiblePlaces.com)

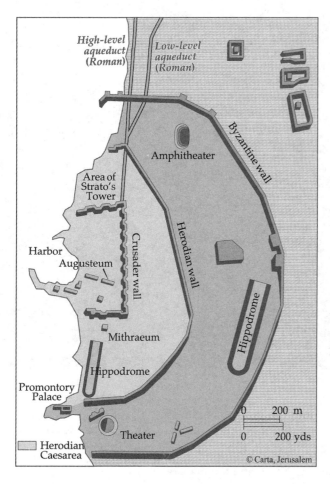

High-level
aqueduct
(Roman)

Low-level
aqueduct
(Roman)

Amphitheater

Byzantine wall

Area of
Strato's
Tower

Harbor
Augusteum

Crusader wall

Herodian wall

Mithraeum

Hippodrome

Hippodrome

Promontory
Palace

Theater

0   200 m

0   200 yds

Herodian
Caesarea

© Carta, Jerusalem

Fig. 3.8. Map of Caesarea
Maritima (Map prepared by
Carta, Israel Map and Pub-
lishing Company, Ltd.)

centuries, their underlying organization goes back largely to Herod. (See
plate 6.)

From the city's very beginning, a
key structure deviated from the unifying orthogonal pattern: a temple. Located on an artificial platform roughly
11.5 meters above sea level in the center of the city, the temple faced west,
toward the water. It would thus have
been one of the very first features of
the city seen by those arriving by sea.
Given its highly visible location, it is
almost certainly the temple dedicated
to Augustus and the goddess Roma
mentioned by Josephus (*War* 1.414;
Ant. 15.339). It stood on an impressive platform that measured approximately one hundred meters along the
coast and ninety meters wide. Because
a church, a mosque, and then another
church were built atop it, the temple
itself is poorly preserved, but it appears to have been 46.4 meters long
and 28.6 meters wide with Corinthian
columns.[27] It was apparently the first
temple of the imperial cult in the Near East and one of the earliest
anywhere in the empire.

Also visible from sea would have been the Promontory Palace,
so called because it was built on a small point of land jutting out into
the water (fig. 3.9). Two thousand years worth of waves have worn
away much of it, but it appears to have been a two-story building with
two wings, the Lower Palace and the Upper Palace. Its luxurious nature is evidenced by the peristyle court with rectangular swimming
pool (35 by 18 meters) that stood at the center of the Lower Palace,
just a few meters from the sea. The Upper Palace, which was likely a
post-Herodian addition, also had a sizable peristyle courtyard (64 by
42 meters). Its various rooms contained gardens, mosaics, a Roman

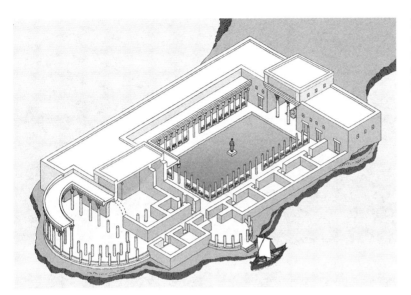

Fig. 3.9. Reconstruction drawing of Herod's Promontory Palace at Caesarea Maritima (Reconstruction drawing by Leen Ritmeyer)

bath, and an exedra, and a miqveh was located just outside one of its entrances. The building is the most likely candidate for the praetorium of Herod mentioned in Acts' account of the questioning of Paul (23:35).[28]

Adjoining the Upper Palace to the northeast was a lengthy, oval-shaped structure (310 meters long, 68 meters wide) with seating on all but its northern side (fig. 3.10). It was clearly designed for sports and shows, but whether it was a hippodrome intended primarily for horse and chariot competitions or a stadium for foot races is uncertain. The building may be the "amphitheater" that Josephus mentions stood south of the harbor (*Ant.* 15.341), though some scholars have suggested that Josephus was mistaken, pointing to an oval indentation in the ground in the northeastern part of the city as a more likely location.

South of the Promontory Palace stood a theater that, like the temple, was oriented to the west and not wholly aligned with the city's grid pattern (fig. 3.11). Although its lower portions were cut directly into the underlying rock, like Greek-style theaters, for the most part it was built according to Roman conventions. Its seating area (*cavea*) formed a half circle with a diameter of eighty-five meters that could have held some thirty-five hundred to five thousand spectators. The thirty-meter-wide orchestra at the base of the cavea completed

Fig. 3.10. Hippodrome or stadium at Caesarea Maritima (Photo courtesy of Sean Burrus)

Fig. 3.11. Roman-period theater at Caesarea Maritima (Photo courtesy of Todd Bolen/BiblePlaces.com)

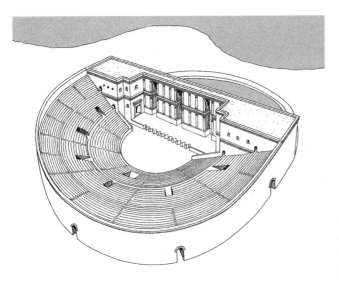

Fig 3.12. Reconstruction drawing of theater at Caesarea Maritima (Reconstruction drawing by Leen Ritmeyer)

the half-circle shape, differing from the circular orchestras of earlier Greek theaters. The stage appears to have had a back wall, or *scaenae frons,* also a Roman element (fig. 3.12). The structure thus appears to have been the earliest Roman-style theater in the area and one of the first outside the Italian peninsula. Its construction followed that of the first permanent theater in Rome by only a few years.[29]

The city's harbor facilities were no less impressive than the rest of it. The earlier community of Strato's Tower had built piers for maritime visitors, but the site's natural harbor capabilities were limited. Herod constructed his own new harbor, and the ample finds discovered by underwater archaeologists demonstrate that his final product was the most technologically sophisticated harbor of its day. His workers built two long breakwaters (one stretching 500 meters, the other 180), leaving an opening between the two as the harbor's entrance. Constructing the breakwaters on the sea floor required the use of hydraulic concrete made from volcanic ash (*pozzolana*) imported from the Bay of Naples area. Herod's engineers filled wooden frames with this concrete and sank them to the bottom of the sea, where they hardened into blocks. These blocks were massive—one measures 11.5 by 15 meters, with a height of 2.4 meters. Their impressions are still visible on some of the timber archaeologists have recovered from their frames. Concrete blocks beyond the breakwater may have functioned as bases for statues, lighthouses, or towers, such as the one Josephus mentions

Fig. 3.13. Roman-period aqueduct at Caesarea Maritima, originally constructed by Herod, with channels added by Hadrian (Photo courtesy of Todd Bolen/BiblePlaces.com)

that honored Augustus's son Drusus (*War* 1.412; *Ant.* 15.336). Herod's harbor was not the first in the Mediterranean that had required extensive underwater work, but it was the most massive in scale.[30]

Storage facilities must have been located adjacent to the harbor, though none remain from the Herodian period. A number of *horrea* (warehouses) employing Roman barrel vaults once thought to date to the city's foundation are now generally attributed to the late first century C.E. A sewer system utilized seawater to wash away the city's refuse, according to Josephus (*Ant.* 15.340–41). The city relied on aqueducts for freshwater (fig. 3.13). The aqueduct familiar to modern visitors dates to later decades of the Roman period, but a less well known one running to Mount Carmel may be Herodian.

Samaria-Sebaste

Herod also honored the emperor by rebuilding Samaria, the ancient capital of the northern kingdom, and naming it Sebaste, the Greek equivalent of the Latin title Augustus. The king placed six thousand settlers in his refounded city among the mixed population of Samari-

Fig. 3.14. Roman street in lower Sebaste, former capital of northern kingdom (Samaria) rebuilt by Herod the Great (Photo courtesy of Todd Bolen/BiblePlaces .com)

tans, pagans, and perhaps Jews who already dwelled there (*War* 1.403; cf. *Ant.* 15.296–98). He surrounded the acropolis with a 3,700-meter wall that incorporated older Hellenistic defenses and included approximately thirty rectangular and circular towers. At the city's highest point, he built a temple to the emperor, elevating it further with a four- to five-meter artificial platform. This temple was smaller (33.5 by 24 meters) than that at Caesarea Maritima but still would have been the most visible feature of the city. A set of stairs 24 meters wide connected it to a large (83 by 72 meters) forecourt lined with double colonnades. Impressive buildings surrounded the temple complex, including storage facilities, a rectangular building with an apsidal central hall, and a rectangular house with a peristyle courtyard, bath, frescoed walls, and a mosaic floor. If the Roman-style forum, a central rectangular plaza integrated into the street system, dates to Herod's time, it would have been among the first in the Roman East (fig. 3.14). It, too, was located on a raised platform and surrounded by porticoes, with an adjacent basilical structure that may also have Herodian origins. A rectangular stadiumlike structure (205 by 67 meters) at the city's northeastern edge probably dates to Herod. It contained a massive courtyard surrounded by Doric colonnades five meters wide, and red and yellow paneled frescoes adorned its interior walls.[31]

Banias and Other Cities

The imperial temples at Caesarea Maritima and Samaria were joined by a third at Banias (*War* 1.404; *Ant.* 15.363–64), which also received the name Caesarea.[32] Herod's son Philip would later change its name to Caesarea Philippi. If the imperial temple is the one depicted on Philip's coins, as is commonly believed, then it had a four-column Ionic facade. Possible candidates among the buildings excavated at Banias include one with an opus sectile floor, opus reticulatum walls, and cavities in the walls to support marble facing, and another with *opus quadratum* construction. Some scholars have pointed farther away,

Fig. 3.15. Possible Augusteum at Omrit in northern Israel, presumably built by Herod the Great (Photo courtesy of J. Andrew Overman)

suggesting that the temple to Augustus, or Augusteum, stood some 4.5 kilometers southwest at Omrit (fig. 3.15). An impressive temple built atop a podium there is contemporaneous with the reign of Herod.[33]

Other cities in Herod's kingdom also experienced his largesse. At Hebron, Herod built a rectangular compound (34 by 59 meters) that is known as the Tomb of the Patriarchs. One of the best-preserved Herodian structures, it is associated with the Cave of Machpelah, the traditional burial site of Abraham, Sarah, and other ancestors of Israel (*War* 4.529–31; *Ant.* 1.237, 343, 345). The ashlars of its bottom courses are clearly Herodian, and the pilasters decorating its outer walls provide an idea of what those of the Jerusalem Temple would have looked like. A similar enclosure to the north at Mamre likewise preserves Herodian pilasters. Construction also occurred at Esebonitis (*Ant.* 15.295), which is usually associated with Hesban, and Anthedon, which was renamed Agrippias (*War* 1.87, 118; *Ant.* 13.357). Galilee received relatively little of the king's attention. He most likely built the royal palace in Sepphoris that was raided after his death (*Ant.* 17.271), but if he made other investments of resources in the region, they are no longer known. The most notable change in the area was the establishment of a veterans colony to the south at Gaba (Tel Shosh), a strategic location at the northwestern entrance to the Jezreel Valley (*Ant.* 15.294; *War* 3.3).[34]

Desert Fortresses and Palaces

In addition to building cities, Herod constructed a series of fortresses and palaces in the Judean desert, the Jordan River valley, and the Transjordan. Some of these were old Hasmonean possessions that he renovated, while others were wholly new. They were intended to serve as places of retreat and, if need be, refuge, and they reflected the same extravagance and exorbitant spending characteristic of his other projects. Architectural fragments, columns, fortifications, mosaics, frescoes, opus sectile, elements of Roman baths at Doq, Phasael, Callirhoe, Hyrkania, and Alexandrium likely derive from Herodian palaces. Other identifications are more secure. Kypros, a rebuilt Hasmonean palace southwest of Jericho, was named for Herod's mother, while Machaerus is famous as the site of John the Baptist's imprisonment by Antipas. Jericho, Herodium, and Masada, however, provide perhaps the best examples of the king's luxurious quarters and sturdy defenses.[35]

Jericho's year-round temperate climate offered Herod a suitable locale reasonably near Jerusalem for winter retreats (fig. 3.16). Because an earthquake had severely damaged the Hasmonean palace there in 31 B.C.E., Herod built three of his own with peristyle courtyards, decorations of frescoes and simple mosaics, Roman-style bathing facilities, and Jewish ritual baths (fig. 3.17). One palace stood to the north of Wadi Qelt and another to its south, while the third extended across it, with a bridge connecting its one northern wing to three southern ones. This third palace illustrates well the combination of local and Roman elements typical of Herod's buildings. Like the other two, it employed the mud brick construction common to the Jericho region. Unlike them, however, it also incorporated the technique of opus

Fig. 3.16. Colonnaded courtyard, part of Herod's third palace at Jericho, first century B.C.E. The walls would have been frescoed and the floor paved. (Photo courtesy of Todd Bolen/BiblePlaces .com)

Fig. 3.17. Stepped pool at Jericho (Photo courtesy of Hillel Geva, the Israel Exploration Society)

reticulatum. Its gardens were reminiscent of those of Roman villas, and its rooms were decorated with frescoes in the Second and early Third Pompeian styles as well as with molded stucco and mosaics. Columns lined two courtyards, and one room, apparently the main dining hall, was floored with opus sectile. The complex contained two Roman bathing complexes, one of which used barrel-vault technology, had a large stepped pool as its *frigidarium* (cold water pool), and included a huge (92 by 40 meters) swimming pool.

Approximately 1.5 kilometers north of the palaces, Herod constructed a very unusual sports facility. Its elliptical shape (320 meters long by 80 meters wide) suggests a hippodrome, but the 3,000-seat semicircular cavea at its northern end sets it apart from other known hippodromes and stadiums. This theater-style seating was backed by a large artificial mound topped by a rectangular structure with a central courtyard. The purpose of this unique design is unknown.[36]

Herod built another palace-fortress on a hill twelve kilometers southeast of Jerusalem, naming it Herodium (*War* 1.419–21; *Ant.* 15.323–25). Though the hill had a flat summit and required no additional leveling, Herod brought in large quantities of fill to build up its sides, creating the volcano shape visible today. He encircled the summit with a thick, thirty-meter-high casemate wall with towers facing each of the four directions. Inside the circular wall was a peristyle rectangular building that would be converted by later users into a synagogue, a residential area with Roman-style mosaics, frescoes, and bathing facilities, and storage chambers. The complex was the largest palace in the Roman world at the time of its construction, surpassing in size even the residence of the emperor (fig. 3.18).

Other buildings stood outside the walls, and a monumental staircase led from the summit to the base. North of the hill stood a cluster of structures now known as Lower Herodium. The palatial complex there included a swimming pool and bathhouse. The pool's use was made all the more pleasurable by the region's hot, dry climate, and the colonnaded garden around it further accentuated the luxury of the royal lifestyle. A small circular building in the pool's center recalls the round structures depicted in Roman wall paintings of swimming pools. The bathhouse southwest of the pool was the largest built by Herod. A marble washbasin found there bore a carving of the mythological figure of Silenus. Between the palace and the pool

Fig. 3.18. Aerial photograph of Herodium (Photo courtesy of Todd Bolen/BiblePlaces .com)

stood a long terrace (350 by 30 meters) that resembles a sports facility but is atypical in size for both horse and foot racing tracks. Adding to its odd nature was a nearly square (15 by 14 meters) building at the western end with engaged columns and a stepped pool. As with the course at Jericho, the purpose of the structure is an enigma.

The circular palace atop Herodium was reminiscent of Augustus's mausoleum, descriptions of which may have reached Herod, and some have suggested the king designed the site with his own tomb in mind from the start. Josephus reports that he was buried there but does not specify exactly where (*War* 1.667–69), and scholars have long debated whether the summit or Lower Herodium would have been a more suitable location. In recent years, excavators have identified a limestone building on the mound's northeastern slope as the site. With a circular upper level and a conical roof, it resembled the Tomb of Absalom in Jerusalem. They point to a fragment from a large carved red limestone sarcophagus found there as the king's own burial receptacle. The sarcophagus bears no inscription, and although sarcophagi of its size were uncommon in the region, they were not unprecedented. Thus there is still some room for question regarding the sarcophagus and the structure, but the most likely interpretation is that they were indeed associated with the grave of Herod.[37]

The best known of Herod's fortresses is Masada (*War* 1.237; *Ant.* 14.296), made famous by Josephus's account of the Roman siege there in 73 or 74 C.E. (*War* 7.275–303). The site had previously been a Hasmonean stronghold. Herod strengthened its defenses by constructing a lengthy (approximately 1,300 meters long) casemate wall with twenty-seven watchtowers and adding storage facilities and cisterns large enough to hold sufficient provisions for long-term occupation (fig. 3.19). He also expanded the living quarters. The most remarkable of the new residential buildings was a palace perched on the cliff face of the northern promontory looking out over the Dead Sea, the desert, and the

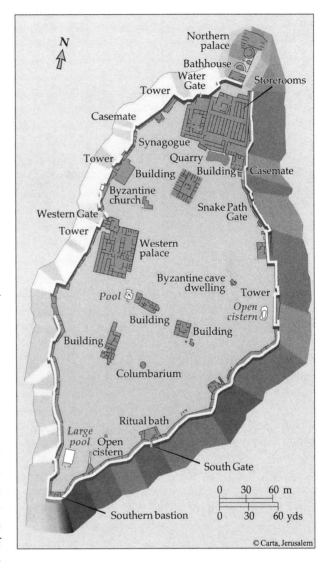

Jordan Rift valley (fig. 3.20). Built on three levels, the Northern Palace spanned thirty-five vertical meters. The summit level consisted of a semicircular balcony backed by living space; the middle level eighteen meters down was dominated by a circular building surrounded by rooms; and the lowest level supported a square hall and a Roman-style bathhouse with an *apodyterium* (entrance and dressing room), *tepidarium*

Fig. 3.19. Map of remains at Masada (Map prepared by Carta, Israel Map and Publishing Company, Ltd.)

Fig. 3.20. Reconstruction
drawing of the Northern
Palace at Masada (Recon-
struction drawing by Leen
Ritmeyer)

(warm room), *caldarium* (hot room), and a miqveh that served dual purpose as a frigidarium (cold pool). All three levels were decorated with
columns, frescoes, and mosaics.

Other Roman bathing facilities were found on the plateau itself, not far from the Northern Palace. A colonnaded courtyard led to
a rectangular building that also had bathing facilities with an apodyterium, tepidarium, frigidarium and miqveh, and caldarium, the latter
of which had a vaulted ceiling. The pillars of the bath's hypocaust are
still well preserved. This structure, like others at Masada, included a
black and white mosaic with geometric designs as well as fresco and
stucco decorations.

A second palace stood at approximately the midpoint of the plateau's western side. Known as the Western Palace, it was structured
around a large room with columns and pilasters, many of them in the
Ionic style and painted red and black, and an artistically impressive
mosaic of geometric and floral designs. An entrance chamber with a
mosaic floor gave way to a bathing complex that included a heating
chamber, a room with a tub and basin, and a miqveh but lacked the
Roman-style elements found elsewhere at the site. The palace apparently had a second floor, and two additional wings were later added
to it.[38]

Herod's Coins

Few of Herod's subjects would have had more familiarity with his palaces than glimpses from the outside and from afar, and only those near the cities would have recognized the extent to which he was appropriating Greek and Roman architectural styles. For many, the most immediately visible material evidence of Herod's reign would have been his coins (fig. 3.21). Like other Roman client kings, Herod struck his own currency, issuing multiple denominations seemingly modeled on Hellenistic numismatic standards. Only a small minority (estimated at 2 percent) bore dates. Because these are most commonly found at Sebaste, they were likely minted there in the three-year interval between Herod's arrival in Palestine around 40 B.C.E. and his conquest of Jerusalem. Many of their designs appear to have been copied from Roman coins: a helmet and shield; an aphlaston, a nautical instrument for measuring wind; what may be an apex, a hat associated with Roman augurs; a tripod and bowl; a winged caduceus. The undated majority of his coins were likely struck at Jerusalem and bear

Fig. 3.21. Coins of Herod the Great: At left, a prutah with "Of King Herod" in Greek (year 3, or 37 B.C.E.). Second from left, reverse of prutah with "Of King Herod" in Greek; obverse depicts tripod table flanked by palm branches. Middle, obverse depicts palm branch; reverse with aphlaston and "Of King Herod" in Greek. Second from right, coin depicts anchor with "Of King Herod" on obverse; on reverse, a double cornucopia with caduceus. At right, half-prutah with eagle; on reverse, cornucopia with Greek "Of King Herod." The eagle on this coin is the first use of a figural image on a Jewish coin. (Copyright David Hendin, used by permission)

designs such as a table, cornucopiae, a galley, an anchor, and what may be a vine. Perhaps the most surprising symbol was that of an eagle, the sole example of zoomorphic imagery on Herod's coins and a possible reference to Herod's erection of a gold eagle over the gate to the Temple (*Ant.* 17.150–52). None of Herod's coins bore his bust, but their Greek inscriptions included his name and kingly title, often in abbreviated form. All were bronze; for silver, his kingdom relied primarily on shekels and half-shekels from Tyre.[39]

Stone Vessels and Ossuaries

Herod's reign is notable not only for its remarkable amount of state-sponsored construction but also for changes in everyday practices among commoners that left their mark in the archaeological record. The extensive quarrying of limestone required by Herod's building projects in Jerusalem seems to have prompted the widespread usage of limestone vessels (fig. 3.22). A variety of forms existed, from jar stoppers and mugs to serving ware like kraters, mugs, and bowls to large storage jars. Most were intended to hold liquids but even small stone tables have been found. The use and manufacture of these vessels quickly spread beyond Jerusalem to other parts of Palestine. The Gospel of John (2:6) associates them with purity practices, and later rabbinic sources (*m. Betzah* 2:3; *t. Shabbat* 16:11) explain that their nonporous character made them incapable of conveying impurity in the way ceramic vessels could. Their presence at a given site is thus a strong indicator of the presence of Jewish inhabitants. Because purity con-

Fig. 3.22. Collection of stone vessels from the Burnt House in Jerusalem (Photo courtesy of Hillel Geva, the Israel Exploration Society)

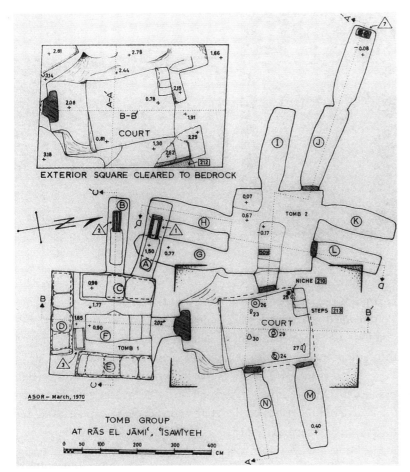

Fig. 3.23. A typical ossuary tomb plan from Isawiyeh, a small village in the north-eastern part of Jerusalem, Herodian period (Line drawing courtesy of the ASOR Archive)

cerns were increasingly widespread in the late Second Temple period, identifying with confidence the particular sectarian leanings of users of stone vessels is difficult, though they included Pharisees and the inhabitants of Qumran. Although larger jars and tables are found only in wealthy homes, smaller vessels have been discovered in more modest residences, demonstrating that both rich and poor used them.[40]

Another practice that seems connected with the increased amount of stone work in Jerusalem was the creation of ossuaries. These small sarcophagi were usually made of limestone, though occasionally clay was used, and were intended for secondary burial. This practice, the regathering of a deceased person's bones after sufficient time (approximately a year) had passed for the flesh to decay, is at-

Fig. 3.24. Decorated ossuary with rosette design, from Isawiyeh (Photo courtesy of the ASOR Archive)

tested in the Bible (Gen 50:24; Exod 13:19), but appears to have increased in the late Second Temple period. The creation of ossuaries as individual receptacles was an innovation that appears to have begun in Jerusalem, where hundreds have been found. Their use spread throughout much of Judea and extended north into Galilee (fig. 3.23).

The ossuary form itself may have been influenced by the Persian practice of burying bones in *astodans* or the Roman use of decorated boxes to hold the ashes of the cremated. Scholarly explanations for the practice of secondary burial vary. Some suggest that the gathering of bones was intended to prepare the deceased for physical resurrection, while others associate it with the belief that the decay of flesh facilitated the expiation of sins. Another proposal attributes the practice to increasing notions of individual identity due to Hellenistic influence and a resulting hesitance to mix multiple sets of bones in common charnel pits (fig. 3.24).[41]

Aside from coins, ossuaries are the single most common source of inscriptions in the late Second Temple period. Many name the interred, and some provide additional details such as age, place of residence or origin, and names of family members. Most inscriptions are in Hebrew or Aramaic, though approximately a third are in Greek and a few are in Latin, providing important evidence for the growing epigraphic usage of those languages. Ossuaries with such inscriptions show how Greek and Roman cultural influences mingled with Jewish customs not only in daily life but also in the rituals marking death.[42]

Fig. 3.25. View of Herodium from the lower city, showing columns from a structure in the lower city (Photo courtesy of Sean Burrus)

The Death of the King

King Herod's own demise occurred in 4 B.C.E. Josephus provides a vividly stylized description of the symptoms leading up to his death (*War* 1.656–73, 2.1–100; *Ant.* 17.168–323): fever, itching, intestinal pain, swollen feet, infection, breathing difficulty, and worms. After a bath at Callirhoe failed to rejuvenate him, he retired to Jericho, where he died. A funeral procession made up of his family and troops carried his body to Herodium (fig. 3.25).

Despite his considerable achievements and the indelible imprint his construction projects left on the land, Herod was in many ways a figure who was rejected by the populace. He had nine wives, drowned one of his sons, and lived a life of great excess. Even though he brought Judea into greater dialogue with the cultural currents of the Roman Empire and made the Second Temple one of the wonders of the ancient world, his devotion to Rome and its leadership put the region on a rocky path as his successors and their subjects adjusted to new political realities.

CHAPTER 4

Khirbet Qumran and the
Dead Sea Scrolls

The site of Khirbet Qumran is located on the northwestern shore of the Dead Sea, twenty-one kilometers east of Jerusalem and twelve kilometers south of Jericho (fig. 4.1). Situated on a marl terrace at the foothills of the Judean Wilderness alongside the Dead Sea, the lowest spot on earth, at an elevation of 338 meters below sea level, Qumran is also one of the driest places in the world, receiving less than 50 millimeters of rain annually. The scenery may appear beautiful to the visitor today looking eastward to the hills of Moab and Edom and westward to the hills of Judea, but the climate is unrelenting in its harshness and the temperature in the long summer can often reach above 120 degrees Fahrenheit. The absence of potable water near the site—the closest spring for drinking water being in Jericho—made living there a real challenge. Capturing the winter runoff from the hills to the west and redirecting it to the site ranks as one of the main technical achievements of the ancient settlers. Water from the spring at the neighboring site of Ein Feshka was too brackish to consume and hence was used only for agriculture and industry, a suggestion made by the original excavator.

Although the site was known to nineteenth-century explorers Louis-Felicien Caignart de Saulcy, Claude Conder and Herbert Kitchener, James Finn, Guillame Rey, Ernest Masterman, and Charles Clermont-Ganneau among others, as well as Gustaf Dalman at the beginning of the twentieth century, it did not really attract any serious attention until the discovery of the Dead Sea Scrolls in 1947. It was only in 1949 that Roland de Vaux, of the École Biblique et Archéologique Française de Jérusalem, and G. Lankester Harding, the chief inspector of Jordanian antiquities, set out to explore and excavate Cave 1; their soundings there confirmed that indeed the scrolls circulating on the open market had been removed from that very lo-

Fig. 4.1. Aerial photograph of Khirbet Qumran settlement (Photo courtesy of the ASOR Archive)

cation.[1] They had been put on the market by the Bedouin shepherds who had discovered them and were reputed to have come from caves near the Dead Sea (fig. 4.2). The archaeologists also managed to conduct a brief survey of the site and excavate two graves. Their first expedition began in 1951 and was followed by two major campaigns in 1953 and 1956. The preliminary results of this work were for the most part published in French and reported in *Revue biblique,* the journal of the École Biblique, and were only later summarized in the publication of the Schweich Lectures delivered before the British Academy in 1959, first published in French in 1961 and subsequently in English in 1972 and 1973.[2]

The site of Qumran, located below and to the east of the closest caves, was first occupied in the Iron Age II period, the eighth–seventh century B.C.E. during the heyday of the Judean monarchy. The main building from this period was a large rectangular structure with a row of rooms built on the east side of a courtyard (fig. 4.3). A large cistern was attached to an enclosure on the west side of the building (Locus 110) and was filled with runoff water and remained in use till the end of the settlement. In the later periods of use it was filled by water chan-

Fig. 4.2. The caves at Qumran (Photo courtesy of Sean Burrus)

nels connected to an aqueduct. The long wall in the southeast is also from this early phase and separates the large area to the south of the site. This earliest stratum of occupation came to an abrupt end in 586 B.C.E. with the destruction of the First Temple and fall of Judea at the hands of the Neo-Babylonians.[3]

De Vaux's publications basically held sway until recently partly because there has been no final publication of any of the materials since his days and there has been little access to the finds by others with interest in them. Although his chronology has been challenged on any number of grounds, his original thinking on such matters is worth repeating briefly. His earliest phase of the reoccupied site, late Hellenistic, he labeled Period Ia (circa 130–100 B.C.E.), and it consisted of the Iron Age building noted above, which was rebuilt and re-

Fig. 4.3. Plan of the Qumran settlement.
Major features include: (1) tower; (2) scriptorium;
(3) kitchen; (4) refectory; (5) larder; (6) kiln;
(7) pottery workshop; (8) cisterns and ritual baths;
(9) former ritual baths; (10) aqueduct; (11) stables;
(12) courtyards. (Drawing courtesy of the ASOR
Archive)

occupied, the earlier cistern that was filled by a new channel, and two
rectangular pools next to it (Loci 117, 118). Rooms were built around
the cistern and some of the courtyard walls were reused. De Vaux also
dated two pottery kilns to this phase of occupation (Locus 66).[4] His
next phase, Period Ib (circa 100–31 B.C.E.), which is late Hellenistic to
early Roman, was the time in which the sectarian community took definitive shape at the site beginning in the reign of Alexander Jannaeus
(103–76). Most of the features that we discuss below are dated to this
period: the two-story watchtower (Loci 9–11) along with the north
gate, which dominates the east of the site (de Vaux's "main building"),
the small stepped pool to the northwest (Locus 138), and the potters'
workshop in the southeast. The western sector is dominated by the
old Iron Age cistern. The so-called assembly hall is situated on the
south side of the main building, which had a pantry attached to it
(Locus 86) full of more than a thousand dishes. De Vaux identified a
toilet in a room of the main building (Locus 51), which opened on to

two stepped pools or ritual baths (Loci 49, 50). In the southeast of the main building were the two pottery workshops (Loci 64, 84) and the large stepped pool (Locus 71). The rooms in the west were workshops, storerooms, and industrial installations. The water system was greatly expanded during this period: water was directed through an aqueduct from the Wadi Qumran and into the settlement to supply all pools, entering from the northwest. When there were heavy rains a sluice gate (Locus 137) was there to restrain the heavy flow of water to the settlement. The end of this expansionist phase was brought about in the view of de Vaux by the great earthquake of 31 B.C.E. (*War* 1.370–80; *Ant.* 15.121–47).[5]

De Vaux's Period II (4 B.C.E.–68 C.E.) commenced after a hiatus of more than twenty years, which he based on numismatic evidence. The site was badly disturbed by the earthquake and fire, and when abandoned it was also badly damaged by water since the aqueducts and channels were no longer functioning. The site was reoccupied by the same group of settlers. Several of the pools went out of use along with other features, and the tower on the north side was reinforced with a stone rampart. In the secondary building workshops, ovens, and silos were installed. The roof of the assembly hall was also re-built (Locus 77) at this time and the area on the second floor was now used for meals. In the center of the main building de Vaux identified the room known as the "scriptorium" (Locus 30), and amid the collapse from above was discovered what were identified as writers' tables, plastered over mud brick. The presence of inkwells in the debris, relatively uncommon in excavations, led him to identify the room as a place where scrolls were copied. This view has been questioned in some quarters, but in the main it has survived such challenges. Modifications to the water system have also been noted. The site came to a violent end when in de Vaux's view the Romans destroyed it in 68 C.E. during the course of the Great Revolt.[6]

Embedded in de Vaux's presentation of the archaeology of the site, and more explicitly stated in his Schweich Lectures, is the thesis that the occupants of the settlement were Essenes, sectarians who wrote many of the scrolls discovered in the caves and who adhered to extreme rules of purity, abhorred marriage, held communitarian views, and were known from ancient sources (including Josephus, Philo, and Pliny).[7] It is a testimony to de Vaux's insightful understanding of the unique nature of the site and surrounding caves that his views, though challenged in many quarters in recent years, have survived. Of the 900 or so scrolls and fragments of scrolls identified in the caves surrounding Qumran only 220 preserve part of the present Hebrew Bible and what is known as the Christian "Old Testament Apocrypha."[8] The Jewish Bible was not yet completely formed when the scrolls were written, and the remainder of them include a large variety of texts and genres, many of which are sectarian in character, such as texts detailing rules to be observed, laws to be followed, calendars, eschatological writings, and new commentaries—in short, aspects of Jewish thought that we would otherwise have little knowledge of. In the discussions here we follow de Vaux's lead in many respects while offering several new refinements to his chronology and details of the excavation as well. We also offer support for the view that many of the scrolls were hidden by residents of the site who were living there at the time of the first destruction of Qumran in 9/8 or 4 B.C.E., or when the Romans advanced on the eve of the Great Revolt. Since some of the scrolls predate the founding of the community we cannot resolve definitively how they came to be deposited in the caves unless it was the first sectarians who brought them.

The Scrolls and Qumran

It is precisely the extraordinarily dry climate that made it possible for the scrolls that were found in the eleven caves to the south, east, and north of the site to be preserved. The first scrolls were discovered in 1947 by Bedouin shepherds (fig. 4.4). We call them the Dead Sea Scrolls because they were found near the site on the Dead Sea, even though we know today that many of them predate the founding of the site in the late Hellenistic period and therefore must have originated elsewhere. Even those that are contemporaneous with the settlement of the site need not necessarily have been composed or copied there. Though more than thirty additional caves in the area have been located, these have produced mostly ceramics and other nonwritten remains. Nearly 90 percent of the scrolls are written on parchment, which is produced from animal skin, probably goatskin. A bit more than 10 percent are written on papyrus, and one unique document, the Copper Scroll, is incised in metal (fig. 4.5).[9]

Fig. 4.4. Bedouin shepherds who discovered the Dead Sea Scrolls (Photo courtesy of the ASOR Archive)

Fig. 4.5. The Copper Scroll, one of the Dead Sea Scrolls found in the caves surrounding Qumran, purporting to locate hidden Temple treasures (Photo courtesy of the ASOR Archive)

The original group of seven manuscripts that first came to light wound up in Israeli hands quite by accident. Hoping to make some quick cash, the Bedouin turned over the scrolls to a dealer from Bethlehem named Kando, who sold the first four from Cave 1 to Mar Athanasius Samuel, metropolitan of the Syrian Orthodox Church (fig. 4.6). Those manuscripts were the great Isaiah Scroll, the Community Rule (Manual of Discipline), the Pesher (Commentary on) Habakkuk, and the Genesis Apocryphon. They turned up on the market in the United States in 1954 and were sold to Israel through a third party for $250,000, with Yigael Yadin serving as the secret representative of Israel. Eliezer Sukenik, a biblical scholar and archaeologist at Hebrew University (as well as the father of Yadin), purchased the other three scrolls, consisting of Hodayot, or Thanksgiving Hymns, the War Scroll, and a partial copy of Isaiah, directly from Nasri Ohan, who served as an intermediary for the Bethlehem dealer Feidi al-Alami, in 1947. All of these scrolls were soon published and set the background for the fuller analysis of the written materials that were purchased on the market and recovered from further excavation and survey (fig. 4.7).

We discuss the discovery of the scrolls first since there can be no doubt that many of them are related to the site of Khirbet Qumran.

Fig. 4.6. Mar Athanasius
Samuel of Saint Mark's Monastery, Jerusalem, Metropolitan of the Syrian Orthodox
Church, looking at the great
Isaiah Scroll of Qumran
as it appeared at an exhibi-
tion of the first scrolls in the
Duke University Chapel, 1950
(Photo courtesy of Duke University Archives)

Fig. 4.7. Typical biblical
scroll found in caves adjacent
to Khirbet Qumran (Photo
courtesy of the ASOR
Archive)

Indeed, an example of the now familiar and unique cylindrical "scroll jars" that were first discovered in Cave 1 has also been found at the site of Qumran in the settlement itself. Similar jars have now been found at nearby Jericho and Masada.[10] Moreover, much of the pottery in the caves may be dated to the same time as the various phases of the site, and the typology of the pottery found in the caves is very similar to the pottery found in the settlement, though there are some forms that are unusual and unique to the region along the Dead Sea shores and up to the site of Hellenistic-Roman Jericho. In the main the types of everyday wares are similar to what is found in Judean sites, though the clays for such vessels at Qumran are different. Noteworthy too is the absence of imported wares, Western and Eastern Terra Sigillata.[11] And except for a few scrolls that predate the origin of the ruin at Qumran the dating of most of the scrolls also fits within the date range of the history of the site. That is not to suggest that all the scrolls were necessarily written or composed in Qumran or that other parties could not have hidden some of them in the caves on the eve of the destruction of Jerusalem. But to dismiss the scrolls, especially the sectarian ones, as providing a probable literary and social context for understanding the ruin itself would be to ignore the obvious. As Jodi Magness has put it: "Why should we disregard the scrolls or use only part of the evidence instead of all of it—especially when . . . the scrolls and our ancient sources provide evidence that complements the archaeology? And as we shall see, archaeology establishes the connection between the scrolls in the caves and the settlement at Qumran."[12] So let us consider the archaeology of Qumran in the light of recent discussions about the dating of the settlement, the interpretation of the ruins, and the relationship between the ruin and the eleven caves that have produced what we know as the Dead Sea Scrolls.

In agreeing to discuss the archaeology of Qumran along with the history of the deposition of scrolls in the nearby caves we open up the question of whether the Essenes or a group of them could have been responsible for the resettlement of the site. We perforce also reopen the debate about the chronology of the site, the dating of the scrolls, and how they came to be deposited there. Since some of them predate the history of the settlement we must be open to the fact that all of the scrolls did not originate at Qumran; and since a number of those that predate the community there have ideas that find a common thread with later sectarian views—for example, Jubilees and the special calendar in it, or 4QInstruction or Sapiential Work A, a kind of wisdom instruction similar in form and content to Ben Sira or Proverbs, especially Proverbs 22:17–24:22, which shares some common themes reflected in the Community Rule—we may safely conclude that there was another setting for such views well before the establishment of what we know as the Qumran site around 100 B.C.E. or a bit later.[13]

Interpretations of the Archaeology

The archaeology of Khirbet Qumran has become a source of much debate in recent years. Until the discovery of the scrolls in the nearby caves in 1947 the site had not been associated with the Essenes, although this idea was first implied by Pliny (*Nat. Hist.* 5.73), who simply says they lived west of the Dead Sea. Joan Taylor, in support of Pliny, has suggested that at the very least he had heard that some Essenes lived by the Dead Sea.[14] The leading scholars of the early years after the discovery—Eliezer Sukenik, Miller Burrows, Andre Dupont-Sommer, Frank Moore Cross, Jr., Geza Vermes, and Roland de Vaux—by 1956 all had adopted what became the regnant view for many years, namely, that the settlement of Qumran below the caves was occupied by the Essenes and that the community was founded by dissident Zadokite priests who broke away from the Jerusalem establishment in the mid–second century B.C.E.[15] Although this view no longer holds complete sway, recent scholarship has made it possible to conceive of multiple communities of sectarians who might fall under the heading of Essenes or the Yahad, one group of which lived at Qumran well after 100 B.C.E.[16] We need not believe any longer that there was only one group of Essenes confined to Qumran, a fact made abundantly clear in two documents, the Damascus Document (CD) and the Community Rule (1QS), that presuppose at least two groups, one marrying and the other celibate (compare also Philo and Josephus). Today, the debate over the archaeology of the site not only has led to a revised occupational chronology but also has renewed discussion of whether the caves and the site may be related, and hence whether the scrolls from the caves—none have been found at the site—may be used to understand the site itself. But we begin with

a consideration of some of the newer interpretations of the site, all of
which depend on the material remains uncovered in the excavation of
the site and not on the scrolls.

Norman Golb has been the most persistent voice arguing that
the scrolls were hidden in the caves alongside Qumran after the fall
of Galilee in 68 C.E. He believes along with many followers that the
settlement was a fort.[17] The absence of legal documents in the corpus
of scrolls and letters at the time of his writing led him to believe that
the military inhabitants of Qumran were party to the hiding of the
documents in the caves and that the corpus itself reflected on the Jerusalem establishment that produced them. Golb's view received unexpected support from Yitzhak Magen and Yuval Peleg when they proposed that the site was originally a military outpost for maintaining
security on the Dead Sea shoreline, though they contend that from 63
B.C.E. onward it functioned as a center for the manufacture of pottery.[18] An important inference drawn from their work, however, is
that the site of Qumran was an integral part of the local economy of
the Dead Sea region, but as we shall see, participating in the regional
economy did not necessarily mean that the material culture of the site
was the same as its neighbors. Indeed, selected provenience studies of
Qumran pottery have shown conclusively that some of it was made
from clays imported from Jerusalem. Magen and Peleg, however, argue that the sophisticated water system, including most of the ritual
baths, was devised for the collection of sediments at the bottom of
the cisterns and reservoirs for the production of some vessels.[19] Moreover, the idea that there were only twenty to thirty residents at the site
and all were potters is not convincing and does not take into account
the large number of ritual baths, ten in all, as well as other communal installations, not to mention the fact that the caves were used for
living also.[20] Magen and Peleg contend that refugees fleeing Jerusalem during the Great Revolt took their synagogue scrolls with them
to Qumran, where they found a group of potters who had convenient
vessels ready for hiding scrolls rescued from the Romans. A number
of scholars have suggested that some of the caves were suitable places
to live, especially during the times of the year when the heat was so
excessive. Escaping to the relative cool of the caves is understandable
when the outside temperature reached well above one hundred degrees Fahrenheit.

A much debated alternative, proposed by Pauline Donceel-Voûte and Robert Donceel in 1994, is that the site was a *villa rustica,* or agricultural settlement.[21] These authors had been appointed to prepare the material from the original excavation for final publication, and they were very much impressed with the high quality of many of the small objects in the finds, especially glass. Their suggestions met with immediate opposition, partly because the soil at the site is not good for agriculture, which was possible only nearby at Ein Feshka, and because of the absence of aspects normally associated with a villa rustica, such as mosaics, wall paintings, stucco, and a true Roman-style bathhouse as opposed to ritual baths.[22] Magness also noted how the location of Judean villas was in urban places like Jerusalem or close to sources of freshwater, such as Jericho or Ein Gedi.[23] The Donceels ignored some of the communal features of the ruin, and identified the so-called scriptorium (Locus 30) as a dining room, so that many considered their case unconvincing. Their effort to focus on the site itself and its finds, however, led others to follow, which in turn resulted in other theories.

Another team introduced a related proposal in 1994, that Qumran was a commercial entrepôt, a customhouse, trading post, or caravanserai.[24] This theory is based on the supposition that Qumran was situated along a major trading route, but the idea met with strong resistance, especially since in antiquity the level of the Dead Sea would have risen to the cliffs alongside the site.[25] An underlying assumption of this proposal, however, was compelling: that Khirbet Qumran was not as isolated as many previous scholars had thought. This is precisely the theme that Jürgen Zangenberg also emphasized in 2004 by pointing out that anyone living at Qumran could easily have trekked back to Jericho, connecting there with a major transregional road that led to Jerusalem in the west and Amman/Philadelphia to the east.[26] It is true that a convincing case for non-isolation has been made, based on the string of contemporary sites on both sides of the Dead Sea in the time when the site was occupied, in the late Hellenistic–early Roman period, and on the kinds of pottery forms that find parallels elsewhere, but none of this gainsays the notion that some sectarians could have lived there utilizing some of the local resources at their disposal while at the same time living a unique lifestyle that focused on ritual purity, study, and communal living. We believe those aspects of the

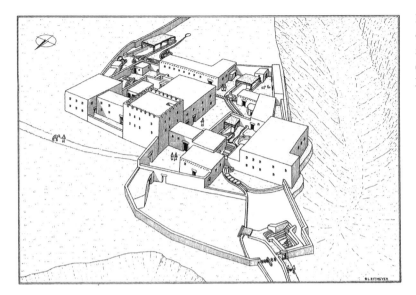

Fig. 4.8. Reconstruction drawing of Qumran, featuring a ritual bath at lower right (Reconstruction drawing by Leen Ritmeyer)

site are reflected in the nature of the buildings, installations, especially the ritual baths, and layout of the site, as well as some of the unique aspects of the ceramics found there (fig. 4.8).

Another major point of view on the nature of the site was proposed by the late Yizhar Hirschfeld in 2004.[27] He argued that the Essenes lived in multiple places in the Judean wilderness, in the manner of the followers of John the Baptist, and that a number of them went to Ein Gedi where they lived as hermits.[28] Hirschfeld rejected the idea that the water level of the Dead Sea was too high for a main north–south road to have existed alongside Khirbet Qumran, and therefore he saw a direct connection from Jerusalem to Jericho to Ein Gedi passing along the site. He argued that Qumran was built as a fort by the Hasmoneans and that the complex provided a kind of safe passage for travelers along the road. It also served as a place for safeguarding royal revenues.[29] In the time of Herod the Great, Hirschfeld suggests, the site was rebuilt as a fortified manor by a Herodian elite who might have belonged to a priestly family and who had close ties to the royal family. As one can easily see, this view is very similar to the one that proposed a villa rustica but takes into account the large number of ritual baths and chalk-stone vessels found at the site that were impervious to ritual defilement. Like other scholars Hirschfeld was not bothered by the absence of the trappings of a more fanciful lifestyle, such as mosaics like those found in the Jewish Quarter excavation of Herodian Jerusalem. As for the relationship between the site and the caves, he offers the following explanation: Sadducean priests fleeing Jerusalem during the time of the Great Revolt, in a convoy of pack animals loaded with scrolls, found assistance at Qumran with a friend and fellow priest who helped to hide the scrolls in the adjacent caves.[30] In our view this theory strains credulity. At less than 4,500 square meters, with a small community center, Qumran could hardly be called an elaborate manor house, and no mosaics, frescoes, or a Roman bathhouse have been found. Finally, why would the Sadducees hide sectarian documents that did not accord with many of their views?

A middle-of-the-road position on these competing views was recently put forward by Jean-Baptiste Humbert, the person in charge of the final publication of all remaining materials from Qumran.[31] What Humbert now says is that the early stages of the settlement indeed reflect a secular phase when, he claims, there was a country house there. By the middle of the first century B.C.E. or so, when it became an Essene community site, however, the complex had been reconfigured into a communal settlement. He argues that, lacking the palaces and elaborate buildings that we find in Jericho and elsewhere, and having no domestic baths or domiciles, for at least several periods the Essene hypothesis "remains the most likely explanation" of the material remains.[32] His position takes account of most of the data, though the date at which the communal and religious character of the site took shape still remains contested.

Other scholars also would like to understand the site of Khirbet Qumran in its larger regional context, as one among a number of sites along the Dead Sea shore up to Herodian Jericho. Among the more important of these sites were Ein Feshka, Ein Gedi, Ein Turaba, En Boqeq, En ez-Zara, each of which had an adequate water supply, and places connected to Qumran by paths such as Khirbet Mazin and Ein el-Ghuweir. There are also the more well known sites associated with the Hasmoneans, Herodians, and Zealots such as Masada, Hyrkania, and Jericho.[33] Scholars mention these sites to argue that Qumran was not so isolated as previous generations have maintained, and it was thus an unlikely site for a withdrawn sectarian community. It is true that Qumran was not isolated. We can no longer say that the region around it was devoid of activity and habitation in the century and a half that some of the Essenes or Yahad group or their leaders would have lived there. It is obvious too that if these other sites existed, then there was trade, freshwater, and food available for survival. That is not to say that it was easy to live in this area, the lowest spot on earth. But the sectarian community did not choose to live exclusively at the Dead Sea. They lived in Jerusalem and in other towns and villages, and some, like Menahem the Essene, were even honored by Herod the Great (*Ant.* 15.372–73). Today the so-called Essene Quarter on Mount Zion, originally identified by Bargil Pixner, is being excavated by Shimon Gibson (fig. 4.9). It may be that the leaders elected to set up headquarters or an initiation location in the desert, believing that they were fulfilling the long-standing biblical ideal of seeking God's presence and truth in the wilderness, just as the Israelites of old had done in Sinai.[34] Those who lived in Jerusalem among the "corrupt" still engaged with their neighbors and shared their message with many of them. So the regional context is relevant, but that does not eliminate the possibility, or probability, that an Essene community, possibly one

Fig. 4.9. Excavation of the Essene Quarter on Mount Zion (Photo courtesy of James Tabor)

of several, chose to live in the "wilderness" of the Dead Sea at Khirbet Qumran.

Even in light of these new theories, it is impossible to ignore the evidence of the 900 different manuscripts that have been discovered in the caves. Although no scrolls have been found at the site, Weston Fields, director of the Dead Sea Scrolls Foundation in Jerusalem, reports in his history of the discovery that de Vaux had seen and wanted to buy a number of blank parchment scrolls that had surfaced on the market in relation to the finds from Caves 4 and 5. De Vaux believed they supported his idea that scrolls were copied or written at the site. "Otherwise," he said, "why would they have blank pieces of parchment there?"[35]

Current Views

The fact that after sixty years a good many aspects of de Vaux's views on the original excavations have survived is a testimony to his good judgment and careful work. Nonetheless, a new consensus has begun to emerge in regard to the site even though we still await final publication of much of the material. The site of Qumran was first settled in the late Iron Age, the eighth to seventh centuries B.C.E., based on the discovery of three eighth-century royal jar handles stamped *la-melekh* (literally, "for the king"). No doubt the site functioned as a stronghold in the Jordan Valley, having a military and agricultural function. After a hiatus of nearly five hundred years, the next stratum de Vaux labeled Ia, 130–100 B.C.E., early in the Hasmonean era. After so many years and despite the lack of a final publication, based on careful stratigraphic analysis and a more refined knowledge of the ceramic typology of the period, Jodi Magness has offered a revised chronology of the site of Qumran that we find persuasive. Let us summarize the two main positions and then offer comments on the particulars, leaving out the Iron Age settlement. The new chronology has established the founding of the community around 100 B.C.E., thereby eliminating de Vaux's Period Ia. Although this is only a difference of some thirty years, lowering the dates has the effect of placing the rupture between the sectarians and the Jerusalem establishment in a different historical setting. Magness, in fact, is quite open to lowering it a bit more in the light of her ceramic dating, which others have accepted also, and in light of the numismatic evidence. In addition, de Vaux's cutoff of 31 B.C.E. for Period Ib in the time of the great earthquake has also been lowered by Magness to 9/8 B.C.E., a change of more than twenty years. His dating of the end of Period II to 68 C.E., and the end of the sectarian settlement, however, has stood the test of time, though Joan Taylor would extend the presence of Roman soldiers a bit longer.

One of the main reasons de Vaux's dating of the founding of the community has not held up through the years is the fact that no coins have been found that may be definitively related to his Period Ia. Like many other archaeologists of his day, de Vaux tended to publish mostly whole pottery, so that while we still await final publication of the full ceramic corpus from the excavations, what we know about what he published suggests a much later chronology for the re-founding of the site, sometime in the first century B.C.E. Humbert has proposed that in de Vaux's Period Ia the site functioned as a non-sectarian agricultural community, and did not change over to a sectarian, Essene, occupation until after 57 B.C.E., when the site was destroyed by the Roman governor Gabinius, or in 31 B.C.E. after the great earthquake and when Herod took control of the Dead Sea region and Jericho.[36]

Magness's evidence for lowering the chronology of Period Ib focuses on the hoard of Tyrian silver tetradrachmas recovered in Locus 120, most dating to between 126 and 9/8 B.C.E.[37] Magness believes the hoard was buried in advance of some impending danger and never retrieved even after the site was reoccupied. Most scholars today do not believe that the site was abandoned after the earthquake of 31 B.C.E., and hence the latest coins of 9/8 B.C.E. may provide the date for the end of Period Ib, which is supported by a layer of ash, pointing to destruction by fire. A similar terminus is also suggested by the events of the last days of the reign of Herod the Great and the accession of Archelaus in 4 B.C.E. Judging from the silting of the site, its abandonment was of very brief duration; the burial of the hoard probably belongs to the post-31 B.C.E. portion of Period Ib. As a result we may now reassign de Vaux's Ia materials to the pre-31 B.C.E. phase of Period Ib.[38]

The final period of occupation at Qumran then began around 4 B.C.E. and lasted until 68 C.E. when the Romans, led by Vespasian, destroyed the site.[39] De Vaux had arrived at this same date range for

Period II on the basis of the 94 revolt coins found at the site.[40] Taylor
has refined our understanding of the end of Qumran, however, relying on both coins and literary evidence, agreeing that Vespasian captured Qumran and burned it in 68 C.E.; she has also suggested that
while searching the caves for refugees and booty, the Romans came to
Cave 4, the site of the majority of fragments, and intentionally ripped
them up. Other nearby sites, at Machaerus and Masada, survived until
71 and 73 C.E. Finds such as a legionary brick and coins at the associated agricultural site of Ein Feshka suggest that although it was partially destroyed in 68 C.E., non-locals occupied it for some time well
after 70 C.E., no doubt laborers and gleaners who worked the date
palms.[41] Getting control of the date and balsam plantations along the
road from Jericho to Ein Gedi after 68 C.E. was a major concern of the
Roman army, which could well have used Qumran during those years
as a military stronghold to guard the pass near Qumran and "exploit
whatever economic resources still existed."[42]

The Settlement and Community Center

Despite the recent debates over the chronology of the site and its character, ample evidence indicates that Khirbet Qumran was a sectarian
site after 100 B.C.E., even taking into account newer theories concerning the multiplicity of Essene communities in Judea and the possibility that a core group settled near Essene Gate on Mount Zion during
the Herodian period. Moreover, in light of recent discussions there is
no doubt that the site of Qumran was much more fully part of the regional setting and that its material cultural remains reflect that world
also. All of this may be inferred from the archaeology of the site. The
fact that the distinctive communal character of some of the buildings
and the unique group of ten ritual baths may be dated to the earliest
phase of occupation, after 100 B.C.E., is evidence that it was a small
religious community.[43] Its size, taking into account that the majority lived in the nearby caves, was between 150 and 200 souls, though
some could have resided in the community center above Loci 1, 2, and
4, where there is a staircase to a second floor that no longer exists.[44]
Hirschfeld, using a population coefficient of 20 for a tenth of a dunam, came up with a population of only 20, based solely on the premise that all inhabitants would have lived at the site in a large building

complex.[45] As mentioned earlier, scholars have been careful to note that the everyday pottery in the caves and at the site not only is of the same date range (Periods Ib–II) but is also of the same character and undecorated type.

The largest room at the site is the so-called assembly hall or dining room (Locus 77), which covers an area of 99 square meters (22 by 4.4 meters). It has been identified on the basis of the pantry that is attached to it on the southwest (Locus 86), which produced a cache of more than a thousand pieces of kitchenware that collapsed onto the floor during the earthquake of 31 B.C.E. Magness has suggested that the dining hall was moved at this time to a second story above Locus 77, one of several stories at the site at this later stage of Period Ib.[46] Near the large assembly hall may be found what is identified as a kitchen (Loci 38 and 41) with several fireplaces in it. The large assembly hall could accommodate between 120 and 150 individuals, depending on how one calculates seating capacity. It is very difficult to dismiss the communal character of this space, and although some critics have argued that it could have been a dining area used for serving laborers or slaves, it is more reasonable to assume that it could have been a place of assembly and celebration of religious rites.[47] Humbert was so impressed with the orientation of the hall and the contents of the adjacent pantry that he conjectured that the vessels might have been used for the Feast of Shavuot, or fall harvest festival, since the odd sizes of the vessels made them suitable for liquids, grains, and fruits.[48] The other main structure at the settlement is the tower near the entrance to the north of the main building. It is massive in size and two stories in height, with a revetment wall around it. It no doubt served as part of a defensive stronghold or military outpost at one time and is dated usually to the presectarian phase, or Period Ia. Its use in the next phases of occupation is not at all clear, but since it is so central to the site it must have served some important function.

Among the most important indicators of sectarian occupation of the settlement is the ten ritual baths, or *miqvaot* (fig. 4.10).[49] To be sure, the presence of several large pools, or reservoirs, and the aqueduct point to the ingenuity and technological savvy of the occupants. Considering the location of the site in the middle of the desert, having an adequate supply of water is paramount, and Loci 110 and 91 could provide enough water for up to 200 people during the dry

Fig. 4.10. Stepped pool at Qumran, southeast of the main building, showing damage from earthquake (Photo courtesy of the ASOR Archive)

season, spring to fall.[50] The excessive size of the ritual baths and the sheer number of them, in light of the accepted estimate of the population (150–200), underscores the centrality of purity rules for the inhabitants. The presence of small partitions in several of them in their upper portion also points to a special care for separating the pure from the impure. Numerous scholars have pointed to the similarity of the Qumran ritual baths to the ones found in the Jewish Quarter of Jerusalem where priestly families lived and needed the baths to purify themselves before consuming the priestly offerings. Their presence at Qumran may relate to the communal meal that the sectarians consumed, if we look to the literature for possible explanation.[51] The presence of these ritual baths in such number and with such size in our view eliminates many of the proposals that would offer any variation of the villa hypothesis. The stepped pools are also situated in places where purification might be required and where impurity might be in-

curred. For example, two are located near the entrance to the two dining areas (Loci 48 and 49), in front of the room with a toilet, and near
the potters' workshop (Locus 71). The one near the northern entrance,
Locus 138, may be intended for the people who contracted an impurity
outside the compound, similar in a way to the ritual baths outside the
southern Temple Mount steps where pilgrims entered.[52] The stepped
pools would have been covered with roofing of mud brick, thatch,
and wood beams, so that the water would remain cool in summer, and
perhaps for reasons of modesty. All of these factors point to a community with a great concern for purity.[53]

The unique character of the site of Qumran is also partially reflected in the perimeter, where a long wall that runs north–south close
to 140 meters separates the settlement itself from the approximately
1,000 burials in the cemetery to the east. In addition, there is a second wall, a kind of boundary wall that runs intermittently for 500
meters along the shoreline from the Wadi Qumran to the springs of
Ein Feshka. Joan Branham and Jean-Baptiste Humbert, among others, have convincingly argued that the inner wall acts as a kind of
screening device to separate out the pure from the impure, heralding
the sacred space of the compound.[54] The boundary wall functioned as
a kind of *erub,* or Sabbath limit wall. In view of the revised, later chronology of the site advanced by numerous scholars to the first century
B.C.E., the long wall, and its extension southward, the reuse of the
large cistern in the settlement, and the cemetery are contemporaneous with the origins of the settlement around 100 B.C.E. or a bit later.
The significance of this chronology is quite clear, that the intent of
the long wall was to separate the pure from the impure world of the
cemetery to the east and to point to the settlement as the place of the
ritually pure community of believers. Branham has also suggested that
the break of two meters in this wall, to a point near a sort of vestibule
giving access to the large cistern, might have served as a location for
a burial party to enter a fixed point in the settlement where a group of
mourners could purify themselves (11QT 50:4–8). The low long wall
thus enabled the settlers at Qumran to identify themselves simultaneously in the two polar opposite states of pure and impure, the cemetery being the site of impurity and the settlement the site of purity.
We find analogous situations in the Jerusalem Temple, the sectarian
site of the Therapeutae in Egypt (Philo, *Contemp. Life* 32–33), and in

the many communities of Jews that used ritual baths from around 100 B.C.E. onward. In the words of Branham: "Interpreting the wall as a symbolic device of liminality, in turn posits Qumran itself as a liminal threshold for those seeking transition (spiritually or ritually) from an imperfect world to one more *halakhically* resolute."[55] This understanding of Qumran comports well with our view that recognizes the profane character of the regional context for the site, accommodating the idea that Qumran was not hermetically sealed from that world but rather envisioned itself apart from it, living in a state of purity.

The close proximity of the remains from the cemeteries that adjoin the community settlement at Qumran as well as their dating to the period of the settlement indicate that those buried there were affiliated with the inhabitants of the site, and that their manner of inhumation was most unusual for the period they date from, namely the end of the Second Temple period. The graves are well organized and carefully dug and nearly all are solitary—each shaft is a primary burial for a single individual. This is in contrast to the popular and contemporaneous practice of burial in family tombs with loculi and secondary burial, very often into ossuaries. The unique aspect of the burials and design of the cemeteries suggest an intentional differentiation from the more ordinary forms of Jewish inhumation at this time.[56] In the main cemetery, all were male; a small number of women and children were interred in a smaller, extension cemetery. Singular interment in shaft tombs is rare but not unheard of, with close parallels at the cemetery of Khirbet Qazone on the southeast shore of the Dead Sea, at Ein el-Ghuweir, south of Qumran, and even in Jerusalem, at Beit Zafafa, as well as a few other places.[57] Rachel Hachlili rejects the idea of intercommunal influence and maintains that the inhabitants' choice of this type of burial reflected their ideas of afterlife and was quite intentionally different from the dominant form of family burial at the time. The very fact that the individuals buried in the cemeteries at Qumran were not interred with their ancestors, a practice honored in ancient Israel and early Judaism for more than a millennium, places the emphasis on the individual over the family or larger unit. Hachlili concludes: "The residents of Qumran did not think of themselves as families. They also did not practice secondary burial in ossuaries, a common custom in the first century C.E. as evidenced by finds in Jerusalem and Jericho. These divergent practices are consistent with the identification of Qumran with one of the Jewish sects of the Second Temple period."[58] In our view the most likely candidate to be identified with those who inhabited Qumran is the Essene sect, even though the Essenes had numerous groups and were not localized in one place.

As we have seen, Golb, Magen and Peleg, Hirschfeld, and others have noted that no scrolls have been found at the site and consequently suggested that no connection exists between it and the caves.[59] Nonetheless, we believe that there is a connection between the site of Qumran and the caves where the scrolls have been found. The site itself illustrates the unique lifestyle of the Essenes, and the close proximity of the caves, especially Cave 4, which produced fragments representing more than half of the scrolls, offers strong evidence to link them with the site. The absence of scroll remains from the site itself can possibly be explained by the fact that it was destroyed by fire in 68 C.E., which meant that any scrolls there would have been consumed in the conflagration. A number of blank parchment pieces were among the scrolls that turned up and were sold by the Bedouin finders in the 1950s, adding weight to the assumption that many of the scrolls were copied at the site (fig. 4.11).[60] Also, the Qumran settlers, anticipating

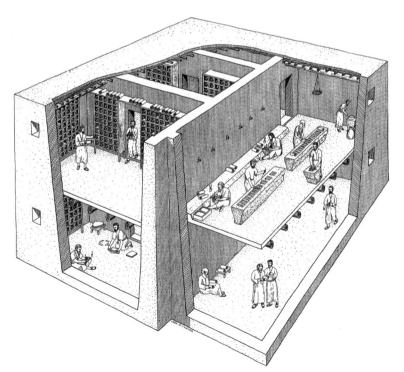

Fig. 4.11. Room for copying scrolls (Scriptorium) at Qumran (Reconstruction drawing by Leen Ritmeyer)

the looming struggle with the Romans, could have hidden the scrolls from the advancing armies to preserve them. Some have suggested that this might also explain the circumstances for hiding scrolls taken from the Temple in Jerusalem. But this hypothesis assumes that whoever lived at the site of Qumran, Essenes or others, would have had to have been supporters of those who came from Jerusalem to hide the scrolls, and that leaves us with understanding the site only as a villa or manor that was somehow connected to the Jerusalem elite or priesthood who would have wanted to save the Temple's scrolls. If scrolls were taken from Jerusalem to be hidden in the nearby caves, it could hardly have been done in secret, unless of course it happened after the destruction of the site in 68 C.E. On the other hand, if inhabitants from the Essene Quarter in Jerusalem or from one of their other communities feared that their scrolls would be endangered and destroyed by the Romans then they could possibly have brought them down to their fellow sectarians in Qumran who would have helped them hide them in the caves.

Other important factors to consider are the kinds and chronology of the pottery found at the site and in the caves, the relative absence of imported wares, and most important the meaning of the relatively rare use of the cylindrical jars for scroll storage in the caves and their appearance at the site. In addition, the ovoid-shaped jars found in abundance at Qumran also lend themselves to easy storage of written materials because of the large mouth, in contrast to the more common bag-shaped storage jars that dominate in the Roman period. Rachel Bar-Nathan and other scholars have successfully pointed out in recent years that the distinctive scroll jars are not unique to Qumran and have been found especially at the nearby site of Hasmonean-Herodian Jericho (90 B.C.E.–73 C.E.), some fourteen kilometers north of Qumran, and at Masada to the south, even possibly in Jerusalem at Qalandiya.[61] She also suggests the possibility of a common pottery workshop for both sites based on typological and provenience analysis. At Jericho there is a new and relatively small influx of imported wares in the Roman period, especially Nabatean wares, also documented at Qumran, which she says demonstrates that Qumran was not isolated from its surroundings. Bar-Nathan notes that the scroll jars are particularly well suited to archival use, since it was so easy to put one's hand inside, and that their presence at other sites does not

Fig. 4.12. Discovery of masses of pottery lying on the floor of the pantry in early excavations at Qumran (Photo courtesy of the ASOR Archive)

mean that the jars could not have served other uses as well. These interpretations, however, do not undermine the theory that an important segment of the Essene community could have occupied the site of Khirbet Qumran; rather, they serve as important reminders that even the Essene leadership could not be totally isolated from the surrounding culture that they were fighting so hard to change, if not in real time then in metahistorical time, that is, after the end of time.

The variety of forms in the pottery found at Qumran and the nearby caves suggests that together they represent a single corpus of everyday wares, with special types such as the scroll jars, that testifies to a common population inhabiting both the caves and the site below (fig. 4.12). The dating of the Qumran pottery falls well within the suggested time frame of the community, circa 100 B.C.E. to 68 C.E. The near absence of imported wares, especially Eastern Terra Sigillata A, however, may point to a certain hesitancy to utilize objects that would normally be associated with the wealthy and elite Jewish and non-Jewish aristocratic class, though the cost of importing such items may have been a factor as well. In addition, the dearth of imported materials of this sort certainly adds to the evidence against identifying the site of Qumran as a palatial villa. Moreover, the use of the cylindrical jars in which scrolls were stored, together with the presence of ovoid storage jars, both of which are more or less limited to the Qumran-

Jericho-Masada region, seems to be related to the purity issues that are most usually associated with the Essenes and their literature. The more common bag-shaped jars with narrow necks and loop handles are not found at Qumran, and Magness has argued convincingly that the reasons for this are that the ovoid and cylindrical jars had much wider openings and therefore could be used more efficiently for the storage and pouring of pure foodstuffs and liquids without danger of contamination due to pouring. A stone ladle, for example, could be easily inserted into the mouth of a cylindrical or ovoid storage jar but not the more common bag-shaped jar. Magness goes on to say that their distinctive shape also made them readily identifiable to those who were mindful of these legal concerns.[62] Since so many of the jars were found in the caves, there is no doubt that pure foodstuffs and drink were stored there as well. Storing sacred writings in jars goes back to biblical times (Jer 32:13–14), and is even practiced to this day by pious Jews who bury jars holding well-worn scrolls in a *genizah,* or permanent storage area, or who salvage the burned remains of Torah scrolls from fires and bury them or permanently store them in ceramic containers. The ovoid jar has been used in modern times for such a practice.

The larger question, which we have already referred to, is this: Does the archaeology of the site of Khirbet Qumran point to its occupation by a group of sectarians known collectively as the Essenes, or in the direction of some others, perhaps a select group such as those who occupied Jericho or Masada? From the corpus of pottery we may conclude that although the ceramic evidence is suggestive of a particular group sensitive to purity concerns, its similarity to other sites in the region and use of clays from the Jerusalem area demonstrates that the occupants of the site did not sever their ties with Jerusalem or totally distance themselves from their surrounding culture as much as others have suggested through the years. In our remarks on "common Judaism" below we point out the numerous lines of continuity that undergird all of the major sects of the late Second Temple period, Pharisees, Sadducees, Essenes, and even Zealots. Many Essenes lived in Jerusalem and villages in Judea (*War* 2.124), and the Community Rule and Damascus Document were intended for more than one community of sectarians. Hence, despite their disdain for the establishment and the Temple community in particular the Essenes still could live among the people and hold to their unique views. When Hillel the Elder, who lived at the end of the first century B.C.E. and overlapped with part of the career of Jesus, preached "Do not separate yourself from the community" (*m. Aboth* 2:5), he was giving voice to the view that Jews still should remain united in community despite strong political or theological disagreements. The statement attributed to Hillel seems to preserve a memory or awareness of the withdrawal of some sectarians from the community, and it could well be a veiled reference to the settlement at Qumran.

Aspects of Common Judaism

Despite the many differences between the Essenes and other groups of Jews in the Second Temple period, Pharisees, Sadducees, and Zealots, there were also strong elements of continuity among them, many common ideas that were based on biblical sources and that pointed ahead toward rabbinic Judaism. Despite the harshness of some of the disagreements among the main Jewish sects, there was a sense that all remained committed to God's Torah, though they disagreed what that written Torah was; what they agreed upon was observance of the Law, circumcision, and the core of the Shema: to love God with all one's heart and soul (Deut 6:4–9). Josephus also praises the commonality of Jewish practice at the turn of the era, although elsewhere (*Ant.* 13) he describes the three main *haireseis,* or philosophical schools among Jews: "Unity and identity of religious belief, perfect uniformity in habits and customs, produce a very beautiful concord in human character. Among us alone will be heard no contradictory statement about God, such as are common among other nations, not only on the lips of ordinary individuals under the impulse of some passing mood, but even boldly propounded by philosophers; some putting forward crushing arguments against the very existence of God, others depriving Him of His providential care for mankind. Among us alone will be seen no difference in the conduct of our lives. With us all act alike, all profess the same doctrine about God, one which is in harmony with our law and affirms that all things are under His eye" (*Against Apion* 2.179–81).

This notion of a "pluralistic" Israel, surely written to impress Gentile ears, nonetheless offers an alternative perspective on diversity in Second Temple Judaism, what our colleague E. P. Sanders has called "common Judaism." In our enthusiasm to acknowledge diversity and sectarianism, we need to be reminded of some of the commonalities that undergirded all groups, including ultimately the Jesus movement within Palestinian Judaism.

The discoveries at Qumran can shed light not only on sectarian differences therefore, but also on commonalities. From such texts as the Temple Scroll and the MMT Scroll (literally, "Some of the Works of the Torah"), also known as the "Halakhic Letter," which was probably intended for the priests in Jerusalem delineating the differences between the two groups, we can observe aspects of the beginnings of later rabbinic law. In the MMT Scroll, in particular, it becomes evident that the sect's halakhah (or law) shared certain key ideas with what must have been Pharisaic legal arguments of the time. The complex biblical hermeneutics utilized by the sectarians, including their extensive use of intertextuality, anticipate the methods used by the later rabbis, and are based on the Persian-period intertextual biblical traditions.[63]

The many scrolls found near Qumran also shed light on literary activity in the last few centuries of the Second Temple period. In addition, careful examination of the transmission of some of the scrolls has clearly pointed to a pre-Qumran setting for the "community" or "Yahad."[64] Both the evidence for a pre-Qumran setting for some of the scrolls and the dating of some of the manuscripts to a pre-Qumran period offer a full agenda for future studies that would focus on determining their original setting. One such recent study went so far as to suggest that the origin of the sectarian community was in early post-exilic times.[65] Whatever the origin of the sect, the early scrolls and many of the copies of biblical scrolls were almost certainly brought from elsewhere, possibly to be rescued from the destruction of Jerusalem, though as we have argued this does not mean that all other scrolls were brought to the caves of Qumran from elsewhere. The distinctively sectarian documents all date to the period of settlement at Qumran and no doubt relate to the unique history and ideology of the community, some of whose members made their home in the ruins below the caves, or possibly at another location in the Dead Sea region, as some scholars now maintain, as well as in other places in Judea including Jerusalem (fig. 4.13).

Fig. 4.13. Reconstruction of Khirbet Qumran, showing its proximity to the Dead Sea (Reconstruction drawing by Balage Balogh)

Many of the Scrolls contain books or fragments of books that were to become part of the present Hebrew Bible, some 220 in all. It is no surprise that the Pentateuch is so well represented in the corpus. The Book of Deuteronomy is first among the five, found in 29 manuscripts; only Psalms is found more frequently, in 36 manuscripts. The third most attested book in the Qumran library is the Book of Isaiah, which is found in 21 manuscripts. Not unexpected is the fact that the only other books represented in double digits are those in the rest of the Pentateuch, namely Genesis, Exodus, Leviticus, and Numbers. In all, 202 copies or fragments of biblical books are represented, or around 25 percent of the total. The statistics surely inform us about the important place of biblical books in the lives of Second Temple Jews from Jerusalem or Judea and surely something about the people who lived in Qumran. The sum total of all the manuscripts also demonstrates the richness of literature that was available, mainly in Hebrew and Aramaic, outside what was to become the Hebrew canon of Scripture in the early centuries C.E. In this connection the absence of any copies or fragments of the Book of Esther is noteworthy. Though it may be the result of happenstance, Esther is the only book in the Hebrew Bible that does not mention the name of God; nor does it mention the city of Jerusalem, the festivals, and many Jewish laws and practices. The feast of Purim that is associated with the book, likewise, is never mentioned in any Qumran text either. Although its absence could be due to sheer chance, perhaps it was its lack of piety or because it celebrates a victory of Diaspora Jews that caused the Essenes to reject it.[66]

Among the remainder of the manuscripts are many of the Christian Old Testament Apocrypha, a new corpus of Jewish pseudepigrapha, and the rewritten Torah. Other texts deal with the cycle of Jewish worship and holidays, especially the Sabbath in the framework of the solar calendar of the sect. All of these materials testify to the centrality of biblical texts and biblical figures in the Jewish literature of the turn of the Common Era, to the rich variety of genres found in the sectarian library, and to the belletristic character of the entire corpus both sectarian and nonsectarian. The amazing variety and number of compositions associated with both the Qumran and Jerusalem communities point to an unprecedented and unique moment in Jewish history and to a literacy rate that probably exceeds many other cultures in antiquity. The assumption is that there was a decent if not large audience for the literature that could appreciate it, at least orally in some form. All of this compositional activity occurred well in advance of the finalization of the Jewish canon of Scripture in the early centuries C.E.

Moreover, the great variety of types of writing reflected in the Qumran corpus shows that the sectarians as well as most other Jewish groups including the Jesus movement were more or less in accord about the Pentateuch and Prophets, although the Kethubim, or Writings, were still in a state of some flux in the first century C.E. The copious use of quotations from Jewish scripture in the New Testament, as seen for example in the Gospel of Matthew and the Book of Revelation, further confirms that even sectarian groups like the early Christians relied on the same scriptures as the elite establishment. The common Judaism that was emerging at this time was based on a commonly held library of texts, still with the sense that Scripture was unfulfilled and incomplete, thus allowing openings for apocalyptic groups such as the sectarians who lived in Qumran and other Yahad groups and the early Christians to base their visions of the future on the biblical text.

CHAPTER 5

From Herod to the Great Revolt

Herod's reign had united almost all of the land of Palestine, but his death brought about its division and a period of fluctuating boundaries and political statuses. For most of the first century, territory shifted back and forth between rulers appointed by the Roman emperor. These appointees were initially all sons of Herod, but Roman reliance solely on client kings to administer the region proved short lived. Within a few years, Judea and Samaria were converted into a Roman province overseen by Roman governors, an arrangement that lasted for most of the period leading up to the first Jewish revolt, while members of the Herodian dynasty ruled over other parts of the territory. Neither the Roman governors nor the Herodian client kings had access to the vast resources that Herod the Great had possessed, and the pace of construction of Roman monumental architecture slowed considerably. No building projects in the early decades of the first century seem to have matched Caesarea Maritima or Jerusalem in scale, but even smaller projects like those at Sepphoris, Tiberias, and Banias were highly significant in reshaping the landscape to display Roman cultural influence and domination as well as the political stature of their sponsors (fig. 5.1). Ultimately, the combined strains of Roman rule and internal divisions led to ruptures in Jewish society and the Great Revolt, a war followed within a few decades by the dissolution of the Herodian dynasty and the annexation of the entire region as a Roman province.[1]

The Division of Herod's Kingdom

A glimpse of the turmoil ahead was visible in the unrest that broke out soon after Herod's death (fig. 5.2). A Passover riot in Jerusalem was suppressed by Herod's son Archelaus, reportedly resulting in the deaths of three thousand people, some of them on the Temple Mount (*War* 2.10–13; *Ant.* 17.213–18). Roman forces arriving in Jerusalem from

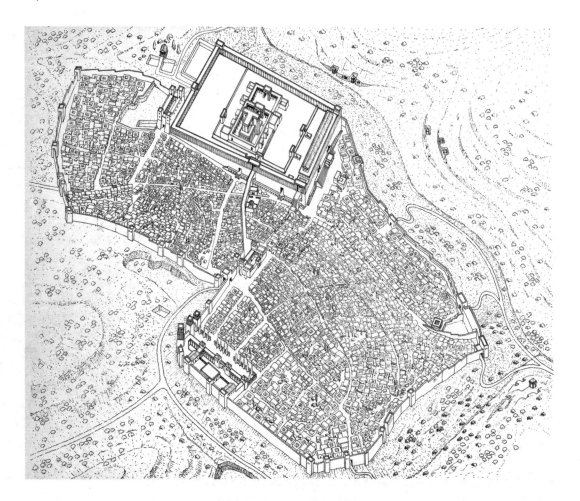

Fig. 5.1. Reconstruction of Jerusalem during the time of Jesus (Reconstruction drawing by Leen Ritmeyer)

Syria prompted a violent reaction that led to their own besiegement in Herod's palace and considerable damage to the porticoes of the Temple (*War* 2.39–54; *Ant.* 17.250–68). In Galilee, Judas, the son of the earlier rebel Hezekiah, led an uprising, while the royal slave Simon started a revolt in Perea. Elsewhere, a shepherd named Athrongaeus attempted to seize power, and even some of Herod's own Idumean troops lurched toward rebellion (*War* 2.55–65; *Ant.* 17.269–85). The troubles escalated enough that Varus, Roman legate of Syria, intervened, marching south to Jerusalem and Idumea and reportedly razing several towns along the way (*War* 2.66–79; *Ant.* 17.286–98).

Struggles for power in Palestine also occurred in the imperial court as Herod's sons vied for their father's throne. Faced with the

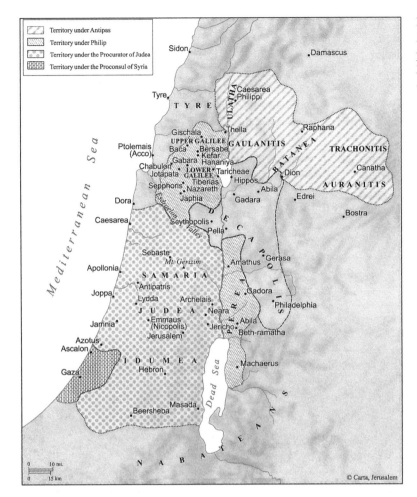

Fig. 5.2. The division of Herod's kingdom (Map prepared by Carta, Israel Map and Publishing Company, Ltd.)

confusion created by multiple versions of Herod's will, Augustus decided to divide his kingdom three ways. The emperor declined to bestow the highest title of *basileus* (king) on any of Herod's sons, at least for the moment. Instead, he named Archelaus an *ethnarch* (ruler of a people), with the promise that effective rule might eventually lead to his elevation to king. The ethnarchy of Archelaus included Judea, Samaria, and most of the coastal cities, though Gaza was attached to the province of Syria, along with the Decapolis cities of Gadara and Hippos. Antipas and Philip were granted the lesser title of *tetrarch* (ruler of a fourth). Antipas received Perea, the area east of the Jordan River between the Decapolis and the Nabateans, and Galilee, while

Table 5.1. The Herodian Dynasty

Ruler	Area	Dates
Herod the Great	most of Palestine	37–4 B.C.E.
Archelaus	Judea and Samaria	4 B.C.E.–6 C.E.
Antipas	Galilee and Perea	4 B.C.E.–39 C.E.
Philip	Iturea and Trachonitis	4 B.C.E.–34 C.E.
Agrippa I	territory of Philip	37–44 C.E.
	Galilee	39–44 C.E.
	remainder of Herod's territory	41–44 C.E.
Herod of Chalcis	Chalcis	41–48 C.E.
Agrippa II	Chalcis	48–53 C.E.
	Batanea, Trachonitis, and Gaulanitis	53–90s C.E.
	parts of eastern Galilee, Perea	61–90s C.E.

Philip took possession of the regions north and northeast of Galilee—Batanea, Trachonitis, and the area around Banias (*War* 2.94–100; *Ant.* 17.318–23).[2]

Archelaus's rule was too brief to make a widespread impact on the archaeological record. Excavators have, however, positively identified the site of a new city he built and named for himself (*Ant.* 17.340). An inscription found at Khirbet el-Beiyudat, roughly 12 kilometers north of Jericho, declares, "You are now entering Archelais." A 280-square-meter mansion there included a large courtyard divided by a row of columns, storage and living rooms, and a two-pooled miqveh. Nearby, a massive ashlar tower had walls that were more than a meter thick. Stone vessels in both the palace and the tower confirm that their occupants were Jewish.[3] At Jericho, changes in Herod's third palace might be attributed to Archelaus, in light of Josephus's report that he rebuilt a palace there after it was destroyed in the tumult following Herod's death (*Ant.* 17.340), but the site's primary excavator thinks it more likely they were initiated by Herod himself.[4]

The best-known archaeological remains from the ethnarchy of Archelaus are his coins. The weights of his various denominations appear to have been modeled on the Roman standard, rather than the Greek/Seleucid standard that Herod the Great had used. This change likely reflected an awareness that Roman influence had permanently eclipsed the Greek political dominance of early generations, and it was copied by other members of the Herodian dynasty when they struck their own coins. Archelaus's numismatic inscriptions included his title of ethnarch and his dynastic name Herod, rather than his Latin name Archelaus. Some of his coins' symbols were quite close to those on Herod's coins, such as cornucopiae and an anchor, while others, like a vine and galleys, were completely different.[5]

Little else is known of the reign of Archelaus, other than that by 6 C.E., his subjects had tired of his harsh hand. Both Jews and Samaritans sent envoys to Caesar to complain of his excesses. Caesar promptly deposed him, exiling him to Vienna and confiscating his property. The territories of Judea, Samaria, and Idumea were henceforth governed by a Roman official (*War* 2.117, in contrast to *Ant.* 17.354–55, which says they were joined to the province of Syria).

The Impact of Antipas

The longer reign of Antipas (4 B.C.E.–39 C.E.) left more extensive archaeological remains (fig. 5.3). Antipas devoted considerable energy to construction projects in Galilee.[6] Josephus reports that Antipas rebuilt Sepphoris after Varus burned it down in the chaos following Herod the Great's death (*War* 2.68; *Ant.* 17.289), though no archaeological corroboration of that destruction has been found. If evidence of damage to the city is lacking, however, evidence of its development

Fig. 5.3. Herod Antipas ruled Galilee and Perea from 4 B.C.E. to 39 C.E. The coin at left is dated to 39/40 C.E.; the reverse has a palm tree and "Herod the Tetrarch" in Greek. The coin at right, dated to 29/30 C.E., also reads "Herod the Tetrarch," and includes the name of the mint city, Tiberias, on the reverse in a wreath. (Copyright David Hendin, used by permission)

Fig. 5.4. Water reservoir at Sepphoris, part of a larger Roman-period water system; this section post-dates Antipas (Photo courtesy of Eric Meyers)

in the first century C.E. is abundant. Settlement on the city's acropolis and its western summit began to grow, spilling over onto a plateau to the east that became the primary area of expansion in the second and later centuries. Excavators of a basilical building on the eastern plateau date its foundation and the beginnings of the city's orthogonal road plan to the first century, although others suggest a later date.[7] An aqueduct was built to ensure an adequate water supply for the city's increased population, which likely numbered between 8,000 and 12,000 (fig. 5.4).[8] Though an origin during the reign of Antipas has been proposed for a Roman-style theater on the western summit holding 4,500–5,000 seats, majority opinion dates it to the late first or early second century C.E. Disagreement over the theater's date hinges on stylistic considerations and the interpretation of unpublished ceramic evidence from under its foundations. (The theater is discussed further in Chapter 10.)

Fig. 5.5. Bronze prutah of Herod Antipas, struck at Sepphoris (I B.C.E./I C.E.). Obverse depicts a palm tree with the name Herod, and the reverse shows grain of barley surrounded by "Tetrarch, IV." (Copyright David Hendin, used by permission)

Antipas named his new city Autocratoris, a name that honored the imperial title of Autocrator, the Greek equivalent of the Latin Imperator or, alternatively, a reference to the city's independent (literally, "self-ruling") status (fig. 5.5). The city appears to have been the only one in the empire to receive that name, which never gained wide usage. Aside from one passage (*Ant.* 18.27) Josephus always refers to the city as Sepphoris, and most later sources use its Hebrew name, Zippori, or its second-century C.E. Greek name, Diocaesarea.

In 20 C.E., Antipas issued a series of coins that announced his foundation of a new city in Galilee.[9] Like Sepphoris-Autocratoris, the new city bore a name honoring the emperor: Tiberias, after the recently acceded Tiberius. Also like its sister city, Tiberias appears to have been the only one in the empire with its particular name. The new city was located at approximately the midpoint of the western shore of the Sea of Galilee. Built on the site of old tombs, Antipas had to force settlers to live there (*Ant.* 18.36–38; cf. *War* 2.168). Despite initial difficulties in attracting inhabitants, the city's population grew to approximately the same size as Sepphoris.

Most of the archaeological findings from ancient Tiberias have been unearthed on the southern side of the modern city. A gate with two adjacent round towers is usually attributed to Antipas, though some have suggested that it actually dates to the late first or the second century C.E. (See plate 7.) A *cardo,* a north-south street, running parallel to the lake has also often been associated with the city's earliest years, as has a recently discovered Roman theater at the foot of Mount Berenice. Whether such structures date to the time of Antipas or to subsequent early rulers is not clear. Recent excavations have uncovered a villa decorated with columns, opus reticulatum, and marble that may be the palace of Antipas (*Life* 65, 68). If so, the use of marble in such an early context would be unusual; Palestine was not fully integrated into the marble network until after the revolt. Josephus mentions other public buildings; by the time of the first revolt, the city had a sizable *proseuche,* or building for prayer (*Life* 277), hot baths (*Life* 85), and a stadium of some sort (*War* 2.168, 3.539; *Life* 92, 331). A nine-meter-thick curved wall and another nearby wall found at the modern Galei Kinneret Hotel could be the remains of the stadium.[10]

Antipas's efforts were not wholly limited to Galilee. In Perea, he renamed Betharamptha, which had also suffered in the revolts after Herod's death (*War* 2.59), as Julias (*Ant.* 18.27; *War* 2.168) and probably used it as the region's administrative center. The location of this Julias is not clear, and little has been found in the archaeological record east of the Jordan River that can be securely associated with Antipas. (This Julias should not be confused with the distinct community of Bethsaida-Julias, which is discussed below.)

Antipas struck his coins in Galilee, minting his first issues in Sepphoris and all subsequent ones in Tiberias. Galilee was predominantly Jewish, as evidenced by the widespread use of stone vessels and the occasional discovery of miqvaot as well as the writings of Josephus, the Gospels, and later rabbinic texts. Antipas's coins reflect sensitivity to the religious sensibilities of his subjects. They bore no portraits of the ruler himself, the emperor, or pagan deities, instead bearing images such as a wreath, a reed, or palm trees. Most were inscribed with the name of his city Tiberias, though the final series of coins, issued in 39 C.E., swapped this epigraphic reference for an inscription naming and honoring Gaius, who had replaced Tiberius on the throne.[11]

The economic effects of Antipas's city building remain a point of considerable debate. Some scholars have argued that such massive construction projects must have had a negative impact on villages and small towns. The cities, they suggest, would have drained food and other resources from the countryside, resulting in shortages for many communities. In their view, smaller independently owned farms must have given way to larger estates. The building of two cities would have necessitated a high tax rate, the collection of which would have been facilitated by the increased monetary supply that resulted from the striking of coins by Antipas. The combined result of such changes would have been the creation of cycles of debt, land loss, and poverty for the masses. For most commoners, according to this line of reasoning, developments in Antipas's reign resulted in economic crisis and exploitation.[12]

Noting that such proposals are often based more on particular social-scientific theories than on the archaeological evidence itself, other scholars have offered a very different picture of first-century Galilee. In their view, the emergence of cities would have stimulated the region's need for foodstuffs and other products, and farmers and artisans would have benefitted from the increased level of demand. Precise information about the level of taxation under Antipas is lacking, but what does seem clear is that the very modest amount of coinage he struck would not have moved the economy to a new level of monetization; a mixed economy based on both barter and buying had been the norm since the influx of large amounts of Hasmonean coinage a century earlier. Villages such as Jotapata, Khirbet Cana, and Capernaum show indications of economic vitality, not decline, with increases in community size and in production of olive oil, textiles, and pottery. While the Gospels and other ancient literary sources refer to absentee landlords and tenant farmers, neither they nor the archaeological record provide sufficient data to trace shifts in patterns of ownership or crop production. To be sure, poverty was widespread throughout the ancient world, but if it increased suddenly and dramatically in Galilee because of the policies of Antipas, such developments are not clearly attested in the archaeological record.[13]

What is clear is that Antipas's construction of cities marked the introduction of a new level of Greco-Roman cultural influence in Galilee. By their names alone, the cities pointed to the power of the emperor. The introduction of orthogonal street planning arranged civic space in the style of the Romans, and monumental civic architecture appeared for the first time, if not in his reign then in the decades that immediately followed. Even so, this growth of Greco-Roman culture should not be exaggerated; it is best understood as foreshadowing of the more dramatic developments that would follow in the second and third centuries C.E.[14]

The Reign of Philip

If Antipas had named cities after the emperor and Archelaus after himself, their brother Philip combined these approaches, changing the name of Banias from Paneas, which honored the Greek deity, to Caesarea Philippi (*Ant.* 20.211; Mark 8:27; Matt 16:13). The name distinguished this Caesarea from his father's coastal city, though second- and third-century coins show that it was later abandoned for Caesarea Paneas. The city served as the location for Philip's mint, and the tetra-style temple appearing on his coins is usually interpreted as Herod the Great's temple to Augustus.[15] Caesarea Philippi at this point appears to have been only a modest city; excavations suggest that its area was quite small and had few residential structures.[16]

Philip's city-founding activity extended beyond Caesarea Phi-lippi. At some point he built walls around the village of Bethsaida and renamed it Julias. One wonders if Jesus' disciple Philip, who hailed from Bethsaida according to John 1:44, was named after the tetrarch. According to Josephus (*Ant.* 18.27–28), Bethsaida's new name honored Augustus's daughter Julia. Noting that Julia was disgraced by charges of adultery in 2 B.C.E., some have suggested that Josephus's report is confused and that Bethsaida's new name actually recognized Augus-tus's widow Livia, who had become a member of the Julian family and taken the name Julia at his death. Ultimately, it is difficult to determine with certainty when and for whom Philip renamed Bethsaida.[17]

Nor is it clear exactly where Bethsaida-Julias was located, though excavators at et-Tell have argued that is the most likely candidate. They suggest that a rectangular basalt building at the site was a shrine to Livia built by Philip, identifying its various rooms as typical components of a temple: a porch, *pronaos* (entrance chamber), naos (main room), and *opisthodomos* (back room). As supporting evidence, they point to nearby discoveries of a female figurine that they identify as Livia and a bronze incense shovel, which they argue indicates the presence of the impe-rial cult. Other scholars, however, question the architectural compari-son to a temple and note the lack of votive gifts, dedicatory inscrip-tions, animal bones from sacrifices, and other indisputable evidence of a temple cult. Some also note that et-Tell's location, a kilometer and a half north of the Sea of Galilee, seems to conflict with ancient refer-ences suggesting that Bethsaida was a lakeside town. The excavators have defended their identification of the site with claims that the water level was higher in antiquity and would have stretched to et-Tell, while critics counter that a water level that high would have inundated parts of other known first-century communities and submerged the known ancient harbors scattered around the lake.[18]

Regardless of whether Philip built an imperial temple, he defi-

Fig. 5.6. Two portrait coins of Herod Philip, the first Jewish ruler to place his portrait on coins. Left obverse depicts Augustus with legend "Of Caesar Augustus," and the reverse has a portrait of Herod Philip and legend "Of Philip the Tetrarch" (1/2 C.E.). (Copyright David Hendin, used by permission)

nitely found a way to honor the emperors that distinguished him from both his father and his brothers. He depicted the emperor and members of the imperial family on his coins, making him the first Jewish ruler to employ numismatic images of humans (fig. 5.6). Coins minted early in his reign portray Augustus on one side and Philip himself on the other, while others depict the emperor and a tetrastyle temple. Images of Tiberius later replaced those of Augustus, and depictions of the temple varied among the different issues. A three-denomination series struck in 30/31 C.E. makes Philip's relative stature clear: the largest portrays Tiberius, the medium size depicts Livia, and the smallest bears the image of Philip himself.[19]

Such images would not have offended the majority of Philip's subjects, who were Gentiles. A sizable minority, however, were Jews, particularly in the area immediately northeast of the Sea of Galilee. Archaeological evidence of Jewish inhabitants has been found most notably at Gamla, in the form of stone vessels and one of the earliest known synagogues, as well as at et-Tell, which has also yielded fragments of stone vessels.[20]

The Two Agrippas

When Philip died in Bethsaida-Julias in 33–34 C.E., he left no heirs. Upon the client king's death, Tiberius attached his territory to Syria, though this would prove to be only a temporary arrangement; the area soon shifted to Agrippa I. Agrippa, grandson of Herod the Great, had been educated in Rome but left the city after squandering his wealth and falling into debt. Through the efforts of his sister Hero-

Fig. 5.7. Coins of Agrippa I, grandson of Herod the Great. At left, obverse has portrait of Caligula, reverse has distyle temple with two facing figures and the legend "The Great King Agrippa, friend of Caesar" (42/43 C.E.). Center coin (37/38 C.E.) has portrait of Agrippa I on obverse; reverse has his son Agrippa II on horseback. The coin at right, dated to 41/42 C.E., was originally intended for circulation in Judea, which was added to the territory of Agrippa I in 41 C.E. The obverse depicts an umbrella-like canopy and "Of King Agrippa"; the reverse has three ears of barley. The canopy served as a sign of royalty. (Copyright David Hendin, used by permission)

dias, who was married to Herod Antipas, he received an appointment of *agoranomos* (market overseer) in Tiberias around 34 C.E. Agrippa soon departed Tiberias for Syria and then left Syria for the island of Capri, where he lived with Tiberius until the emperor imprisoned him for infelicitous comments about the positive political prospects of Gaius (Caligula). When Tiberius died and Gaius ascended the throne, he remembered Agrippa's support. He appointed him king over Philip's territory in 37 C.E. and gave him Antipas's territories two years later (*Ant.* 18.252; *War* 2.183). In 41 C.E., the new emperor Claudius expanded Agrippa's territory further with the gifts of Judea, Samaria, and northern parts of the Golan (*Ant.* 19.274; *War* 2.214–17). Agrippa thus ruled over a sizable kingdom, albeit only briefly (fig. 5.7).[21]

Agrippa's best-known construction project was the "Third Wall" in Jerusalem. A minority of scholars argues that this wall ran roughly along the northern border of the present Old City. Most, however, opt for a considerably larger expansion of the city's boundaries. They suggest that the wall stretched as far as 450 meters north of the present wall and pointing to several segments of a major wall discovered in that vicinity. If the latter position is correct, the new fortification practically doubled the size of the city, which now included Bezetha, just north of the Temple Mount. Agrippa did not complete the wall; Josephus attributes suspension of its construction to the king's death in one passage (*War* 2.218–19) and to Roman demands to cease work in another (*Ant.* 19.326–27). Jewish rebels later

Fig. 5.8. Coins of Agrippa II. Obverse of coin at left (83/84 C.E.) has a portrait of Domitian; the reverse depicts Tyche-Demeter holding ears of grain in the right hand and a cornucopia in the other, with the title "King Agrippa." The coin at right, not dated, has a bust of Nero on obverse; on the reverse is an inscription naming Caesarea Paneas as the mint, with a legend that reads "In the time of King Agrippa, Neronias." (Copyright David Hendin, used by permission)

finished it during the revolt (*War* 5.147–59). Remains of several towers have been found, though nowhere near the ninety that Josephus claims. Even after the city's expansion, numerous buildings remained outside its walls. Agrippa built a new aqueduct for the city, probably in response to population growth (*Ant.* 19.328–31).[22]

Agrippa also sponsored other projects. He funded games in Caesarea Maritima (*Ant.* 19.343), where coin finds from his reign date the renovation of the hippodrome, or stadium, adjacent to the Promontory Palace.[23] Numismatic evidence also suggests that he built a sizable (1.6 hectares) road station at Archelais with colonnaded porches decorated with pilasters and a miqveh.[24] Agrippa donated a theater, amphitheater, portico, and baths to Berytus (Beirut), where he also paid for gladiatorial games (*War* 1.422; *Ant.* 19.328, 335–37).

Agrippa's coins reflect the steady increase of Roman influence on numismatic designs, with some modeled on coins issued in the city of Rome itself. Many portrayed the emperor and members of the imperial family, while still others bore the image of Agrippa and his family, including his son Agrippa II, the future king (fig. 5.8).[25] If, as has been suggested, the *phi rho* on one of his lead weights is an abbreviation for "friend of Caesar" (*philoromaios*), the title would make sense in light of his friendship with the emperor (Philo, *Against Flaccus* 25, 40).[26]

Agrippa died after a short sickness in 44 C.E. Both Acts (12:20–23) and Josephus (*Ant.* 19.343–52) blame his demise squarely upon hubris. According to Acts, when Herod did not reject acclamation as a god by the people of Tyre and Sidon, an "angel of the Lord struck him down, and he was eaten by worms and died." In Josephus's version, Agrippa was greeted as a deity by the audience at a spectacle in Caesarea Maritima, accepted the flattery, and immediately fell ill with an abdominal disorder, dying five days later.

His son Agrippa II was only seventeen at the time (fig. 5.9). Claudius waited until he had aged four more years before awarding him the territory of Chalcis in 48 C.E. after its previous ruler, Herod of Chalcis, died. After the death of Agrippa I, Herod of Chalcis had been placed in charge of the Jerusalem Temple's administration and given the authority to appoint the high priest. Now, Claudius transferred those powers to Agrippa II, giving him influence and power in Jerusalem even though his territory did not include Judea. In 53 C.E., Claudius removed Chalcis from Agrippa's domain but assigned him territories in the Golan Heights (*War* 2.247; *Ant.* 20.137–38). Nero later gave him Tiberias and Taricheae in eastern Galilee and Julias and surrounding villages in Perea (*War* 2.252; *Ant.* 20.159). After Agrippa's death, which probably occurred some time in the 90s C.E., the Romans returned Galilean and Perean territories to the province of Judea and annexed his northern territories into the province of Syria. He had been the longest reigning of the Herodian client kings.[27]

Josephus writes that Agrippa II "embellished" Banias (*War* 3.514). An aqueduct there may date to his rule, and a palatial complex almost definitely does. The palace was massive, covering perhaps as many as ten thousand square meters and including a basilical building, courtyards, and vaulted passages. Its floors and walls were decorated with real marble, reflecting greater access to the stone than earlier Herodian kings had had. The city's cardo dates to the first or second century and thus may also be associated with the king. The excavators suggest that it was during Agrippa's reign that Caesarea Philippi acquired enough residents to be considered a true city rather than simply a governmental center (fig. 5.10).[28]

In contrast to his father, Agrippa II almost always refrained from depicting himself on his coins. If the bust of a ruler appeared on an obverse, it was that of a Flavian emperor. Pan and other deities adorned the reverses of many coins, though smaller denominations include non-anthropomorphic images such as cornucopiae, a palm tree, an anchor, and corn. A few of his coins have Latin inscrip-

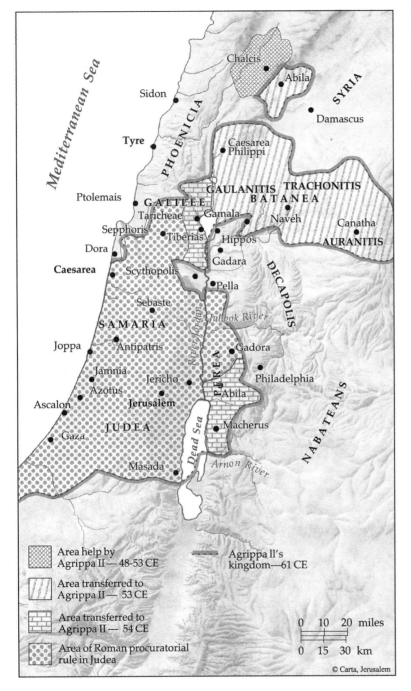

Fig. 5.9. The kingdom of Agrippa II, or Roman Palestine (Map prepared by Carta, Israel Map and Publishing Company, Ltd.)

Mediterranean Sea

Chalcis
Abila
SYRIA
Sidon
PHOENICIA
Damascus
Tyre
Caesarea
Philippi
Ptolemais
GAULANITIS TRACHONITIS
BATANEA
GALILEE
Taricheae Gamala
Naveh
Sepphoris Canatha
Tiberias AURANITIS
Dora Hippos
Caesarea Gadara DECAPOLIS
Scythopolis
Pella
Sebaste
Jabbok River
SAMARIA
Joppa PEREA
Antipatris Gadora
Jamnia Philadelphia
Jericho
Azotus Abila
Ascalon Jerusalem
Macherus NABATEANS
Gaza JUDEA
River Jordan
Masada Dead Sea
Arnon River

Area help by
Agrippa II — 48-53 CE
Agrippa II's
kingdom—61 CE

Area transferred to
Agrippa II — 53 CE

Area transferred to
Agrippa II — 54 CE

| 0 | 10 | 20 miles |

| 0 | 15 | 30 km |

Area of Roman procuratorial
rule in Judea

© Carta, Jerusalem

Fig. 5.10. Cult shrine at
Banias, or Caesarea Philippi
(Photo courtesy of Sean
Burrus)

tions, a feature that would have sharply distinguished them from most
of the Roman East's Greek-bearing coins and one that his subjects almost certainly would have interpreted as a strong statement of Roman
identity. As a loyal client king, Agrippa contributed troops to Rome's
effort to suppress the Great Revolt, and he advertised the Roman victory by placing images of Nike, goddess of victory, on his coins, a
choice reminiscent of coins issued by the Romans themselves that proclaimed *Judea Capta* ("Judea Captured").[29]

Prefects and Procurators

Most Herodian client kings had Roman counterparts ruling other
portions of Palestine as provincial governors. After the deposal of
Archelaus, Judea and Samaria were placed under direct Roman rule
as the province of Judea, and remained in that status for the rest of
the century, with the exception of the three years in which Agrippa I
held all Palestine (41–44 C.E.). After the death of Agrippa I, Galilee
was added to the province, though some of its eastern communities
were later parceled out to Agrippa II. Palestine's Roman governors
are commonly known as procurators, though in fact they held the
different title of prefect until the reign of Claudius. Many provinces
had Roman senators as governors, but Judea's were only of equestrian

rank, an apparent reflection of the province's low stature and high propensity for unrest.[30]

No Roman legionnaires were regularly stationed in the province in the pre-70 C.E. period. Instead, the Romans relied on auxiliary troops, primarily local recruits from Caesarea Maritima and Sebaste (*Ant.* 19.356–66, 20.122, 20.176; *War* 2.236). These units were stationed in Jerusalem, mainly at the Antonia Fortress overlooking the Temple Mount, and Caesarea Maritima. The total number of Roman troops in the province of Judea was quite small; when Agrippa I died, it consisted of only five cohorts and one cavalry unit, or approximately three thousand men (*Ant.* 19.365; cf. *War* 3.66). In times of serious trouble, the governor had to seek aid from his higher-ranked colleague, the legate of Syria, who commanded three to four legions.[31]

The Roman military and administrative contingent proclaimed its presence and authority through the striking of bronze coinage. Some governors issued no coins at all, while others, like Pontius Pilate, struck a considerable number (fig. 5.11). The physical quality of the procuratorial coinage varied widely, from crudely manufactured misstruck pieces to elegant specimens that are still well preserved. In adherence to eastern Mediterranean custom, these coins bore Greek, rather than Latin, inscriptions. Likely minted in Jerusalem, they have been found largely in Judea and Samaria and had only limited circulation in Galilee. None bore the name of the governor who issued them, but they can nonetheless be identified with particular prefects and procurators through their inscribed dates, which name the regnal year of the current emperor. A coin dated to the seventeenth year of Tiberius (30 C.E.), for example, was obviously struck by Pilate. The designs of these coins were far less provocative than they could have been, as they bore no busts of the emperor or prefect. Instead, most had images that provincial residents would have regarded as traditional, such as a palm tree, palm branches, lilies, cornucopiae, vines, and a wreath. Only a few departed from this pattern. Pilate issued coins with images of a *lituus* and a *simpulum,* implements used for Roman cultic acts, while Felix's coins had the regional motif of a palm tree on one side but spears and shields on the other, militaristic imagery that was likely intended as a reminder of Roman might. The consistent avoidance of anthropomorphic and zoomorphic imagery may have reflected sensitivity to Jewish unease with figural representation (fig. 5.12).[32]

Fig. 5.11. Coins of Pontius Pilate. Left, an inner wreath on obverse; on reverse, augur's wand and Greek legend "Of Tiberius" (30/31 C.E.). Coin at right depicts three bound ears of grain, with the legend "Julia, the queen" in Greek (Julia Olivia was the mother of Tiberius); the reverse depicts a libation ladle surrounded by the legend "Of Tiberius Caesar" (29/30 C.E.). None of the coins of procurators carried their own names. (Copyright David Hendin, used by permission)

Fig. 5.12. Ossuary of Caiaphas, the high priest, during
the time of the trial of Jesus
(Photo courtesy of the Israel
Antiquities Authority)

Fig. 5.13. Inscription of
Pontius Pilate at Caesarea,
the only known attestation of
the name of the governor of
Judea who ordered the crucifixion of Jesus (Photo courtesy of the Israel Museum)

The Romans made Caesarea Maritima the administrative capital
of the province, bolstering its status as the most Romanized city in the
eastern Empire. The governors took over Herod's Promontory Palace, and its eastern wing and peristyle courtyard appear to have been
added by the new administration. This complex may be the "praetorium of Herod" in which Paul was questioned (Acts 23:35). Elite residences elsewhere in the city took on the Roman
trappings of colored plaster and mosaic decorations, and the city grew in size and population.[33]

Only one of the first-century governors is
mentioned in the city's many Roman-period inscriptions (fig. 5.13). A dedicatory inscription of Pontius
Pilate is partially preserved on a limestone slab that
was later reused as a step in the theater. The Latin
inscription reads:

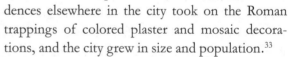

[——]s Tiberieum
[-P]ontius Pilatus
[praef]ectus Iuda[ae]e
[———]

No small amount of effort has been spent trying
to reconstruct and understand this inscription. The

identification of "Pontius Pilate" is clear enough, as is the reference to his title of prefect of Judea. The "Tiberieum" has traditionally been interpreted as a shrine dedicated to the emperor. If that reading is correct, then the building's construction may have gone against the preferences of the emperor himself, who often declined divine honors.[34] It conceivably could have been some other sort of building dedicated to the emperor.

The Growth of Jerusalem

Whether under client king or prefect, Jerusalem continued to grow in the first century. The city was impressive, even by Roman standards, as illustrated by Pliny the Elder's description of it as "the most illustrious city in the East" (*Natural History* 5.70). Recent estimates of its population range from "a few tens of thousands" to more than two hundred thousand, with one hundred thousand being a common estimate. Whatever the correct figure, the number of people present would have swollen much more during the three annual pilgrimage festivals.[35] The city's water needs were too great for its traditional springs, leading to further development of its aqueduct system. Pilate's use of Temple funds for aqueduct construction sparked protests, while the later work by Agrippa I seems to have been uncontroversial (*War* 2.175–77; *Ant.* 18.60–62).

The Temple dominated the city physically, politically, and economically, and as would be expected, the areas adjacent to it underwent extensive development. Large buildings, some of them elite residences, sprang up below its southern gates, and shops occupied the few meters separating the western retaining wall from the north–south thoroughfare running parallel to it. Though this road seems to have been built by Herod the Great, it was repaved in the first century, judging from the dates of coins found underneath it.[36]

Josephus refers to several examples of prominent civic architecture in Jerusalem, though their locations remain unknown. A xystus, usually thought of as a porticoed area devoted to exercise and athletics, west of the Temple Mount was joined to it by a bridge (*War* 2.344, 5.144, 6.325, 8.377). Josephus implies that a hippodrome stood not far from the Temple (*War* 2.44; *Ant.* 17.254–55). Whether the structure was built by Herod or one of his successors is not known.

Fig. 5.14. Pool of Siloam,
Jerusalem, south of Temple
Mount, where pilgrims
ascended to enter the Temple
after ritual purification (Photo
courtesy of Todd Bolen/
BiblePlaces.com)

Another public project was the renovation of a first-century
B.C.E. pool in the southeastern part of the city (fig. 5.14). The pool
received a new pavement of limestone ashlars. Fed by runoff water
and the nearby Gihon spring, the pool had steps leading into it on all
sides and a colonnaded walkway to the north. Over two hundred meters long, this pool could have been used by hundreds of people at a
time. Given its location on the slope above the Kidron Valley and near
the end of the Tyropoeon Valley, it is very likely the Pool of Siloam referred to by Josephus (*War* 5.140; cf. John 9:7). (The nearby pool also
known as the Pool of Siloam that is located at the entrance to Hezekiah's Tunnel actually dates only to the Byzantine period.) Another pool
from the late Second Temple period located north of the city where
the Church of Saint Anne now stands has been identified as the Pool
of Bethesda. Ronny Reich concludes that pilgrims used both it and
the Pool of Siloam for ritual immersion and that they found numerous ways to guard their personal modesty.[37]

Fig. 5.15. Stone vessels from the Burnt House, Jerusalem (Photo courtesy of Hillel Geva, the Israel Exploration Society)

The wealth of many of the city's residents is reflected in the remains of their houses, which were destroyed in the revolt. (See plate 8.) Lavish residences stretched across the Upper City toward the Temple Mount. Many of these buildings were quite large, and some appear to have had second stories. Molded stucco and painted plaster decorated their walls, particularly in the dining rooms. Some painted walls imitated marble panels, while others bore architectural, floral, and geometric motifs. Some houses even had images of living things, showing a flexible attitude toward the traditional Jewish prohibition of representational art. Stucco moldings, for example, include the shapes of a rabbit, an antelope, a lion, and perhaps even a pig. One painted wall in a residence on what is now called Mount Zion depicted birds. More distinctively Jewish designs were also found, including a menorah carved into the plastered wall of a house in the eastern Upper City, one of the oldest known depictions of the Temple candelabrum. Mosaics adorned the floors of these houses, some of them multicolored, others black and white in a style common elsewhere in the Roman world. Geometric and floral designs were omnipresent in these mosaics, with rosettes being especially common, and figural representation appears to have been entirely absent.[38]

Miqvaot are common finds in these houses, as are a variety of stone implements, ranging from utensils to serving pieces to large

Fig. 5.16. Everyday pottery from the Burnt House, Jerusalem (Photo courtesy of Hillel Geva, the Israel Exploration Society)

storage vessels to entire tables. Both miqvaot and stone vessels reflect a high level of concern with ritual purity, and the proximity of these houses to the Temple strongly suggests that priestly families occupied them (fig. 5.15). A stone weight found in the so-called Burnt House, an excavated structure destroyed by the conflagration of the revolt, confirms this for one residence; its Semitic inscription, "of Bar Qatros," likely refers to the Qatros priestly family. However, it is surprising to note the paucity of imported vessels in the Burnt House. Excavator Hillel Geva notes the presence of only two amphoras, sherds of several lamps, and a few other pieces (fig. 5.16).[39]

In some domiciles, however, imported fine pottery and wine amphorae demonstrate a familiarity with luxury goods. The families that lived in these Jerusalem houses had a propensity for decorated tablewares, both foreign and locally produced. A new style of cooking pan also appears, one found elsewhere primarily at elite dwellings such as the Herodian palaces. Its flat shape reflects the clear influence of Italian-style casserole pans. The combination of these Italian pans, elegant tablewares, and frescoed triclinium-like dining rooms suggests Romanophile tendencies, at least on the level of dining and living customs.[40]

Wealthy residents of Jerusalem continued the custom introduced in the Hasmonean period of burying the deceased in elaborately decorated tombs, some of them accompanied by impressive monuments. Such tombs are found on all sides of the walled city. Among the bet-

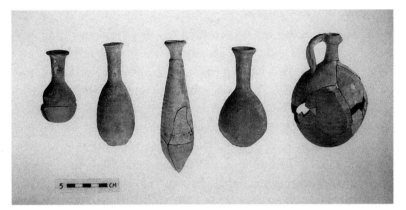

Fig. 5.17. Typical pottery found in a Jewish tomb from the early Roman period at Isawiyeh, Jerusalem (Photo courtesy of the ASOR Archive)

ter known today are the Tomb of Absalom, with its famous cone-shaped monument, and the adjacent tomb of Jehoshaphat, clearly visible down in the Kidron Valley from the eastern limits of the city. West of the city, a foundation for a monument is clearly visible in front of what is often called Herod's family tomb, in the modern park adjacent to the King David Hotel.[41] To the north, not far beyond the Third Wall, stood the Tomb of Queen Helena of Adiabene, often called the Tomb of the Kings. The queen was a convert to Judaism who had relocated to Jerusalem (*Ant.* 20.17–95). Her tomb was marked by three pyramids on its top, a Doric frieze with acanthus leaves, wreaths, and grapes, and an elaborately decorated facade with attached Ionic columns. The traveler Pausanias considered this tomb noteworthy enough to mention along with the mausoleum of Halicarnassus as among the most beautiful tombs he had seen (7.16.5). Mount Scopus was also the site of impressive burials, such as that of Nicanor, whom inscriptions identify as a donor to the Temple. Other decorated tombs in Jerusalem's necropolis included the Sanhedrin Tomb, the Tomb of the Grapes, and the Tomb of the Frieze. Tombs like these, with outer decorations visible to passersby, advertised the stature of the deceased and their families and contrasted sharply with the hundreds of more simple rock-cut tombs found elsewhere around the city (fig. 5.17).[42]

Constructing Jewish Identity Under Roman Rule

Such opulent demonstrations of wealth were not common in most of the rest of Palestine, particularly the Jewish areas. For example, imported slipped dishes of the types found in Jerusalem houses had been common earlier at Galilean sites, but they are absent from first-century C.E. strata, where undecorated, locally produced vessels take their place. Galilee's ceramic profile differs in this regard from those of adjacent pagan sites, however, which continued to import the red-slipped plates and bowls known as Eastern Sigilatta A. Thus, trade networks that could have provided Galileans with red-slipped pottery were still in place, but Galileans ceased importation of those wares. Similarly, the imported Italian-style pans found in elite Jerusalem houses and Herodian palaces are far less common in Galilee and other areas. In contrast to Jerusalem, most predominantly Jewish communities showed a strong preference for simple pottery from regional workshops, many of them relatively new centers of production that had appeared only in the previous century. Such a preference might indicate a desire by those in smaller communities to differentiate themselves from the wealthy, often Romanized tastes of the region's elites or a desire to rely on Jewish artisans, rather than pagan potters; the two explanations are not mutually exclusive, of course.[43]

Another notable pattern is reflected in the usage of lamps. In the late Second Temple period, a new form of lamp became common, the so-called Herodian lamp, which had a spatulated, knife-pared nozzle attached to a round, molded body and little or no decoration (fig. 5.18). Herodian lamps are found mostly at Jewish sites, though some examples have also been found at predominantly pagan sites. Neutron activation, X-ray fluorescence, and micromorphological analyses show, however, that lamps recovered at Jewish sites in Galilee differ in provenance from those appearing at Gentile sites. Although Herodian lamps at Gentile sites were produced at nearby regional workshops, those at Jewish sites, in contrast, were produced primarily by Judean workshops near Jerusalem. Galilean Jews thus preferred to import Herodian lamps from the south rather than rely on those manufactured at closer workshops. This reliance on Judean potters reflects the cultural affinity that linked Jews in both the south and the north.[44]

An increased interest in ritual purity illustrates how relatively new practices functioned to help construct a strong sense of distinctively Jewish identity. The use of stone vessels that had begun in the previous century continued to spread throughout the Jewish parts of

Fig. 5.18. Selection of Herodian lamps from the Burnt House during Jerusalem excavations (Photo courtesy of Hillel Geva, the Israel Exploration Society)

Palestine. Vessels and fragments have been discovered at dozens of sites in Judea and Galilee, and archaeologists have found evidence for sixteen large-scale production centers as well as smaller house-based workshops in the two regions. In Galilee, for example, workshops have been discovered at Reina and Bethlehem (the latter not to be confused with the Judean Bethlehem). Stone vessels are generally absent from sites in Samaria and Gentile areas, however.[45] Ritual baths also continued to multiply in Judea and, to a much lesser extent, to Jewish areas to the north. They varied considerably in their particulars, differing in size and the presence or absence of a storage pool (otsar) and an inner partition. Several hundred appear in diverse settings, having been discovered in large cities and small villages, in private and public contexts, near agricultural installations such as winepresses and olive presses, in houses big and small as well, in association with synagogues and at the entrance to the Jerusalem Temple complex.[46] The interest in purity reflected by ritual baths and stone vessels continued beyond the destruction of the Temple in 70 C.E., and we will return to the topic in Chapter 8.

The Jewish practice of secondary burial also extended well beyond its point of origin in Jerusalem. It is difficult to gauge how quickly it spread, but by the middle of the first century C.E. it was well established at Jericho, where an ossuary inscription mentions Agrippina, the wife of Emperor Claudius. Limestone ossuaries have been discovered at other sites in Judea, Samaria, and Galilee, though not all sites have them (Qumran, for example). Though the date of their introduction in Galilee is unclear, they were definitely in use there by the end of the first or the early second century C.E. and may well have appeared several decades earlier.[47]

Such commonality in material culture underscores the shared cultural identity held by many Jews throughout the different regions of Palestine. It reflects an increasing emphasis on ethnic and religious distinctiveness in response to growing imperial domination by the Romans. As widespread evidence of shared practices, these features provide strong support for reconstructions of early Judaism that emphasize the common elements that bound Jews together, even in the midst of the diversity reflected in ancient literary sources.[48]

CHAPTER 6

The Great Revolt and the Bar Kokhba Rebellion

Unlike the Second War against Rome (132–135 C.E.), also known as the Bar Kokhba Revolt), the Great Revolt (66–74 C.E., also known as the First Jewish War) had its own eyewitness and historian in the person of Josephus ben Mattathias. Josephus wrote his fullest accounting of the Great Revolt in his first publication, *The Jewish War,* around ten years after the end of the revolt and during the reign of Titus (79–81 C.E.), son of Vespasian. Josephus finished his longer and more expansive project, *Jewish Antiquities,* which dealt briefly with the Great Revolt, during the reign of Titus's brother Domitian (81–96 C.E.) along with his autobiography, *The Life,* and his apologetic treatise in which he explains Judaism, *Against Apion.*[1] All the while that he pursued these writing projects he was ensconced in a villa in Rome, where he was a citizen of the city and a client of the imperial family, the Flavians, whom he supported; hence his appellation "Flavius Josephus."[2]

As commander of the Galilean forces in 66 C.E. only recently returned from Rome and as a member of the priestly aristocracy, Josephus at first was a supporter of the Jewish cause and a defender of his people. His seemingly abrupt change of heart after the defeat of his force at Jotapata (Yodefat) in 67 C.E. (*War* 3.141–288, 355–408) justified earlier misgivings of the Zealots, especially John of Gischala, who had thought all along that Josephus's real motive was to make peace with Rome and hence had made several attempts against Josephus (*War* 2.585 ff.). As a result later Jewish historians have had their difficulties in positively assessing the career of Josephus. The fact remains, however, that we are heavily dependent on him in any discussion and assessment of the Great Revolt, and we need not reject his pro-Roman point of view out of hand since there were other, significant sectors of society that had, for many years, embraced a peace policy. Zuleika Rodgers understands Josephus's views on this matter to have derived from his priestly, aristocratic leanings and his condemnation of monarchy in *Jewish Antiquities*.[3] We will explore some of these complexities as we consider the causes and outcomes of the Great Revolt and decide when we can and cannot rely on his witness.[4] Regardless of what one thinks about Josephus, there is no more important corpus of writings about Jewish history in Roman times than his, and they provide a unique opportunity for the modern reader to comprehend the past from a particular point of view.

Moreover, there are no more important events in the history of Israel in the Second Temple period and after than the two wars with Rome, which have left such an imprint on the land itself and on the memory of the Jewish people. The material remains of the two wars that have been recovered in the archaeology of the major sites associated with those wars provide an invaluable resource for assessing the impact of those events on both the land and the people. They provide a vivid testimony to the reality of war and allow the contemporary historian to evaluate the accuracy of what we learn from ancient sources. So much of what we know about these years comes from this database that we accord it a special place. Judging from the literary sources, especially Josephus, his pro-Roman stance has often influenced his point of view and presentation of the narrative. In any case, the Roman occupation of Palestine in 63 B.C.E. had met with resistance from the outset, and from that time many of the lands taken by the Hasmoneans had been returned to Gentile inhabitants.[5] The economic situation too of the rural Jewish population did not improve under Roman domination, and after the death of Herod the Great uncertainty over the fate of the country and concerning the leadership of his three principal heirs only increased. The estrangement of the people from both their own leadership and the outside leadership of Rome, in particular after the death of the popular Jewish king Agrippa I in 44 C.E., could only lead to more and more tension.

Josephus attributes the emergence of the Zealot or war party to the legal incorporation of Judea into the Roman provincial system in 6 C.E. (*War* 2.117). It was at this time that Judas the Galilean (son of Hezekiah, whom Herod had fought as a bandit in Galilee a half century before), who had organized a revolt in Galilee after Herod's death, urged his compatriots not to accept the new procurator, Coponius (6–9 C.E.), who assumed power with the authority to impose the death penalty and collect taxes in behalf of Rome (*Ant.* 18.1–10). Often called bandits or brigands by the Romans (at least so Josephus designates them—the Greek term is *lestai*), the Zealots became identified with the group known as extreme patriots dedicated to preserving the independence of the Jewish nation. The use of the term "bandit" or "brigand" represents the Roman point of view in describing all resistance fighters as such extremists. The Zealots were not an organized army but a group of individuals from a common social class lower than the Herodian family and priestly caste who, for a variety of socioeconomic and theological reasons, opposed the new status quo. The Sadducees made up the priestly establishment (*Ant.* 18.16–18) and had everything to gain by cooperating with Rome, which was depending on them and the high priest to keep the people from joining the growing band of rebels.

Galilee and Sepphoris

We do not intend to take the reader on a detailed review of the war in all its complexities. Rather, having outlined in broad strokes the main causes of the revolt, we will focus on a few aspects only to get a better sense of its centrality to the history of the Holy Land for Jews and Christians. We say this because the first century is so important for the emergence of those two traditions, and the destruction of Jerusalem in 70 C.E. is so central to their fate, not to mention a major turning point in the relations between them. To all intents and purposes the disruption caused by the revolt and subsequent shifts in demographics led to formative changes in both religions, which in the short term left the local Jewish leadership to reconstitute itself in Galilee and the Christian leadership to redefine itself in the west. But this is getting ahead of the story. Let us first begin with what happened in Galilee when the war broke out.

We begin with the story in Galilee since this is the region that had been most independent of Jerusalem in the centuries before. Only after the conquest of the Hasmoneans in the late second or first century B.C.E. did Galilee become more attached to the Jerusalem and Temple bureaucracy. The degree to which the Galilean population was sympathetic or opposed to the Herodian leadership of Antipas or Agrippa I or II is also difficult to assess for the seventy years leading up to the Great Revolt. When the revolt began in 66 C.E. the only way for the Judean priest-based leadership to maintain control was to consolidate its influence over its own region and settle on a strategy to do the same in the north. The Jewish leaders in Judea came up with a simple plan: to limit the insurgency in the hopes of stalling for time to accommodate with Rome for the longer haul. Pharisees, the priestly establishment (the Sadducees) and especially the high priest Ananus (Hanan) and remnants of the royal family, and other wealthy citizens joined together to quash the Zealots (*War* 2.651–54).[6] The activity of this provisional coalition helps us to understand the position of Josephus himself and hopefully allows the reader the possibility of a more sympathetic or more tolerant view of his writing. So in a way Josephus's appointment to the command of the Galilean force in 66 C.E. can be understood as part of a larger policy of accommodation to Rome as well as a tactic of limited engagement with the Romans (*Life* 115–18), and, Jotapata being the main exception, keeping tension to a minimum. The forces under Josephus's command in Galilee were used mainly to control the general situation, but he did have a private army with him as a kind of bodyguard (*War* 2.583).

The success of this policy in Galilee by the provisional government in Jerusalem is no doubt partially the result of the fact that Galilee had been ruled earlier by Herod Antipas and afterward in two parts, first by Agrippa I, with the main city of western Galilee, Sepphoris, accountable to the governor in Caesarea, and with eastern Galilee, and subsequently by Agrippa II after 54 C.E., who governed from Tiberias and Taricheae. When the high-priestly-dominated provisional government in Jerusalem (*War* 2.562–68) began to reassert itself in taking over affairs in Galilee in the summer of 66 C.E. by trying to replace Josephus (*War* 2.626–31; *Life* 189–335), it became quite clear that the coalition that included the Pharisees wanted to reassert its control there to impress Rome of its good intentions and ability to maintain order so that a workable compromise could be found in the future.

Sepphoris, the capital of Galilee in the time of Antipas and Jesus and now of western Galilee, was the prime target of such a strategy. At first the citizens of the city resisted the policy of accommodation so much that they were allowed to shore up their walls (*War* 2.574). And when John of Gischala sought to bring Sepphoris and also Tiberias (*Life* 102–13) into the war and challenge Josephus's command (*War*

2.629), we learn that Josephus initially had a hard time winning support for his position. The Sepphoreans even hired a group of mercenaries led by a brigand named Jesus (*Life* 104–11) to protect them from
other groups of Galileans, especially John of Gischala, who had tried
unsuccessfully to get them to join forces with him (*Life* 123–24).

After giving up his command, Josephus's role in bringing over
Sepphoris to a pro-Roman stance after the battle of Jotapata is not entirely clear. The end result, however, was that Sepphoris did not join
in the revolt and adopted a peace policy that was unique for the country. Alternatively, some believe that Sepphoris was always staunchly
anti-revolt because of its aristocratic population.[7] This is a narrative
in which literary sources join with recent archaeological evidence to
clarify the inconsistent reports in Josephus. One such instance is the
report in which Josephus says that the Sepphoreans repulsed his attack
aimed at bringing in towns and cities that were hesitant to join the
Galilean forces under him. In speaking of this he notes that he himself had strongly fortified Sepphoris and that is why it was impreg-
nable, all the while insisting he had already abandoned the Galilean
cause (*War* 2.61; *Life* 188).[8]

Be that as it may, the end result was that the city decided to
adopt a pro-Roman stance that eliminated any need to join forces with
Josephus or fight against the Romans. The Greco-Roman heritage of
the city and its expansion under Antipas, when it became "the ornament of all Galilee," along with its strong priestly presence and aristocratic leanings doubtless contributed to this decision. In any case in
68 C.E. that decision is commemorated in the minting of coins that
bear the legend "Eirenopolis-Neronias-Sepphoris" (fig. 6.1). These
coins date to the fourteenth year of Emperor Nero, in which the inhabitants of Sepphoris declared their loyalty to Vespasian and the Roman Senate. Once designated "City of Peace" (Eirenopolis), Sepphoris put behind it the revolutionary attitudes that some of its citizens
had held about the revolt (e.g., *War* 2.574, 629; *Life* 188, 203). The numismatic evidence clearly points out that by 68 C.E. the city was pretty
well united in its pro-Roman stance and had given up the prospect of
joining with other revolutionaries in Galilee. We may speculate how
the sobriquet "City of Peace" came to be placed on a city coin. It certainly commemorates how the city welcomed Vespasian and the army
in peace. It may also be a play on the expression in Zechariah 8:3 re-

Fig. 6.1. Bronze coins from Sepphoris. Coin at left shows two cross-cornucopias with caduceus between, and the Greek legend "In the time of Vespasian in Irenopolis-Neroneas-Sepphoris"; reverse has, in Greek, "Year 14 of Nero Claudius Caesar" (67/68 C.E.) in a circle inside a wreath. The coin at right has a nearly identifiable Greek inscription, and cornucopias are replaced by the letters "SC," an abbreviation for SENATVS CONSVLTO. (Copyright David Hendin, used by permission)

ferring to Jerusalem as the "City of Truth." As Sepphoris was one of the principal cities of Agrippa II, there remained, no doubt, a strong royalist contingent in the population. Similar coins were struck in Banias (Caesarea Philippi), which served as the capital city of Agrippa II (*Ant.* 20.211).[9]

One further note about Sepphoris is in connection with this singular moment in the Great Revolt when the major Jewish city in Galilee decided to support a policy of accommodation to Rome. There was a large fort on the western summit that had existed since late Hellenistic times, which the Duke excavations at Sepphoris spent many years uncovering (fig. 6.2). It was built on bedrock and had wide walls to support a serious superstructure, and there were even several ritual baths in the basement to allow the troops to adhere to the laws of purity. During excavation it became quite clear that the fort went out of use sometime in the first century, when its superstructure was taken down and its basements were filled in systematically. Careful examination of the ceramics in that fill point to the end of the Second Temple period, and it is quite plausible that, in coming to a decision about adopting a pro-Roman policy after seriously considering joining the revolt, as a sign to Vespasian and the Roman army of their good intentions the Sepphoreans took down the fort, buried it under meters of fill, and converted the area to an open space. As a symbolic gesture it would have been very dramatic. What could possibly follow to emphasize the great significance of such an act? The issuance of the "City of Peace" coins with the sobriquet "Eirenopolis" constituted such a gesture, and it had the blessing of the emperor as well.

Fig. 6.2. A computer-generated reconstruction of the fort at Sepphoris by BBC Television (By permission of Eric Meyers and BBC-TV)

Matters were not all so peaceful in other corners of Galilee. Tiberias was the scene of bitter fighting and factional disputes (*Life* 32–39). The city council (*boulē*) consisted of the wealthier citizens who were pro-Roman, while the poorer elements of society were eager to join the war. It was the destitute class led by one Jesus ben Sapphias (*Life* 66, 134) that set fire to the palace of Herod Antipas there, which was decorated with images of animals. Those who joined the revolution were understandably distrustful of Josephus's background and hence suspicious about his intentions as general of the northern command. A similar story may be told about nearby Taricheae just northwest of Tiberias where elites and the lower classes clashed. But it was in the remoteness of the Upper Galilee where revolutionary fervor boiled over and brought John of Gischala, Josephus's primary rival in the north, to prominence (*War* 2.588; *Life* 372), with John even challenging him in Tiberias. John survived the surrender of his hometown, Gischala, and escaped in 67 C.E. to Jerusalem, where he went on to lead the extremist wing of the Zealot party. That faction immediately ousted the moderates in the central provisional government (*War* 4.138–46) and replaced them along with the high-priestly families that supported them and elected a new high priest by lot (*War* 4.152–57).

The Battle at Jotapata (Yodefat)

One of two major engagements in the north between the Jewish forces led by Josephus and the Romans occurred at Jotapata, which, after Jerusalem, receives the longest treatment by Josephus (*War* 3.145ff.). The excavations there, unlike the excavations in urban Sepphoris, reveal the formation of a first-century Galilean rural town (fig. 6.3).[10] The walled town extends over 5.5 hectares, with a third of it built into the steep eastern ridge of the rounded hill where a third of the population resided—the remainder of the inhabitants lived on the plateau below (fig. 6.4).[11] Mordechai Aviam describes the results of seven years of work there in this manner: "Five residential areas were excavated, revealing modest private dwellings, cisterns, ritual baths (*miqvaot*), storage places, cooking ovens, pressing surfaces for agricultural processing, pottery kilns, an oil press in a cave, . . . loom weights, spindle whorls, clay vessels, stone ware and coins. In Field X part of a luxurious mansion was uncovered with frescoed wall and floors. The latest coins found on the floors date to the reign of Emperor Nero."[12]

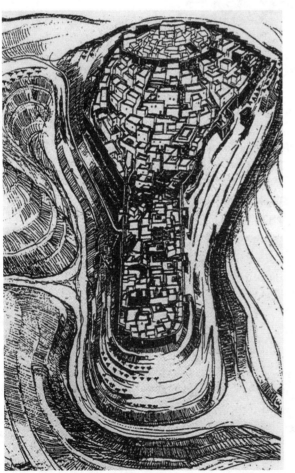

Fig. 6.3. Reconstruction drawing of Jotapata, or Yodefat (Drawing courtesy of Mordecai Aviam)

The first important point to note is that the numismatic evidence corresponds to the date of the battle in Josephus and to the issuing year of the "City of Peace" coins in Sepphoris. The second point to emphasize is that at one and the same site we have modest domiciles alongside an elegant one, which illustrates something we have already noted, namely, that it is very difficult to identify particular groups easily in the absence of written remains. We know from a late source that Jotapata was settled by the priestly family of Miyamim, and we might conjecture that the family lived in the fancy domicile but there is no way to prove that. Josephus confirms the importance of the

Fig. 6.4. A ritual
bath at Jotapata in
a family domicile
(Photo courtesy of
Mordecai Aviam)

Fig. 6.5. A defensive wall at Jotapata
revealed during
excavation there
(Photo courtesy of
Mordecai Aviam)

twenty-four priestly courses, the families who administered the Temple service in two-week intervals, and he took pride in being a member of the first of them (*Ant.* 7.365–68 and *Life* 2).[13] The priestly clans or families are usually associated with the upper strata of society, and the site of Jotapata is tiny and rural and most of the homes excavated thus far are rather modest. With the discovery of the one villa with frescoed rooms, the picture we derive from the Jotapata excavations thus is very important for showing how different social strata lived together in a small rural setting and urges caution in thinking of rural sites in the countryside as representative of only a more lowly stratum of society.

The siege at Jotapata was the second bloodiest battle of the Great Revolt after Jerusalem; the excavations have uncovered much that illuminates the struggle and its setting (fig. 6.5). First among those items is the fortification wall(s) that also accords with Josephus's

Fig. 6.6. A collection of ballista stones from Jotapata (Photo courtesy of Mordecai Aviam)

notation that Jotapata was the first of the towns he fortified in Galilee (*War* 3.158–59). Remains of an earlier, late Hellenistic phase of the fortification wall were uncovered, parts of which were strengthened during the early Roman phase. There is a huge tower on the northern extension of the wall and a smaller tower to the west. A casemate wall was laid over the earlier wall and even over a kiln, suggesting haste in extending the wall, and one large tower and two and a half rooms have been preserved in the casemate. These rooms were filled by the defenders to prevent the Romans from entering with a battering ram, and a ballista stone was found in one of the rooms amid the fill. Other sections of the fortification wall were excavated in four other areas. An underground shelter containing evidence of the battle was found in it including arrowheads, ballista stones, and human remains indicating that it was used during and after the battle in 67 c.e. (fig. 6.6).[14] The manner of construction of the last early Roman phase, the placement of the casemates, all point to a hurried construction with a sense of urgency, showing that it was intended for the battle mentioned in Josephus. In addition the expedition also located the assault ramp on the northern slope to accommodate the siege machines (*War* 3.163–65). In all, seventy arrowheads of the trilobate kind were found, five from the floor of the frescoed room. Fifteen catapult arrowheads were also recovered from various parts of the site, along with thirty-five ballista stones, an iron spear point, the tip of a Roman dagger, and fragments of Roman army equipment.

The excavation of Jotapata also revealed many human remains that allow us to imagine the horrific ending of the siege and loss of life in the battle. A surprising aspect of the archaeology of the Great Revolt is the scarcity of human remains at the sites where major battles took place (fig. 6.7). At Masada only a few skeletons were found in the northern palace, while more complete ones were found in a cave below the cliffs; in Jerusalem only the remains of an arm were discovered in the Burnt House; and at Gamla only a single jawbone was recovered.[15] At Yodefat in one cistern in Field VIII two adults and a child were recovered; in the southern part of the residential area the skeletal remains of twenty people were found, also in a cistern, with evidence of violent trauma inflicted on some of them. The cistern was not fully excavated. Other skeletal remains were uncovered from the site as well that give vivid testimony to the final end of the city.

Fig. 6.7. Silver coins of the Great Revolt. At left is a shekel showing a ritual chalice with staff, and three pomegranates on the reverse with the Hebrew inscription "Jerusalem, Holy." Middle coin is a half shekel with the same motifs struck in 66–68 C.E., with "Jerusalem the Holy." At right is a silver shekel from year three of the First Jewish Revolt (68–69 C.E.). (Copyright David Hendin, used by permission)

Josephus reports that there were forty thousand victims (*War* 3.338), but Aviam estimates a maximum of seven thousand inhabitants in the town at the time of the final battle, including refugees from the fighting in Galilee. Of these, he suggests a total of two thousand would have died while another twelve hundred might have been taken captive. He understands the evidence of the skeletons in the cisterns as the result of leaving corpses unburied for a considerable time, and suggests that survivors returned much later to remove the bones from the streets and buried them in caves and cisterns.[16] According to Josephus, when the Romans broke into the town via the northern wall, he sought refuge in a large pit or cistern where he came upon others who had also hidden themselves there. When they were subsequently discovered Josephus's companions threatened to kill him if he were to surrender. Then, as the story goes, Josephus persuaded them to draw lots to commit mass suicide. As fate would have it, according to Josephus's retelling, he drew one of the last two lots, whereupon he and one other person both fled and abandoned the plan. Josephus was soon found and taken to Vespasian and boldly predicted that Vespasian and his son Titus would one day become emperor (*War* 3.399–409).[17] Whatever the veracity of the Josephan narrative, the excavations at Yodefat have provided abundant physical evidence that sheds new light on the revolt in Galilee just before the citizens of nearby Sepphoris came to their historic decision to not join the war effort. In respect to the mass suicide component of the narrative, there has been much skepticism about it in view of the fact that Jewish law explicitly condemns suicide. The critical literature, however, has focused on the purported mass suicide at Masada in view of the notoriety of the dig and the place of Masada as a symbol of nationalism in Israeli culture, a topic we will discuss below.[18]

Gamla, "City of Refuge"

The other great battle in the north occurred at Gamla, a Jewish village located in the southern Golan Heights overlooking the Sea of Galilee, which like Jotapata is described in great detail by Josephus (*War* 4.1–83). (See plate 9.) Originally loyal to the Romans when it was in the hands of King Agrippa II, as refugees from the revolt fled there it soon became a rebellious enclave: "For the town was crowded with refugees because of the protection it offered, which was proved by the fact that the forces previously sent by Agrippa to besiege it had made no headway after seven months" (*War* 4.10). Josephus's description of the site reveals that he was personally and intimately acquainted with it.[19] When Vespasian besieged the village Josephus was already a prisoner of war, having fallen into the hands of the Romans at Yodefat just a few months earlier. Vespasian allowed his prisoner Josephus to accompany him on his subsequent exploits, including the capture of Gamla. As to the credibility of the story of the Roman siege of Gamla and Josephus's presence during it, Danny Syon, one of the most recent excavators of the site, claims that Josephus's knowledge of Gamla is too accurate for him not to have actually been there (*War* 3.407).[20] Gamla became the scene of one of the greatest battles of the war, and like Jotapata, it was never rebuilt, so it remains one of the best-preserved Jewish villages in all Israel. Fourteen seasons of excavations and conservation beginning in 1976 have led to many important finds that illuminate aspects of the war and the events that occurred there. No massive skeletal remains have been found at the site, however, so whether there was a mass suicide at Gamla remains an unsolved problem.[21]

Because Gamla was abandoned after the battle and never resettled, its remains offer an unfettered glimpse into Jewish life in a small village in the last decades of the Second Temple. Remains of the Hasmonean period dating to Alexander Jannaeus's activity there (*War* 1.103–6; *Ant.* 13.394) have not been well enough isolated, but we may date many of the typical Jewish finds to the later Hellenistic period, after 100 B.C.E.: four ritual baths, one of which stands at the entrance to the synagogue, 258 stone vessel fragments, and perhaps even the synagogue at that time, along with thousands of Hasmonean coins, though they remained in circulation for a long time.[22] No traces of the Roman siege camps have been found at the site, no doubt because Vespasian did not spend a long time there and the siege works would have been constructed of wood and perished long ago.

Although Josephus claims to have fortified the town by building a wall in the time of his command in Galilee (*Life* 37; *War* 4.9), excavation has demonstrated that what he probably accomplished was to close the gaps between clusters of preexisting houses and buildings on the eastern edge of town and to build a second wall behind some of them. The round tower located at the highest point in the wall was constructed in an earlier period. It is not clear when the twin towers below the synagogue and the round tower were added, but they are built over an older Hasmonean structure. Since few arrowheads and ballista stones were found in this area it appears that the Romans focused their attack closer to the top of the wall near the synagogue.[23] Though a siege ramp has not been definitively identified, a large filled trench below the round tower has been tentatively suggested as the logical place where the Romans first breached the wall and where such a ramp would have existed. The breach is located in a building just below the synagogue and it is the only one uncovered by the excavation. The original thickness of the wall was 0.7 meters, which was strengthened to a thickness of 2.05 meters. Farther down the slope the wall reached a thickness of 4 meters. Two other locations where concentrations of ballistas and arrowheads were found are also suggested as having been breached.

Heavy concentrations of weapons were found in various locations at the site: 2,000 ballista stones, 1,600 arrowheads, mostly trilobate, 100 catapult bolts, and, in an alley near the twin towers, the remains of a Roman officer's equipment—helmet, cheek guard, strip armor. The defenders depended on roof rollers, millstones, and the like to throw at the invaders. Among the most significant finds of the site, from the western quarter of town, is a small group of seven coins minted at Gamla and all made from the same obverse die; two dies were used for the reverse. On one side the coin bears an imitation of the well-known Jerusalem silver shekel illustrating one of the Temple utensils, which first appeared on Jerusalem silver shekels in 66 C.E.

One additional coin minted at Akko-Ptolemais was found with these examples, and it was made in honor of Vespasian's landing there several months before the siege of Gamla. The inscription on the Gamla coins begins on the side with the Temple vessel and continues on the back, reading: "For the redemption of Jerusalem the H[oly]." The Gamla Revolt coins were thus produced during the siege or just before it. The ability to mint coins suggests a high degree of organization and unity among the rebels, which contradicts the view that they were divided and easy prey for the Romans. The inhabitants at Gamla under the most difficult conditions also remembered the holy city of Jerusalem and were clearly aware of the original intentions of the war.

The siege of Gamla began in October 67 c.e. (*War* 4.4–7, 10), at which time Josephus looked upon the site he had once fortified as part of Vespasian's train. But the residents misjudged badly the strength of the Roman force, and the town was taken. When the Romans entered the breached walls only two female survivors were found (*War* 4.81–84). No complete human skeletons have been recovered from all the years of working at the site; only one jawbone was identified. This leads to the suggestion that the Romans would surely have collected their dead and cremated them; they might well have allowed Jewish escapees to come back and bury the remains of their dead in a cave or mass grave that has yet to be discovered. Neither the relatively steep terrain (about 30 degrees) nor the lack of skeletal evidence supports an interpretation of mass suicide at Gamla, although this is what Syon and Josephus claim happened: "At Gamla, however, a very real battle took place, at the end of which, when there was no more hope, 'they flung their wives and children and themselves too into the immensely deep artificial ravine that yawned under the citadel. In fact, the fury of the victors seemed less destructive than the suicidal frenzy of the trapped men; 4,000 fell to Roman swords, but those who plunged to destruction proved to be 5,000'" (*War* 4.79–80).[24]

We shall discuss the synagogue at Gamla in another chapter, but first we offer a few words on the pottery. The final publication of pottery from the 1976–1989 excavations adds another dimension to the study and understanding of Gamla for the nearly two centuries of its history. Andrea Berlin has presented the data from those years in a handsome recent volume.[25] In it she offers new insight into the trade patterns of the inhabitants, and their habits in dining and food selection that may or may not relate to religious practice. She infers also that the earlier population was more cosmopolitan than the later one, judging from the pottery. The late Hellenistic population was more inclined to use imported vessels than the first-century community. Her volume is recommended for anyone wanting to learn more about the site and everyday life there.

Jerusalem and Masada

The war in Galilee was confined to the years 66–67 C.E., and with the escape of John of Gischala to Jerusalem the internal dissension among the different Jewish parties reached an intolerable level. With the Zealots taking charge of the appointment of a new high priest by lot, the provisional government of the moderates came to an end. Even Simon ben Gamaliel's attempts to gather moderates around him failed, resulting in a reign of terror by John with the aid of the Idumeans (*War* 4.283–300) and his subsequent rise to supreme leader of the rebels. During this time Vespasian took all of Perea and the Jewish centers in the heart of Judea. Fighting was temporarily suspended, however, in June 68 C.E., with the death of Nero, until the question of succession could be settled.

This respite was hardly a time for the rebels to come together. Rather, it was an opening for one Simon bar Giora to challenge John's rule, which resulted in a new and more bitter civil war. The internecine battles led Vespasian to intervene again in May–June 69 C.E., when he conquered more of the Jewish heartland, but not Jerusalem or the three Herodian fortresses of Masada, Herodium, and Machaerus that the Zealots had taken.[26] But on July 1, 69 C.E., in Rome, after the Romans' internal hostilities relating to the imperial succession ceased, Vespasian was declared emperor and his son Titus was appointed to direct the war effort in the East against the Jews. When Titus set out to besiege Jerusalem yet another rebel group made its move to take control of the revolt, led by a lower priest by the name of Eleazar ben Simon. Now there were three groups of Jewish rebels fighting one another and yet pledged to defend the city from Rome: the Zealots, the Sicarii, and the followers of Simon bar Giora (*War* 5.22–26). This was an impossible situation for the rebels, and Titus's siege of Jerusalem began in 70 C.E., a few days before Passover.

Fig. 6.8. Destruction debris from 70 C.E. on the street below the Western Wall, Jerusalem. At left are the remains of a row of shops. (Photo courtesy of Sean Burrus)

Under his command Titus had the Fifth, Tenth, and Fifteenth legions and the Twelfth if he needed it. It was the Twelfth legion that had been defeated in the north under the command of Cestius Gallus at the outbreak of the revolt. During the ensuing days of Passover John's followers murdered Eleazar (*War* 5.98–105) and joined hands with Simon bar Giora when it became necessary to repulse the Romans after they began to construct the siege works and ramparts. The Roman forces succeeded in breaching the "Third Wall" in late May and the "Second Wall" soon after, which left the Temple itself, the lower city, and the upper city still in the control of the rebels (*War* 5.302–31). Finally Titus focused on the Antonia Fortress, which in former times was the place where Roman soldiers deployed to watch over their Jewish subjects; it was taken by Titus and his troops at the end of July. Soon after, on August 6, the daily sacrifice in the Temple was terminated, and at the end of August 70 C.E., on the 9th of Av, the anniversary of the destruction of the First Temple, the Romans captured

Fig. 6.9. An inscription reading "To the place of the trumpeting," from the southwest corner of the Temple, where a horn was sounded to announce the beginning of the Sabbath and festivals (Photo courtesy of the Israel Museum)

the Second Temple and burned it to the ground (*War* 6.257–59), dismantling other portions and leaving only the Western Wall partially standing (fig. 6.8). The upper city fell in early September, and nearly all of the inhabitants of Jerusalem were killed or sent into forced labor; John and Simon were taken to Rome as prisoners in triumphal procession.

Vivid reminders of the destruction of the Temple have been recovered from excavations along the Western Wall, where its collapse is evident from the debris on the north–south street running alongside it. Hillel Geva writes: "Most imposing are the piles of collapsed masonry from the Temple Mount walls, which have been exposed at its foot. Stones flying from high above crashed onto the shops below, even penetrating the flagstones of the street along the western temenos wall. There was evidence that the shops were burned before being covered in the collapse."[27] Among the most dramatic finds at the southwest corner of the Temple Mount was a Hebrew inscription on a cornerstone from the top of the wall reading, "To the place of the trumpeting . . ."; in other words, where the beginning of the Sabbath (and holidays) would be announced with the blasts of a trumpet (fig. 6.9).[28] Josephus writes that "it was the custom for one of the priests to stand and to give notice, by sound of trumpet, in the afternoon of the approach, and on the following evening of the close, of every seventh day, announcing to the people the respective hours for ceasing work and for resuming their labors" (*War* 4.582–83). Some scholars have suggested adding "for announcing" since there is a break in the inscription after the letters *lhk* [*ryz*], which results in the reading.[29]

Also offering vivid testimony to the final days of the Temple are the skeletal remains of a young woman from the so-called Burnt House (fig. 6.10). All that remained of the woman's corpse was her forearm and hand, stuck under the debris where the house was destroyed and burned, her body no doubt removed for reasons of proper burial or for sanitation. Since so few skeletal remains have been recovered in the excavations of Jerusalem, these remains suggest that Roman soldiers might have removed corpses after the fall of the city, though Geva has recently proposed that the house may have been burned and the body of the woman removed by Jews during the period of the siege, prior to the Roman invasion of the Upper City.[30] The

Fig. 6.10. The Burnt House, Jerusalem, during excavation (Photo courtesy of Hillel Geva, the Israel Exploration Society)

rest of the house also provided abundant clues to the last days of its existence. Small objects lay strewn throughout the rooms of the mansion, the most outstanding feature of each space being a heap of broken objects: stone vessels, stone tables, and pottery, possibly signs of the action of Roman looters discarding unwanted belongings on the floor, and in one room a spear was leaning against the wall in a corner (Room 3), no doubt left by one of the original occupants.[31]

Remains of the Burnt House also shed light on the socioeconomic level of priestly families living in the shadow of the Temple (fig. 6.11). Inside the house an inscription on a stone weight was found that read "belonging to the son of Qatros." Recently Joshua Schwartz has challenged the older view of Nahman Avigad, and endorsed the view of Ronny Reich that the Qatros priestly family was not necessarily engaged in the production of incense for the Temple.[32] Rather,

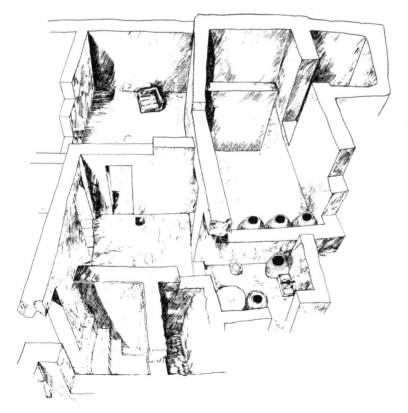

Fig. 6.11. Reconstruction of the Burnt House (Reconstruction drawing courtesy of Hillel Geva, the Israel Exploration Society)

the weights uncovered in the house may be related to the task of accurately weighing the tithes and to a lesser extent heave offerings for priestly families.[33] Determining the precise weight for the priests was a religious obligation, and Schwartz rejects Reich's view that careful weighing of the tithes could have been related to interpriestly strife between wealthy and poor priests.[34] The fact that the weights are made of chalk stone made them impervious to ritual defilement, but we find chalk stone vessels at Qumran and in most Jewish settlements of the period that may or may not have priestly families living there.[35] The point is this: without the inscription on the weight itself identifying a well-known priestly family, all that might have been learned about the occupants of the Burnt House relates to the enormous size of the domicile, the high level of its building style with mosaics, stucco, private ritual baths, and more, and that it was destroyed in the Great Revolt. At the same time we know that not all priests were wealthy. As for the material remains of the Great Revolt, we simply caution the reader once again that we are dependent mostly on literary sources to sort out the internal dynamics of that struggle. We are in much better shape for the Second Jewish War thanks to the discovery of many written remains in the Bar Kokhba caves.

The internal wars among the Jews in the final years of the fight for Jerusalem and fall of the Temple led later generations to ascribe the legend of Yochanan ben Zakkai's escape in a coffin from the city to this period as a way of explaining Jewish survival.[36] As a result of his miraculous escape Ben Zakkai is said to have won permission from Vespasian to relocate the Sanhedrin and rebuild Jewish life at Jamnia (Yavneh), where he is assumed to have been responsible for many reforms in Judaic practices that were required in the absence of the Temple. In one tradition he is said to have predicted Vespasian's rise to be emperor, just as Josephus had predicted when he was taken prisoner at Jotapata. Those who did survive the war in general went on to Jamnia or headed to Galilee to resettle and rebuild their lives. As for the last of the Jewish rebels, the most extreme of them, the Sicarii, had left Jerusalem for Masada rather early in the war when one of their leaders was murdered after going into the Temple to offer sacrifice wearing royal robes. Some seventy years after the death of Herod the Great, in 66 C.E., the rebels captured the fortress of Masada from a small Roman legionary garrison that had been there for many years.

The Zealots' Last Stand: Masada

Masada is a fortress located on the edge of the Judean Wilderness on the western shore of the Dead Sea, some 25 kilometers south of Ein Gedi; it lies on top of an elevated plateau and runs 800 meters north to south and 300 meters east to west, a sheer drop of 440 meters to the level of the Dead Sea (fig. 6.12). Like Gamla it was originally built in the Hasmonean period, probably in the time of Jannaeus (103–76 B.C.E.), and excavations have produced many coins of his and pottery from the late Hellenistic period. The fortress was greatly enlarged and upgraded by Herod the Great, who used the site as a convenient and elegant getaway spot. Scientific excavations were conducted by Yigael Yadin in 1963–1965, when nearly the whole site was uncovered under the aegis of the Israel Exploration Society and the Israel Defense Forces, which greatly assisted in all the work at every level. The last Jews to occupy the site were the Zealots and Sicarii who fled Jerusalem and adapted the palatial spaces to their own purposes, and it is to their brief stay there until 73 or 74 C.E. that we now turn.

Fig. 6.12. Aerial view of Masada (Photo courtesy of Todd Bolen/BiblePlaces.com)

At Masada the rebels took over all of the Herodian buildings, palaces, bathhouses, and fortifications and converted them and the casemate wall into living spaces, with ovens, new dividing walls, and benches inserted into the old spaces. The rebels' construction may be described as modest at best, intended to serve the ordinary needs of the people in their daily lives. The rooms that were added last to the perimeter wall were the least well built, using small stones, with thatched roofs of branches and old textiles, plaster made of mud, and floors of beaten earth—a far cry from the lavish style of Herod's days. Ritual baths were apparently built at this time also, as well as a small synagogue, where texts that included biblical manuscripts were found.[37] Whether there was a synagogue in the Herodian period or not is a point that is still debated, but Yadin was of the opinion that even in Herod's day the building served his family as a place of worship. In any case, the Zealots made major alterations to the space: they did away with the anteroom, closed off a small space in the northwest corner, added new columns in the east, and added benching on three sides.[38] The space could hold up to 250 people, and the entrance was on the east, facing Jerusalem. The casemate wall served as the main place of residence for the newly arrived rebels, modifying the space by adding thin walls making small cells, adding baking ovens, stoves, and silos and using old columns for tables and carved ashlars for chairs; more distinguished refugees and military personnel might have resided in the palaces.[39] When the site was too crowded, temporary quarters were built inside the casemate near the inside walls. Amnon Ben-Tor estimates the rebel population to have been about one thousand on the eve of its collapse.

After the fall of Jerusalem in 70 C.E., Titus decided to keep the Tenth Legion in Judea along with some auxiliary units to deal with the remaining strongholds and pockets of resistance at Herodium, Machaerus, and Masada (*War* 7.5) and to maintain order (fig. 6.13). With the subsequent collapse of Herodium and Machaerus, the Roman army under the command of Flavius Silva focused on Masada with approximately 8,000 to 13,000 troops, 5,000 of them members of the Tenth Legion and the rest auxiliary units that were used to build the siege ramp and the camps, supply water and food, and provide other support functions.[40] Ben-Tor estimates that the Roman army would have required 16 tons of food and 26,000 liters of water every

Fig. 6.13. The Roman siege camp at the foot of Masada on the eastern side. The Dead Sea appears in the background. (Photo courtesy of Todd Bolen/BiblePlaces.com)

day. The closest spot for water was Ein Gedi, 25 kilometers to the north, with some of it brought by Jews (*War* 7.278). The rebels were well supplied above on the "rock" and made use of dried foodstuffs from Herod's days kept in the large storerooms, water in the great cisterns that was diverted and collected during the rainy season, and even a stash of arms left over from Herod's time (*War* 7.295–300). Silva therefore decided to commence at once with the construction of the siege ramp to attack the fortress wall. Required for the general task were some 40,000 cubic meters of stone for the eight camps, siege wall, and ramp. The siege wall was 4,500 meters long, 1.6 meters wide, and 3 meters tall. The siege ramp at Yodefat took about 47 days to build, the Gamla ramp took roughly 33 days, and the various ramps in Jerusalem approximately 18–21 days; Masada would have taken about 20 days. Adding to this would be the time for the construction of the stone platform at the top of the ramp for the battering ram, transport of wood and soils for the ramp, and other technical problems, bringing the total up to 50–60 days.[41] The rebels did not stand idly by as these preparations were undertaken, shooting arrows and discharging slingshots at the workers and soldiers, who returned fire with ballista stones weighing anywhere from 0.5 to 17 kilograms, though most were under 4 kilograms. All manner of equipment has been found at the site: scale armor, swords and scabbards, arrows and arrowheads, pommels, belt fittings, helmets, shields, bows, spearheads.

Since the final publication of findings from Masada a debate has arisen about the date when the fortress fell. The traditional date was usually taken to be 73 C.E. However, two papyri discovered at the site along with an inscription regarding the career of Silva suggest a date in the spring of 74 C.E.[42] A much larger debate has arisen over the precise nature of the rebel collapse and whether Josephus's tale of mass suicide can be taken literally. Once the Romans had successfully breached the wall of the fortress with a battering ram, it was clear to the rebels that the end was near and would be horrific. They were led to this conclusion by a certain Eleazar, who in his first rousing speech recommended self-destruction: "setting before his eyes what the Romans, if victorious, would inflict on them, their children and their wives" (*War* 7.320), and arguing for the rebels to choose death over slavery (*War* 7.336). When his words did not touch the hearts of all the rebels he renewed his appeal and went on to defend the idea of "self-immolation" on the Indian model (*War* 7.351–57). Finally the rebels were overpowered by his words and with haste set out to accomplish the deed (*War* 7.389 ff.). Ten men chosen by lots set out to kill the remaining group and accomplished the task with wives and children clinging together as families: "Wretched victims of necessity, to whom to slay with their own hands their own wives and children seemed the lightest of evils!" (*War* 7.393). Only two women and five children escaped by hiding, according to Josephus, and it was they who informed the Romans of the sad end. The Roman soldiers, upon hearing what had happened, "instead of exulting as over enemies . . . admired the nobility of their resolve and the contempt of death displayed by many in carrying it, unwavering, into execution" (*War* 7.405–6).

How the end came about and whether the lots discovered by Yigael Yadin in his excavations are the same as those described in Josephus's account of the mass slayings of 960 souls has become a matter of some controversy, as has the absence of human skeletal remains, similar to the situation at Jerusalem, Jotapata, and Gamla.[43] Apart from the three skeletons found in the northern palace, the rest of the skeletal remains that were recovered in the caves below all show signs of predation, possible evidence that animals carried them to their final location. In addition pig bones were found with some of them, suggesting that they might have been non-Jews. An alternative theory explaining the absence of skeletal remains is that the Romans could well have taken the rebels captive.

Yadin referred to the discovery of eleven ostraca or lots on the northern track that led to the storerooms and the administration building as the most important find of the entire dig.[44] Upon each of them was inscribed a name, apparently all written by the same hand, in his view. Yadin speculated that these were the names of the last defenders of Masada who had been selected to slay all the rest of the survivors, 960 in all. The Eleazar who had delivered the two memorable speeches was identified by Yadin as none other than Eleazar ben Yair, whose name appears on one of the ostraca, the remainder being the names of his commanders. From those lots Eleazar had to determine the order of their final round of deaths. According to Yadin, "it is this which brings the recruits of the armoured units of the Defense forces of modern Israel to swear the oath of allegiance on Masada's heights: 'Masada shall not fall again.'"[45]

A rather stinging criticism of Yadin's work at Masada has emerged from a sociologist at the Hebrew University, Nachman ben-Yehuda. He contends that Yadin adopted the story of the mass suicide there only as a way to create a national myth of heroic resistance, which was imperative for the State of Israel and its frame of mind in the early 1960s.[46] Ben-Yehuda follows in a long line of critics, beginning with Stewart Alsop, who coined the phrase "Masada complex" to describe a siege mentality against a hostile world that threatened the security of Israel.[47] In any event, the story of the Zealots' heroic last stand at Masada has been embedded in the hearts of most Israelis and tourists who have seen the site, even though suicide in Jewish law is strictly forbidden.[48] However the Zealots met their end in Masada, there were no further such incidents in Palestine till the Second Jewish War with Rome, the Bar Kokhba Revolt in 132–135 C.E. As a result Jewish life turned inward and focused on the challenges that came forward at Jamnia.

Consequences of the Revolt

One immediate consequence of the revolt was that Judea became an independent Roman province under the administration of a governor of praetorian rank. As a result of this changed status the Tenth Legion Fretensis was stationed in Jerusalem, on the western hill near the entrance to the city. A pottery workshop has been discovered along the ancient road to Jaffa at the entrance to the city, which produced pottery and bricks for the soldiers and functioned through the second century C.E.[49] Modern research has estimated that the revolt resulted in a loss of up to a third of the Jewish population, which meant that its economic effect was immeasurable. According to Josephus, lands that had belonged to the populace and to the royal family—the royal estates—now belonged to the emperor, and those who worked the land became, to all intents, tenant farmers, though private ownership is suggested by other sources.[50]

The deprivation of a measure of independence, destruction of the Temple, and massive loss of human life, however, did not mean the end of Jewish life by any means. In many ways the most creative period in Jewish history was yet to happen, as the synagogue developed to replace the Temple and prayer to substitute for Temple sacrifice. The Essenes of Qumran did not resurface, and their extreme views regarding purity did not take hold among the populace. Although the party of the Sadducees may have disappeared, their influence lived on in other ways. The priests were redistributed in the newly settled communities of Galilee and in the Diaspora, and we even have a number of later inscriptions that mention where the priestly families relocated. They found other ways to exert their influence with their unique background and training, such as contributing to the development of synagogue liturgy, perhaps even preparing the *targumim,* or translations of the biblical readings, since they had priority in the Torah reading.[51] The royal family, however, had little further influence, though Agrippa II remained important, since he continued to reign until his death in the 90s. Josephus went to Rome and wrote his memoirs and account of the revolt (*Ant.* 18–20 and *War* 1–2). Vespasian, in gratitude, gave him a large tract of land in Judea, and Titus presented him with the royal estate in the Jezreel (*Life* 216). Except for the Roman historian Tacitus's *Histories,* book 5, little is known about the Great Revolt from Gentile authors. For Jews, however, it was an epochal event that ended the Second Jewish Commonwealth and is commemorated today in the observance of a fast on the 9th of Av by traditional Jews. On the other hand, the reconstruction begun at Jamnia ensured that the legacy of the Pharisees and other Jews who had participated in the reformulation of Judaism would survive and shape the future of the Jewish people for all time to come. In a way, out of tragedy came triumph and a new beginning.

Part of this new beginning, according to Jewish tradition, was a result of Yochanan ben Zakkai's unwillingness to go along with the Zealots' insistence on dying rather than surrendering to the Romans, and his subsequent escape from Jerusalem during the revolt and meeting with Vespasian, where he won approval to establish a rabbinic academy at Jamnia. Scholars have referred to this story as a "founding myth of rabbinic Judaism."[52] It is similar to the story of Josephus being taken prisoner after the fall of Jotapata, meeting with Vespasian, and predicting his imminent rise to emperor (*War* 3.392–408). The importance of these stories cannot be overemphasized, even though we are unable to verify the historicity of either the Josephan narrative or rabbinic legends. What we can glean from them is that each story has a distinct purpose. In the account of Jotapata and Josephus's miraculous escape from death we observe the historian justifying his subsequent life as an author and favorite of the Flavians far away from the homeland in Rome. In the Talmudic versions of the story of Yochanan ben Zakkai (*b. Gittin* 56b; *Avot of Rabbi Nathan,* 4), we may observe the pragmatic outlook of the rabbis whose pro-Roman views were accommodationist at heart, intended to win approval for the establishment of a Torah academy in the small town of Jamnia on the Coastal Plain.

The Bar Kokhba Revolt, 132–135 C.E.

While Jewry in the land of Israel was in the process of reconstituting itself after the Great Revolt, at Jamnia and many other locations, Jewry in Diaspora lands, especially North Africa, Greece, and Italy, was reshaping itself as well. The synagogue was the institution that bound all of them together, as did a commitment to tradition in the form of the Hebrew Bible and a common form of Jewish practice that embraced dietary restrictions, a different calendar including holidays and the Sabbath, and an attachment to the land of Israel, which, by virtue of the Jews' leaving it, had become a kind of ideal. The emerging corpus of religious law in Israel and Babylonia was at a remove from most Diaspora communities. It was only much later that the leadership of Israel and Babylonia managed to exert a major influence on the Diaspora. Those who chose to leave after 70 C.E. and settle new lands or join existing Jewish communities could not have imagined that another revolt and a major uprising would occur so soon after and put Jews in the Roman world in a most uncomfortable position. Nonetheless, this is precisely what happened during the reigns of Trajan (98–117 C.E.) and Hadrian (117–138 C.E.).

With as much as a third of the Jewish population of Judea having been killed during the Great Revolt, one can only imagine the kind of hostile feelings Jews held for the Roman rulers, whether they lived in the homeland or in the Diaspora. No doubt many concluded that God had forsaken them, while others placed their hopes on a future redeemer or messianic leader who could one day reestablish the glory of the past. However, both the homeland and the Jewish Diaspora remained unusually quiet for some time, until 115–117 C.E., when unrest broke out under Emperor Trajan after his campaign against the Parthians in 115 C.E.[53] While he was away in the east Jews rose up in revolt in Egypt, Cyrenaica, and eventually Mesopotamia, in each location turning on their Gentile or pagan neighbors. Ancient sources provide details of the atrocities Jews committed against Gentiles, as fighting raged all the way to Cyprus. In Egypt, where Jews apparently won an early battle against the Roman prefect, M. Rufinius Lupus, they were ultimately defeated in Alexandria.[54] Several papyri provide direct evidence of the struggle in Egypt, noting at first the initial victory of the Jews and their subsequent defeat at the hands of the "Hellenes" after they received support from additional troops.[55] In Cyrenaica the rebellion was led by someone the Jews hailed as their king, called Lucuas by Eusebius and Andreas by Dio.[56] The rebellion was finally crushed in Mesopotamia by General Lusius Quietus, who, somewhat later, was appointed governor of Palestine. The rebellion did not apparently spread to Judea, where the arrival of a second legion to complement the Tenth Legion provided a successful buffer against further uprisings.[57]

Some speculation as to why such widespread antagonism mani-

Fig. 6.14. Bronze coin with Hadrian shown on the obverse, and the legend "The Colony Aelia Capitolina, the foundation" on the reverse (Copyright David Hendin, used by permission)

fested itself at this time has focused on the millenarian aspects of the rebellion. The economic and social position of the Jewish minority in the affected areas was not good, and the feelings that had emerged during the Great Revolt were never far below the surface, as we know especially from the Bar Kokhba Revolt that erupted some fifteen years later in Hadrian's reign.

The Second War against Rome, as it is also known, is a decisive and singular event in Jewish history. The Diaspora Revolt under Trajan cannot be considered a major cause of the Bar Kokhba Revolt, but they both had at their core the sense of Jewish dissatisfaction with the status of Jews in the empire and their abiding hope to reestablish some semblance of the independence of years before. Without the account of an eyewitness historian like Josephus, who was directly involved with the Great Revolt, reconstruction of events in the Bar Kokhba war is dependent on numerous sources. Rabbinic tradition (*Genesis Rabbah* 64:10) attributes the outbreak of hostilities to Hadrian's change of heart about rebuilding the Jerusalem Temple, a not very likely explanation. Pseudo-Spartianus in his *Historia Augusta* reports that Hadrian's ban on circumcision or genital mutilation (*Vita Hadr.* 14.2) inflamed the Jewish community, leading to open warfare. However, there is no real way to know whether this decree came before the outbreak of hostilities or in response to them. The historian Dio Cassius in his *Roman History* (69.12) points to Hadrian's plan to refound Jerusalem as a Roman colony with a new pagan temple and call it Aelia Capitolina as the precipitating cause (fig. 6.14). This final reason would seem to be the most likely scenario for opposition to Hadrian, as there could be no greater affront to Jewish sensibilities than to make the holy city a pagan shrine. Just as the pious ones in the time of the Maccabees rose up to oppose the spoliation of the Temple by Antiochus IV, no doubt so did a group of pious Jews rebel against the desecration of their beloved city.

Fig. 6.15. Second Revolt coins. Left, a temple flanked by the name Jerusalem in Hebrew, and on the reverse a lulav bunch with ethrog, and the words "Year two of the freedom of Israel" (133/134 C.E.). The large bronze coin in the middle features the name Jerusalem in a wreath; on reverse, a large amphora and "Year one of the redemption of Israel" (132/133 C.E.). Coin on right depicts a flagon and willow branch on obverse, a possible reference to Sukkot, with the inscription, "Eliezer the priest"; reverse has "Simon" in almond wreath. (Copyright David Hendin, used by permission)

Thus some sixty-two years after the fall of Jerusalem, a leader by the name of Bar Kokhba arose to lead a campaign against Rome. Coins from this period bear his first name, Simon or Shimon, together with his title among fellow Jews, Nasi, or Prince (fig. 6.15). The coins with this title are marked on the reverse "Year one of the redemption of Israel" or "Year two of the liberation of Israel." Strengthening Bar Kokhba's claim to be a messiah is the title "Prince" and the support reportedly given him by Rabbi Akiba, who is quoted as saying, "This is the King Messiah."[58] Some of his followers understood Numbers 24:17 to refer to him in a positive way ("A star shall go out of Jacob"—Bar Kokhba means "Son of the Star" in Aramaic), and a text recovered from Nahal Hever nearby (XHev/Se 30), the only letter intended for Simon bar Kosiba (his original Aramaic or Hebrew surname), shows that some Jews attributed to him charismatic or messianic qualities.[59] (Bar Kokhba was the positive interpretive name; Bar Koziba, "Son of a Liar," is the pejorative name given in some Jewish sources to denigrate his messianic pretensions.) Yadin's excavation of the so-called Bar Kokhba caves has shed light on the makeup and nature of Bar Kokhba's followers, and many of the items recovered there show that they were a pious group. The letters in particular help reveal the language, culture, and legal system in place at the time, just as the Mishnah was beginning to take shape (fig. 6.16).

Fig. 6.16. A letter from Bar Kokhba to Joshua, son of Galgola, from Wadi Murabbaat (Photo courtesy of the Israel Museum)

Researchers are fairly united in assessing the damage caused by the war as more devastating than the first revolt, and it also had long-lasting effects. At the conclusion of the war Hadrian omitted the normal formula in reporting to the Senate of Rome: "All is well with me and the legions" (fig. 6.17). This omission underscores the extent of the following the revolt must have had in the Jewish community and Bar Kokhba's popularity, which he could not have achieved without Akiba's public endorsement. Cassius Dio's summary of the war's end in his *Roman History,* while greatly exaggerated, states the extent of the destruction of villages (around 985) and outposts (about 50) and the total destruction of Judea. He does not mention Galilee, and there is little to no physical or literary evidence for the war in the north, though recent archaeology in the region has hinted that it may have reached that far.[60] Dio mentions also that nearly 600,000 men perished in the war. Other sources note that captives of the Roman army were sold as slaves and the economy of the country wiped out. Many Jews who had not migrated to the north and Galilee after 70 C.E. did so at this point, marking another significant shift in the demography of the Holy Land. Galilee became the epicenter for yet another Jewish

Fig. 6.17. Bronze bust of
Hadrian from Tel Shalem
(Photo courtesy of the Israel
Museum)

period of reconstruction and creativity, which in the course of two or
three generations, at most, succeeded in turning the catastrophe into
a critical turning point that resulted in an era of great literary output
and reconciliation with Rome.

The artifacts and letters recovered from a series of caves in the
Judean wilderness have provided scholars and historians with a vivid
glimpse of the last days of the Second War with Rome, when Simon's
officers and soldiers fled after the fall of Bethar to escape from the
Romans and take refuge in these remote caves overlooking the Dead
Sea and the Jordan Valley. Others who sought to hide from the Romans fled to the Shephelah or to the Hebron area and carved out hiding places for themselves in the soft limestone. Jerome, aware of these
conditions, wrote in his *Commentary on Isaiah* (2.15): "And the citizens of
Judea came to such distress that they, together with their wives, their
children, their gold and their silver, in which they trusted, remained in
underground tunnels and deepest caves." Some of those who had not
joined in the rebellion, like residents of Ein Gedi, earned the wrath
of their leader, as is apparent when Simon wrote to them: "You live
in ease, eating and drinking Israel's goods, and have no care for your
brethren." Thirty-five refuge caves have been found dating to the end
of the revolt; scrolls and other documents have been found in nine of
them. Skeletons were found in five refuge caves, and some scholars
believe that the report in rabbinic literature (*Lamentations Rabbah* 1:45)
mentioning that starvation had led the rebels to consume human flesh
is true.[61]

Not surprising, however, and more compelling to us, is the
fact that most of the rebels appear to have been observant Jews, judging from the phylacteries (prayer boxes attached to the arm and fore-
head) that were found and the reference in one letter urging an officer to leave early enough so that he could arrive to meet with Bar
Kokhba before the onset of the Sabbath; another letter asks the commander at Herodium to accommodate his troops over the Sabbath.
Two other letters mention the Four Species necessary to observe the
Feast of Booths or Tabernacles. In addition, economic documents reveal that the rebels also observed the sabbatical year. Even the textiles
preserved in the caves indicate that they adhered to biblical and rabbinic standards of manufacture. Among the types of textiles recovered were nearly complete tunics, mantles, a child's linen shirt, sheets

of linen, and bundles of unspun wool and linen. Study of these items has revealed that none of the textiles violated the biblical prohibition of using two different types of cloth together (the laws of *shaatnez*).[62] Detailed examination has also shown that men and women wore different colors as well and had a variety in decoration. Of special interest was the identification of tassels from prayer shawls, which receive even fuller treatment in the Talmud (*b. Menahot* 38–52). Even the verses in John 19:23–24 are illuminated by the examination of the tunics; their description of Jesus' tunic as seamless and woven from a single cloth piece can be understood to refer to a very special kind of garment, since most of the known tunics from the finds are woven from two pieces.[63] On the other hand, some of the artifacts recovered reveal that the rebels also participated in the surrounding culture: pictorial images abound on the metal objects, though some appear to have been defaced, and there are stone vessels used for purposes of ritual purity. Some of the papyri, especially those from the Nahal Hever, provide valuable insights into the early development of Jewish law and employ legal terms and formulas used in later rabbinic literature. All of these finds may be related to conditions in the months of August and September 135 C.E.

The letters relating directly to Bar Kokhba discovered in the caves number twenty-five and are written in three languages, Aramaic, Hebrew, and Greek.[64] Only about half of these were excavated by archaeologists; the rest came to light in the antiquities market in Jerusalem where they were offered by some Bedouin seeking to make money. At least one document seems to support the supposition that Bar Kokhba was indeed a messianic figure, for he is called both "Prince of Israel" and "Beloved Father."[65] Among the most important other documents found in the caves are a cache of letters relating to one Babatha, daughter of Simeon son of Menahem, written principally in Greek but also in Aramaic, Judean, and Nabatean. These thirty-five letters wrapped in a leather pouch tell us of Babatha's two husbands and provide a rich genealogy of her family. They even tell us about her father's purchase of a plot of land in the village of Mahoza in the district of biblical Zoar on the southern tip of the Dead Sea. One of the documents actually records the deed of purchase by Simeon and also how he subsequently gave it to his wife, Miriam. It goes on to list all the various items in the land, houses, courtyards, groves, and

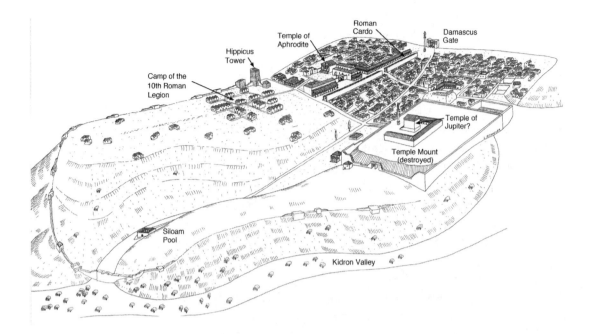

Fig. 6.18. Diagram of Aelia
Capitolina (Drawing courtesy
of Leen Ritmeyer)

more. We even have Babatha's marriage contract (*ketubah*), though we
cannot tell if it was from her first or second marriage. Two other marriage documents were found in other caves. The amount of legal information in these and other documents and the degree to which they
inform us about later rabbinic laws and tractates is simply stunning.
They also provide significant insight into how Jewish people on the
borders of the Holy Land used Roman law to their benefit as well.

　　Jerusalem was likely never captured by the rebels during the Second War against Rome, and it became known as the Roman colony of
Aelia Capitolina, named after Hadrian's family and Jupiter (fig. 6.18).
Jews were banned from the city and faced the death penalty if they
tried to enter. Jerusalem was thoroughly paganized, with new temples erected and dedicated to Jupiter and Aphrodite, plus a statue of
Hadrian as well. Jewish sources record that both during and just after
the war circumcision was banned along with most aspects of Jewish
practice, and public figures were persecuted and tortured in public.
Those martyrs mentioned in rabbinic literature are today remembered
annually in a special service on the Day of Atonement. These religious
edicts appear to have stayed in force until Hadrian's death in 138 c.e.
An arch dedicated to Hadrian following his second acclamation as im-

perator was discovered twelve kilometers south of Beth Shean and testifies to his importance in suppressing the revolt; it is dated to a time when the Roman Senate no longer dedicated such arches in the provinces. Most of Judea's villages that have been surveyed or excavated appear to have been razed after the suppression of the revolt. The Romans also expunged the name of Judea from the provincial designations, heretofore called Provincia Judaea, henceforth calling it Provincia Syria Palaestina. The demographic shift from Judaea to Galilee that began with the First Revolt further increased as Galilee became the all-important focus of Jewish life.

CHAPTER 7

The Emergence of Christianity

Archaeological discoveries of recent decades have shed enormous light on the world of Jesus and the movement he started (fig. 7.1). We have already seen examples of how they inform our understanding of Jesus' social setting in our discussions of Herod the Great's introduction of Roman architecture to the Near East and the changes his son Antipas brought to Galilee. Sometimes they have helped us to understand more specific issues such as architectural features mentioned in the Gospels, as with the recently excavated pool south of the Old City that is likely related to the Pool of Siloam (John 9).[1] Other times excavations uncover new information about public figures, as with the Pilate inscription at Caesarea Maritima.[2]

On occasion, archaeological finds vividly illustrate the customs and practices described in ancient sources. An excellent example is a boat hull recovered in 1986 from the mud of the Sea of Galilee near Kibbutz Ginnosar (fig. 7.2). The "Galilee boat" dated to the first century B.C.E. or C.E. and measured over eight meters long and two meters wide. Its basic shape resembles that of a sailing vessel depicted in a first-century C.E. mosaic at Magdala (Taricheae).[3] Made of low-quality timber, branches, and wood reused from earlier crafts, it hints of the economic challenges that faced fishermen. The right size to carry a bulky seine net for fishing, it probably required only a handful of crew members but could have carried up to fifteen people. It is thus the sort of boat suggested by Gospel stories of Jesus and his disciples traversing the lake. Its construction especially illuminates one such pericope, that of Jesus stilling the storm (Matt 8:23–27; Mark 4:35–41; Luke 8:22–25). Mark notes that when the storm began, Jesus was sleeping in the stern. The hull of the recovered boat demonstrates that its stern was relatively deep and thus a suitable place for passengers to take shelter, especially if it was also the location of its main deck, which would have carried the dragnet.[4]

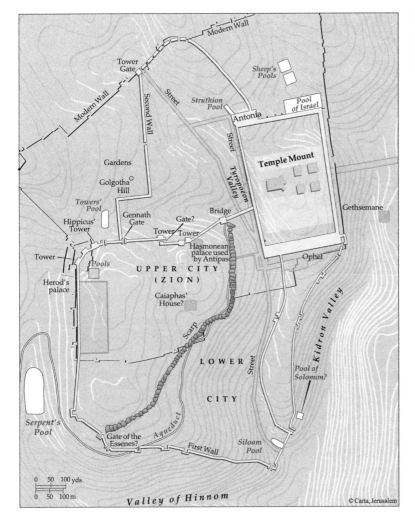

Fig. 7.1. Jerusalem in the time of Jesus (Map prepared by Carta, Israel Map and Publishing Company, Ltd.)

Another story that has been greatly illuminated by archaeological data is that of the wedding at Cana in which Jesus famously turned water into wine. According to John (2:1–11), the water was held in six massive stone jars, each of which held twenty or thirty gallons. The use of stone vessels to protect liquids from ritual impurity is an element of Jewish culture that is much better understood after the uncovering of stone vessels at so many sites in Palestine. Less often observed is the fact that archaeology helps us understand not only the "purification rites" referred to in John but also the socioeconomic context im-

Fig. 7.2. Boat recovered from the Sea of Galilee, first century C.E. (Photo courtesy of Todd Bolen/BiblePlaces.com)

plied by the story. Excavations have demonstrated that large jars such as these were associated primarily with elite residences; John's description of their size thus further underscores the impression of extravagance and wealth that other details of the narrative (such as the presence of a wine steward and servants) suggest.[5]

A more dramatic discovery comes from a tomb at Givat ha-Mivtar in Jerusalem, where the remains of a crucifixion victim were found, the only anthropological evidence for crucifixion ever discovered. An ossuary there with the inscription "Yehohanan, the son of Hagakol" contained the skeletal remains of a child and an adult male as well as a bone from another adult, the latter perhaps included mistakenly when the bones were gathered up for secondary burial. A bent iron nail pierced the adult male's right heel, with a piece of olive wood still attached to it. The legs of the man (presumably Yehohanan) were broken, a fact that recalls John's claim that Roman soldiers found it unnecessary to break Jesus' legs because he had already died (19:18), although whether Yehohanan's limbs had been broken before his death or during the removal of his body from the cross is impossible to determine. The lack of traumatic injury to his arms suggests that they may have been tied, rather than nailed, to the cross.[6]

We are also in a better position to understand biblical descriptions of Jesus' burial place because of the excavations of numerous

Plate 1. Aerial view of the Temple Mount (Photo by Todd Bolen/BiblePlaces.com)

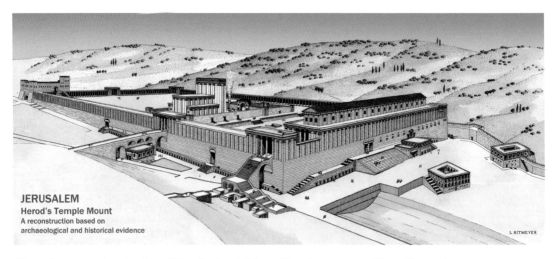

Plate 2. Reconstruction drawing of Herod's Temple Mount (Drawing courtesy of Leen Ritmeyer)

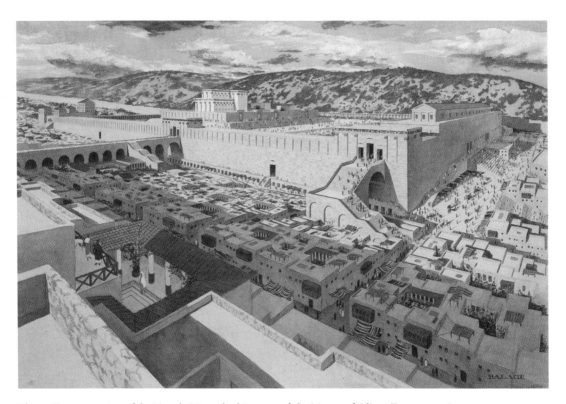

Plate 3. Reconstruction of the Temple Mount looking toward the Mount of Olives (Reconstruction drawing by Balage Balogh, from *Excavating Jesus,* HarperSanFrancisco, 2001; permission to reprint by John Dominic Crossan and Jonathan L. Reed)

Plate 4. A street in ancient Jerusalem, south of the Temple Mount (Reconstruction drawing by Balage Balogh, from *Excavating Jesus,* HarperSanFrancisco, 2001; permission to reprint by John Dominic Crossan and Jonathan L. Reed)

Plate 5. Interior of Herod's Temple, as pilgrims celebrate a festival (Reconstruction drawing courtesy of Balage Balogh)

Plate 6. Reconstruction of first-century Caesarea Maritima (Reconstruction drawing by Balage Balogh, from *Excavating Jesus,* HarperSanFrancisco, 2001; permission to reprint by John Dominic Crossan and Jonathan L. Reed)

Plate 7. Reconstruction of first-century Tiberias (Reconstruction drawing by Balage Balogh, from *Excavating Jesus,* HarperSanFrancisco, 2001; permission to reprint by John Dominic Crossan and Jonathan L. Reed)

Plate 8. Reconstruction of a wealthy priest's home in Jerusalem (Reconstruction drawing by Balage Balogh, from *Excavating Jesus,* HarperSanFrancisco, 2001; permission to reprint by John Dominic Crossan and Jonathan L. Reed)

Plate 9. Reconstruction drawing of the destroyed town of Gamla (Reconstruction drawing by Balage Balogh, from *Excavating Jesus,* HarperSanFrancisco, 2001; permission to reprint by John Dominic Crossan and Jonathan L. Reed)

Plate 10. Reconstruction drawing of a first-century courtyard house at Capernaum (Reconstruction drawing by Balage Balogh, from *Excavating Jesus,* HarperSanFrancisco, 2001; permission to reprint by John Dominic Crossan and Jonathan L. Reed)

Plate 11. Partially reconstructed synagogue at Nabratein, looking south (Photo courtesy of Eric and
Carol Meyers)

Plate 12. A reconstructed synagogue at Khirbet Shema, looking east (Photo courtesy of Eric Meyers)

Plate 13. Reconstruction drawing of the House of Dionysos at Sepphoris (Reconstruction drawing by Balage Balogh, from *Excavating Jesus,* HarperSanFrancisco, 2001; permission to reprint by John Dominic Crossan and Jonathan L. Reed)

Plate 14. Herakles and Dionysos (also known as the Symposium of Herakles and Dionysos), from the central panel of the mosaic floor at the Dionysos mansion (Photo courtesy of Eric and Carol Meyers)

Plate 15. The "marriage" of Dionysos and Ariadne, from the mosaic at the Dionysos mansion.
Eros crowns the reclining god with a wreath, as Ariadne sits holding a basket of fruit.
(Photo courtesy of Eric and Carol Meyers)

Plate 16. The drunkenness of Herakles, from the Dionysos mansion mosaic. A small fragment of Dionysos processing in a chariot appears in left panel. (Photo courtesy of Eric and Carol Meyers)

Plate 17. From the House of Dionysos mosaic, on the northern side of the triclinium framed in an acanthus medallion, a portrait of a beautiful woman, possibly Aphrodite, dubbed "the Mona Lisa of the Galilee" (Photo courtesy of Eric and Carol Meyers)

tombs. The Gospels describe how Joseph of Arimathea, a rich man (Matt 27:57) and a member of the Jewish council (Mark 15:43; Luke 23:50), took Jesus' body and placed it in a tomb—one that he himself owned, according to Matthew (27:60). When the women visited the tomb on the first day of the week, they found that the sealing stone had been rolled away (Matt 28:2; Mark 16:3–4; Luke 24:2; cf. John 20:1). Relying only on the text, it might be difficult to envision this sort of tomb entrance and rolling stone, but archaeological finds illustrate it perfectly. Several tombs with large circular sealing stones have been discovered around Jerusalem and others at the Judean site Horvat Midras and at Hesban in Jordan. The stones were often set into a groove in the ground to facilitate their rolling to open and close the entrance. In the late Second Temple period, these round sealing stones were quite rare, much less common than square and rectangular blocks that were simply plugged into tomb entrances. The use of circular stones was limited to social elites—people much like the character Joseph of Arimathea.[7]

We might expect to find ample archaeological evidence of the early Christians themselves (however "Christian" is defined), especially in light of the strong literary evidence of their presence in Roman Palestine. The unfortunate reality, however, is that such evidence has proved elusive thus far. Despite occasional claims of the discovery of artifacts associated with early Christians or even biblical figures, the fact is that the material culture of the earliest followers of Jesus is extremely difficult to identify, precisely because it was largely indistinguishable from that of other Jews. In fact, not until the fourth century c.e. does Christianity become widely discernible in the archaeological record. A review of Christianity's ancient roots in Palestine, religiously motivated efforts to find sacred sites and objects, and modern scholarly attempts to identify artifacts associated with earliest Christianity reveals just how arduous—and surprising—this particular archaeological quest can be.

Jesus and His Movement

Although scholarly debate surrounds most aspects of the life of Jesus, the basic geographical parameters for his activity suggested by the Gospels are generally accepted: the bulk of his ministry occurred in

Galilee, he may have traveled to adjacent areas, and his more limited time in Judea (whether one adult trip to Jerusalem as per the Synoptics or multiple trips as reported by John) culminated with his execution around Passover. Jerusalem aside, Jesus' activity seems to have been limited to villages, small towns, and rural areas. Thus, the Gospels claim that he preached in the synagogue of his home village of Nazareth, attended a wedding in the Lower Galilean village of Cana, and spent considerable time preaching and teaching in the area around the Sea of Galilee, choosing Capernaum as a sort of home base (Matt. 9:1 refers to it as his "own city"). His disciples and followers were drawn from communities like Capernaum, Bethsaida, and Magdala. Various accounts place him in the territories associated with the surrounding pagan cities—the districts of Tyre and Sidon (Matt 15:21–28; cf. Mark 7:24–30), the villages of Caesarea Philippi (Mark 8:27–33; cf. Matt 16:13–23), the region of the Decapolis (Mark 5:1–20; Luke 8:26–39; Matt 8:28–34; Mark 7:31)—but not one claims that he entered into any of the city centers. Likewise, he reportedly passed through the region of Samaria but is not said to have gone to Sebaste, the ancient city of Samaria that Herod the Great had renamed in honor of the emperor.[8]

Despite Jesus' mobility within Galilee, the region's own cities of Sepphoris and Tiberias are conspicuously absent from the Gospel narratives; only Tiberias is mentioned (John 6:1, 23, 21:1), but not as a place that Jesus visited. Scholars have offered several possible solutions for why the Gospels ignore the two cities. Sepphoris, we must remember, was within a reasonable walking distance of Jesus' home village of Nazareth, and Tiberias would have dominated the western side of the lake where Jesus spent so much time. Some have suggested that perhaps Jesus visited these cities but was so poorly received that the early Christian community had little reason to preserve stories of those visits. Others have argued that Jesus avoided the cities because he was offended by their budding Greco-Roman culture. As we have noted in earlier chapters, however, the true floruit of that culture was in the centuries following him. On the other hand, it may be that the mere presence of a city name honoring the Roman emperor was enough to garner his disapproval. Still others have suggested that Jesus was appalled by the economic pressures that the cities' construction placed on the region's masses, but that argument, too, is debatable in the absence of clearer evidence for a thoroughgoing economic crisis. Perhaps Jesus avoided the cities of Antipas because his own values clearly brought him into conflict with those of the Herodian dynasty, and the fate of John the Baptist illustrated for all to see what criticism of the Herods could provoke.[9]

As for Jerusalem, the Gospels' descriptions of Jesus' activities there are rich in detail, sometimes so much that they conflict. They note numerous specific places where events purportedly took place: the upper room of the Last Supper (Mark 14:15; Luke 22:12); the Garden of Gethsemane where Jesus prayed and was arrested (Mark 14:32; Matt 26:36); the house of the high priest where he was tried (Luke 22:54–62; John 18:15); the site where he was delivered over to Pilate and presented to the crowd (Mark 15:1–15; Matt 27:1–26; Luke 23:1–25; John 18:28–19:16); Golgotha, where he was crucified (Mark 15:22; Matt 27:33; Luke 23:33; John 19:17); the new tomb, where he was buried (Mark 15:46; Matt 27:60; Luke 23:53; John 19:41); and the village of Bethany, where he ascended into heaven (Luke 24:50–51).

Our primary source for what happened after Jesus' death among his first followers is the book of Acts. Without entering into the thicket of issues regarding its historical accuracy, we can note the traditions Acts preserves. Jesus' followers and their converts lived communally, gathering in houses and worshiping in the Jewish Temple (2:44–47, 5:42). The movement spread to the city of Samaria (8:4–25), cities west and north of Jerusalem (8:40, 9:36–43), Caesarea Maritima (10), and into the Diaspora.

Other sources corroborate the general claim that Jesus' followers were based in Jerusalem. Paul was familiar with James the brother of Jesus, Cephas (presumably Peter), and John as key leaders in the Jerusalem church (Gal 1:17–19, 2:1–10); planned to bring the Jerusalem church a collection of money gathered from Diaspora churches (Rom 15:25–32; 1 Cor 16:3; 2 Cor 8–9); and knew of other churches in Judea (Gal 1:22; 1 Thess 2:14). Josephus describes the execution of James by the Sadducean high priest Ananus in Jerusalem, around 62 C.E. (*Ant.* 20.197–203).[10]

The ultimate fate of the Jesus movement in Jerusalem is murky. Writing in the fourth century, Eusebius (*Church History* 3.5.3) and Epiphanius (*Panarion* 29.7.7–8, 30.2.7–9; *On Weights and Measures* 15) claim that Jewish Christians fled Jerusalem to escape its destruction in the Great Revolt and resettled across the Jordan in Pella; Epiphanius refers to the group as Nazareans, Jewish Christians disparaged by the Church Fathers for their Jewish practices. The accuracy of claims of a flight to Pella is highly questionable, and no archaeological evidence in Pella supports the presence of a Jewish-Christian group at such an early date. In fact, Eusebius elsewhere contradicts his own report of the depletion of Jerusalem's Christian community by suggesting that "until the time of the siege by Hadrian there was an extremely significant Church of Christ at Jerusalem, which consisted of Jews" (*Proof of the Gospel* 3.5.108) and providing a list of bishops that stretches from the Bar Kokhba Revolt back to James (*Church History* 4.5). A church remained in Jerusalem after the second revolt, he writes, though in contrast to the earlier one it was predominantly Gentile, and he provides names of its bishops, too (*Church History* 5.12, 6.10–11, 39, 7.14, 28.1, 32.29). Such references reflect Eusebius's concern with apostolic succession, and the facts behind them are often difficult to determine in the absence of additional evidence, but at the least they preserve traditions of ongoing Christian activities in Jerusalem in the preceding centuries.[11]

Jerusalem was not the only important church in Roman Palestine. In the early third century, Caesarea Maritima began emerging as an important intellectual and political center for Christianity.[12] Origen visited in around 215 C.E. and moved there from Alexandria circa 232, and he was soon joined by other Christian scholars. A century after Origen, Eusebius became bishop of the city, and he frequently refers to predecessor bishops.[13] By that time, the political circumstances of Christians in Palestine and elsewhere in the Roman Empire had changed dramatically thanks to the sympathy of Emperor Constantine, of whom Eusebius was the chief biographer.

Christian Holy Sites and the Life of Jesus

When Constantine turned his favor upon certain streams of Christianity, it brought rapid change to Palestine. No less a figure than Constantine's own mother, Helena, arrived in about 326 C.E. to identify the sites associated with the sacred stories of the life of Jesus and other biblical characters (fig. 7.3).[14] By far the most famous of the holy sites she identified are those of Jesus' crucifixion and resurrection. Finding the supposed exact spots required extensive digging, making Helena's project an early and crude example of an archaeological excavation. Her son recognized the sacred space by building the Church of the Holy Sepulcher, a later version of which stands today. One ancient tradition credits Helena with another remarkable discovery: the True Cross that Jesus was nailed to.[15] Whether Helena's identifications of the sites of Jesus' death and burial were correct is debatable, but her theory is not without merit. The area she designated would have been outside the city walls in the time of Jesus, and as modern visitors often discover, it was indeed the site of several late Second Temple period *kokhim* (burial niches). Verifying for sure that Jesus' followers laid his body in a *kokh* there is impossible, but the site is the most likely contender for his tomb.

Fig. 7.3. Architectural fragment of stone from church at Pella with pelican and menorah, Byzantine period (Photo courtesy of the ASOR Archive)

Some scholars hailed the discovery in the 1970s of a drawing of a ship and an inscription on the stone wall of an ancient cave (now Saint Vartan's Chapel) below the Church of the Holy Sepulcher as proof that Christians venerated it as a holy site even before Constantine. The inscription, although difficult to read, was interpreted by Pierre Benoit as *domine ivimus* ("Lord, we went"), a phrase that he regarded as an allusion to the Latin rendering of Psalm 122:1 (per chapter numbering in the Masoretic Text): *In domum Domini ibimus,* or "we shall go to the House of the Lord." Magen Broshi followed Benoit's reading and argued that the inscription represented "the joyous exclamation of [Christian] pilgrims who sailed from the western part of the Empire and finally reached the Holy City." The ship, in his view, was nothing less than a depiction of the sort of vessel that transported Christian travelers to the Holy Land, sketched by the hand of one such passenger (fig. 7.4).[16] In a detailed study, however, Shimon Gibson and Joan E. Taylor review a number of other possibilities. Reconstructing the inscription is a challenge, but in any case, the word *domine* ("Lord") was applied to a very wide range of parties in the Roman period and was most definitely not limited to use as a Christian title for Jesus. Gibson and Taylor demonstrate the high degree of nautical accuracy in the drawing and suggest that it was created by a sailor in the second century C.E. They question why a drawing of a ship cannot simply be a drawing of a ship, rather than evidence for pilgrimage or a symbolic reference to the church. Last, they raise the possibility that the stone with the drawing is in secondary usage—that is, that it came from

Fig. 7.4. Drawing of a small Roman sailing vessel from Saint Vartan's Chapel below the Church of the Holy Sepulcher, first century C.E. (Drawing courtesy of the ASOR Archive)

elsewhere in the city and happened to end up in this particular cave for use in a building project. Fortunately, the inscription and drawing (both somewhat altered through restoration efforts) can still be viewed today, allowing visitors to make up their own minds.[17]

The Church of the Holy Sepulcher was just one of many shrines that came to dot the area as Christians developed the notion of a "Holy Land" (fig. 7.5). Helena also established churches at Bethlehem, on the Mount of Olives, at the base of Mount Sinai, and at Mamre. By the time Egeria, a Christian pilgrim, visited Palestine around 381–384 C.E., numerous other holy sites had been identified, and Byzantine-period sources comment on places like Mount Tabor (purported site of Jesus' Transfiguration), the Mount of Beatitudes, and Tabgha (purported site for Jesus' multiplication of the loaves and fish). This association of specific sites with particular Bible stories was an ongoing process that has continued into the modern period. The current route of Jerusalem's Via Dolorosa (the "way of suffering"), which Christian pilgrims tread to commemorate and reenact Jesus' walk to Golgotha, was fixed in the 1700s, replacing earlier routes with Byzantine-period origins.[18]

One of the most visited sites today was not identified until 1883, when the British general Charles Gordon became convinced that what is now known as the "Garden Tomb" was the actual burial spot of Jesus, rather than the Church of the Holy Sepulcher (fig. 7.6). Taking his cue from biblical references to Golgotha, translated by the Gospel

Fig. 7.5. The Church of the Holy Sepulcher in Jerusalem, traditional site of the burial of Jesus, photographed in 1875 by Tancrede Dumas (Photo courtesy of the ASOR Archive)

writers as "the place of the skull" (Matt 27:33; Mark 15:22; John 19:17; cf. Luke 23:33), Gordon was convinced that the topography of Jerusalem looked like a skeleton with the head at the site of the Garden Tomb. It did not hurt his argument that an adjacent cliff face bore superficial resemblance to the eye and nose sockets of a skull; modern visitors often find jarring the juxtaposition of this ancient supposed

Fig. 7.6. The Garden Tomb, an alternative site for the burial of Jesus (Photo courtesy of Sean Burrus)

Golgotha with the bus station at its base. While the Garden Tomb has repeatedly proved itself an ideal setting for Christian pilgrims to contemplate and meditate on the significance of events in Jerusalem for their faith, archaeologists are unanimous in their appraisal of the tomb itself. It dates to the Iron Age, perhaps the eighth or seventh century B.C.E., and is thus not a plausible candidate for the grave of Jesus.[19]

The issue of Jesus' burial place illustrates the sometimes complex relationship of archaeological investigation to efforts to "authenticate" holy sites. Although archaeology suggests that the Church of the Holy Sepulcher *may* mark the spot of Jesus' grave and that the Garden Tomb most certainly does *not*, it does not settle with certainty the question of where Jesus' followers laid his body. Archaeological excavations can rarely identify where events described in the Bible happened and thus often can neither confirm nor disconfirm the traditions that underlie holy sites. Nor can archaeology prove or disprove the historicity of many biblical stories, and in any event, most archaeologists working in the area today are occupied with entirely different research questions. Ultimately, the value of holy sites depends on judgments of faith, not findings of the spade.

Evidence of Early Jewish Christianity?

Nonetheless, the difficulty of authenticating holy sites and identifying early Christianity in the archaeological record has not prevented
scholars and clerics from trying. Among the best-known attempts
are those of the Franciscan scholars Bellarmino Bagatti, Emmanuele Testa, Stanislao Loffreda, and their colleagues, who claimed to
have found evidence of Jewish Christians at several sites. In their argument, the Jewish Christian movement traced its roots directly back
to Jesus' own circle, and it constituted the Church of the Circumcision mentioned by Eusebius. Proponents of this view have argued
that the *minim* ("heretics") at Sepphoris, Kefar Sikhnin, Kefar Nevoraia (Nabratein), and Capernaum mentioned in rabbinic references
must have been Jewish Christians (*t. Hullin* 2:22–24; *b. Avodah Zarah*
16b–17a, 27b; *Qoheleth Rabbah* 1.8, 7.26).[20]

This theory placed considerable weight on the discovery of inscriptions of names corresponding to personalities in the Gospels and
of various markings that were interpreted as Jewish-Christian symbols. When Franciscan scholars led by Bagatti excavated the five-
hundred-tomb necropolis of Dominus Flevit on the western slope of
the Mount of Olives in 1953–1955, they unearthed 129 ossuaries with
such names as Yehudah, Shimeon, Martha, Miriam, and Yehosef.
Some ossuaries were marked with crosses and x's, and one had been
carved with a *chi rho* monogram of the sort that became a Christian
symbol after Constantine. The excavators regarded the names as evidence that early Christians had named their offspring after key members of Jesus' circle. In their view, the ossuaries provided proof that
Jewish Christians had lived and died in Jerusalem in the decades between Jesus' death and the city's destruction.[21]

The Franciscans were not alone in interpreting archaeological
finds this way. Their arguments were similar to those accompanying a
discovery in 1873 southeast of the city on the Mount of Offense (Batn
el-Hawa). Construction there had opened up a tomb holding thirty
ossuaries with mostly Aramaic inscriptions. Several of the names
carved into the ossuaries were familiar to readers of the New Testament, such as Shimon, Martha, Yeshua, Salome, Yehudah, and Iesous.
Some ossuaries were marked with crosses, including one that closely
resembled the Latin cross of later centuries. Their publisher, Charles
Clermont-Ganneau, regarded the names and symbols as indicators of

an early Christian community.[22] In 1945, only a few years before the Franciscan excavations at Dominus Flevit, the renowned archaeologist Eliezer Sukenik had commented on the presence of similar names on ossuaries discovered in the Jerusalem suburb of Talpiyot. Sukenik argued that two of those inscriptions reflected grief over the death of Jesus. One read *Iesous Iou* and the other, *Iesous Aloth*. Sukenik interpreted *Iou* in the first inscription as "woe" and tentatively suggested that *Aloth* should be understood as a form of the Hebrew and Aramaic verb *alah,* to wail or lament. Sukenik suggested that such inscriptions provided "the earliest records of Christianity in existence."[23]

Subsequent scholarship has not affirmed these interpretations. As the number of recovered ossuaries has grown to the thousands, it has become increasingly clear that such names were common in ancient Judaism (a fact already evident in the writings of Josephus and the rabbis). Rather than the Gospels illuminating the ossuary inscriptions by serving as the source for their names, the ossuaries illuminate the names in the Gospels by showing just how typical they were for their time period. Sukenik's interpretations of the Talpiyot inscriptions have been rejected; *Iou* appears to be from *Ioudou,* which would make the inscription read "Jesus son of Judah," and *aloth* is typically understood as either a name or perhaps a nickname related to the Hebrew *ahalot,* "aloes." Many of the markings on the Dominus Flevit ossuaries that the excavators regarded as Christian crosses were more likely masons' marks meant to indicate how to align the lid or where to place a decoration or inscription, or, alternatively, marks added by family members to distinguish a particular ossuary from others. The *chi rho* would become an important reference to *Christos* in the fourth century and later, but in earlier periods it could serve as an abbreviation for any number of words prominently employing those letters (*chreston,* "good," and some form of *charasso* for "scratched" or "sealed" are standard explanations). The Latin cross from the Mount of Offense is better explained as a Christian addition in the Byzantine period, perhaps by someone reusing the tomb, than as the marking of a first-century Jewish Christian anticipating the symbolic conventions of several centuries later.[24]

Some scholars question the automatic identification of *minim* with Jewish Christians. A few rabbinic passages do seem to attest the presence of Jewish Christians, such as those recounting a story set in Sepphoris of a Jacob from Sakhnin telling Rabbi Eleazar about Yeshu ben Pantera, generally understood to be Jesus (*t. Hullin* 2:22–24; *b. Avodah Zarah* 16b–17a). The Birkat ha-Minim, or "maledictory prayer against the heretics" that rabbinic sources claim was added to the Eighteen Benedictions of synagogue liturgy in the second century C.E., may have been directed at such Christians who sought to participate in synagogue services. Rabbinic references to minim are sometimes ambiguous, however, leading some scholars to argue that "minim" was an indeterminate enough term to include a variety of Jews with beliefs and practices that the rabbis regarded as heterodox, not just Jewish Christians. If those scholars are correct, then passages mentioning minim provide a weak foundation for an argument of a substantial Jewish-Christian presence in Roman Palestine.[25]

Fig. 7.7. A Greek inscription found beneath the modern Basilica of the Annunciation in Nazareth: "On [the] holy place [of] M[ary] I have written there" (Drawing courtesy of the ASOR Archive)

Claims of Jewish-Christian artifacts also extended to include pre-Constantinian architecture. During excavations conducted in conjunction with the erection of the modern Basilica of the Annunciation in Nazareth, Bagatti and his team discovered a remarkable series of earlier buildings (fig. 7.7). They uncovered portions of a Crusader church that had been built atop an even earlier mid-fifth-century church, as well as a monastery associated with two caves, the significance of which will be discussed below. The fifth-century structures had been erected over a third-century C.E. stepped pool and the destroyed remains of a sizable structure in use in the third and early fourth centuries, a building that the excavators identified as a Jewish-Christian synagogue. The bedrock was pocked with cavities and depressions that had served late Hellenistic and early Roman houses as foundation holes, agricultural installations, and storage space.[26]

Now known as the Grotto of the Annunciation and the Martyrium, the two caves were venerated by Christians in antiquity. The Grotto of the Annunciation is named for the site of Gabriel's appearance to Mary (Luke 1:26–38), and the Martyrium takes its name from the excavators' theory that it commemorated the martyrdom of Conon, a Christian from Nazareth killed under Emperor Decius (249–251 C.E.). This suggestion was based on the assumption that a Greek mosaic inscription to its south from the fifth-century church recording a "Gift of Conon, Deacon of Jerusalem," reflected homage to the martyred Conon by a later Christian of the same name.[27] Graffiti in the Grotto of the Annunciation were undatable, but the excavators believed Christian inscriptions carved into plaster in the Martyrium to be pre-Constantinian. They also interpreted floral motifs in that cave's plaster as depictions of paradise, though most scholars would now identify them as common decorations of no symbolic significance.

The earliest layer of plaster in the Martyrium bore Greek prayers such as "Christ Lord, save your servant Valeria" and "Jesus Christ, Son of God." The excavators dated the layer to the third century c.e., but their proposal is highly debatable. Their key evidence is a small bronze coin found beneath the third layer of plaster. Most of its inscriptions are worn away, but the imperial bust on its obverse and the Victoria on its reverse are clear enough. Bagatti suggested that it depicted Constans (337–350 c.e.) and argued that its presence indicated that this layer had been applied by the middle of the fourth century at the latest; the two layers below it with Christian graffiti would thus be even earlier. Others dated the coin to the early years of Constantine (306–337 c.e.), positing a possible pre-fourth-century date for the bottom layers of plaster.[28] Yet dating the third layer of plaster on the basis of this single coin is tricky. Determining whether the coin was minted by Constantine or his son is difficult enough, but in either case it would provide a fixed date only for the earliest possible application of the plaster, not the latest. If the coin is an issue of Constantine, the plaster would date to his reign or afterward, making a fourth-century date for the earlier layers of plaster also possible. If it were issued by Constans, the range of dates for the first two layers would extend even further into the fourth century. This wide time span makes the attribution of the Christian graffiti to the third century questionable, though not impossible.

The limestone and marble architectural fragments that Bagatti interpreted as a Jewish Christian synagogue included column bases, capitals, and drums as well as moldings, doorjambs, thresholds, cornices, and chunks of plaster from the walls. Many of the fragments bore graffiti obviously written by Christians, mostly in Greek, although two were in Aramaic and at least one was in Armenian. The most famous of the inscriptions is the XE/MAPIA found on a column fragment. Bagatti believed the first word to be an abbreviation for *chaire,* "hail," making the inscription "Hail, Mary." Others have suggested that it could just as easily be read *Christe,* making the inscription "Christ, Mary."[29] Various other markings and images

adorned the fragments, including crosses, a boat, and a man in armor with a spear. Although these inscriptions have sometimes been treated as late-Roman period, it is more likely that many of them, at least, are Byzantine. As Taylor points out, the Armenian inscription in particular is unlikely to predate the fifth century.[30] Additional graffitied plaster pieces from the building were found in the stepped pool discovered below the nave of the fifth-century church under a mosaic with a *chi rho* inscription that is itself still earlier (fig. 7.8). The red, green, and brown plaster chunks bore Greek and a few Syriac inscriptions. The excavators interpreted one Greek inscription as "Lord" (*kyrie*) and found "John" and "Amen" in the Syriac ones.[31]

For the excavators, the pool itself is a strong indication of lengthy Jewish-Christian use of the site. The plastered pool of 2 by 1.95 meters dates to the third century and had seven steps, five of them cut into bedrock and two built of stones and mortar. The shape of the pool closely resembles a miqveh except for one feature, a circular sump in its northeast corner. The plastered sides of the miqveh bore crude depictions of boats, crosses, ladders, nets, and other items that the excavators interpreted as Jewish-Christian symbols. Bagatti regarded the pool as a baptismal basin and proposed the same identification for another seven-stepped plastered pool with a sump beneath the nearby Church of Saint Joseph.[32]

Bagatti's interpretation of these pools has been strongly contested. The presence of a sump in each is a challenge to their identification as miqvaot, and the one at the Church of Saint Joseph has mosaic tiles in the bottom, a feature unparalleled in other ritual baths. Taylor points to the discovery of a metal knife blade in a niche of the pool in the Basilica of the Annunciation as an indicator that the basin was in fact an agricultural installation, perhaps a vat for squeezing grapes, though this identification is not without its own problems, in that wine

Fig. 7.8. This Greek inscription from a Byzantine-period synagogue at Sepphoris is frequently identified as Jewish-Christian because of the chi-rho monogram at the right end of the bottom line (Drawing courtesy of the ASOR Archive)

and oil vats typically lacked steps and there is no obvious adjacent surface for threshing or crushing. As for the carvings in the pool's plastered sides, Taylor persuasively argues that there is little reason to interpret them symbolically, suggesting that they may be nothing more than the scrawlings of children. Whatever the significance of the pools and their carvings, there is no evidence for their use for baptism.[33]

Determining how all of the different phases of occupation beneath the Basilica of the Annunciation relate to each other is difficult. For Bagatti, it was self-evident that Jewish-Christians had associated the site with events in the life of Jesus and his mother Mary early on, visiting the caves and gathering to worship. The pool attested to their practice of baptism, and the architectural and plaster fragments with graffiti showed that they had constructed a synagogue-church that was later destroyed for the fifth-century Byzantine structures. However, very few scholars now appear to be persuaded by Bagatti's identifications of various markings and images as Jewish-Christian symbols, thus rejecting evidence that was central to his thesis.[34] Even if the pool under the nave mosaic is indeed a miqveh, the structure built atop it, however interpreted, need not be associated directly with it. If the pool is interpreted as an agricultural vat of some sort, then Bagatti's argument for specifically Jewish-Christian usage is damaged even further. If Bagatti has rightly dated the architectural fragments to the late Roman period, then their interpretation as parts of a synagogue would be reasonable, but the question that then arises is how the graffiti that are indisputably Christian relate to that building. If the architectural fragments and Christian graffiti are from the same phase of usage, then the building was obviously some sort of church. The later the various graffiti are dated, however, the less reason there is to associate them with the earlier phases of the public building. The evidence could be explained by the construction of a fourth-century church atop a Roman-period synagogue, making use of its elements, or by the conversion of a synagogue to a church. Either explanation seems more reasonable than Bagatti's own thesis. Little aside from the bedrock layer and its various installations predates the third century C.E., and there is no reason to suggest an ongoing religious function dating back to the first century.

The case for several centuries of continuous Christian usage for a series of structures at Capernaum is stronger, though there, too, they fall short of being conclusive. Archaeologists Virgilio C. Corbo, Stanislao Loffreda, and Emmanuele Testa excavated a domicile that they claimed to be none other than that of Peter, and thus a house that Jesus himself visited. All of the canonical Gospels report that Jesus preached and worked miracles at Capernaum, and some refer to it as his home (Mark 2:1; Matt 4:13, 9:1). (See plate 10.) Capernaum is traditionally regarded as the hometown of Peter, Andrew, James, John, and Levi/Matthew (Matt 4:13–22, 9:9; Mark 2:14, though John 1:44 and 12:21 identify Bethsaida as the home of Andrew and Peter). The Synoptics claim that Peter's house was the site where Jesus healed not only Peter's mother-in-law but also many of the city's sick and demon-possessed (Mark 1:29–34; Matt 8:14–15; Luke 4:38–39; cf. Matt 17:25). If the excavators' interpretation of the house is correct, then it provides a tangible link with the historical Jesus and his disciples.

The structure in question is thirty meters south of the well-known limestone synagogue. Its location is marked by a glass-bottomed modern church that overlooks the remains of a fifth-century octagonal church. The octagonal church was constructed atop an earlier fourth-century church with Christian graffiti that itself was built around a well-attended room from an earlier house. It is this house that the excavators identified as Peter's home. They argued that Jewish Christians continued to meet in it for over two centuries after the time of Peter before completely renovating it in the fourth century, at which point it became a *domus ecclesiae,* or "house of the church." They emphasize the importance of reports of Byzantine-period pilgrims who recorded the presence of a house associated with Peter. Egeria, writing in the late fourth century, marveled that "in Capernaum the house of the prince of the apostles has been made into a church, with its original walls still standing" (fig. 7.9)[35] The sixth-century pilgrim from Piacenza also visited what he believed was Peter's house, referring to it as a "basilica" (*Itinerarium Antonini Placentini* vii). The archaeologists suggest that three of the building's graffiti include the name Peter, establishing a direct connection between it and the church mentioned in the pilgrim literature.[36]

The house was originally built in the early first century B.C.E. and was definitely in use in the following century, making its occupation contemporary with Jesus and Peter. Made of basalt with fieldstone floors, it contained grinding stones, hand mills, and presses and

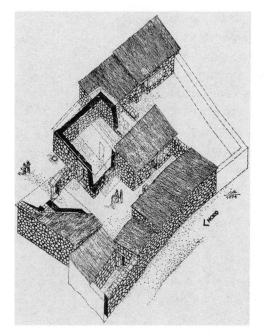

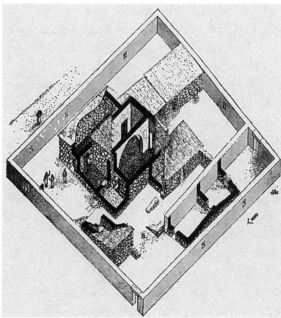

Fig. 7.9. Isometric view of the Insula Sacra at the time of Jesus, Capernaum (Drawing courtesy of the Franciscan Printing Press, Jerusalem)

Fig. 7.10. Isometric view of the fourth-century C.E. domus ecclesiae, Capernaum (Drawing courtesy of the Franciscan Printing Press, Jerusalem)

looked very much like other non-elite late Hellenistic and early Roman residences in Capernaum. In the late first century C.E., however, it underwent atypical renovation, and its ceiling, walls, and floor were extensively plastered. At least two additional layers of lime plaster were later applied. The site's excavators placed considerable weight on these changes, arguing that they indicate that already the house served as a point of assembly. Joan E. Taylor has questioned the dating of the plaster, and she has rightly pointed out that it is not necessary to posit a public function to explain plaster floors. Although this house appears to have been the only one in the western part of Capernaum to have such floors, wealthier homes in the eastern part of the site contained them. Changes in the pottery found in the house, however, also point to a new function. Although the earliest stratum contained cooking and serving wares, vessels from later centuries are limited primarily to storage jars, suggesting that the building ceased to be a simple domicile.[37]

In the fourth century, the house underwent additional significant changes. It was expanded, and the earlier plastered room (the "venerated hall," in the excavators' parlance) was decorated with red and white plaster with floral and geometric designs, with an arch constructed across its middle. Several new rooms were built around it, and an enclosure wall surrounded the entire complex. The preservation and spatial centering of the earlier room suggest that it was regarded as important.

The plastered walls of the "venerated hall" were marked with dozens of graffiti, in which the excavators identified 151 Greek, 13 Syriac, 10 Aramaic, and 2 Latin inscriptions. Some are Christian (such as "Christ, have mercy"), but many are difficult to decipher, and Testa's identifications and interpretations are often highly doubtful. For example, Testa regarded the Greek inscription on one plaster fragment as *moulou* (from *moulos,* mule) and argued that it illustrated the importance of the mule as an early Christian symbol. James F. Strange, however, notes that such a reading requires a very odd morphology of characters. If one turns the inscription upside down, he points out, the morphological problem disappears and the inscription appears to read not *moulou* at all but *doulou.* Testa identified three references to Peter, but his readings of two have been disputed, and whether the third refers to the apostle or the name of a pilgrim is debatable. Testa dated these graffiti to the late second to the fourth centuries, which would suggest that the house was an object of pilgrimage only 150 years after Jesus. Here, too, there is room for disagreement, since it is not always clear when plaster with graffiti should be attributed to the fourth-century renovations and when to an earlier period.[38]

Ultimately, the archaeological evidence for identifying this structure as the house of Peter can be described as largely circumstantial: the series of structures dates back to a residential building from the right time period that later underwent an unusual transformation. Whether one should regard that earliest residence as the actual house of Peter depends on how much weight is placed on the centrality of one of its rooms in the designs of later structures, when the graffiti is dated and how it is interpreted, and whether the building should be equated with the House of Peter mentioned in Byzantine pilgrim accounts. The site could mark where Peter's house actually stood, or it could mark where later Christians mistakenly thought it stood, or it could even be associated with a church altogether distinct from the House of Peter mentioned in literary sources (fig. 7.10).

Why is it so difficult to identify with much confidence Christian churches from the earliest centuries of Christianity? The answer lies in the passages cited from Acts earlier in this chapter. The first Christians typically gathered in private houses, domiciles indistinguishable from those of their neighbors. Only in later centuries might such a house be renovated to better host communal meetings. It is to such a modified structure that archaeologists sometimes apply the afore-mentioned term "domus ecclesiae," of which the oldest example in the East is a third-century C.E. structure at Dura Europos in Syria.[39] The absence of church buildings dedicated solely to worship in the Roman period is also in accord with evidence in Patristic sources that many early Christians worshiped in synagogues. According to Church Fathers critical of the practice, Christians were apparently attracted by the "awesomeness" of those buildings, their holiness as a place where the Hebrew Torah and Prophets were read, and perhaps also the prestige of synagogue leaders who could heal and do wonders.[40] The aforementioned Birkat ha-Minim may have been directed at such worshipers.[41] Architecturally distinctive church buildings were largely a post-Constantinian development.

The Sensationalization of Ossuary Inscriptions in the 2000s

The House of Peter is not the only archaeological finding that some associate directly with Jesus' closest followers. In 2002, the Biblical Archaeology Society announced with great media fanfare the discov-ery of an ossuary it alleged to be the burial receptacle of James, brother of Jesus, known as "James the Just" in later Christian tradition. Its inscription reads *Yaakov bar Yehoseph bar Yosef achui Yeshua*. Translated most literally, this means "Jacob son of Joseph brother of Jesus," but the fact that New Testament references to Jesus' brother Jacob have traditionally been translated into English as James explains why the box is called the James ossuary. The ossuary's owner, later revealed as the lifelong antiquities collector Oded Golan, claimed to have pur-chased it on the antiquities market some decades earlier. It had sat in his apartment, he claimed, before he showed it to epigrapher André Lemaire. Upon seeing its nineteen-centimeter Aramaic inscription, Lemaire had immediately recognized the potential significance of its clustering of names.[42]

Little differentiates the ossuary from the hundreds of others found in the vicinity of Jerusalem (fig. 7.11). It is typical in appearance

Fig. 7.11. James Ossuary (Photo courtesy of Lori Woodall)

and is unornamented except for the faint outlines of incompletely carved rosettes on one long side and the inscription on the other. The side with the rosettes is weathered and displays unusual pitting, with numerous small, very shallow holes in its surface. Its exact provenance is unknown, although its owner claims to have been told that it came from the Silwan district in East Jerusalem.

The ossuary itself is undoubtedly ancient, but the antiquity of the inscription faced almost immediate challenge. Some scholars granted the antiquity of the first three words, "James son of Joseph" but questioned the authenticity of the final two, "brother of Jesus," arguing that a different hand had carved them and suggesting that they had been added to increase the ossuary's value on the antiquities market. Others rejected the entire inscription, a position that gained favor when it was pointed out that the shapes of its letters seemed to have been modeled after already published ossuary inscriptions with the names Jacob, Joseph, and Jesus.[43]

Defenders of the ossuary's link to James the Just, such as Hershel Shanks of the Biblical Archaeology Society and New Testament scholar Ben Witherington, reject such arguments and emphasize the striking convergence of biblical names. All three names were common among first-century C.E. Jews—Shanks himself notes two other examples of "Jesus son of Joseph" ossuaries—but the reference to a sibling was unusual (though not unprecedented), suggesting that James's brother Jesus was someone of stature and importance.[44] The ossuary's promoters insist that the clustering of these particular names with these specific familial relationships makes it statistically feasible that the ossuary once contained the bones of James the Just. According to a calculation by Tel Aviv University statistician Camil Fuchs that Shanks and Witherington highlight, it is 95 percent likely that only four individuals in first-century Jerusalem named James would have had a Jesus as brother and a Joseph as father.[45]

Even if for the sake of discussion we were to accept the 95 percent probability, then by the statistician's own argument there were likely three other men named James who had fathers named Joseph and brothers named Jesus, in addition to James the Just. By this logic, it is actually statistically *unlikely* that the ossuary had held the bones of James the Just and more likely that it held those of one of these other individuals. Other statistical arguments are no more convincing. Lemaire devised his own figure, based on assumptions that Jerusalem had a population of eighty thousand, half of whom were male; that two generations should be factored into the data pool; and that the sample of names known from Jerusalem is statistically representative of first-century Jews throughout Palestine. According to his calculation, approximately twenty first-century Jerusalemites had the right names and familial relationships.[46] Such odds again would suggest that the ossuary is unlikely to have been associated with James the Just and far more likely to have held a different James. Regardless, Lemaire's assumptions are questionable, and different figures at any point would result in a very different final statistic. Using an alternative estimate for the city's population, for example, would seriously change the calculation, as would expanding the sample size of individuals to include the rest of Palestine's population of several hundred thousand. James was from Galilee, not Jerusalem, after all, and individuals from that and other regions were likely buried in Jerusalem on occasion. Given such gaps in our knowledge, there is no way to adequately control for such variables, making these types of statistical arguments extremely misleading in their seeming authoritativeness.[47]

In 2003, a committee of experts appointed by the Israel Antiquities Authority declared the inscription a forgery. Among the factors that led to their conclusion were irregularities with the ossuary's patina, a thin layer of encrustation that develops over time. When police searched Golan's residence and storage facilities, they found tools they identified as forgery implements and numerous forged antiquities. Authorities alleged that Golan was deeply involved in the creation and selling of faked antiquities, including the Jehoash Inscription, which purportedly records temple repairs by King Jehoash (2 Kgs 12). After a seven-year trial, the Jerusalem District Court ruled in March 2012 that the evidence was insufficient to prove that Golan had forged the ossuary. The 475-page verdict emphasized, however, "This is not to say that the inscription on the ossuary is true and authentic and was written 2,000 years ago." Despite complaints that the Israel Antiquities Authority bungled the investigation, and defenses of the inscription's genuineness by Shanks and Witherington among others, the archaeological community has almost unanimously rejected it.[48]

Even if the entire inscription were determined to be authentic and the identification with the biblical James somehow indisputably established, the ossuary would add little to existing scholarly knowledge. The existence of neither James nor Jesus is in serious question, and James's burial in Jerusalem is claimed by Eusebius (*Church History* 2.23, quoting Hegesippus). The primary new information would be that James or those in his circle had sufficient means to purchase a stone ossuary, a cost that exceeded the resources of many Jerusalemites but that was not exorbitant either. It would also mean that his family or followers had opted to incise that ossuary in a Semitic language rather than Greek, thus conforming to the epigraphic trends of the city, an interesting but not earth-shattering discovery.

An even more remarkable set of claims was made in 2007 when documentary filmmaker Simcha Jacobovici announced that a tomb excavated in 1980 in Talpiyot was nothing less than the family tomb of Jesus of Nazareth, asserting further that an ossuary found inside it marked *Yeshua bar Yehosef* had held the bones of Jesus himself. Six of the ten ossuaries from the tomb were inscribed, five with Semitic inscriptions and one with Greek, and in addition to *Yeshua bar Yehosef,* they included other names well known to readers of the Gospels: *Yoseh, Yehudah bar Yeshua, Mattiyah, Maryah.* Another was marked with an inscription initially interpreted as the name *Mariamene* [also called] *Mara,* although another proposed reading renders it *Mariame kai Mara,* or Mariam and Mara. Jacobovici argued that because mitochondrial DNA sampling of the bone remains in the *Yeshua bar Yehosef* ossuary and those from the *Mariame kai Mara* ossuary proved that the individuals interred in them had not been maternally related, they were likely husband and wife. The most sensible interpretation, he claimed, was that the ossuaries demonstrated that Jesus of Nazareth had been married to Mary Magdalene. Yehudah son of Yeshua, whose bones were placed in another ossuary, had been their child, while the nearby Yoseh was Joses, brother of Jesus (Mark 6:3; cf. 15:40, 47). Because the Israel Antiquities Authority had lost one of the ten ossuaries, Jacobovici suggested that the James ossuary bought by Golan had originated here, connecting this ossuary controversy to the earlier one. As had the proponents of the James ossuary, Jacobovici supported his claims with statistical arguments, and biblical scholar James Tabor strenuously argued that Jacobovici's conclusions were credible.[49]

The implications of these claims were enormous. If accurate, then the question of Jesus' marital status had been resolved and what had seemed fanciful speculation about a sexual relationship with Mary Magdalene had been confirmed. Most significantly, the Christian theological claim of the physical resurrection of Jesus had been archaeologically disconfirmed by the discovery of the box in which his fleshless bones had been deposited a year after his death.

Despite popular attention, however, this chain of arguments gained no traction in the scholarly community, as nearly every link was shown to be tendentious. The tomb had been discovered in considerable disarray, its contents scattered and broken. Only three of the ten ossuaries were intact, and the one misplaced by the Antiquities Authority was broken and uninscribed, probably misplaced precisely because of its unremarkable nature and not resembling the largely intact James ossuary in any way. Bones and bone dust from different burials were mixed in the tomb, and the excavator suggested that as many as thirty-five individuals could have been interred there, though this number was an estimate rather than an actual count of distinct sets of remains.[50]

Whether appropriate DNA sampling would even be possible for bone remains found in such a state is questionable. In any case, the argument that DNA tests demonstrated a marital relationship between Yeshua bar Yehosef and Mariame is completely unpersuasive.

As Christopher Rollston has pointed out, the woman named Mariame could have been related to any of the males in the tomb through a variety of familial relationships (sister, half-sister, wife, and so on), and there is no reason to assume that she was married to Yeshua bar Yosef. The inscribed names were all common in early Palestinian Judaism, and without inscriptions with more familial information, it is impossible to determine the various relationships between the individuals buried there. Just as there was no reason to assume Yeshua and Mariame were married, neither was there any reason to assume that Yoseh was brother of Yeshua.[51]

Given the frequency with which these names appear on ossuaries and in literary sources, the conclusion that they belonged to the individuals named in the Gospels is forced. Mary, in its variations, was one of the most common female names in Jewish antiquity; fully half of known named Jewish women in ancient Palestine were called some version of either Mary or Salome.[52] Because the *Mariame kai Mara* inscription did not include a reference to a place of origin, there is no reason to associate it with Magdala, and because none of the inscriptions included a geographic reference, it is impossible to link any of the individuals buried in the ossuaries to Nazareth or anywhere elsewhere in Galilee.

A final challenge to the tomb's identification as the family tomb of Jesus is the question of why his family would have owned a tomb in Jerusalem, rather than Galilee. One need not accept Gospel traditions of burial in a tomb belonging to Joseph of Arimathea (Matt 27:57–61; Mark 15:42–47; Luke 23:50–56; John 19:38–42) or of Jesus' resurrection to recognize that the scenario proposed by Jacobovici is highly unlikely. A simpler explanation of the data is that the tomb was representative of late-first-century practices of secondary burial, and the names in its inscriptions were typical; nothing indicates an association with Jesus of Nazareth or provides a basis for an elaborate theory about his family members and their final resting places.

The Megiddo Inscriptions

Given all the scholarly energy devoted to finding artifacts reflecting Jewish Christianity, it is ironic that the clearest archaeological evidence for Christians in pre-Constantinian Palestine was left by Gen-

Fig. 7.12. Megiddo Church
mosaic (Photo courtesy of the
Israel Antiquities Authority)

tiles associated with the Roman army. Excavations in 2005 at Kefar
Othnay, an ancient village adjacent to Tel Megiddo and Legio, headquarters of the VI Ferrata legion, discovered a remarkable facility that
serviced the nearby Roman camp. According to the excavators, ceramic and numismatic finds show that the building was used in the
third century and abandoned by the early fourth century. Domestic
and storage pottery suggests a residential function, while ovens and
military bread stamps demonstrate that it included a bakery. Astonish-
ingly, a rectangular room in its western wing appears to have served as
a gathering place for Christians.[53]

The evidence for communal usage comes from the room's mosaic floor (fig. 7.12). Of the mosaic's four panels, two have only geometric designs but the others bear surprising Greek inscriptions. The
southernmost panel includes two inscriptions with women's names.
One reads, "Akeptous the God-lover has offered the table to God Jesus Christ as a memorial," making extremely early epigraphic use of
abbreviations known as *nomina sacra* (sacred names) for the reference to
"God Jesus Christ." The other urges, "Remember Primilla and Cyri-
aca and Dorothea, and also Chreste." The northern and largest panel
includes a central medallion with two fish and a Greek inscription
identifying the mosaic's donor as "Gaianus, also known a Porphyrius,

centurion, our brother." The four panels flank a stone pediment that likely supported the table given by Akeptous.

Taken together, the inscriptions not only clearly reflect the presence of Christians among the Kefar Othnay and Legio communities but also demonstrate that they were allowed to meet in what was apparently a military or government building. No less than a Roman centurion sponsored the laying of the mosaic. At least one female member of the community was wealthy enough to donate a table, and others are remembered for their own important roles. The public tone of the inscriptions, the reference to Gaianus as "our brother," and the injunction to remember key women indicate that an organized group utilized the room, not merely a small number of private individuals. The presence of a "table" for "God Jesus Christ" suggests that Christians took the Eucharist there, and the images of fish may be intended as Christian symbols. In church history, the third century is often known for the occasional Roman persecution of Christians, but at Megiddo we find strong signs of a thriving and secure community that included Roman soldiers. The most indisputable Roman-period archaeological finds associated with Christians in the Holy Land is thus found in what many would have regarded as the most unlikely of quarters.

The Archaeology of Palestine and the
Study of Early Christianity

Attempts to link specific artifacts directly with Jesus or other important Christian figures like James excite popular interest but have usually failed to convince the majority of scholars, as have most efforts to identify Christian names and symbols in first-century c.e. inscriptions. Over time, the reception of claims to have found Christian gathering places in Roman-period strata at Nazareth and Capernaum has been mixed at best. The difficulties such arguments encounter raise important questions about the types of information archaeology can provide. If Jesus and his earliest followers held the same names as countless of their Jewish contemporaries, how could scholars even hypothetically recognize epigraphic references to them? Suppose an inscription were unearthed that referred to a Mary and specified that she was from Magdala. Given how extraordinarily popular variants of the name Mary were, even this inscription would be difficult to associate definitively with the biblical Mary Magdalene. Similarly, one wonders what epigraphic content could irrefutably demonstrate that an ossuary had been used by Christians. Possible answers are imaginable, such as a prayer directed to "Lord Jesus" or a reference to "Jesus the messiah," but it would take this level of explicitness to make the case persuasively, and thus far such examples are lacking. Identifying markings, symbols, and pictures, whether on ossuaries, cave walls, or architectural fragments, as specifically Christian seems nearly impossible in the absence of such direct and unmistakable accompanying epigraphic evidence. The lack of recognizably Christian inscriptions in the Roman period hinders efforts to identify buildings used by Christians. It is precisely because of its exceptional nature and explicitly Christian content that the Megiddo mosaic is so important. One hopes that future excavations will recover other evidence so clear, but it is likely that archaeology's chief contribution to the understanding of the genesis of Christianity will continue to be the ongoing illumination of its broader cultural milieu.

CHAPTER 8

Early Judaism and the Rise of the Synagogue

For a very long time the dominant view on the rise of the ancient synagogue has been that it originated during the time of the Babylonian exile, after 586 B.C.E., when the Judeans who were deported to Mesopotamia and were thus bereft of the Jerusalem Temple learned new ways to approach God without sacrifice. In other words they learned to pray in the small groups that gathered together in exile, as in Ezekiel's *miqdash meat* (11:16), or "little temple," or the "dwelling place" (*meon*) of Psalm 90:1.[1] Later rabbinic tradition understood Ezekiel's "little temple" as referring to the beginnings of the synagogue (*b. Meg.* 29a). In antiquity, however, the common view was that Moses invented the synagogue, a view supported by Philo (*On the Creation of the World* 128; *The Life of Moses* 2.215–16) and Josephus (*Against Apion* 2.175; *Ant.* 16.43–44). Such a view came to dominate presumably because Moses is credited in the Hebrew Bible with giving the Torah to the people and reading it to them (for example, Exod 24:7; Deut 5:1, 31:11). The association of the reading and interpretation of Scripture with Moses is one of the main factors that led to the centrality of the place of the Bible in the early development of the synagogue in the Second Temple period and even the post-70 synagogue in Galilee, a view already reflected in the Jerusalem Talmud (*y. Meg.* 75a).[2]

An important variant on the idea that the synagogue emerged after the destruction of the Temple in 587 B.C.E. is the one that associates the early synagogue with the city gate, some even pushing the idea back to the pre-exilic era.[3] As the place for conducting important decision making, rendering judgments, reading Scripture, and proclaiming laws (Neh 8), the city gate's importance cannot be overstated. But it seems to us that positing the city gate as the main reason for the creation of the "early" synagogue rather explains how the Torah came to be associated with certain communal activities but not necessarily with what we might call worship. The septennial reading of Scripture on Sukkoth when certain rituals were performed (Deut 31:9–13), the reading of and interpretation of the Law when Ezra read it also on Sukkoth (Neh 8), and the reading of the Law by the priests, Levites, and other officials (2 Chr 11:7–9) quite naturally leads to the conclusion that increasing weight was given to the centrality of Torah in the Second Temple period. As one might expect, such an activity ultimately was reflected in the late Second Temple period in the earliest known synagogues in Palestine where reading of the Torah was essential. Anders Runesson calls the earlier Second Temple examples "village assemblies" and the later Second Temple examples "voluntary associations."[4] In respect to the synagogue as a voluntary association he suggests that Jewish society became more decentralized as reading and interpreting the Torah became more essential to non-Temple worship.[5] The synagogue in ancient Palestine thus emerges quite apart from the central authority of the government, and after the corpus of authoritative scriptures had taken its more or less fixed form except for the Kethubim, or Writings. In other words, by late Hellenistic times there would have been a synagogue of the Essenes (Philo, *That Every Good Person Is Free,* 81–82) "where the young sit ranked in rows below the elders," a synagogue of Freedmen (Acts 6:9), and many others. And we may assume also with Philo (*On the Special Laws* 2.62) that a knowledgeable person would read from Scripture on the Sabbath and with Josephus that in addition to reading from Scripture, study of it was also a central part of Sabbath service (*Against Apion* 1.42; *Ant.* 16.43–45).[6] As we shall see below, the oldest synagogues from the land of Israel may now be dated to the first century B.C.E.

The Pre-70 C.E. Synagogue in the Diaspora

The situation in the Diaspora is quite different, and the oldest attested buildings outside the land of Israel are in Delos, from the first century B.C.E., and Ostia, Italy, from the first century C.E. In Ptolemaic Egypt and later in Egypt, there are twelve inscriptions and papyri that identify the existence of structures known as *proseuchai,* or synagogues or prayer structures. Runesson suggests that some of them could originally have been temples and only later were identified as places of worship or proseuchai.[7] Though all are attested in the corpus of Greek inscriptions and papyri from Egypt, their physical remains have mostly never been located, nor have the inscriptions published over half a century ago been rediscovered. Peter Richardson has recently republished much of this inscriptional evidence supplemented by a number of papyri and presented them in a convenient form.[8] He agrees that the epigraphic data confirm that this corpus refers to synagogues as actual buildings in Egypt even though the archaeological evidence for them is lacking.[9] Whether the synagogues were once temples or were simple places of worship where a non-Temple liturgy began to emerge earlier than in Palestine, we do not know for certain. The terminology suggests as much, but given the limited nature of the data we cannot speak with authority on the matter in regard to Egypt.

The literary evidence for Diaspora synagogues is very ample and together constitutes yet another database for assessing the Jewish communities there. There is even mention in rabbinic literature of the great synagogue in Alexandria that was of such great size that the leader of worship standing on a raised dais had to lift a kerchief in order to signal the congregants when to respond with the appropriate "amens" and the like.[10] Philo mentions this synagogue as well and calls it the largest and most magnificent one in all Alexandria (*On the Embassy to Gaius* 143). The fact is, however, there is no archaeological attestation for any such kind of building till the much later Byzantine period at Sardis and possibly elsewhere.[11]

Although it is beyond the scope of this volume to deal with the many mentions in literary sources of synagogues in the Diaspora, we will briefly discuss the two pre-70 C.E. synagogues for which the archaeological evidence is strongest, one in Ostia, near Rome, and the other in Delos, in the Cyclades (fig. 8.1). The Delos synagogue was excavated in the early twentieth century, and only recently has a consensus about it being a synagogue emerged.[12] Probably built in the mid–second century B.C.E., or at the latest a century later, and surviving in the second century C.E., the Delos synagogue is located on an island in the Aegean lying southeast of the Greek mainland. The synagogue is situated on the eastern shore near a residential area and gymnasium, inland from the harbor. L. Michael White has questioned whether the

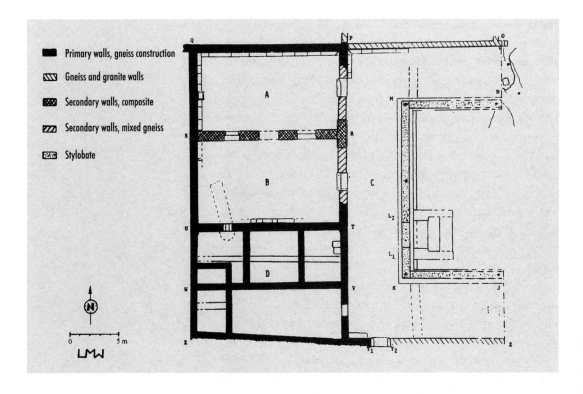

Primary walls, gneiss construction

Gneiss and granite walls

Secondary walls, composite

Secondary walls, mixed gneiss

Stylobate

Fig. 8.1. Plan of the synagogue at Delos. Room A functioned as the main assembly hall; benches are marked along two of the room's walls at upper left, with a chair in the middle of the western wall. (From Lee I. Levine, *The Ancient Synagogue,* Yale University Press, 2000)

synagogue was originally built as a synagogue or was rather a house that was later converted to a synagogue, and his view has met with reserved approval by Lee I. Levine.[13] A strong case for either has been made on the basis of archaeological and epigraphical evidence. There is a marble chair that could possibly be identified with the Seat of Moses for the elder of the congregation; it is oriented east toward Jerusalem; and there is a cistern that may have served as a ritual bath. The inscriptional evidence, however, is even more compelling. There are four inscriptions that mention the most-high God: "Theos Hypsistos." And there is the inscription with the use of the term *proseuche.*[14] The absence of a Torah Shrine should not be a problem since most early synagogues do not have them. Close to the synagogue, some ninety meters north, two additional inscriptions from the third or second century B.C.E. have been recovered that point to the presence of a Samaritan community.[15] Inscribed on marble stelae, the texts contain several inscriptions honoring two benefactors of the community of

Delos, calling themselves Israelites "who make offerings to the sacred Argarizein," which is taken by most to refer to Mount Gerizim, the sacred mountain of the Samaritans.[16] It is not clear whether the Jews mentioned in Josephus (*Ant.* 14.213–17) are Samaritans or not; and it is not clear that the benefactors refer to fellow Samaritans or to local Gentiles who had contributed to the local Samaritan community.

The building purported to be a synagogue was identified as such by the original excavator, and most descriptions follow that.[17] It has a courtyard to the east, facing the sea (C), and there are three parts to the structure. The southern part (D) contains a series of four or five small rooms that provide access to the cistern or ritual bath; the large middle room (B) has three entrances to it and functioned as the main hall in front of the assembly hall (A), which contained benches on two walls and the carved marble seat already mentioned that faced east. The benches and marble seat—possibly a seat of Moses—facing east are reminiscent of Galilean synagogues and support the identification of the assembly hall as a prayer hall. Although we have rejected the idea that the building was originally a house that was converted to a synagogue in the first century B.C.E., it is still possible that it could have had a secular function in its earliest phases. That it became a synagogue can hardly be doubted any longer, and so it is the earliest by far in the Diaspora.

The synagogue at Ostia, the ancient port of Rome, is one of the most beautiful and most important ones in the Diaspora. Unfortunately, the synagogue that is preserved today dates to the fourth century C.E. and later, and we will have to conjecture whether or not reports of an earlier one beneath it are to be taken as accurate accounts of an earlier structure.[18] Runesson has been very forceful in his argument for a mid–first century C.E. date, and Levine also has endorsed such a view.[19] Dieter Mitternacht has the most complete discussion of the issues that extend to the epigraphical remains as well as a full consideration of the archaeology.[20] Since there is no final report on the excavations, and there is ongoing work at the site by White and others, it is not impossible that we will have a more definitive idea in years to come. In any event the floor plan of the synagogue is this: it is 24.9 by 12.5 meters and may have included a *bema,* or raised platform, on the curved western wall and could have also had benches.

Synagogues in the Land of Israel

In turning to the archaeological remains of ancient synagogues in the Land of Israel, we must identify this small corpus as among the most important databases for understanding the rise of early Judaism in relation to the rise of early Christianity. The excavation of synagogues all over the Land of Israel and in the Diaspora, especially those of the late Second Temple period, has produced important results. Pre-70 C.E. Palestinian synagogues have been excavated and/or identified at Masada, Gamla, Herodium, Qiryat Sefer, Modiin, Magdala (Taricheae), and possibly Jericho; others are identified in historical literature at Dor, Caesarea, Capernaum, Bethsaida, Nazareth, and elsewhere. Diaspora examples from the first century B.C.E. and C.E. or earlier have been previously noted. Both Palestinian and Diaspora synagogues are mentioned in first-century literary sources, such as Philo and Josephus, and in epigraphic remains such as the Theodotus inscription (fig. 8.2).

We begin this discussion by quoting the inscription in full: "Theodotus, son of Vettenos, priest and *archisynagogos*, son of an archisynagogos and grandson of an archisynagogos, built the synagogue for the reading of the Law and for the teaching of the command-

Fig. 8.2. The Theodotus synagogue inscription, Jerusalem (Photo courtesy of the Israel Museum)

ments and [built] the guest-house, and the [other] rooms, and the water fittings [installations?] for the lodging of those in need of it from abroad, [the foundations] of which were laid by his fathers and the elders and Simonides."[21] The inscription, which is dated to the first century c.e., points to a number of features that we may clearly associate with the pre-70 synagogue. First we may say that the term "synagogue" is used to indicate both a social grouping (congregation) and a building with special features. Second, the name "Vettenos" would most likely identify the synagogue as a place for Jews who came from Rome.[22] Theodotus built it, and his ancestors together with the elders and one Simonides founded it some three generations earlier. In addition the text states that three of the main functions of the pre-70 synagogue were these: the reading of Scripture, studying the commandments of the Torah, and providing hospitality to visitors, many of whom were no doubt pilgrims, but not necessarily for the exclusive use of Theodotus's own community. Note also the mention of "water installations" or "fittings," which could possibly refer to a ritual bath, though this is by no means clear. The original excavator who found the inscription, Raymond Weil, noted that it had been recovered from a cistern, and a contemporary excavator, Ronny Reich, has pointed out that there were indeed miqvaot and water installations in the area just north of the cistern in which the inscription was found.[23] The presence of ritual baths and this mention in the Theodotus inscription are very suggestive of a relationship between the synagogue and ritual purity. The repeated use of the term "archisynagogos" for priests might be suggestive of a connection with the Temple, and in light of the frequent mentions of synagogues in the written sources there would not appear to be a problem of synagogues existing while the Temple still stood. However, in light of the frequent use of the term "archisynagogos" in later inscriptions both in Palestine and the Diaspora, it hardly suggests more than the priestly lineage of a well-to-do family of Roman background. The allusion in the last line to an earlier phase of the synagogue or congregation, which would have gone back to the first century b.c.e., is also instructive. Moreover, implicit in the text is also the idea that other sorts of activities would have taken place in the synagogue, such as the meetings of the town council or *boule* in Tiberias (*Life* 277–80), as well as the idea that the synagogue also offered simple hospitality not related to pilgrimage and the like.

Fig. 8.3. Reconstruction of
Capernaum synagogue and
village at Sea of Galilee.
Ritual immersion would have
taken place in the nearby lake.
(Reconstruction drawing
courtesy of Leen Ritmeyer)

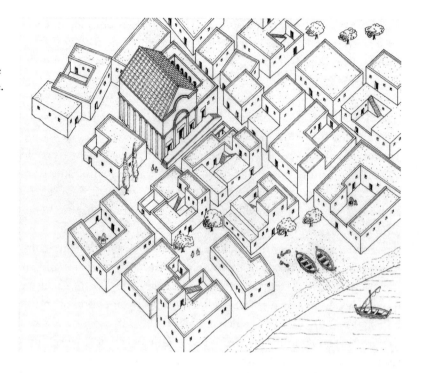

Let us begin with examples from Galilee since we have such a solid literary base on which to build. All of the Gospels refer to Jesus' activities in synagogues, preaching, teaching, and healing, most of them in small towns and villages, which suggests that Jesus avoided the urban centers consciously.[24] The towns mentioned in the Gospels are Nazareth, Capernaum, Bethsaida, Chorazin, Gennesaret, and Magdala (figs. 8.3, 8.4).[25] Among these there are only two possible candidates for pre-70 synagogue buildings and only one for certain.

If the domicile in Capernaum that some identify as Saint Peter's House was indeed a house church in the first century, then it presumably served as a meeting place for Jewish Christians to worship.[26] About thirty meters to the north, under the great limestone synagogue that dates to the Byzantine period, are vestiges of earlier structures that are for the most part to be associated with private domiciles. Some of the features like thick basalt walls and a cobblestone pavement found under the nave of the synagogue suggest an earlier structure, which the excavators posit was the original synagogue of Jesus.[27] Very few scholars have accepted this view, but it should remain

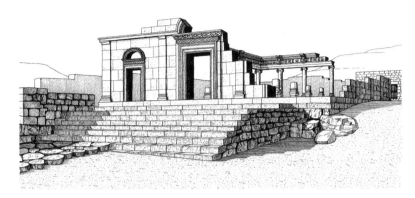

Fig. 8.4. Partial reconstruction of the fourth-century c.e. synagogue at Chorazin, a site mentioned in the New Testament (Mt 11:21; Lk 10:13) (Reconstruction drawing courtesy of Leen Ritmeyer)

a possibility. In any case the precise nature of the proposed synagogue remains unknown.

One of the most stunning surprises in recent years is the discovery of a first-century c.e. synagogue just a few miles south of Capernaum at Magdala, literally on the water's edge of the Sea of Galilee, also known as the Plain of Gennosar. As of this writing no scientific reports have been published, and we are entirely reliant on press releases from the excavators, Dina Avshalom-Gorni and Arfan Najar of the Israel Antiquities Authority and attendance at a public presentation of the discovery at the 2010 American Schools of Oriental Research Convention in Atlanta.[28] The site is associated with Mary Magdalene of the New Testament and is identified with the city of Taricheae. The site was apparently destroyed during the First Revolt and completely buried by debris. However, some archaeologists think it may have survived the Great Revolt and was possibly deserted because of flooding or other natural causes. The main hall of the building is 120 square meters and has stone benches built against its walls. The floor was paved with a simple black and white mosaic with meander design in the corners, and the walls were all frescoed with bright colors in the Pompeian style. Early Roman pottery and stone vessels abound, confirming its pre-70 dating, suggestive even of a date in the middle of the first century b.c.e. But the most exciting discovery is a large limestone piece that is engraved on one side with a seven-branched menorah flanked by two amphorae, with rosettes on top and several early Roman lamps depicted on its sides.[29] The stone is square and is engraved on the three other sides as well and appears to be a limestone pedestal with a triangular base. The four corners on top

of the piece are worked smoothly, possibly to hold a wooden superstructure. It is our view that the stone served as the base for a readers'
platform or table from which the Torah was read. It is situated in the
middle or northern interior of the building, which is oriented south
toward Jerusalem. The menorah depicted on the stone pedestal is one
of a number of examples from the Land of Israel dated to the period
of the Second Temple—the first was a graffito depiction of the Temple menorah from the Jewish Quarter excavation.[30] The high level of
artisanship, the mosaic floor, the oldest in a synagogue, the excellent
quality of the frescoes, all suggest a very affluent community though a
small one, possibly associated with a priestly family. None of the other
synagogues of such an early date can compare to this. Its closeness to
the Sea of Galilee mitigates any need to build ritual baths since immersion in the sea, filled with pure water from the headwaters of the Jordan, would have been sufficient. The same holds for Capernaum.

The other northern synagogue of early date and importance to
be considered is Gamla (fig. 8.5). Before the discovery of Magdala the
Gamla synagogue was considered the earliest in the land of Israel (Judea), dating to the turn of the first century C.E. or slightly earlier.[31]
The synagogue is the largest structure at Gamla and was certainly the
main focus of all communal activities, since there is no other comparable building at the entire site. It is built of local black basalt stone.

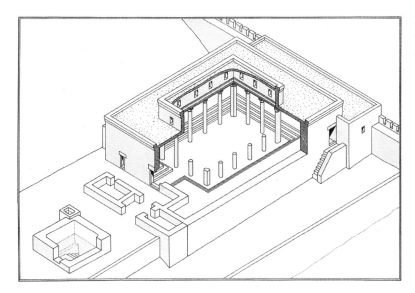

Fig. 8.6. Reconstruction of Gamla synagogue (Reconstruction drawing by Leen Ritmeyer)

Located just inside the eastern perimeter wall of the city, its interior measurements are 13.4 by 9.3 meters. It has three entrances, two on the southwest, one of them leading to the northern aisle, the second leading into the main hall, and one from the east that opens to the east. There is a niche in the northwestern end whose function in unclear. Benches surround the interior on all four sides and there are sixteen interior columns on all sides, though the plan in the Qatzrin Museum in the Golan has eighteen.[32] The column drums supporting the roof were all well made and of high-quality workmanship. In each of the corners were columns with heart-shaped sections, composed of two half columns. The capitals all were of the late classical Doric order. Zvi Maoz conjectures that columns should be restored along the Jerusalem-facing entrance as a propyleum or in the center to hold a podium for the reading of Torah, where there is a row of stone pavers in the dirt (?) floor.[33] Having a podium for the reading of Scripture makes good sense in light of the discovery of the synagogue at Magdala, where the carved stone with a menorah could have served as a base for a reader's platform. A stepped cistern just west of the main entrance has been understood as a ritual bath, and a small channel and basin on the eastern aisle may be understood as a place for washing the hands or feet (discussed below in regard to the early synagogue at Nabratein). The synagogue could have held no more than 250 people:

150 on its benches and perhaps another 100 standing or seated on the floor in the center (fig. 8.6).

Turning south to the Judean desert we direct our attention to the well-known Herodian sites of Masada and Herodium (fig. 8.7). As we have seen in a previous chapter, there is some question about whether the synagogue of Masada was a synagogue in Herod's days. With the large retinue of aides, servants, and others that Herod would have had traveling with him, it is quite possible that the building served a sacred function before the turn of the era. But we cannot be certain. We are absolutely certain of its use as a synagogue during the final stage of the site's occupation by the Zealots and Sicarii, from 66–73/4 C.E. The small rectangular structure, 15 by 12 meters, not unlike the size of the Gamla synagogue, has a small room in the northern corner, 5.7 by 3.5 meters, where fragments of scrolls were found including a rolled scroll with portions of the Book of Deuteronomy and chapters from the Book of Ezekiel. There are five internal columns and benches all around that were added in the final phase and plastered over in the rough style of the rooms in the casemate wall. Its main entrance in the east faces toward Jerusalem.[34] A ritual bath is located close by.

The situation with the synagogue at Herodium is clearer: it was used as a synagogue only by the rebels and was converted from its

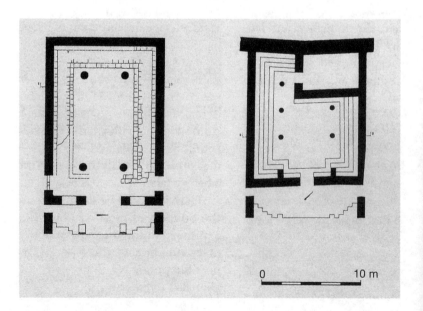

Fig. 8.7. Ground plans of synagogues at Herodium (left) and Masada (Drawings courtesy of the Franciscan Printing Press, Jerusalem)

0 _____ 10 m

prior use as a triclinium in Herod's fortress palace.[35] The Herodium synagogue is slightly smaller than Masada, at 10.5 by 15 meters. In the conversion from banquet hall to worship space four new columns were added as well as benches, some of which were made from the architectural fragments of Herod's palatial building on site. Like Masada, the Herodium building is oblong, with its interior plain and undecorated. The walls at Herodium retained their original plaster stucco and there was no trace of plaster on the benches. Although there is no small room such as the so-called scroll room at Masada, there is an adjoining room at Herodium that could have served as a repository for scrolls and other objects. A ritual bath is situated along the eastern wall near the door. The main entrance as at Masada is from the east, as in the Temple in Jerusalem, a point emphasized by Gideon Foerster, who says this is to be understood in keeping with later rabbinic literature.[36]

There are other notable examples of early synagogues in the foothills of Judea and in the upper Shefelah region, including at Qiryat Sefer and Modiin, which have not been fully published but are worth mentioning. There is no consensus on these, but Levine has included Qiryat Sefer (fifteen kilometers east of Lod) in his list of synagogues dated to the first century C.E. or at the latest to the time of Bar Kokhba.[37] The square hall measures 9.6 meters on each side and is surrounded by four Doric columns and a wide aisle and is paved with well-fitted flagstones; a gabled lintel was found outside it. The facade is constructed of well-hewn ashlars with margins typical of the Herodian period. There are benches on three sides. Stone vessels and early Roman pottery were found on site. Thus, the synagogue would appear to be the first village synagogue found in Judea. Another candidate to be added to this list is Modiin, or Khirbet Umm el-Umdan, which is located near the Latrun junction in the Judean foothills on the road to Jerusalem and is not published.[38] The site, however, has revealed a public structure like the ones at Gamla, Masada, and Herodium, 7 by 12 meters, paved with stone slabs, and with eight columns. A ritual bath was discovered in a room just to the west of the building, which the excavators identify in its first phase as a synagogue and have tentatively dated to the late Hellenistic period, which would possibly make it the oldest synagogue in the Land of Israel.[39] The building was enlarged in the Herodian period to an irregular shape measuring 9.5 by 10 by 11.5 by 13.5 meters, with one column removed; many plaster fragments were found on the floor of this phase in red, white, and yellow. An additional phase dating to between the two revolts has also been identified when the flagstone floor was plastered and a small room added at the northeast.[40] Like Qiryat Sefer this site is also a village synagogue, and most likely coterminous with it. The claim of the oldest synagogue to be found in the Land of Israel was also made by Ehud Netzer, who identified a structure at Jericho as a synagogue and dated it to the mid–first century B.C.E.[41] That building was 16.2 by 11.1 meters, with twelve pillars and benches all around, and a ritual bath nearby.[42] Netzer's views on this subject have not won any sort of acceptance, and Levine has most recently suggested it might have been part of a villa.[43]

All of the examples of pre-70 synagogues we have brought forward have miqvaot nearby. Moreover, each reveals its public or communal character rather dramatically. Even as diversity in building plan is a defining characteristic of these synagogues, we can also observe a great commonality among them: square or rectangular buildings with internal columniation, benches for seating, and in several the entrance lies on the east side. Equally important is the fact that they are devoid of artistic decoration and inscriptions, except perhaps for Magdala where the pedestal is rather elaborately decorated. Moreover, unlike later synagogues, none had a Torah Shrine or a bema, though in several cases, as at Magdala and possibly Gamla, there are hints that the Torah was read in the middle of the hall. The question of sacred orientation toward Jerusalem for this small group of pre-70 synagogues is still too unclear to answer, although several do seem to be intentionally oriented to Jerusalem. All of the pre-70 synagogues are lacking specifically religious features, which suggests that they would have served some community functions in addition to gathering for prayer and Torah study.

The probability that the earliest synagogues were used for communal purposes in addition to religious ones is supported by the fact that the architectural model for the early synagogue was probably the Hellenistic *bouleuterion* or *ecclesiasterion,* where people assembled to decide matters of civic interest or concern. The actions of Jews on the Sabbath in the Caesarea synagogue, which is not preserved, in 65–66 C.E. on the eve of the Great Revolt concerning their status in that city, as reported in Josephus (*War* 2.266–70, 284–92; *Ant.* 20.173–78, 182–84), indicates that a political meeting took place there, in a building that also had a religious function. Note also that the New Testament focuses on Jesus' teaching and preaching in synagogues, as in his Sabbath appearance at the synagogue in Nazareth (Luke 4:16–30), rather than on worship and study; and Torah reading is also the emphasis in regard to Paul's experience in the Diaspora (Acts 13:14–15, 15:21).[44] In addition, the Theodotus inscription informs us not only about the religious-educational nature of the early synagogue but also about its social and communal functions, such as a hospice or inn, as well as about its priestly and administrative leadership. Clearly, the emergence of the synagogue in various locations and diverse forms signified the growing decentralization of Jewish life at this time, even though Herod's rebuilding of the Temple and his expansion of its priestly precincts would underscore the centrality of the holy city and its Temple as well as its unique importance in Jewish liturgy. The irony of the synagogue's development at a time when the Second Temple served as the most important symbol of Jewish religion cannot be overstated. On one hand the emergence of the pre-70 synagogue signifies diversity and decentralization, and on the other hand the Temple signifies uniformity and centralization. Nonetheless, the reality by the end of the Second Temple period was that the synagogue was already a pivotal institution among most Jewish communities and proved to be a key to the continuity of Jewish life after 70.[45]

The Post-70 C.E. Synagogue

After the destruction of the Temple in 70 C.E., the synagogue became the central communal and religious institution of the Jewish community, reconstituted mainly in Galilee (fig. 8.8). Because of the relative paucity of archaeological evidence for synagogues in the pre-70 period, a brief glimpse of the synagogue in the later periods of the Roman era is in order, for not all aspects of the developing synagogue were present in its early precursors.[46] Indeed, it is only after 70 C.E. that its specifically religious character appears in the archaeological record. Levine has raised the issue of the scarcity of synagogue remains from 70 C.E. to 250 C.E., calling it a gap of some two hundred years.[47] While admitting that there are abundant literary sources for

Fig. 8.8. Locations of ancient synagogue remains uncovered in Israel. Many of the structures shown on this map are preserved only in their post-Roman states; as can be seen here, they tend to be concentrated in the north, in the Galilee and Golan, where the vast majority of Jews settled after the two wars with Rome. (Map prepared by Carta, Israel Map and Publishing Company, Ltd.)

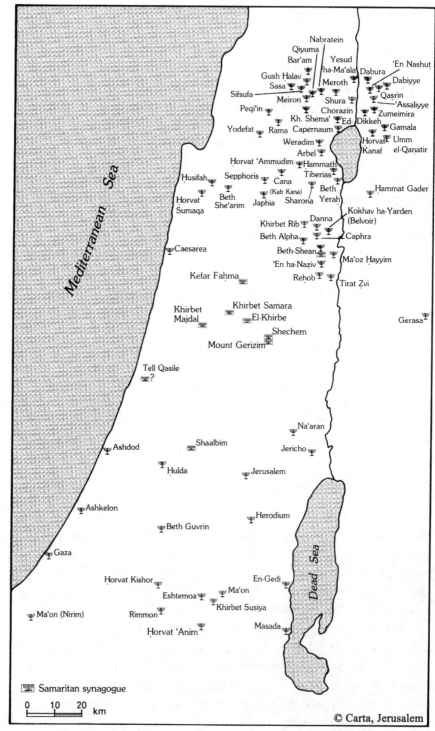

Mediterranean Sea

Nabratein
Qiyuma
Bar'am
Yesud
Gush Halav   ha-Ma'ala   Dabura   'En Nashut
Sasa   Meroth   Dabiyye
Sifsufa   Qasrin
        Meiron   Shura   'Assaliyye
Peqi'in   Chorazin   Zumeimira
        Kh. Shema'   Ed. Dikkeh
Yodefat   Rama Capernaum   Gamala
        Weradim   Horvat   Umm
            Arbel   Kanaf   el-Qanatir
    Horvat 'Ammudim   Hammath
Husifah   Sepphoris   Tiberias
            Cana   Hammat Gader
Horvat   Beth   (Kafr Kana) Beth
Sumaqa   She'arim Japhia Sharona Yerah
                              Kokhav ha-Yarden
        Khirbet Rib   Danna   (Belvoir)
        Beth Alpha   Caphra
Caesarea   Beth-Shean
            'En ha-Naziv   Ma'oz Hayyim
Kefar Fahma   Rehob   Tirat Zvi

Khirbet   Khirbet Samara
Majdal   El-Khirbe   Gerasa
        Shechem
Mount Gerizim

Tell Qasile
?

                    Na'aran
Shaalbim   Jericho
Hulda   Jerusalem

Ashdod

Ashkelon   Herodium
Beth Guvrin

Gaza
                        Dead Sea
Horvat Kishor   En-Gedi
Eshtemoa   Ma'on
Ma'on (Nirim)   Khirbet Susiya
Rimmon
Horvat 'Anim   Masada

🕎 Samaritan synagogue

0   10   20 km

© Carta, Jerusalem

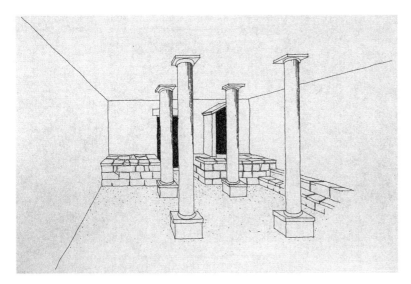

Fig. 8.9. Reconstruction drawing of the interior of a second-century synagogue at Nabratein (Nevoraiah), showing a bema with Torah Shrine at back right (Photo courtesy of Eric and Carol Meyers)

physical structures from this period in the tannaitic, or pre-200 C.E., rabbinic literature, he is hesitant to draw too many conclusions about the emergence of the post-70 synagogue in view of the limited archaeological evidence.[48] Although we freely admit that there is a scarcity of evidence for the early-Roman-period synagogue, we do not want to draw any major historical inferences from this as do others, as seen, for example, in the influential suggestion that Judaism was adrift after the two wars with Rome and only in response to the rise of imperial Christianity did the Jewish community get hold of itself and begin to build synagogues in any significant numbers.[49]

At Nabratein in Upper Galilee, rabbinic Nevoraia, for example, we have one of the earliest post-70 Galilean synagogues, circa 135–250 C.E., Synagogue I, which dates to the second century C.E. and has the earliest bema and possible Torah Shrine; we would not be surprised for other examples from this period to turn up in future excavations and surveys (fig. 8.9). The bema on the southern wall of the Nabratein synagogue clearly indicates the orientation of the building to Jerusalem. Although Jerusalem was no longer a Jewish city at this time, its conceptual significance as the Holy City and thus the focus of worship continued and increased as manifested in the architectural principle of sacred orientation.[50] (See plate 11.)

Another early synagogue has been identified at the site of Hor-

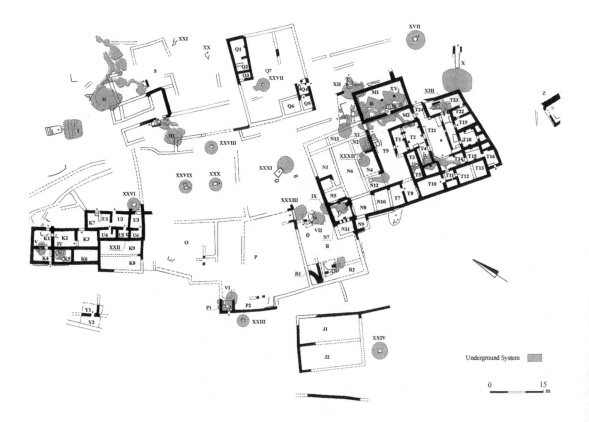

Fig. 8.10. Plan of the village of Horvat Ethri. The synagogue was located at M1, in upper right, with ritual baths near it at XV and T23. (Plan courtesy of Boaz Zissu with V. Essman, S. Pirsky, N. Zak)

vat Ethri, located in the upper Shefelah, roughly thirty-five kilometers southwest of Jerusalem, which may be identified with a village mentioned in Josephus, Caphetra (*War* 4.552–54) that was destroyed in 69 C.E. by the Fifth Legion (fig. 8.10).[51] The structure that has been identified as a synagogue is thirteen by seven meters and is a broadhouse in plan entered from one of the long walls. Three columns are located across the width of the hall to hold the ceiling. In front of the entrance is a courtyard with a ritual bath off to the side. The structure is very similar to the village synagogues described above in the section on pre-70 evidence. Though lacking in any definitive feature that we might identify with synagogues, which is the case with most of our examples, the site is still an excellent candidate for a synagogue that dates to the interwar period (fig. 8.11).[52]

Levine suggests that it was the chaos created by the two wars with Rome that possibly contributed to the destruction or demise of

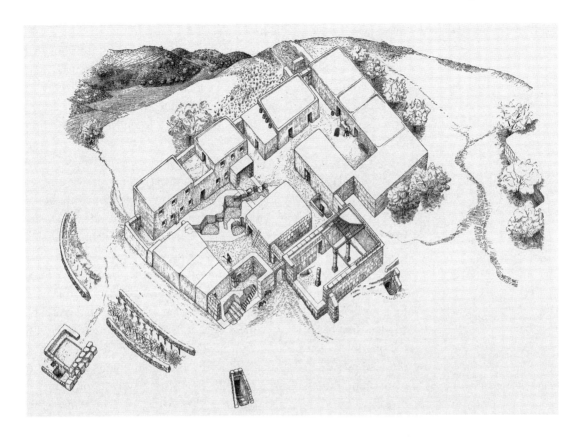

Fig. 8.11. Reconstruction drawing of Horvat Ethri, featuring the synagogue at right foreground with columns inside (Reconstruction drawing courtesy of Boaz Zissu with V. Essman, S. Pirsky, N. Zak)

Second Temple synagogues. That the earlier synagogues were of a different sort from the later, post-70 synagogues is a point we have already made and will emphasize in our presentation of the later data. The internal furnishings and plans of those later synagogues from the third and fourth centuries, and even later, suggest that at that time there was a greater emphasis on the idea of holiness taken from the Temple and less of an emphasis on the communal character of the synagogue. In support of his notion that the two wars wreaked havoc on the land and the people, Levine cites the *Chronicle* of Malalas, which records that Vespasian destroyed a synagogue at Daphne and replaced it with a theater, inscribing on it "from the spoils of Judaea" and doing the same with a synagogue at Caesarea.[53] We may also add to this the possible destruction of a synagogue in Tiberias and Alexandria, and the aftermath of the Hadrianic persecutions a bit later; and we are not hard-pressed to find many other examples of the difficulties Jews faced after 70 C.E.[54] The problem is that we do not have much material evidence for many of these claims, and the literary traditions that report some of these events are not always reliable, something Levine readily admits. At the same time we must emphasize the existence of many early rabbinic (tannaitic) sources, which presuppose the reality of the synagogue as architectural entity in the second and third centuries C.E.[55]

The second explanation Levine advances for the so-called archaeological gap is the possibility that the synagogue at this early stage of development was a domus ecclesiae, or a space in a private home akin to a house-church, which would make it very difficult to identify in a material context, a point we have briefly explained above. Levine dismisses this explanation in the following way: the Palestinian synagogue in the pre-70 era was a communal structure and separate edifice with columns and benches on four sides as at Masada and Gamla, and judging from the Theodotus inscription was a building that could be so identified because of its individual construction. But even though the pre-70 evidence illustrates a number of common features among the examples we have provided, the diversity of buildings and ground plans among the Judean synagogues may also be noted. Some of that diversity can be attributed to the fact that many Jerusalem synagogues were built by Jews who originated in the Diaspora. Levine freely admits, however, that the pre-70 synagogue building could well have survived into the next centuries, since the tannaitic sources for it are so rich and incontrovertible. Both types of synagogues—the domus ecclesiae, or "house-synagogue," and the smaller, village types with columns similar to Synagogue 1 at Nabratein or one like Modiin or its neighbors—could easily have existed side by side in the early post-70 era. Indeed, as advisers to Nazareth Village, Levine and Meyers agreed to such a structure being built at Nazareth among the Roman-period ruins, representing as it were the kind of synagogue that Jesus and his early followers would have known there.[56]

Levine also offers an archaeological explanation for justifying the possibility of a two-century gap in the Palestinian synagogue. Because so many new synagogues were constructed in the late Roman and Byzantine periods, it is not surprising that earlier materials could easily have been discarded during a renovation or building stage. This was certainly the case in Jerusalem, not necessarily in respect to synagogues alone. Herodian construction obliterated much of the earlier phases of occupation in many places. This was especially true where bedrock rises high and is utilized in the later building phase(s). At Khirbet Shema in Upper Galilee, for example, the oldest preserved synagogue is built over a series of bedrock structures and underground cavities that had to be filled in and leveled off in order to build anything over them (fig. 8.12). In the process of constructing the first synagogue building on the site, those structures and their surrounding contexts were virtually erased, leaving it most difficult to reconstruct with any degree of certainty the nature of the earlier materials except for sealed pockets here and there.[57] Looking at the two east–west walls of the later synagogue and the fact that there are abutments in key places, it is possible to conjecture that a house was there before the building of the first synagogue; but it is also possible that there was only a ritual bath, which survives in the southeastern quadrant. In any case, the extensive building operations in the third century made it most difficult to reconstruct fully what the area looked like before. A similar situation existed at Nabratein where cavities in bedrock, underground chambers, and tunnels had to be sealed up when Synagogue 1 was constructed. No doubt these chambers and tunnels had a function, but whatever it was is difficult to recover since the first synagogue and other structures come from a variety of periods and make it nearly impossible to reconstruct the picture of how things looked

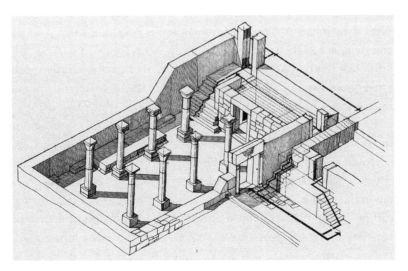

Fig. 8.12. Isometric drawing of Khirbet Shema with traffic patterns (Plan courtesy of Eric Meyers)

Fig. 8.13. Perspective drawing
of Khirbet Shema synagogue.
The Torah Shrine appears at
left in pre-bema stage, and
there is a menorah carved on
a lintel at right. (Drawing
courtesy of Eric Meyers)

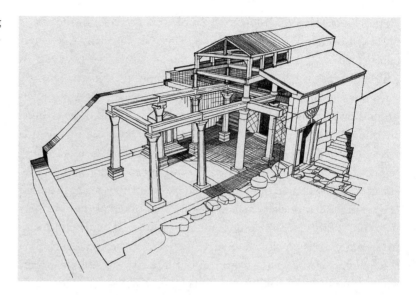

right after 70 c.e. So, Levine has a very strong point in this line of
reasoning, and we believe the accidental nature of the survival of Synagogue 1 (second to third century) at Nabratein makes such an explanation more plausible.

Levine goes on to advance the well-known theory of how the
Palestinian synagogue took on more and more of the holiness and sacrality of the Jerusalem Temple in the course of time. One of the features of the later third-century Galilean synagogues that he points to is
the sacred orientation, directing prayer to the wall facing Jerusalem.[58]
With their interiors oriented toward the holy city and three rows of
columns, it was the southern wall facing Jerusalem that had no columns that was dubbed the "Jerusalem wall" of orientation. Often such
synagogues would have a bema and Torah Shrine to accentuate the
importance of the southern wall of orientation, which was the case
at Khirbet Shema (fig. 8.13) and Gush Halav (fig. 8.14), and each of
the synagogues at Nabratein.[59] In the case of Nabratein, however, we
may associate this pattern with the earliest phase of all its synagogues,
which is why the presentation of Synagogue 1 is offered in such detail in the final publication. If we succeed in making our case for the
earliest phase of Nabratein, then we may say with a good degree of
conviction that the post-70 synagogue assumed these distinguishing
features, namely sacred orientation and a Torah Shrine with or with-

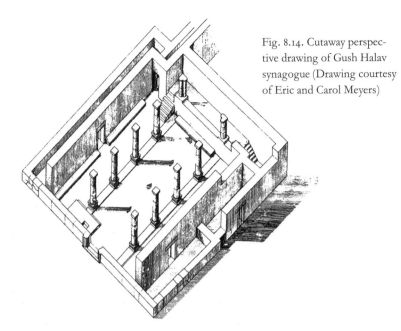

Fig. 8.14. Cutaway perspective drawing of Gush Halav synagogue (Drawing courtesy of Eric and Carol Meyers)

out bema, soon after the two wars with Rome and not later, as Levine was inclined to believe when he wrote his influential book on the history of the synagogue in 2000. This would also support the view that the post-70 synagogue assumed more and more of the sanctity of the Temple at a very early stage when the liturgy of the synagogue was taking final shape. Such a view challenges the consensus that only in the third century or later did the synagogue assume that sanctity.

In regard to Synagogue 1 at Nabratein let us point out also that its measurements as a broadhouse, 11.2 by 9.35 meters, reflect the design pattern and unit of measurement of the standard Roman *pes,* or foot.[60] In addition Doron Chen has noted that the proportion of 4:3 indicates a use of the Pythagorean triangle (3:4:5), which was regularly utilized in antiquity for laying out angles on the ground. If he is correct this would imply that the builders of the first public building at Nabratein employed well-known classical standards and measurements in their work, indicating that the process of Romanization was already at work deep in the heart of rural Upper Galilee in the second century C.E. When the designers made the next phases of the building basilical in layout, Synagogue 2, third to fourth century C.E., with six columns, and Synagogue 3, sixth to seventh century C.E., with eight columns, we may observe the continuing influence of classical architectural style on the local architecture in the Roman East (fig. 8.15).

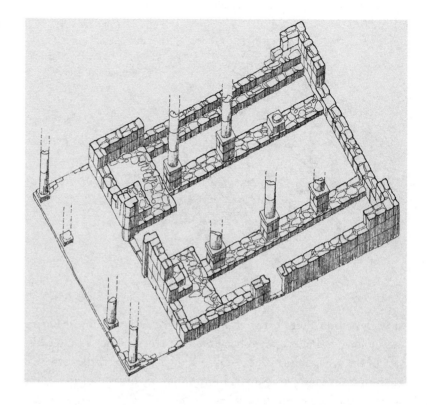

In contrast to the earlier Second Temple synagogues, an important feature of the post-70 synagogue is that its dominant plan is
the Roman basilica, though as noted Synagogue 1 at Nabratein was a
broadhouse. The choice of the basilical form in the first centuries C.E.
is another indication, in addition to what we have already mentioned,
that many Jews found features of Greco-Roman culture congenial. Yet
they did not always relinquish their indigenous architectural traditions
and forms. The fascinating case of the third- to fifth-century synagogue at Khirbet Shema illuminates this point as well. Khirbet Shema,
like Eshtemoa and Susiya in the south, is a broadhouse structure like
Nabratein Synagogue 1, as were many temples in the Semitic world;
its bema, or focus of worship, is on the long, Jerusalem-oriented wall
(fig. 8.16). Yet, with its characteristic columniation, and when viewed
looking east–west rather than to the south, it appears basilical. It thus
exhibits a mixed or hybrid architectural type—its classical basilical
features are derived from Roman building types and its broadroom
plan represents an indigenous form that echoes Canaanite prototypes.

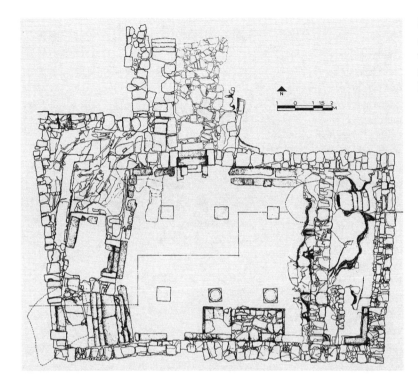

Fig. 8.16. Ground plan of the synagogue at Khirbet Shema with ritual bath detailed at right (Drawing courtesy of Eric Meyers)

This combination of plans meant that the Holy Ark, or Torah Shrine, if placed on the bema of the long southern wall, could not be seen from all directions because the many columns along the main sight lines blocked it. The Khirbet Shema synagogue, although later than the first or second century, is an indication of the creative response of Palestinian Jews to Greco-Roman culture and Hellenistic influence in the rabbinic period. (See plate 12.)

We would add that the Torah Shrine as the focus of worship in late Roman and Byzantine synagogues is likely modeled after the pagan aedicule. An excellent example is the oldest extant Torah Shrine, perhaps the best one in all the Land of Israel, from the late Roman synagogue at Nabratein, Synagogue 2a (fig. 8.17). Its elaborate construction on a raised bema, with columns and rampant lions as well as a place for a chain to hold the Eternal Light, indicates how even more important Scripture had become in the life of the Jewish people at the time when the Mishnah was edited and the canon of the Hebrew Bible was coming to a close.[61] The Torah Shrine after all is a kind of perma-

Fig. 8.17. Interior
view, looking south,
of a late-Roman syna-
gogue at Nabratein
built as a six-column
basilica. The Torah
shrine is at right.
(Drawing courtesy
of Eric and Carol
Meyers)

Fig. 8.18. Pediment
of Torah Shrine from
Nabratein, third cen-
tury C.E. (Drawing
courtesy of Eric and
Carol Meyers)

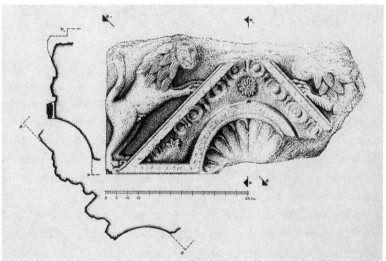

nent house for the Hebrew Bible, and its elevated place on a bema and
decoration give visual testimony to its sacrality and centrality in Jewish worship (fig. 8.18).

Another feature of the developing synagogue, known from ancient art, is the fact that the Torah was read in the rolled "scroll" form.
This may mean that by the third century the synagogue as a Jewish
place of worship differed from the places where the first Christians

prayed—for the Christians read from their new sacred books in the form of a codex, according to the evidence from ancient mosaics and frescoes. However, Christianity in the east was still in the formative stages in the first centuries C.E., as indicated by the absence of a distinct symbolic vocabulary and of any structures that can be identified as having been purposely built as churches. Roman-period synagogues and churches probably looked much the same except for the Torah Shrine and bema in synagogues and the use of the codex rather than scrolls in Christian worship.[62]

With the establishment of the synagogue as the true successor to the Jerusalem Temple, Judaism's ability to move away from the sacred center was made the more possible and easier. Whereas before 70 C.E. there was only scattered evidence for Jewish worship, after 70 we may conjecture that as the liturgy developed and the tractates of the Mishnah and texts of other contemporary writings (for example, the tannaitic midrashim) were written down, there was hardly a place where Jews settled in which we could not imagine a communal gathering place where Torah was read and interpreted and the emerging liturgy recited or chanted. Even though the material evidence for synagogues is somewhat limited, we need not conclude that the two centuries after 70 C.E. were devoid of an appropriate physical setting in which the liturgy could be chanted, the Torah read and interpreted, and communal meetings held. The rise of imperial Christianity after Constantine the Great gave a second impetus to local communities to strengthen their ties to the traditions of the past and to develop new ones in the face of a daughter religion that now became the official religion in the East. All this is to say that the synagogue early on became the major vehicle for allowing Jewish tradition to move and reinvent itself with relative ease. The synagogue, thus, became the place where Jews could worship God wherever they may find God, in the Land of Israel or in the Diaspora, in private houses, elaborate basilicas, or hybrid buildings in which a quorum would gather for prayer and reading the Torah.

It is not surprising then that we believe there was an important stage in the evolution of the synagogue as a purpose-built structure in the two centuries after 70 C.E. Nor do we find compelling recent arguments for the late dating of Galilean synagogues to the Byzantine period, in the light of both material and literary evidence.[63] There is literally no other institution in the history of the Jewish people that

Fig. 8.19. Remains of Khir-bet Hamam synagogue, just north of Tiberias and west of the Sea of Galilee, dated to the late Roman period (Photo courtesy of Uzi Leibner)

has exerted such an important influence on Jewish civilization as the synagogue, and much of its liturgy has been dated to precisely this period; moreover, it has influenced the development of the church and mosque in their own distinct ways. In general it may be said that the synagogue was less decorated with art and sculpture in the earlier periods and devoid of colorful mosaics and figural art, but this may be pure happenstance. The rabbis were very much at home with art throughout the Roman period, and Nabratein in particular in the Roman period has a full range of relief sculptures both inside and outside the synagogues there.[64] The most famous ones are the pair of rampant lions that stood astride the pediment of the Torah Shrine in the second half of the third century C.E., giving a sense of power and authority to the Hebrew scrolls of the Bible housed in the Torah Shrine below. By the Byzantine period, when a ban was imposed against building new synagogues, greater emphasis was placed on the interior of buildings and on repairing old buildings. We find many decorated with colorful

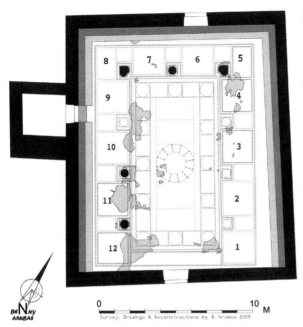

Fig. 8.20. Plan of
Khirbet Hamam
synagogue with
diagram of mosaic
(Drawing courtesy
of Uzi Leibner)

mosaics, including a number with the zodiac as the central theme, as
at Tiberias, Sepphoris, Beth Alpha, and other places (fig. 8.19).

The recent excavations of Uzi Leibner at the Wadi Hamam synagogue in eastern Galilee, however, suggest that decorated mosaics
on synagogue floors were introduced in the Roman period, either at
the end of the third century or a bit later (fig. 8.20).[65] This goes along
well with the excavation and publication of the Dionysos Mansion
and mosaic at Sepphoris, which dates to the third century and is contemporary with the residency there of Rabbi Judah the Patriarch, who
was responsible for the redaction and publication of the Mishnah and
related writings at the beginning of the third century C.E.[66] The overwhelming majority of decorated synagogue mosaics, however, may
be dated to the Byzantine period, or late fourth, fifth, and sixth centuries, the reasons for which lie beyond the scope of this volume.[67]
It should be noted in brief that Zeev Weiss and Rina Talgam, who
wrote the report on the Dionysos mosaic at Sepphoris, do not agree
on who was the owner of the mansion let alone who was responsible
for the commissioning of the mosaic. Since the mansion is on the
edge of the Jewish sector of the western summit, it is unlikely that
it could have been owned or inhabited solely by Gentiles during the

סגרה‎

Fig. 8.21. Portions of mosaic from the Khirbet Hamam synagogue, late Roman period, including a battle scene (at left), and a construction scene (Photo courtesy of Uzi Leibner)

third century C.E. (a fuller discussion of this issue appears in Chapter 10). Indeed, there is no reason to dismiss the idea that the mansion could have been a place where the municipal council, or *boule,* met, a body integrating Jews and Gentiles in decision making as it may have affected the life of the city.[68] Indeed, the Jewish council members in the time of Rabbi Judah the Patriarch are called *boulevtim,* derived from the Greek word for council.[69] The mosaic at the Khirbet Hamam synagogue, depicting workers and artisans and possibly biblical themes, has also challenged many older views about the date when elaborate mosaics were included in the decorative design of synagogues. Heretofore the consensus was that synagogue mosaic art originated only in the late fourth century and later.[70] If Uzi Leibner is correct in his dating of the mosaic and synagogue, and we must await final publication of the finds, not only will the dating of the so-called synagogue be less of an issue, but the date for the beginning of mosaic art with narrative themes from the Bible will be lowered by a significant degree, a century or more (fig. 8.21).[71]

This is only to say that the study of the ancient synagogue today finds itself in a dynamic phase that will surely go on for some time. With renewed excavations being conducted at Taricheae (Magdala), which produced the remarkable first-century synagogue, and at Horvat Kur and Huqoq in the same vicinity, much new information is coming to light about the material culture of eastern Galilee, which will help us better understand what was happening between Jews and Christians at a critical time in the history of both traditions.

The absence of an artistic vocabulary for material culture in the Christian tradition until after Constantine, however, makes this quest very difficult.[72] We saw the earliest evidence for Christian worship places in the preceding chapter, but neither at Capernaum nor near Megiddo in the Kefar Othnay room do any of the spaces have the cross in them.

Purity Concerns: Before and After 70 C.E.

The association of ritual baths and handwashing with purity concerns is an issue of long standing that has surfaced regularly in relation to the analysis of the ancient synagogue and the dispersion of the Jewish people into new lands after the destruction of the Temple in 70 C.E. Recent discussions of purity in relation to the existence of miqvaot in different contexts besides proximity to synagogues, such as in agricultural, industrial, and domestic settings, with a chronological range of about 200 B.C.E. to 600 C.E., have led to a new appreciation for the phenomenon of "non-priestly purity." This practice has to do with eating ordinary food in a state of purity and has been extended to the realm of prayer and reading the Torah, first by Gedaliah Alon and most recently by Eyal Regev.[73] Eating food in a state of purity is also known by the expression "table fellowship" and has been associated with the Pharisees and their Bible study groups known as "havurot." Such a concern also touches upon the most intimate matters between a man and a woman but also extends to areas of daily interaction of a nonsexual kind. Interest in this subject has also been renewed because the number of known ritual baths from the land of Israel has doubled in the past decade, from 300 to more than 850 today, and that number will surely keep rising as new excavations are conducted and new construction leads to the discovery of new sites.[74] In addition, as more and more stone vessels have turned up in excavations of sites from all over the country greater attention has been given to the reason for their occurrence and their association with ritual baths as well.

The oldest literary mentions of non-priestly defilement go back to the late Hellenistic period (first half of the second century B.C.E.) and are found in the Apocrypha. Tobit (2:9) purifies himself after burying his fellow countryman's corpse, and after leaving Holofernes's camp Judith purifies herself of Gentile uncleanness before praying for divine guidance (12:6–10). Similarly, the practice of prayer demanding some form of ritual purity occurs in Pseudo-Aristeas (305–6) and the Third Sibylline Oracle (591–93), which mentions handwashing in the sea as a means of purification, and we have seen several examples of possible features in the early synagogues (Gamla and Delos). As Susan Haber puts it: "In the Diaspora ritual ablutions took the form of sprinkling, splashing, or hand washing."[75] The cisterns and baths found at numerous sites, however, cannot be definitively understood in this way. Haber believes that in the Land of Israel even though the use of stone vessels was widespread, defilement according to biblical standards required total immersion, a suggestion that is rejected by Regev and many others if we are thinking about non-priestly purity practices. The fact that there are so many ritual baths near synagogues does not necessarily mean that ordinary worshipers would bathe adjacent to the synagogue before prayer, following the practice associated with going up to the Temple as pilgrims, in which no one could enter the Temple precincts in a state of impurity (Lev 15:31). Even in one of the smallest synagogues, say for 100–150 souls, it would take hours for the congregation to assemble and enter the synagogue if they were all required to immerse just before entering. The fact that many of these small communities had several other ritual baths in the village could simply imply that there was a general concern for purity in the community. So, for example, while there is a ritual bath ten meters away from the synagogue at Gamla to the southwest, there are also three other ritual baths in the settlement. The same pattern exists in regard to Masada, where the assembly hall/synagogue used by the rebels in 66–73 c.e. had a ritual bath only fifteen meters to the north and there were three other ritual baths from the same period scattered about the site.

The association of Khirbet Qumran with issues of purity comes from the fact that ten ritual baths were found among the ruins. Furthermore, texts associated with the sect call for regular immersion in pure water, especially the Community Rule. Even the well-known Theodotus inscription mentions that there are "water fittings" associated with the synagogue, though it is not clear whether they are for ritual or hygienic purposes since the synagogue also functioned as an inn of sorts.[76] Haber calls attention to the water basins found at Gamla and Masada and raises the possibility that they were used for ritual handwashing, which actually supports Regev's idea of the practice of non-priestly purity, though in the case of Theodotus it was a priestly synagogue.[77] In connection to ritual handwashing we might also add the basin found at the Byzantine-period synagogue of Nabratein (Synagogue 3) with a depiction of the Torah Shrine on it, which could have been used for handwashing or footwashing, the latter still being the orthodox practice today when Levites are called to wash the feet of the Cohanim before they deliver the priestly benediction.[78] In regard to the Diaspora synagogues in the pre-70 era there is simply too little information to draw any concrete conclusions. Nonetheless, washing the hands and sprinkling could well be associated with the known synagogues of Ostia and Delos.

It is logical, therefore, as Regev has assumed in his study, that such an awareness and attention to purity laws cannot be solely related to priests either before or after 70 C.E. In Regev's own words: "those who voluntarily observed purity in order to eat, pray, and read Scripture were seeking holiness in their everyday life."[79] Achieving a sense of personal sanctity, Regev goes on to say, was an effort of the individual to identify the human body as part of the self, an idea that is a direct outgrowth of the biblical concept of the close relationship between body and soul, or *nephesh,* in contradistinction to the Greek dualistic notion of body and soul that presupposes an immaterial soul in a physical body.[80] The Greeks, it should be emphasized, celebrated the human body and hence too much should not be drawn from their dualistic views. That the concern for ritual purity began in the Second Temple period proves that the Temple could not fully meet the religious and spiritual needs of all Jews, especially those who lived far away from Jerusalem. Such a view also permits us to understand the practice of non-priestly purity as a feature that delineates Jewish ethnic boundaries, as in the observance of the dietary laws. But it is precisely the comprehensive nature of the observance of non-priestly purity that enables us to speak of it as a major feature of early Judaism before and after 70 C.E. A large number of ritual baths thus far discovered or excavated in ancient Israel belong to the period after 70 C.E., especially up to 135 C.E. At Sepphoris on the western summit, for example, of more than thirty excavated ritual baths the vast majority are from the middle to late Roman period.[81] While stone vessels are traditionally dated to the Herodian period, from the first century B.C.E. to about 135 C.E., there is increasing evidence that this cutoff date is much too early, a logical assumption in view of the tremendous literary activity associated with the Roman period—the redaction of the Mishnah, the writing of the tannaitic midrashim, the canonization of the Hebrew Bible, and the emergence of the Talmud of the Land of Israel—most of which presupposes the existence of purity concerns and practices. Jonathan Adler, however, whose research is focused on this matter, sees the Sepphoris evidence as anomalous and reflective of the priestly presence at the site. Rather, he argues that both miqvaot and stone vessels pretty much went out of use around 135 C.E., and that is why no synagogues after that time have ritual baths associated with them.[82] But this is precisely the period, as we have argued above, that the ancient synagogue emerged as the main institution of Jewish life in the homeland and doubtless in the Diaspora as well. If in the Second Temple period, therefore, we may postulate a high degree of awareness for and practice of purity issues, albeit for both priestly and non-priestly reasons, all the more may we attribute to the post-destruction era a high degree of purity practice and awareness for many of the reasons given above. The nature of the archaeological evidence for continued use of stone vessels and miqvaot into late antiquity or after 135 C.E., however, in only a number of sites and their absence in synagogues from that period, makes this point an important one for further study. The sanctity of Scripture only increased as the process of canonization came to fruition; and the sanctity of the synagogue only became greater as the liturgy of worship came into being beyond the Torah service.

Toward a Complex Common Judaism After 70 C.E.

The major literary production of the Second Temple period may be said to be the Hebrew Bible in its proto-Masoretic version and the various rewritten forms it took in the corpus of the Dead Sea Scrolls. Not that there were no other types of literature produced (legal, liturgical, secular, midrashic). But it is fair to say that it was the Hebrew Bible or Old Testament as we know it that emerged post-70 C.E. as the predominant document that was to shape the future of the Jewish people. It also shaped the early Christian community along with Christian scripture that was emerging. At this point two significant streams in early Christianity, the Jerusalem church and associated Christian communities elsewhere in Palestine, whose origins predated Paul, and the Diaspora churches founded or influenced by Paul, were coming together. And it is precisely in this time period, from 70 to 200 C.E., that the tannaitic literature of the early rabbis was produced in response to what had been evolving over so many years before, which many scholars associate with the Oral Law. Indeed, many of the Qumran documents are pre- or proto-rabbinic in character, and the whole late corpus of biblical books is full of intertextual components that presage later developments.

We have noted before the usefulness of E. P. Sanders's rubric of "common Judaism."[83] Primary components of that common Judaism were monotheism, reliance of Scripture, especially Torah, and the symbolic centrality of the Temple. While we endorse in the main Sanders's views on this subject we also maintain that other factors also come into play when we define the people who lived in this era. What a person actually did to actualize his or her Jewish practice, for example, and how we identify that, also must be taken into account. Where one lived and what languages one spoke also played significant roles, as did what one consumed at meals. Common Judaism, thus, has common aspects of practice to it, and we have accordingly presented the realia and variety of Jewish life after the destruction of the Temple that pertain to it. Many of these factors also inform the everyday life that underlies the period of reconstitution of the Jewish people and their traditions in Galilee in the ensuing centuries. It may well justify the use of a new term to describe this phenomenon: "complex common Judaism."

In the process of reconstituting themselves in the north and even in places in the south, the newcomers brought with them the traditions of Judea and the memory of the Temple and its elaborate sacrificial system. The so-called Herodian terra-cotta lamp, it has recently been suggested, was taken to the north as well and became emblematic of the ties to the old heartland of the Jewish people, which after the two wars with Rome became more or less off limits.[84] And the Herodian lamps found at the Jewish sites in the north such as Sepphoris, Yodefat, and Gamla were in fact made of Jerusalem clays.[85] In recreating a religious tradition without the Temple and all the ceremonies that went with it, it is not surprising that the Judean experience became a template for the Galileans. The world of learning that had surrounded the Temple and its priesthood was transferred to the academies and to where the Sanhedrin was located, Jamniah, Sepphoris, Tiberias, and other places. The changing demographics of the early to middle Roman and tannaitic period also brought Jews to other municipal locations away from the new centers of gravity in Galilee: to Caesarea Maritima, Beth Shean (Scythopolis), Tyre, Bethsaida, Caesarea Philippi (Banias), and so on. Although so many Jews had left the Holy Land after the two wars and gone to points west in North Africa and Spain, to the north to Greece and Europe, to the east and the academies of Babylonia, and to southern Arabia as well, a strong community remained in Palestine, flourishing until the Islamic conquest and even after. This community produced the Mishnah in those first several centuries after 70 C.E. and its own version of the Talmud, the Talmud of the Land of Israel, the Yerushalmi, that we recognize as playing the pivotal role in transforming Judaism as a Temple-based religion into one that was portable and fully equipped to face the multicultural world of late antiquity along with the religions of Christianity, Mithraism, and continuing robust versions of paganism that lay at the heart of the Roman Empire. One of the major institutional vehicles for allowing the tradition to develop was the synagogue, which was the true successor in every way to the Temple in Jerusalem.

CHAPTER 9

The Archaeology of Paganism

Palestine was distinctive in the Mediterranean world because of the presence of a large number of monotheists (Jews, and to a lesser extent, Christians) among its inhabitants. Nonetheless, pagan cults flourished there throughout the Greco-Roman age, reflecting the same sorts of syncretism visible elsewhere in the ancient world. Some cults had roots that were centuries deep or even older, reflecting the Canaanite, Phoenician, Syrian, Egyptian, Persian, and other influences that had long existed in the area. The advent of Alexander and his successors hastened the influx of Greek deities, a process that had already begun in the Persian period, and Ptolemaic and Seleucid rule not only furthered Hellenistic culture but also renewed older Egyptian and Syrian influences. When the Romans arrived, they brought with them their own traditional deities as well as gods popular elsewhere in their empire, especially eastern provinces like Syria (fig. 9.1).

The result of this mingling of cultures was a remarkably diverse pantheon, with the number of deities represented increasing as the centuries progressed. Many of these deities were assimilated to each other. While the most famous examples of such fusion are the identification of Greek and Roman gods (Zeus as Jupiter, Athena as Roma, Ares as Mars), those classical gods were likewise assimilated to regional and local deities in the Levant as elsewhere in the Mediterranean and ancient Near Eastern worlds. For example, at Baalbek in Lebanon, known in the Roman period by the Greek name of Heliopolis, worship of the ancient god Baal was reconfigured as worship of the Heliopolitan Zeus and then of Jupiter Baal. James B. Rives has noted that this sort of fusion helped the Romans to make sense of the multiplicity of gods in their conquered territories by equating them with their own deities. Similarly, subject peoples also reinterpreted their own deities within the religious frameworks of their rulers, to varying degrees. Assimilating a local deity to a Greco-Roman one not only clarified the place of that deity in the larger pantheon, it might

Fig. 9.1. Temple of Bac-
chus from Baalbek, interior
monumental gateway, second
century c.e. (Photo from the
Library of Congress, circa
1890–1900, courtesy of Todd
Bolen/BiblePlaces.com)

Fig. 9.2. Hellenistic seal
from Tel Kedesh (Draw-
ing courtesy of Sharon
Herbert, University of
Michigan)

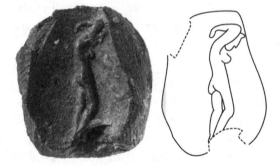

sometimes even raise the stature of a local god. In addition, syncretistic blending of ideas, images, and practices sometimes resulted in new
hybrid deities that differed in notable ways from both their imperial
and their local predecessors (fig. 9.2).[1]

Research on the pagan cults of Palestine faces a familiar limita-
tion: the loss of evidence from earlier centuries, sometimes because of
later construction and sometimes because of deliberate destruction.
The result is that the rich vibrancy of pagan life in the era from Alexander to Pompey is not matched by an abundance of surviving archaeological evidence.[2] Fortunately, considerably more has been pre-

served from the Roman period, particularly the second century C.E. onward, allowing us to get a better glimpse of the vitality and variety of paganism in that era.

Pagan Cults in the Hellenistic Period

Greek influence on local religion was visible in the material culture even before Alexander. Coins minted by various authorities in the last years of the Persian period occasionally depicted Greek deities, some bearing images of Athena in mimicry of the famous coinage of Athens.[3] Statues and figurines reflected not only Persian and Egyptian stylistic influences but also Greek. A pre-Hellenistic limestone head at Tel Zafit, for example, appears to be that of Herakles; a cache of twenty-nine bronze figures from Ashkelon includes Egyptian deities, such as a fourth-century B.C.E. Osiris.[4] Seals also show the influence of Greek mythology; those found in the Samarian cave of Wadi ed-Daliyeh portrayed several classical gods.[5]

Coins continue to be a key source of information about pagan cults in the Hellenistic period (fig. 9.3). This is especially true for the coastal cities, which continued to mint coins well before others in the region even began. Their coins attest to Greek influences, as seen in the images of Tyche, Nike, Zeus, Apollo, and the Dioscuri on those issued by Ptolemais (Akko). Some also bear witness to the ongoing importance of local gods. Ashkelon's coins, for example, depicted the city goddess Tyche, Aphrodite, Astarte, and a dove often interpreted as a divine symbol for the latter goddess.[6]

As for Hellenistic-era pagan inscriptions, the number discovered thus far is relatively small. Most reflect the widespread Hellenistic practice of offering dedications to the gods in fulfillment of a vow. One of the older examples, a third- or second-century B.C.E. inscription at Dan, reads "To the God who is in Dan, Zoilos made a vow," reflecting a very ancient cult's adaptation of that custom. A Ptolemaic-period inscription at the city of Samaria records a dedication of "Hegesandros, Xenarchis and their children to Sarapis Isis," providing evidence of the importance of Egyptian deities and an example of the worship of heavenly couples. From the same period comes an inscription from Jaffa dating to circa 217 B.C.E.; it records either an honorific inscription to Ptolemy Philopator, who is identified

Fig. 9.3. Bronze coin of Dora (modern Dor) featuring legendary founder of the city, Tyche, holding a standard in one hand and a cornucopia in the other, accompanied by the legend "Of the people of Dora, 130," or 66/67 C.E. (Copyright David Hendin, used by permission)

Fig. 9.4. Hellenistic seal of Tyche from Tel Kedesh (Drawing courtesy of Sharon Herbert, University of Michigan)

as a "god" (in Greek, *theon*) and the son of gods, or the dedication of a statue to him by Anaxikles, the king's priest.[7] A second-century inscription found a few kilometers from Akko records a second-century B.C.E. dedication of a votive altar by "Diodotos, son of Penptolemos, on behalf of himself and Philistahis wife and the children" to "the gods who answer prayer," in this case, the Syrian god and goddess Hadad and Atargatis. At Ptolemais itself, an Olympian deity received a dedication, Zeus Soter, circa 130 B.C.E., from a Seleucid governor.[8] A second-century B.C.E. inscription from Scythopolis records a list of the priests of an Olympian deity.[9] A very difficult second-century inscription reportedly found in Jerusalem seems to record an oath by a flute player with the theophoric name Ares and includes reference to "the priests" and "the gods;" an early interpretation rendered it differently as a dedicatory oath to the deity Ares Athletes.[10]

An unusual set of data is provided by the large corpus of sealings found at the Tyrian archive at Kedesh, which went out of use in the mid–second century B.C.E. Mythological images appear in the approximately two thousand sealings, among them the deities Tyche, Aphrodite, Apollo, and Athena (fig. 9.4–9.6). In addition, the Phoenician goddess Tanit, whose worship is so well known from Persian-period finds, is represented here by her traditional symbol, a schematic depiction of a triangular torso with two outstretched arms, topped by a circular head. One inscription refers to the Semitic deity Baal.[11]

Although most cities would have had one or more temples to their favored gods, only a few have been found. One example is a rectangular building with an altar in its accompanying court at the fortress complex at Beersheba in the Negev, a site better known for its much older Iron Age horned altar. Votive offerings associated with the Hellenistic temple include bronze female figures, a bronze bull,

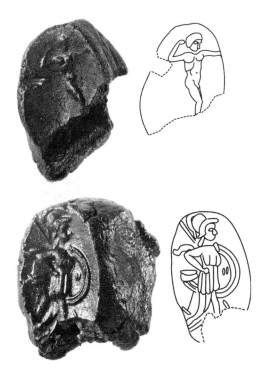

Fig. 9.5. Hellenistic seal of Apollo from Tel Kedesh (Drawing courtesy of Sharon Herbert, University of Michigan)

Fig. 9.6. Hellenistic seal of Athena from Tel Kedesh (Drawing courtesy of Sharon Herbert, University of Michigan)

and reflections of Egyptian influences, such as a sphinx and faience falcon pendants.[12] A shrine at Lachish used in the Persian and Hellenistic periods was built according to a similar design. Because of its east-facing orientation, it has sometimes been called a "solar shrine." Its interpretation has been debated, and although most scholars regard it as a pagan cultic site, others posit that it was some sort of Jewish shrine.[13] The many holy sites associated with Mount Hermon include several that can be dated as early as the Hellenistic period.[14] At Gadara, a second-century B.C.E. prostyle temple with Doric columns may have been dedicated to Zeus, based on a later Roman marble statuette found elsewhere at the site.[15] A limestone statue of a winged Nike at Dor adorned a Doric building from the third or second century B.C.E. that may have been a temple, and a large public building at Hippos underneath a late-first-century B.C.E. temple could have been an earlier temple.[16] Other temples are mentioned in literary sources; Gaza, for example, had one devoted to Apollos (*Ant.* 13.364).

One well-preserved cultic site is at Mizpeh Yamim in Upper Galilee. Initially built in the Persian era, the two-room temple was part

Fig. 9.7. Bronze figurines from the Mizpeh Yamim hoard, late Persian/Hellenistic period: a prancing lion cub, an Apis bull, a recumbent ram, and an Egyptian situla with Phoenician inscription. The ram's pose is a common one in the ancient Near East; the situla was a typical libation vessel used in funerary rites. (Photos courtesy of the Israel Antiquities Authority)

of a modest-sized walled complex at the top of Mount Meiron. In the Hellenistic period, it was an open-air structure, and an altar as well as bones from sacrificed animals (mostly sheep or goats, though with an occasional bovine) have been found there. It is an important exemplar of a site where influences other than Hellenistic predominated, no doubt largely because of its roots in an earlier period. Architecturally, it bore little resemblance to traditional classical temples. Aside from being roofless, it apparently lacked anterior columns, and while the excavators do note three interior columns in its main room, they make no mention of any evidence of the classical styles (Ionic, Doric, Corinthian). Traditional Greek deities are likewise absent. Instead, the cultic objects included a bronze Apis bull figurine and slate representations of Isis, Osiris, and Horus; a nearby building yielded a bronze Osiris (fig. 9.7). A situla was also recovered from the temple; the tear-shaped bronze vessel bore Egyptian inscriptions, depictions of Egyptian deities such as Isis, Nephthys, and the falcon-headed Re, as well as other Egyptian imagery such as a solar boat pulled by jackals. At some point, a Phoenician votive inscription to Astarte was added. Though the situla may have been produced in the Persian period, its use appears to have extended into the Hellenistic period. The temple functioned until the late Hellenistic period, when it was destroyed and its cultic objects damaged, perhaps in conjunction with Hasmonean expansion into the area.[17]

The most commonly found evidence for pagan practices and beliefs comes in the form of figurines and statuettes, some of which have already been noted, and as images on other categories of artifacts.[18] The overall impression they make is again that of diverse origins. Excavations at the coastal city of Dor have recovered the aforementioned statue of Nike and clay and faience figures of gods such as the Egyptian deity Bes, the Greek Pan, and the Phrygian goddess Cybele with her lions. A square lead weight from about 115 B.C.E. bears an image of Tanit on one side and a club, a common symbol for Herakles, on the other.[19] A figurine at another coastal site, Yavneh-Yam, depicts Harpocrates, the Greek god of silence.[20] At Beersheba of Galilee, a female figurine, perhaps of Aphrodite, the base of an Apis figure, and a Horus figure are all made of bronze.[21] In the Huleh Valley, the dig at the wealthy settlement at Tel Anafa uncovered a Pan figurine, a statue that may be of Demeter, and other figurines.[22]

Finds at Mareshah vividly illustrate the range of deities that might be venerated at a single community. An extraordinarily large set of locally produced molded terra-cotta figurines found in its Lower City depict a variety of gods, goddesses, and heroes, including Aphrodite, Artemis, Athena, the Dioscuri, Eros, Herakles, and Kore. Herakles is also represented by a bronze statue that was found near fragments of a marble libation bowl and a carved altar. A fragment of a Greek inscription records the dedication of a statue of an eagle, apparently to Apollo. The Egyptian gods Isis and Harpocrates appear among the figurines, and terra-cotta pillars might be divine representations. For the most part, Hellenistic-style portraits predominate, offering a striking contrast to the eastern and local styles of earlier Persian-period figurines. Because most of the terra-cotta figurines were found in fill, it is difficult to determine their original usage, but the magical function of several lead figurines of humans tied with wire seems clear enough. Limestone tablets also show the influence of magic, bearing prayers to spirits to inflict misfortune on enemies. Local deities are largely missing in the evidence found thus far. Some may have been assimilated to Greek gods; for example, the Edomite deity Qos may have been equated with Apollo. Another possibility is that the worship of traditional gods flourished in the Hellenistic period but is simply not reflected in the media available to us. The extant evidence, however, suggests that to a considerable degree, residents of Mareshah adopted the Greek pantheon as their own.[23]

Paganism in the Roman Period

Several developments in the Roman period make the task of understanding pagan cults somewhat easier than for the Hellenistic era (fig. 9.8). Palestine experienced a change in its epigraphic habit that was typical of the Roman world: as Roman influence grew, the number of inscriptions sharply increased. The result is that we have far more inscriptions than from the preceding centuries, of all types — dedicatory, votive, donor, honorific, civic, and funerary.[24] This increased preference for inscriptions coincided with heightened building activity. Beginning with Herod, the region's rulers and elites introduced Hellenistic and Roman-style civic architecture on an unprecedented scale. As we shall see in the next chapter, in the building boom of the second and early third centuries C.E., numerous cities gained temples, municipal buildings, bathhouses, fountains, and buildings for sports and entertainment such as stadiums, hippodromes, amphitheaters, and theaters. These structures often contained benefactor and other inscriptions that refer to religious practices. Statues also appear to have become more common in the Roman period, and in the second century especially, marble joined bronze and local stone such as limestone and basalt as a medium. Images of deities thus increasingly became part of urban life. Coins contributed further to the raised visual profiles of the gods. Relatively few authorities had struck currency in the Hellenistic period, but dozens of cities issued coins under the Romans, creating new opportunities for local elites to express their views and loyalties. Numismatic depictions of deities usually relied on the standard visual repertoire used throughout the Greco-Roman world, which made representations immediately identifiable, although they sometimes incorporated local touches as well. Many city coins bore images of temples, often thought to reflect architectural details of local shrines. Divine images appeared in other media, such as figurines,

Fig. 9.8. Bronze coins of Banias from the reign of Elagabalus, 218/222 C.E. Reverse depicts Pan playing pipes in the context of a shrine or grotto. (Copyright David Hendin, used by permission)

gemstones, funerary art, in a few cases mosaics, and on the round discus lamps that became popular beginning in the late first century C.E. The survival from this period of more literary sources from a variety of perspectives (pagan, Jewish, and Christian) adds further depth to our understanding of pagan practices and interaction with other groups as well as Jewish and Christian reactions to paganism; one thinks, for example, of how *Mishnah Avodah Zarah* grapples with the difficult issue of how Jews could make sure not to participate in the pagan practices, whether purposefully or inadvertently.[25]

Fig. 9.9. Marble head of the goddess Tyche, Roman period, from Amman Museum (Photo courtesy of Todd Bolen/Bible-Places.com)

The expansion and diversification of the region's pantheon is well attested. Of the classical Greek gods, Zeus was apparently the most popular, although Pan was widely worshiped as well. The city goddess Tyche appears to have been omnipresent, and evidence for worship of the Hellenistic-Egyptian Serapis is abundant (fig. 9.9). Nothing prevented the combination of major gods; alongside several inscriptions to Zeus Olympios at Jerash (Gerasa) we find one to Zeus Helios Great Serapis.[26] Foreign deities appear from locales more diverse than Greece, Rome, Egypt, and Syria. The Cretan god Minos appeared on coins of Gaza, the Phrygian god Men on those of Gaba.[27]

Local deities, however, retained importance, though sometimes in assimilated form. A dedicatory inscription at Qasr Antar on Mount Hermon to the "greatest and holy god" may be a reference to Baal Shamin, as are perhaps the statues of eagles at nearby Har Senaim. At Kedesh, a hexastyle temple with a sizable temenos built in the early second century C.E. (the only fully excavated Roman-era temple in geographical Galilee) also had inscriptions probably associated with Baal Shamin (fig. 9.10). One honored the "holy god of heaven"; the other is only partially preserved, but its reference to the "holy god" might likewise have originally included "of heaven."[28]

Nabatean religion exemplifies the combination of indigenous and foreign influences. Throughout the Hellenistic and Roman periods, the Nabateans continued the millennia-old practice of venerating *massebot,* sometimes erecting single blocks and other times setting up small groups of pillars. They often placed smaller rectangular betyls in niches, some of them unadorned and some with facial features of lines and squares. Larger stones, particularly those square in shape, are typically thought to represent the chief deity of the Nabatean pantheon, Dushara, or, in Greek, Dusares. City coins from the Decapo-

Fig. 9.10. At the remains of a Roman temple at Kedesh, a section of wall standing from antiquity (Photo courtesy of Todd Bolen/BiblePlaces.com)

lis city of Adraa make the association explicit, depicting a betyl with a Greek inscription reading "Dusares, god of the Adraenoi." Worship of that deity spread far beyond Arabia, reaching as far west as the Italian peninsula, and Dushara was often fused with Zeus. Traditional Arabic deities like Al-Uzza, Allat, Al-Kutba, Manatou, and Hubalu were soon joined by foreign ones such as Isis, Apis, Atargatis, Baal Shamin, Tyche, Nike, Hermes, Helios, Dionysos, and Aphrodite. At the Negev trade station at Oboda, the first-century B.C.E. Nabatean king Obodas II was interred and worshiped as Zeus Obodas and Theos Obodas. As illustrated by buildings at Oboda and more famously Petra, temples increasingly joined massebot sites and open-air sanctuaries as venues for worship.[29]

Individual cities enjoyed remarkably diverse pantheons, as finds from Ashkelon illustrate. The chief deity there was the traditional Phoenician goddess Astarte. Coins bear her image as well as that of a dove, one of her attributes. Other city coins depict the Phoenician god Phanebal, the Egyptian deities Isis and Osiris, what may be the Syrian goddess Derketo, the local deity Marnas, and the Greek gods Poseidon, Herakles, the Dioscuri, and Tyche. In an early-third-century C.E. public building, images of deities from across the eastern empire were placed side by side: a relief depicts the Syrian goddess Atargatis; a pillar, the Egyptian couple Isis and Horus; another pillar, Nike standing atop a globe-holding Atlas (fig. 9.11). Greek influences are visible in funerary art: a marble coffin shows the Rape of Proserpine and lead coffins depict Hermes. Painted stucco in a vaulted grave included one medallion containing a Gorgon mask, another with Pan and his pipe, and paintings of nymphs.[30]

Despite the plethora of gods, each city typically had a favored deity whose temple likely outsized others and whose image appeared on its coins with a frequency rivaled only by the local Tyche. For Dor, it was Doros, son of Poseidon. For Scythopolis, it was Dionysos; the city apparently cherished its place in mythology as the burial place for the god's nurse, Nysa (Pliny, *Natural History* 5.18.4, 5.18.74), its inhabitants referring to themselves in inscriptions as "Nysaean Scythopolitans." The magnificent temple built to Zeus Olympios by Neapolis, a structure best known from coins depicting the long stairwell up Mount Gerizim, suggests that he was its major deity.[31]

A city's tastes might change. In the early Roman era, for example, Jerash's largest temple was to Zeus. Inscriptions show that that deity always remained popular, and in the mid–second century C.E., the heyday of temple construction in the region, his temple was thoroughly reworked. This temple was outsized, however, by another that was erected in the second century C.E. to Artemis (fig. 9.12). In what is probably not a coincidence, the frequency of Zeus's depiction on city coins began to decline at approximately the same time. The temple of Zeus was in the city's southernmost sector, but that of Artemis was more centrally located, and it visually dominated the city. Starting from several hundred meters to the east, a lengthy processional way eleven meters wide stretched toward the temple. The road ended in a triple gateway that gave entrance to a propylaea, which in turn led to an exedra. Beyond the exedra was the city's cardo, which was faced by the fourteen-meter-high retaining wall of the temple complex (fig. 9.13). A stairway gave access to the temple outer court, where an even more massive set of stairs led to the upper court. Within this temenos stood a high podium that held the temple itself, a peripteral structure with six columns lining its front. As Warwick Ball has argued, the temple reflected a mixture of influences. The extensive use of Corinthian columns was common among temples throughout the Greco-Roman

Fig. 9.11. Statue of Nike from Ashkelon, part of decoration of the Severan Forum, third century C.E. (Photo courtesy of Todd Bolen/BiblePlaces.com)

Fig. 9.12. Temple of Artemis
from Jerash, 150–180 C.E.
(Photo from the Library of
Congress, circa 1890–1900,
courtesy of Todd Bolen/
BiblePlaces.com)

world, and the temple's placement along the cardo reflected Roman-
style civic planning. The massive temenos and the crowd participation it facilitated, the placement of Syrian niches on the temple gateway, and the spatial emphasis created by the lengthy processional route
were more characteristic of eastern temples. The complex as a whole
was among the most impressive anywhere in the Roman world.[32]

Fig. 9.13. Forum or "elliptical plaza" from Jerash, first century C.E. (Photo from Library of Congress, circa 1890–1900, courtesy of Todd Bolen/ BiblePlaces.com)

The proliferation of sports and entertainment facilities and their associated activities also created additional venues for religious expression. For example, the amphitheater at Beth Guvrin includes a statue niche and two altars, one of them dedicated to the God of Heliopolis. Three bronze curse tablets there record that some gladiators turned to magic for extra help in their contests. At Samaria-Sebaste, altars, statues, and inscriptions are associated with the stadium, including a painted inscription from the early phase appealing to Kore ("May the learned master Martialis and his friends be remembered by the Kore").[33]

Temples were not limited to cities, however. Some were found in village and other rural contexts. From the late first century C.E. until the time of Constantine, numerous temples were built on the long-venerated Mount Hermon, some of them no doubt in association with earlier cults and holy sites that can no longer be identified. These temples differed from most others to their south, typically lacking a row of columns decorating their entrance and avoiding the use of Corinthian capitals. Whereas many temples had triple entrances, these had a single main door. Some were carved straight from the rocky mountainside. The deities they were dedicated to are often unknown because of a lack of inscriptions.[34]

Evidence for the fusion and association of deities of diverse geographical origins goes well beyond the examples already noted. It was not at all uncommon for representations of Tyche to resemble Astarte or Aphrodite, and for that matter the latter two goddesses were occasionally identified with each other. Thus, the Tyche on Dor's coins looks like Astarte, and a clay figurine there could pass for either Astarte or Aphrodite. Shekels from Tyre depicted the Phoenician god Melqart with the characteristics of the hero Herakles, while the local deity Marnas of Gaza took on characteristics of Zeus. At Khisfin, northeast of the Sea of Galilee, we find a Roman veteran's dedication to Zeus Bel, reflecting the combination of an Olympian deity with a Semitic one. Deities with different cultural ancestries were sometimes joined as divine couples, as in a first-century C.E. inscription at Jerash that pairs Hera with the Nabatean god Pakidas.[35]

As was common throughout the Greco-Roman world, conceptualizations of deities reflected a tension between their universality and their associations with particular locations and attributes (fig. 9.14). We find the chief Greek god venerated not only simply as Zeus but also as Zeus Olympios, recalling his famous association with Mount Olympus, at Jerash and elsewhere; as Zeus Akraios, Zeus of the mountaintop, at Scythopolis; as Zeus Arotescios, Zeus of the Heights, at Hippos; and as Zeus of Doliche, a city of Commagene, at Caesarea Maritima.[36]

Fig. 9.14. The Khazneh at Nabataean Petra, in south-western Jordan, usually identified as a tomb monument, but some have identified it as a temple (Photo courtesy of Todd Bolen/BiblePlaces. com)

The long-term garrisoning of significant numbers of Roman troops had a considerable impact on pagan religion in the region, as evidenced at Jerusalem. With the stationing there of the Legio X Fretensis after the first revolt, the city acquired an increasingly Roman character, a process heightened even further when Hadrian declared it the colony of Aelia Capitolina. A coin minted under Hadrian depicts a distyle temple of the Capitoline triad of Jupiter, Juno, and Minerva, an image often taken to represent an actual temple built in Jerusalem. Indeed, Cassius Dio reported the presence of a temple to Zeus (presumably, that is, Jupiter) on the Temple Mount that may be this temple (69.12.1–2). Another temple is attested farther west by Eusebius, who claims that the Romans had covered Golgotha with fill to support a temple of "the impure demon of Aphrodite" (*Life of Constantine* 3.26.3; cf. 4.6.4). Archaeologists have found evidence for some sort of temple at the site of the Church of the Holy Sepulcher in the form of an altar and a temenos wall that extended to what is now the Russian Hospice. Some scholars have rejected Eusebius's association of the temple with Aphrodite and suggested instead that the temple there was the Capitoline temple mentioned by Cassius Dio, whose location of it at the Temple Mount would thus have been erroneous. The city's coins depict Jupiter, Roma, and even the suckling she-wolf from Rome's foundation myth as well as Hellenistic deities such as Tyche, Serapis, and Dionysos. A range of deities is represented in figurines, statues, gemstones, and amulets throughout the city. On Mount Zion, a member of the Legio III Cyrenaica dedicated a monument to Jupiter Optimus Maximus Serapis, and Roman notions of the genius, a guardian spirit, are reflected in Latin inscriptions such as one dedicated to the genius of the legion and another dedicated for the salvation of the emperor to the "*templum* of the genius of Africa." Votive offerings found north of the Temple Mount near the pools that would later be associated with Saint Anne's Church suggest the presence of a healing cult there.[37]

Pagan practices of Roman troops are illustrated by archaeological finds at other sites throughout the region. Near Legio, the Jezreel Valley headquarters of the Legio VI Ferrata, a marble altar depicted a Victory goddess atop a globe and two Latin inscriptions, one a dedication to Serapis for "the salvation and health" of the emperor. The imperial cult is reflected in finds like the splendid bronze statue of Hadrian associated with an army unit at Tel Shalem, south of Scythopolis. Roman epigraphic conventions are reflected in the gravestones of soldiers or veterans, like those at Tiberias and Gabara where the Latin formula DM pays homage to *Dis Manibus,* the deified Manes, the souls of the dead who were the object of Roman domestic cultic observances.[38]

Romans and locals alike participated in the imperial cult, which had spread well beyond Herod the Great's three temples.[39] In the early decades of the first century C.E., Pilate built a shrine to Tiberius at Caesarea Maritima. Among the several inscriptions at Jerash mentioning imperial priests is a donation to the temple of Zeus Olympios asking for the safety of the Sebastoi, that is, Augustus and Tiberius, suggesting that the imperial cult there dated back to the early first century.[40] Other cities also had imperial shrines; according to Epiphanius, for example, a temple to Hadrian was begun at Tiberias, though it was apparently never finished (*Panarion* 30.12.2). Evidence of local practice is scattered across the region: a third-century inscription on an altar at Kedesh; a prayer for the salvation of the emperor on an altar at Har Senaim; a prayer to the Olympian deities for the salvation of Hadrian, "*pater patriae,* savior and benefactor of the world," from an otherwise unknown village in southern Samaria.[41] Coins of the Herodian kings Philip, Agrippa I, and Agrippa II depicted the emperor and members of his family. Those of the last ruler sometimes showed imperial figures participating in cultic activities or in divinized form: Nero's mother Agrippina II as the goddess Fortuna, or Nero's wife Octavia making an offering.[42] The proliferation of civic mints in the second and early third centuries and the increasing importance of imperial mints resulted in widespread circulation of the emperor's image. So, too, did the placement of his statues in cities, a source of tension between Jews and Gentiles as early as the first century, as illustrated not only by Caligula's failed attempt to place a statue of himself in the Jewish temple (*Ant.* 18.261–309; *War* 2.184–203; Philo, *On the Embassy to Gaius* 188, 198–348), but also by incidents such as that in Dor where a youth placed one in the synagogue (*Ant.* 19.300). The honorific naming of cities like Caesarea Maritima, Caesarea Paneas (Banias), Sebaste (Samaria), Diocaesarea (Sepphoris), Tiberias, Flavia Neapolis, and Aelia Capitolina further underscored the emperor's extraordinary status and power. Rabbinic texts attest to Jewish awareness of the imperial cult. The list of "festivals of the Gentiles" in *Mishnah Avodah Zarah* 1.3 includes two traditional Roman holidays, Kalendaei and Saturnalia, and several festivals seemingly associated with the veneration of the emperor: *Kratesis* (probably "Empowering," a reference to commemoration of the emperor's accession), the anniversary of the kings, the day of birth, and the day of death.[43]

A particularly intriguing example of homage to the emperor is found in a Greek lintel inscription from the late second century C.E. at Qazyon in Galilee. The inscription records a prayer for the well-being of Septimius Severus and his sons. Its initial discoverers in the late nineteenth century noted the presence of an altar and carved eagle nearby, and a recent analysis of the area has demonstrated the similarity of the porticoed building from which the inscription comes to a pagan temple. One might normally assume that the inscription was dedicated by pagans if not for the curious identification of its sponsor: "by oath of the Jews." Were Jews participating in a pagan cult, or was the inscribed lintel a goodwill gift of local Jews to the temple of their pagan neighbors? Perhaps the building should be interpreted not as a temple but as a synagogue, as some have argued, although this suggestion is problematic in that it leaves the altar unexplained. However the data are interpreted, they seem to reflect a blurring of boundaries between Jewish and pagan practice.[44]

Pagan Cults at Caesarea Maritima and Banias

The unusually rich corpuses of finds at Caesarea Maritima and Caesarea Paneas (Banias) make them worthy case studies to illustrate how pagan practices are reflected in various media. Caesarea Maritima was the most Romanized city in Palestine from its inception, with the imperial cult tightly woven into its civic culture. Herod the Great had made his temple to Augustus and Roma the city's visual center, and Josephus characterizes the city's colossal statues of that emperor as "not inferior to the Olympian Zeus" (*War* 1.414; *Ant.* 15.339). A few decades later, Pilate apparently constructed his shrine to Tiberius, and a century later someone built a temple to Hadrian, the existence of which we know only through a sixth-century epigraphic reference to a Hadrianeum. A Latin dedication by an Augustalis attests to the presence of an association devoted to the imperial cult. The city's coins depicted emperors in various poses, and several statues of emperors from Hadrian onward have been discovered.[45]

Veneration of Tyche has deep roots in the city's history as well. She adorned coins minted there by Agrippa I as well as later civic issues, holding a rudder to signify the maritime nature of the city or a bust of the emperor.[46] Statues and gems portray her in various forms and poses, sometimes resembling Roma or Astarte, and a bronze cup now at the Louvre depicts her along with Asclepius, Apollo, and Hygieia.

By the late first or early second century, a vaulted warehouse near the shore had been converted into a cultic site devoted to Mithras. The deity was popular among Roman soldiers, and legionnaires and auxiliaries formerly stationed in Syria probably brought his worship to Caesarea. Decorated with frescoes, the Mithraeum had benches for seating along its north and south walls and holes in its roof to allow sunlight to illuminate an altar at the summer solstice. Excavations uncovered an altar, numerous accompanying lamps, and a medallion showing Mithraic scenes, such as Mithras slaying a bull, the foundation myth for the central ritual of the cult. The only archaeological evidence of a mystery religion in Palestine, this is among the earliest known Mithraea in the entire empire. It functioned until the third century C.E.

Finds at the city also exemplify how contests, spectacles, and performances were infused with religious elements. The older hippodrome had an associated shrine, where votive feet have been found. Several statues, including the multi-breasted Artemis of Ephesus, have been discovered in the theater.

The city's extraordinary assemblage of marble statuary and figurines, most of it dating from the second century and later, portrays a full panoply of familiar deities. Alongside Tyche and the emperors appear Aphrodite, Asclepius, Apollo, Dionysos, Athena, the Ephesian Artemis, the Phrygian goddess Cybele, Isis, and Serapis. Many of these deities as well as others like Demeter, Minerva, Nike, Poseidon, and a harbor god appear on coins and gems from the city.

Egyptian deities were important, as evidenced by the statues of Serapis and Isis. A gem has an inscription to One Zeus Serapis, reflecting the fusion of deities, and an early-second-century C.E. papyrus (*P. Oxy.* 1380) preserves an older text that demonstrates the early assimilation of Isis to Hellas and Agathe at the city's predecessor, Strato's Tower. Gems show attributes of Isis, as does a votive foot decorated with a cobra. Her consort Osiris, god of the underworld, was also worshiped in the city; an epitaph asks him to provide the deceased with freshwater.

Evidence of worship of gods popular in Syria is abundant. Several intaglios depict the Syrian Baal, sometimes with a consort. An altar bore this inscription: "Viktor, in fulfillment of a vow, dedicated and built this to Zeus Dolichenos." Another dedication was offered to God Megas Despotes. A late-second- or third-century inscription on a marble votive foot found at nearby Mount Carmel records a dedication by a colonist from Caesarea to Heliopolitan Zeus Carmelos, showing that the Baal of the Syrian city of Heliopolis had been assimilated not only with Zeus but also with the ancient local god of Mount Carmel.[47]

Considerable data are also available for tracing the development of religious practices at Banias, known as Caesarea Philippi early in the first century and as Caesarea Paneas for the remainder of the Roman period. Pan had special status in the city and began appearing on coins as early as the reign of Agrippa II, but he was hardly the only deity honored there. Agrippa's coins also had images of Tyche and Nike, and civic issues sometimes depicted Tyche and Zeus. Inscriptions record dedications to deities such as the Heliopolitan Zeus, Asclepius, the Nymphs, Silenus, and Baal Shamin, and statues or statue fragments have been found of various Hellenistic deities. Caesarea Paneas was also a center for the imperial cult, and some scholars have identified a structure on the terrace as the temple to Augustus and Roma built by Herod (*Ant.* 15.360), though others propose alternative locations.[48]

Thanks to the work of Andrea M. Berlin, the evolution of cultic activities at Banias is better understood than for the vast majority of cities in Palestine.[49] Its association with the goat-footed Pan extends back into the Hellenistic period. Polybius, writing in about 200 B.C.E., commented on the Panion "beneath the cliffs of Mount Hermon" (16.18.2, 28.1.3). The cult of Pan apparently had no building in the Hellenistic period, but visitors frequently dined on the terrace in front of its famous grotto, leaving behind their cooking and dining dishes as offerings. When the city began to expand under the Herodian dynasty, the ceramic repertoire reflected new patterns in worship. Previous pottery at the terrace had been mostly of regional types, but now dishes from farther afield began appearing in increasing numbers. Lamps joined serving and cooking ware as a common offering. From the late first through the third century C.E., the terrace received several additions, including a court for Pan and the Nymphs, another court for Nemesis, and buildings, including one sometimes thought to be a temple to Zeus and Pan, and another often regarded as a temple to Pan and the Goats. Aedicule niches for statues were carved into the cliffside by the cave, and inscriptions and remains from statues show that wealthy donors dedicated gifts to various deities. Ironically, however, ceramic evidence suggests that visits to the site dropped after the construction of the temple. The number of dishes left behind decreased dramatically, and virtually all of those deposited were unused, showing that ritual dining had ceased. In the early third century, patterns in worship changed again when the temple to Pan and the Goats was constructed on the eastern end of the terrace. Visits increased dramatically, and worshipers again offered table and cooking wares, although these, too, were unused, showing that the custom of dining on the terrace had almost completely faded away. By far the most popular offerings were lamps, judging from the nearly three thousand fragments and intact specimens recovered, some of them locally produced discus lamps but most of them small saucer lamps. The terrace and associated buildings remained popular until the cessation of the cult.

That cessation would not come until the Byzantine period. Prior to Constantine, however, pagan practices infused the everyday lives of the people of Caesarea Paneas as they did for many of the region's inhabitants, whether they lived in urban or rural, public or private contexts. Paganism in Palestine experienced the same vitality and exhibited the same syncretistic blending of influences as did pagan cults across the ancient Mediterranean. It also experienced the same fate, increasingly declining as emperors began to give their favor to the church.

CHAPTER 10

The Growth of Greco-Roman Culture and the Case of Sepphoris

Herod the Great, his royal successors, and Roman administrators had introduced Roman architecture to Palestine, but it is not until the post-70 C.E. period that we see the more widespread flourishing of Roman influence in various spheres of material culture. Although the nature of our literary sources—rabbinic texts, early Christian writings, occasionally attentive Roman histories—makes it difficult to offer a detailed chronological narrative of the events of the following centuries, archaeological finds attest to a transformation of urban landscapes, not only in Palestine but elsewhere in the Roman East. The expansion of cities was matched by widespread growth in the size and number of rural settlements in much of the region.

Many of the changes in Palestine's material culture closely correlate to the imposition of direct Roman rule. The client ruler system had apparently outlived its usefulness to the Romans. When Agrippa II died in the 90s C.E., his territory was attached to the provinces of Syria and Judea. The death of the Nabatean king Rabbel II was followed by the bloodless annexation of his territory and its assignment to Provincia Arabia in 106 C.E. After the Bar Kokhba war, Hadrian renamed Provincia Judaea as Provincia Syria Palaestina, a name it would keep until the end of the fourth century, when it was separated into three provinces (Palaestina Prima, Secunda, and Tertia).

The Cultural Impact of the Roman Army

For the first time, Palestine had a sizable long-term Roman military presence. Prior to the Great Revolt, its garrison had consisted of only a relatively small number of auxiliary troops in Judea, with most of them stationed in Jerusalem and Caesarea Maritima. The latter city provided many of the units' recruits, as did Sebaste.[1] After the war, Rome ceased

Fig. 10.1. Roof tiles with stamps of the Tenth Legion Fretensis. The tile at upper left features symbols of a galley and a boar. (Photo courtesy of Hillel Geva, the Israel Exploration Society)

appointing nobles of equestrian rank to govern the region and began assigning senators, a rank that allowed the command of legionary troops. Although most of the Roman army that had descended upon Judea to crush the rebellion dispersed to other areas, the Legio X Fretensis remained (fig. 10.1). Its primary headquarters was in Jerusalem, but smaller outposts could be found throughout the south. In the early second century, the empire deployed a second legion to the region, giving Judea a remarkably large garrison for a relatively small province. Initially this legion was Legio II Traiana, which had arrived in northern Palestine by 120 C.E. Within a few years, it was replaced by the Legio VI Ferrata, which constructed its main base at Legio, adjacent to the village of Kefar Othnay in the Jezreel Valley. East of the Jordan, the new Provincia Arabia was garrisoned by the Legio III Cyrenaica and its auxiliaries, with Bosra as the primary headquarters. Although crises like the Bar Kokhba Revolt required additional troops, for the most part this garrison was sufficient to ensure stability.[2]

The military devoted considerable energy to constructing a system of paved Roman roads. Earlier Roman roads had been limited to a mid–first century route running north from Ptolemais and a road through the Jezreel constructed by Vespasian's forces during the First Revolt. Now, new roads multiplied. One of the first was the Via Nova Traiana linking Syria to the Red Sea, the construction of which greatly facilitated the expansion of the Decapolis cities. The reign of Hadrian was marked by the construction of roads in several parts of Palestine, integrating key cities and military bases with the larger regional road network. These roads were designed primarily to facilitate faster movement of troops, but they were also used by Roman subjects for trade and travel. We can imagine that the mere presence of the roads reminded those who saw them of Rome's military might. Milestones with Latin inscriptions bearing the name and titles of the reigning emperor underscored the message of imperial domination. That milestones were intended as propaganda and not merely as the utilitarian marking of distances is suggested by the fact that they were generally erected only in densely populated areas.[3]

Civic Identity, Roman Identity

Coins and other inscriptions show that numerous cities received titles and statuses proclaiming their Roman affinities. Soon after the first revolt, Caesarea Maritima was elevated to colonial status and became known as Colonia Prima Flavia Augusta Caesarea. In 132, the Romans refounded Jerusalem as the colony Aelia Capitolina (fig. 10.2). Other cities were awarded the status of colony in the century that followed, and a few took the even more prestigious title of "metropolis." Civic names honoring the emperor were common. The new city founded at the bottom of Mount Gerizim in 81 C.E., for example, was named Flavia Neapolis, thus honoring the Flavian dynasty. Other examples include Antipatris, which became known as Marcia Aurelia Antoniana Antipatris, and Eleutheropolis (Beth Guvrin), which became Lucia Septimia Severa Eleutheropolis.[4]

As was typical in the eastern empire, numerous cities minted their own bronze coins in the second and early third centuries, displaying civic pride not only by advertising their city's titles but by adorning the coins' reverses with images of local significance, often principal deities or their temples. This wave of minting activity continued until the final decades of the third century, when the last civic mints in the region shut down. Imperial mints functioned as a source

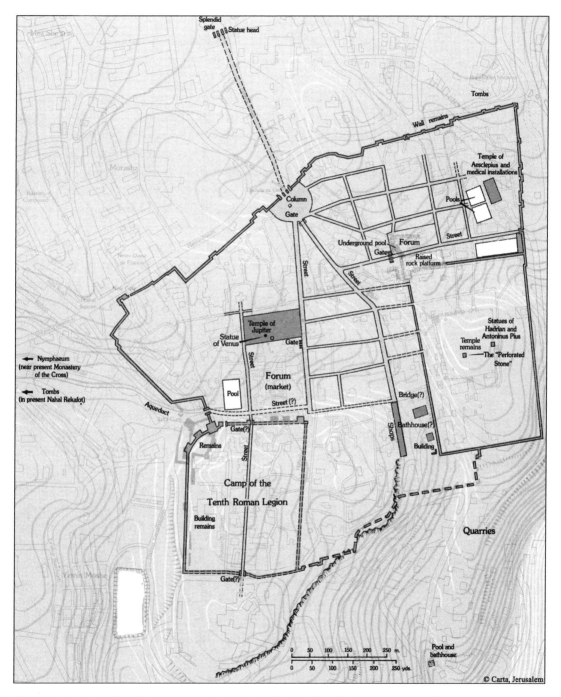

Splendid gate
Statue head

Tombs

Wall remains

Temple of
Aesclepius and
medical installations

Column
Gate

Pools

Underground pool
Gate

Forum

Street

Street

Raised
rock platform

Street

Statues of
Hadrian and
Antoninus Pius

Temple of
Jupiter

Statue
of Venus

Gate

Temple
remains

The "Perforated
Stone"

Nymphaeum
(near present Monastery
of the Cross)

Street

Forum
(market)

Pool

Bridge(?)

Tombs
(in present Nahal Rekafot)

Aqueduct

Street (?)

Bathhouse(?)

Shops

Building

Gate(?)

Remains

Street

Camp of the

Tenth Roman Legion

Building
remains

Quarries

Gate(?)

0   50   100   150   200   250 m.

0   50   100   150   200   250 yds.

Pool and
bathhouse

© Carta, Jerusalem

Fig. 10.2. Aelia Capitolina (Map prepared by Carta, Israel Map and Publishing Company, Ltd.)

of both bronze and silver, and earlier mints of silver coins such as Tyre and Sidon ceased production. Civic and imperial coins alike typically depicted the emperor, serving as an important means of propagating his image.[5]

A standard development in provinces that experienced a large influx of Roman soldiers was an increase in the number and types of inscriptions, and Palestine was no exception.[6] Its remarkably diverse epigraphic corpus includes inscriptions from burials, mosaics, governmental texts, and euergetistic, honorific, and dedicatory contexts. In most cases, these inscriptions were in Greek, demonstrating Hellenism's ongoing influence. Latin was present but relatively uncommon, appearing primarily at Roman colonies like Caesarea Maritima and in government and military inscriptions.[7] Jews made ample use of Greek for their inscriptions but also continued to use traditional languages like Aramaic and Hebrew.[8] Epigraphic use of local languages illustrates how Roman subjects found ways to combine elements of indigenous and imperial cultures. At the extensive Jewish necropolis at Beth Shearim in southwestern Galilee, for example, Greek overwhelmingly dominates the roughly 280 inscriptions, showing that Jewish elites sought inscriptions conforming to the region's epigraphic norm. Some inscriptions were in Hebrew, most notably in tombs associated with rabbinic families. Aramaic, although the common spoken language of Galilee, was rare but present. Even Palmyrene makes an appearance, reflecting the distant origins of the interred.[9]

Papyri also attest to the blending of local and imperial cultures. We have already mentioned the intriguing Babatha archive in our discussion of the Bar Kokhba Revolt. Its thirty-five papyri span the last years of the Nabatean Kingdom and the early decades of the Provincia Arabia and allow us to glimpse Babatha's linguistic and legal contexts. The marriage certificate (*ketubah*) of Babatha and that of her daughter Shelamzion both reflected some of the characteristics of ancient Jewish *ketubot* known from other sources, but their languages differed. Babatha's was written in Aramaic, but Shelamzion's was in Greek. Roman influence is particularly noticeable in the latter. Like other papyri in the collection, it was dated Roman-style by the year of the province and the names of the consuls currently in office. Its scribe identified himself with the Latin loanword *librarius,* and its witnesses signed not in Greek but in Aramaic. Babatha's census declaration from 127 C.E. was dated with a similar formula, and in it she swore by the genius of the emperor that her statement of assets was accurate. That document was written in Greek, but its witnesses signed in Nabatean. When Babatha's second husband died, the *boule* of Petra appointed legal guardians for her son, reflecting Roman law's prohibition of women having legal custody. In fact, the son remained with Babatha, while the guardians were responsible for providing child support. When they sent too few denarii, Babatha availed herself of Roman law by appealing to the Roman governor in Petra. The latest document in the cache, dated to 132 C.E., shows that the amount of the child support payment did not increase. Babatha, it seems, had lost her case. Documents such as these bear vivid witness to the speed with which Roman customs and law mingled with Nabatean and Jewish culture in the newly formed Roman province.[10]

Examples of monumental civic architecture now became common, dwarfing the small number present in the early first century C.E.[11] The ubiquity of these architectural forms functioned as propaganda by creating a widespread network of physical symbols of Roman culture. Many cities were reorganized on orthogonal grids, with cardos, decumani, and other streets intersecting at right angles and sometimes lined with porticoes. A few cities had intersections marked by tetrapyla, large monumental rectangular columns. Some developed market areas in the style of the Roman macellum or the Hellenistic agora, and several acquired the basilical buildings characteristic of Roman cities. A few constructed a monumental arch—or, in the case of cities like Bosra and Jerash (Gerasa), two. Older temples were renovated and new temples appeared. Many cities built new aqueducts and other expansions in water facilities, and some demonstrated their control of water with nymphaea, fountains decorated with statues and relief carvings.

Leisure, entertainment, and sports architecture became very common in the cities. Cities took advantage of their more technologically advanced waterworks by constructing public baths, thus participating in the heyday of bathhouse construction occurring throughout the Roman world. Some of these bathing facilities were quite large, such as the eastern baths at Jerash. In the late first and early second centuries, Roman-style theaters appeared at Pella, Bosra, Jerash, and

Fig. 10.3. Theater at Beth Shean (Photo courtesy of Sean Burrus)

Sepphoris, and by the third century more than thirty theaters of various sizes could be found in the region. Beth Shean (fig. 10.3) and Antipatris received odea, roofed theater-like structures often intended as music halls. A few hippodromes and circuses for races appeared, as did several amphitheaters, the characteristic oval or circular buildings designed for Roman combat sports.[12]

At least some of this construction can be attributed to Roman soldiers. The two legions brought with them engineers, architects, and surveyors who initially would have had more familiarity with these types of buildings than their indigenous counterparts. The large garrison also functioned as a huge labor pool for military-initiated projects.[13] That soldiers served as construction workers throughout the empire is well documented, and occasional inscriptions in Palestine attribute structures to them, such as an aqueduct given to Caesarea Maritima by the emperor Hadrian.[14] At least some of the amphitheaters and bathhouses were constructed to meet the military's

Fig. 10.4. Main street at Beth Shean looking north, with tel in the background and a cutout of a woman directing traffic at right (Photo courtesy of Sean Burrus)

needs; for examples, we can point to the amphitheater at Legio and the bathhouse at the Roman camp at Tel Shalem, near Beth Shean (fig. 10.4). Roman officers, whether active or retired, sometimes sponsored the construction of monumental civic architecture. An inscription at Jerash, for example, records the gift of a veteran to help with the construction of the city's southern theater.[15] Some Roman subjects were skeptical of this overlay of imperial architecture and infrastructure. In the mid–second century C.E., Rabbi Shimon bar Yohai reportedly observed, "Everything that the Romans have built, they have built for themselves: market places, to house prostitutes, baths to pamper themselves, and bridges to take tolls on them."[16]

Recognition of Roman roles in construction and sponsorship, however, should not obscure the widespread participation of local subjects in creating new cityscapes. Inscriptions show that elites, both as individuals and in conjunction with civic councils, paid for many of the region's building projects, demonstrating their desire to participate in the empire-wide culture of euergetism. Obviously, local workers provided much of the labor. A rabbinic text preserves concerns about whether it was appropriate for Jews to help build basilicas, stadiums, and bathhouses (*m. Avodah Zarah* 1:7).

We can better understand how individual cities adopted these Roman styles by briefly considering some specific examples. Caesarea

Maritima maintained its role as a chief exemplar of Roman architecture. Its new aqueduct has already been mentioned. The second century also saw the renovation of its theater and the construction of a circus. The city's enormous corpus of inscriptions records the construction of many other buildings of various types, including a shrine to Hadrian.[17] Beth Shean gained an amphitheater, a second bathhouse, a palaestra, a nymphaeum, a basilica, propylaea, colonnaded streets, and plazas in the second century and a theater and a new temple in the next.[18] Both of Samaria's cities saw similar construction. Neapolis (literally a "new city") was overseen by a huge temple to Zeus Olympius built on the northern peak of Mount Gerizim. In the second century, the city received a hippodrome and a large theater, and a century later an amphitheater was built inside the hippodrome.[19] At Sebaste, new buildings, colonnaded streets, a bathhouse, a theater, an aqueduct, and various shrines joined a forum and basilical building that may have dated as early as the first century C.E.[20]

Jerusalem: From Jewish City to Roman Colony

Jerusalem, the most Jewish of cities in the pre-70 C.E. period, was largely reconfigured along Roman lines as the Legio X Fretensis settled in, likely encamping in its western section. As we have seen, the refoundation of the city as Aelia Capitolina helped precipitate the Bar Kokhba Revolt, and the Roman victory in that conflict was followed by the prohibition of Jews from even entering the city. It is uncertain how long this edict was enforced, but it is clear that the city lost its Jewish character, with the rubble of the Second Temple bearing witness to Rome's abolition of the Jewish sacrificial cult. As the city was rebuilt, a new plan emerged that would permanently influence the city's configuration. The famous Madaba Map, a sixth-century mosaic depicting Christian holy sites, provides a stylized but basically accurate depiction of the main streets.[21] A tripartite arched gate underneath today's Damascus Gate was the primary northern entrance to the city. Adjacent to the arch was a square plaza from which two streets extended into the city, the primary cardo toward the Roman camp on the city's southwestern hill (now called Mount Zion) and a secondary one through the Tyropoeon Valley toward the western side of the Temple Mount. The city's main decumanus appears to have followed the route now marked by the Street of the Chain and Da-vid Street. Reused ancient paving stones in secondary usage are still visible in some places. One forum was located north of the Temple Mount, and remnants of its pavement are known as the Lithostratos. Later Christians mistakenly associated its arch with Pilate's presenta-tion of Jesus before the Jerusalem crowd, giving it the name the Ecce Homo ("Behold the man") arch. Another forum was located in the area now known as the Muristan.[22]

The Cultural Setting of Sepphoris

Aside from Jerusalem, Sepphoris perhaps best illustrates the transfor-mation of a modest town into a major urban center, especially among Jewish cities, and for that reason we will consider it in depth. As we have seen, much of the early debate prompted by the renewed excava-tions there in the 1980s focused on the extent to which Herod Antipas had succeeded in rebuilding Sepphoris and making it "the ornament of all Galilee" (*Ant.* 18.27). Some scholars argued that Sepphoris had already become a major urban center by the time of Jesus, with a fully operational theater, the primary components of a Roman civic center, and a vibrant pagan community. One popular treatment in the early 1990s assumed that the city in the time of Antipas and Jesus was in fact full of pagans, depicting a temple on the western summit (despite a complete lack of evidence for that location), suggesting that the the-ater was fully functional, and arguing that Jesus' teachings were influ-enced by his attendance at theatrical events there.[23]

In our view, however, the significant expansion of the site into a major urban center with civic architecture and evidence of a Gen-tile population occurs in the second century. Rather than being an early-first-century structure, the theater was one of a number of pub-lic buildings that were introduced in the second century (fig. 10.5). Hebrew University and Duke University teams excavated significant portions of it in the 1980s, working with the Jewish National Fund to clean it out. They found no data supporting its existence in the time of Jesus, and the head of the Hebrew University team, Zeev Weiss, adheres to a second-century date, as do we.[24] Judging from the coins minted at the site a Capitoline temple was erected during or shortly after the reign of Hadrian (117–138 C.E.), who appointed a Gentile ad-

Fig. 10.5. Theater at Sepphoris (Photo courtesy of
Eric and Carol Meyers)

ministration to run the city. At this time also the Sixth Legion was stationed nearby at Legio. And a major trans-Galilee east–west Roman
road was constructed just north of the site and marked by milestones.
By the reign of Antoninus Pius (138–161 C.E.), the city was renamed
Diocaesarea in honor of Caesar and Zeus.[25] All this is to say that both
the numismatic evidence and the material culture on the ground indicate that the character of Sepphoris dramatically changed in the period after the Second Revolt. The introduction of the theater is coterminous with those changes.

    With room for forty-five hundred spectators, the theater is lo-
cated on the steep northern slope of the western summit and nearly
touches the northern end of the Dionysos mansion, which stands at
the easternmost end of the western summit. Normally one would expect the theater to be in the center of the civic landscape, but at Sepphoris, as at many other places, topography has had as much an influence as the urban grid. Built according to the Roman model, the
theater is seventy-four meters in diameter and has five entrances,
three *vomitoria* around the *cavea,* and two *parodoi* leading to the orchestra. Only the foundations of the *scaena* and the stage survive (thirty-
five by six meters), though many architectural fragments were found,
indicating that the *scaena frons* was elaborately decorated. Large sections of fresco were also recovered indicating that painted lime plas-

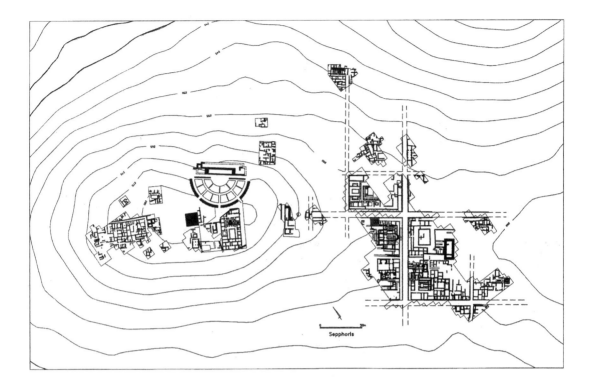

Sepphoris

ter adorned many parts of the theater, as was the case with the eastern *parodos.* The theater went out of use in the fifth century. The theater at Sepphoris is considered midsize and similar to the ones at Sebaste and Gerasa. We should not assume that theater performance in the provinces included classic comedy, tragedy, or satire. No doubt the emphasis would have been on mime, pantomime, and farce. Performances would also have included acrobats, jugglers, and clowns.[26]

Recent work in the Lower City east of the summit has proved beyond any doubt that it became the main focal point of expansion in the second and third centuries (fig. 10.6). Indeed, with the cardo and decumanus there along with major monumental buildings, an eastern bathhouse, a lavishly decorated Roman villa with an Orpheus mosaic, a forum and basilical building, a palatial structure or monumental building identified as a possible library or archive, and most recently a temple and *temenos,* not to mention the shops in the porticoes attached to the major streets, it is hard to overstate the case for major expansion at this time.[27] And there is no doubt that the Lower City was the

Fig. 10.6. Plan of Sepphoris, upper and lower city (Drawing courtesy of Eric and Carol Meyers)

Fig. 10.7. Reconstruction drawing of the House of Dionysos at Sepphoris (Reconstruction drawing courtesy of Leen Ritmeyer)

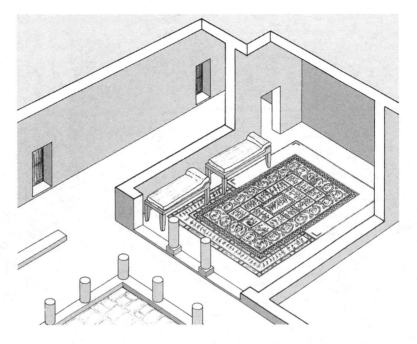

civic center of Sepphoris by the beginning of the second century C.E., and the associated structures there along the two main thoroughfares provide a rare glimpse into the functioning and character of the city in its developmental stage in the Roman period. It is still a bit early to more fully characterize those activities, as the ongoing excavations of the Hebrew University bring to light new material every season.[28]

Nonetheless, for the purposes of our discussion, we choose to focus on the House of Dionysos (fig. 10.7), the large mansion that abuts the theater and stands atop the western summit at its easternmost point. The house is named for the beautiful mosaic carpet in it that has Greek inscriptions and depictions of Dionysos and other mythic figures. Despite its portrayal of Greek deities, the villa lies at the very heart of the area where a distinctive Jewish population has been identified in the Roman period. It is truly an integral part of the domestic complex that is situated on the western summit adjacent to the area of the Duke University excavations, which have uncovered around thirty miqvaot along with other clear signs of Jewish ethnic identity in the domiciles there. Among those other items are stone vessels, lamps with menorot, incense shovels, and even some ostraca and mosaic fragments with Aramaic on them.[29] The combination of classical Greek and Jewish elements makes the house a logical candidate to assess the multicultural aspects of the site. (See plate 13.)

The House of Dionysos is a large palatial mansion, approximately 23 by 48 meters, located just south of the theater. Its northern end was hewn into bedrock. At the very heart of the building is a peristyle courtyard, north of which is a large triclinium or dining room or banquet hall. The northern end has a series of rooms intended for domestic activities, including a latrine and washroom; the floor of the latrine was made of white mosaic with a Greek inscription *hygeia* ("health"), made of black tesserae within a simple frame. A bench in the latrine ran along two walls, and under it there was a drain for sewage. The largest unit of the building is the triclinium, which is bordered by two corridors with rooms to the west and east of them. The function of those rooms is not clear, but they could have been guest rooms. The banquet hall is 9.2 by 6.9 meters and lies just north of the peristyle courtyard; its main entrance was on the south via the three entrances there. A metal grate was found near the northern wall and points to an opening for light and ventilation there. The triclinium was decorated with the lavish mosaic with which we have come to associate the name of this house. The mosaic is T-shaped, and those seated or reclining on *klinae,* or banquettes, in the plain white portion of the mosaic could view the scenes in the rest of the mosaic from their positions. In a way the mosaic carpet constituted a form of entertainment for those gathered around; they could look at the various panels and scenes and talk about them. To the south of the dining area was the peristyle courtyard, which measured 14.5 by 11.6 meters, flanked by colonnades on three sides. The central part was paved with flagstones and its aisles with mosaics poorly preserved. The building also had a southern wing, beyond the courtyard built on two levels, the lower one declining with the slope to the south. This section of the building is least well preserved and is 22.5 by 12.5 meters.

The date of the Dionysos mansion was determined by careful excavations and examination of the coins sealed under the mosaic floor and in key portions of the foundations of the villa along with the pottery found in key probes throughout the building. Its dating is consistent with the chronology for the expansion of the civic center in the Lower City. All of the pottery collected from these probes may

Fig. 10.8. Part of the mosaic floor at the Dionysos mansion. At left is a triumphal "procession" of Dionysos: the young god is seated in a chariot and holds a sacred staff, accompanied by two satyrs playing the double-flute. The panel at right depicts the drunkenness of a bearded Herakles, whose club rests on a table at left as he is held by a female follower (Maenad) and male follower (Satyr). (Photo courtesy of Eric and Carol Meyers)

be dated to the early and middle Roman periods, first to third centuries C.E. The early Roman pottery and some of the earlier coins along with older fresco fragments suggest that there was some other structure(s) here before the Dionysos house was built. The date of its construction based on all of the above along with stylistic and architectural considerations is the late second century or early third century C.E. The House of Dionysos with its famous mosaic is thus dated to precisely the time when Rabbi Judah the Patriarch, Ha-Nasi, is said to have lived at the site during the reign of Caracalla (198–217 C.E.). Rabbi Judah is credited with editing or overseeing the publication of the Mishnah at Sepphoris at this time, which was the major literary achievement of the Jewish community after the Bible.

The villa was in continuous use throughout the Roman period, until it was destroyed in a great earthquake in 363 C.E. The destruction debris in the building was unmistakable: brownish orange to brownish gray earth with large quantities of fallen ashlars in it, along with many fallen architectural elements. None of the many coins found in the debris dates later than the time of Constantius II (351–361 C.E.).[30] This timeline for the duration of the house is also consistent with the picture we have of the domestic area on the western summit, which also suffered great damage as a result of the earthquake of 363 C.E. More than anything else this conflagration marks the end of the Roman era, which was followed by an equally expansive and flourishing time, the Byzantine era, during which Christianity became far more visible and influential.[31]

We turn now to the wonderful mosaic itself, which captures so much of the cosmopolitan or Greco-Roman atmosphere of the city in the third century. (See plates 14–17.) The central panel of the mosaic features the drinking party or symposium between Dionysos and Herakles with fifteen surrounding panels. Several of those panels also feature aspects of Dionysos's role as a deity of feasting, drinking, fertility, and revelry. The Greek labels that accompany most scenes facilitate our understanding of the individual panels, as in the case of the word "drunkenness," which is attached to a scene of the bearded hero Herakles in a drunken stupor, attended by two devotees (fig. 10.8). Do the labels presuppose that only Greek speakers dined here, or do they suggest a bilingual audience and that they served to introduce or guide the visitor to understand the meaning of the legend or myth? Or are they merely reflections of the dominance of Greek for all sorts of inscriptions in the Hellenistic East? If the latter, then we might infer that they were more decorative than meaningful. But we will return to this issue in a bit. Surrounding the fifteen Dionysos panels is a frame of twenty-two acanthus-leaf medallions with a background of black tesserae. The depictions in them feature hunting scenes with wild animals and naked *erotes,* or cupids, often holding bow and arrow. On the two ends, north and south, the bust of a female is presented, the one on the north described as a masterpiece of mosaic art and labeled by journalists "the Mona Lisa of the Galilee" (fig. 10.9).[32] The third component of the mosaic carpet is the border or U-band panels, one across the southern end, the others on the eastern and western sides. The southern panel features a Nilotic scene, quite charming but of an early Byzantine date representing a repair and quite out of character with the rest of the mosaic. The western decorative panel contained a procession of mortals preparing for Dionysiac festivities. The eastern panel is less well preserved and presents other aspects of the Dionysiac procession: a boy rides a gray goat and in front of him a woman plays the *aulos* (fig. 10.10). What is most interesting is the dis-

Fig. 10.9. The "Mona Lisa of the Galilee": detail (possibly Aphrodite) from the mosaic in the House of Dionysos (Photo courtesy of Eric and Carol Meyers)

Fig. 10.10. From the Dionysos mosaic, a Dionysiac procession depicts a young man mounted on an ass being led by a man to the right. In the center is a man carrying two wicker baskets filled with grapes and greenish leaves. At right a woman in a red tunic clasps a duck. (Photo courtesy of Eric and Carol Meyers)

cussion of the meaning and intent of the mosaic and the question of who lived in this house. To these matters we now turn.

The mosaic's rich iconographic program may have been intended as more than sheer ornamentation. Even if we assume that visitors to the room were ignorant of the contents and meaning, the Greek labels assist at the very least in identifying many of the main themes of the life and myth surrounding Dionysos. The U-shaped side panels, in addition, seem to promote the celebration of the Dionysiac mysteries; and the dominant motif of the Symposium and drinking may serve to advance the idea that it is good to maintain a balance between moderate and excessive drinking. It is noteworthy that Rina Talgam and Zeev Weiss in their presentation of the mosaic ultimately disagree about who might have lived in and used the villa. It is to their credit that they present opposing ideas in the hopes of broadening the discussion about visual materials so laden with iconography.[33] Their disagreement provides an opportunity to further explore the dynamics of urban life in Sepphoris at a key moment in its history.

The siting of the villa on the eastern end of a domestic area that was exclusively Jewish, overlooking the theater to the north, raises all sorts of issues. The size and magnificence of the mansion, not to mention the content and themes of the mosaic, suggest that a person of power and substance lived there; or it could have been a kind of guesthouse and place of residence for some sort of official. The most important resident of Sepphoris at the time of its construction was Rabbi Judah the Patriarch, and although there is no specific information that can assure us that he lived there, Weiss at least leaves open the possibility that he did.[34] Talgam on the other hand says that the mosaic's iconographic program is so sophisticated that it obliges us to accept that it was built by pagans for pagans. Weiss believes that the decision to build an elaborate new mansion near the Jewish quarter and away from the civic center implies a conscious desire to be close to the Jewish area, and this interpretation is one among several that should be given serious consideration. Indeed, the life of Rabbi Judah is such that not only was he involved in a major publication enterprise of rabbinic literature at this time but rabbinic legend claims that he was friends with the Roman emperor, Caracalla, who was well disposed to the Jewish community.

It is not entirely clear if the municipal government reverted to Jewish control at this time, but a coin or medallion minted at Sepphoris and featuring Caracalla commemorates an accord between the Roman Senate and the city that hints at such a change (fig. 10.11).[35] Yaakov Meshorer has pointed to the fact that the boule at this time consisted of numerous individuals including Jews—the Talmud of the Land of Israel calls them boulevtim—and suggests that the boule might even have been the Sanhedrin, a reading of the coin legend that is disputed by a few.[36] Given the location of the House of Dionysos in a Jewish domestic area and the likelihood that its extravagance had few if any parallels elsewhere in the city, one can imagine that Rabbi Judah was familiar with it or perhaps even that the municipal council met in it. All of this suggests that just sixty-five years after the Second War with Rome the Jewish community was very much at peace with Rome and completely at home with the Greco-Roman culture of that world.

The presence of so much pagan art in the city at the time of Rabbi Judah has even led at least one major scholar, Sacha Stern, to suggest that the Patriarch sacrificed in behalf of the Roman emperor, citing a rabbinic source.[37] The textual reference, while quite explicit in its use of the term *maqrivim,* "to sacrifice," depends on much ancil-

Fig. 10.11. A medallion and coin commemorating a treaty of friendship and alliance between the Holy Council of Sepphoris and the Senate and people of Rome, depicting the emperor Caracalla (Copyright David Hendin, used by permission)

Fig. 10.12. Two minia-
ture statuettes found in a
domestic area of Sepphoris:
Prometheus, with an eagle
tearing at his liver, and Pan,
holding a musical instrument
in his right hand and a stylized cluster of grapes in his
left. Pointed ears mark this
figure as the young shepherd
god. (Photo courtesy of Eric
and Carol Meyers)

lary material found at the site in Jewish contexts, such as the bronze
statues of Pan and Prometheus, which though found in a Jewish context do not necessarily indicate Jewish worship of those deities (fig.
10.12). Stern's view of the background of Rabbi Judah, however, as
a local Galilean aristocrat, is more to the point.[38] Stern points out in
this regard that in Asia Minor local leaders would be expected to offer
sacrifices to the local cult, and as a local leader, Rabbi Judah might be
expected to have acted in the same manner, especially in light of the
textual support he identifies.

Whatever the case may be, we need not conclude that whoever
sponsored the mosaic was necessarily as informed about the Dionysos
cult and myth as was the designer himself. Such themes were popular throughout the Roman world and are most appropriate in the context in which we have found them. It is less important to determine
whether Rabbi Judah lived in the House of Dionysos than to recognize that he was at home and comfortable in the Romanized world in
which he lived. Moreover, in the urban environment of third-century
Palestine, Sepphoris was a logical place to undertake the challenge of
organizing and redacting the rabbinic literature of the day. Always an
elite activity, it hardly could have taken place in a small agricultural

Fig. 10.13. Roman-period lamps from Sepphoris depicting human and mythological figures (Photo courtesy of Eric and Carol Meyers)

hamlet or village. The synergy created by the Greco-Roman environment, with its multicultural and energetic civic programs, was the only kind of setting in which such literary activity could have occurred.

The elite character of the summit as an excellent place to live is also borne out by the upscale nature of a number of the domiciles in the Jewish quarter. The houses contemporary with the House of Dionysos produced hundreds of discus lamps decorated with human and mythological figures as well as erotic scenes (fig. 10.13).[39] Several houses produced large numbers of ceramic incense shovels, which may testify to the priestly background of some of the inhabitants; the shovels were probably used for the purposes of fumigation, while at the same time maintaining their symbolic value as a reminiscence of the priestly class.[40] The size of the domiciles also testifies to their relative elegance—though all were devoid of mosaics in the third-century phases—with some approaching the size of the large houses in Jerusalem.[41] All of the houses had ritual baths along with a regular supply of stone vessels, and some of the lamps recovered had menorot on them and one had a Torah Shrine. These Jewish symbols were found right alongside erotic art on discus lamps and miniature bronze statues of Pan and Prometheus. The occupants of these domiciles on the western summit were completely at home in the contemporary Greco-Roman culture that came to dominate the urban landscape in the middle Roman period.

The Rabbis and Greco-Roman Art

The case of Sepphoris and the opulent mosaic from the House of Dionysos, not to mention the rich array of pagan imagery that we find on terra-cotta lamps, bronze statues, and so on in Jewish areas of the site, raises the issue of what the rabbis' attitude to figurative art was in the rabbinic period. The older view of the situation is that it was in violation of the Second Commandment, a view held even till very recently in the Jewish community that most often understands itself as being heir to a legacy in writing and books and not heir to a rich visual legacy.[42] A text from *m. Avodah Zarah* 3:4 provides an entry point to a brief discussion of this issue.

> Proklus, the son of Philosophus, asked Rabban Gamaliel who was bathing in Acco in the bathhouse of Aphrodite. He said to him: "It is written in your Torah, 'and nothing of the devoted [forbidden] thing should leave to your hand'" [Deut 13:18]. "Why are you bathing in the bathhouse of Aphrodite?" He answered him: "One ought not respond in a bathhouse." When he came out Rabban Gamaliel said to him: "I did not come into her borders, she came into mine! People do not say, 'Let us make a bath for Aphrodite,' but rather, 'Let us make Aphrodite an ornament for the bath.' Moreover, even if they would give you a large sum of money, you would not approach your idol naked and suffering pollutions, and urinate before it; yet this goddess stands at the mouth of a gutter and all the people urinate before her.[43]

We are not sure whether such a conversation ever occurred, and we do not know who Proklus was or even whether he was Jewish or

Fig. 10.14. Burial catacomb (Catacomb 14) of Rabbi Judah the Patriarch, at Beth Shearim (Photo courtesy of Todd Bolen/BiblePlaces.com)

not. The text, however, is tannaitic and from the time of Rabbi Judah. Rabban Gamaliel was an early tannaitic sage who lived in the mid–first century C.E. and was titular leader of the rabbinical caste. The point of the story is to indicate the limits of participation in Gentile, idolatrous society. So long as the statue of Aphrodite was decorative in the bathhouse, especially since it is placed next to a public urinal, Rabban Gamaliel's bathing next to it cannot be assumed to have been idolatrous.[44] That the sage was comfortable going to a public bathhouse is never in doubt. Even though the rabbinic tractate *Avodah Zarah* goes into minute detail about the idolatrous practices of the Gentile community, so long as Jews were not in danger of participating in them it was permitted. Judging from the above text and the teachings of the rabbis on this subject, their attitude toward pagans and paganism in general must have been fairly tolerant.

The Jewish village and necropolis of Beth Shearim offers an instructive case in respect to the acceptance level in rabbinic circles of pagan art. The site was the original home of Rabbi Judah the Patriarch before he moved to Sepphoris when he became ill; and he was buried there along with many of the sages of the country. From that time forward, early third century C.E., the necropolis at Beth Shearim became the main location for the burial of the sages (fig. 10.14). The major excavations there were carried out in the 1950s by the Israel Exploration Society and Hebrew University.[45] The finds date mainly to between the second and fourth centuries C.E. The walls of the catacombs as well as many of the carved sarcophagi present a world of art that is full of pagan images in both naive art form and highly developed sculpted form as well. Many of the decorative motifs are borrowed from Roman funerary art. Among the most common are hanging wreaths, heraldic eagles, and schematic heads of bulls, hunting scenes, and a bearded figure depicting a Greek god.[46] Among the most dramatic portrayals is that of Leda and the Swan in relief on a sarcophagus from the mausoleum of catacomb 11 (fig. 10.15). It is worth noting that in catacomb 14, where Rabbi Judah is buried, there are no images of humans or animals, though many of the coffins are very costly in execution and many have elaborate decorative motifs. Nonetheless in other catacombs in the necropolis figural images including those of humans abound, and animals are very common. In the large mausoleum adjoining catacomb 11, aboveground and in full view for all to see, lions, an eagle, and wolves are carved in full relief in the decorative arch of the entrance.[47] This shows that there was a

Fig. 10.15. Burial sarcophagus depicting the myth of Leda and the Swan, Beth Shearim (Photo courtesy of Todd Bolen/BiblePlaces.com)

range of attitudes toward visual art at Beth Shearim. The burial place of Rabbi Judah in particular suggests that there was even a significant difference between his home at Sepphoris, which was among the most Greco-Roman cities of Palestine, with pagan images common in Jewish contexts, and his immediate subterranean environment in catacomb 14, which was decorated in a more conservative style lacking in figural art. We should also mention that among the Jewish symbols found in the tomb chambers the menorah and Torah Shrine are attested, the menorah being the most common.

In sum, we may understand the urbanization and Hellenization of the Holy Land after the two devastating wars with Rome in a more positive light when we take into account the case study of Sepphoris and in general the creativity of the Jewish people during this era of recovery, as is evidenced at Beth Shearim. What happened in the second and third centuries c.e. is not unlike what happened in the period after the first destruction of the Jerusalem Temple by the Neo-Babylonians in 586 b.c.e. One of the results of that tragedy was the editing of the Primary History, a first edition of the Hebrew Bible if you will (Genesis to 2 Kings). Moreover, the seventy years in Exile then also allowed the Jewish community to learn to live in the Diaspora without the Temple and to develop new ways of approaching God, among them being prayer in small gatherings that led to the development of the synagogue. Similarly, in the context of a new form of Roman rule, despite the bitter past, the Jewish community in those centuries after the two revolts made peace with Rome and with themselves. The dominant Greco-Roman culture of the day provided fertile ground in which literary and spiritual developments could flourish. The codification of the Mishnah and the appearance of rabbinic commentaries by the beginning of the third century c.e. were only some of the signs of the positive response to tragedy. Over time the Jewish community also codified its teachings into the Talmud of the Land of Israel, which by the end of the fourth century had taken full shape, despite the negative impact of the great earthquake of 363 c.e. and the resulting demographic decline.[48] That the Jewish community's creativity occurred in the larger context of the Roman Empire, with its Greco-Roman cultural ambiance, should not be surprising. In defining themselves against the Other, Jews learned also how to define themselves in their own rich cultural heritage. The rise of imperial Christianity after the victory of Constantine the Great in 312 C.E. hardly resulted in a period of decline for the Jewish community in the Holy Land either.[49] Rather, despite new restrictions against synagogue building, Jews began to decorate their synagogues with colorful mosaics, often with pagan motifs such as the zodiac. And despite a ban against Jews serving in public office and other restrictions in the Byzantine era, the Jewish community in ancient Palestine thrived well into late antiquity, till the dawn of the medieval period.

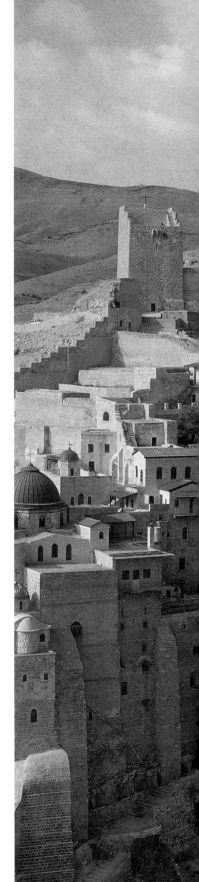

CHAPTER 11

After Constantine
Beyond the Roman Period

When the armies of Constantine and Maxentius clashed at the Milvan Bridge in 312 C.E., it must have seemed to participants and observers alike as simply the most recent in the long list of battles for Rome's throne. Constantine's victory outside the city's walls, however, had repercussions that few could have fully anticipated, because it marked the beginning of the political accession of the church and the decline of Greco-Roman paganism (fig. 11.1). From early in his rule, Constantine very deliberately positioned himself as the protector and benefactor of particular expressions of Christianity, and his admirers attributed his success at the Milvan Bridge to a vision he received from the Christian god on the eve of the battle. The following year, he and Licinius, the co-emperor who ruled the Roman East, met in Milan and issued the famous Edict of Toleration, reversing Diocletian's policies of persecution of Christians and officially legalizing the religion. In 324 C.E., Constantine emerged victorious from a civil war with Licinius, gaining control of both halves of the empire and bringing Palestine into his domain. The centuries between his reign and the Arab conquest are known as the Byzantine period, so-called because of his transfer of the imperial capital to the ancient city of Byzantium, which he refounded as Constantinople. Constantine's Christian sympathies resulted in radical changes in Palestine's landscape. It shifted from being one province among many to being the center of the empire's sacred geography. The fact that Palestine was home to the places where Jesus had walked, worked, and died as well as the setting for other biblical stories and characters gave it special status as the "Holy Land."[1]

The Church of the Holy Sepulcher and the other churches Constantine built in conjunction with his mother Helena's visit were the first of many, as the veneration of holy sites evolved to include the cult of the saints and their relics (fig. 11.2). By the end of the Byzan-

Fig. 11.1. Bronze coin of Constantine the Great, minted in Constantinople. Constantine appears on the obverse with titles in Latin, and the reverse has the inscription "GLORIA EXERCITVS" [Glory of the Army]. (Copyright David Hendin, used by permission)

Fig. 11.2. Church of the Holy Sepulcher today (Photo courtesy of Sean Burrus)

tine period, approximately four hundred churches and chapels had appeared in Palestine and Jordan. This network at first served primarily the needs of pilgrims. As more and more of those pilgrims chose to remain in the land of the Bible, churches were increasingly built for parish use. Some pilgrims were ascetic monks whose withdrawal from society led to the creation of over one hundred monasteries, particularly in the desert regions. In terms of Christianity's visibility and prominence in the region's material culture, the difference from the previous three centuries is notable.[2]

Other examples of the increasingly visible displays of distinctively Christian identity included inscriptions and Christian symbols, most notably the cross. Such expressions often vividly displayed the ongoing influence of Roman culture. When Christians epigraphically honored their leaders, public figures, and key benefactors and epigraphically memorialized the dead, they were appropriating a largely Roman custom, just as Jews were doing. Interestingly, Greek retained its place as the epigraphic language of choice and Latin largely faded from use. The mosaic floors of churches and other buildings reflected considerable continuity with the artistic themes of preceding centuries, although the appearance of biblical characters in a few cases, such as Jonah on a floor at Beth Guvrin, marked a new development. A small number of churches were organized according to a wholly new architectural schema, the shape of a cross, but most reflected an adaptation of Roman sensibilities. A handful had octagonal or circular designs, seemingly influenced by the form of Roman mausolea and perhaps round palaces. Despite their variations (single or multiple apses, the number of columned aisles, the presence or absence of a narthex), the overwhelming majority were in the rectangular shape characteristic of the Roman basilica, a form so dominant that the term itself ultimately became thoroughly associated with church architecture.

Although the emergence of architecturally distinct synagogues had begun in the Roman period, it was the Byzantine period that witnessed their widespread proliferation. Over one hundred were built, and not even an imperial edict in the sixth century prohibiting their construction seems to have slowed down the building boom (fig. 11.3). Although the designs of these synagogues varied, particularly in the placement of the entrances (on the wall facing Jerusalem or opposite it) and focal points of worship (on a long wall or short one), they, too, reflected an adaptation of existing architectural forms, both the basilica and, in some cases, pagan temples. To some extent, their architecture developed in dialogue with the newly appearing church buildings, as well. Their mosaic floors, like those of churches, reflected further evolution from the designs of the Roman period. To the modern observer steeped in the overly simplistic view of Judaism as aniconic, one of the most striking features of some of these mosaics is the comfort with figural depictions, whether of Abraham and Isaac or Helios and the signs of the zodiac, images sometimes placed on the same mosaic. Perhaps because of their need to define and express Jewish identity in a context in which a rival religious group with its own very different interpretation of Jewish history was dominant politically, Jews made even more frequent use of symbols. Menorahs, Torah shrines, and images such as the shofar, the lulav, the ethrog, and incense shovels appear frequently in mosaics, reliefs, carvings, and elsewhere. Jews also made increasing use of inscriptions, most notably in synagogue and funerary contexts, although in contrast to Christians they used Aramaic and Hebrew scripts alongside Greek. Similarly, Samaritan inscriptions employed Samaritan.[3]

These trends are exemplified by the fourth-century synagogue at Hammath Tiberias that was built atop a Roman-period public building of some sort. The synagogue contains Aramaic, Hebrew, and Greek

Fig. 11.3. A lintel from the synagogue at Nabratein, with Aramaic inscription dating the rededication of synagogue to "494 years after the destruction (of the Temple)," or 564 C.E. (Photo courtesy of Eric and Carol Meyers)

inscriptions and Jewish and astrological symbols. Its large mosaic floor includes a panel with a circle of figures representing the twelve signs of the zodiac, each identified with a Hebrew label. At the center of the signs is Helios the sun god and his chariot, while depictions of the Four Seasons, also accompanied by Hebrew inscriptions, adjoin the outside of the circle. Jews gathering in this synagogue to worship were clearly not troubled by figural representation, even of a mythological figure like Helios. The panel north of the zodiac shows a Greek donor list flanked by two lions, while the opposite panel depicts a Torah shrine between two menorahs, a shofar, an incense shovel, a lulav, an ethrog, and myrtle and willow branches. On this floor, Jewish identity is represented by both this latter cluster of what were becoming classic Jewish symbols as well as the comfortable appropriation of Hellenistic and astrological imagery. In the fifth century, a basilical synagogue replaced the fourth-century broadhouse plan.[4]

In sheer numbers, both synagogues and churches became far more common in Palestine than pagan temples had ever been. Temples had appeared primarily in sizable cities, although occasionally in more rural settings. Synagogues and churches, however, were a part of the landscape in both major cities and minor villages, in areas of both dense and relatively sparse settlement. Even small communities might have multiple churches or synagogues. Both Judaism and Christianity integrated worship, public assembly, and monumental display at the level of individual communities in ways unprecedented for the region (fig. 11.4).

The ubiquity of these buildings and the heightened use of inscriptions and symbols make it far easier to map out approximate ethnic

zones of settlement for the Byzantine period than for the Roman. The greatest number of churches is clustered around Jerusalem and Bethlehem, although many are found in other regions as well. Synagogues, too, appear in a variety of locales, and the significant number in Judea indicates that Jews never fully abandoned the region. Most, however, appear in eastern Galilee and, to a lesser extent, the Lower Golan, reflecting the demographic shift of Jewish life northward after the two revolts. Galilee continued to be the primary home of the emerging rabbinic movement, whose presence is attested in occasional inscriptions using the title "rabbi." In western Galilee, churches seem to mark the limit of Jewish settlement.[5] Pagans were widely dispersed, although perhaps most visibly present in the coastal cities. In some communities, Jews, Samaritans, Christians, and pagans lived side by side (fig. 11.5). Capernaum provides one of the more enduring examples of coexistence, its fifth-century basalt octagonal church just a short walk away from the gleaming white limestone synagogue (fig. 11.6).

Fig. 11.4. Mar Saba Monastery, Judean Desert, founded fifth century C.E. (Photo courtesy of Todd Bolen/ BiblePlaces.com)

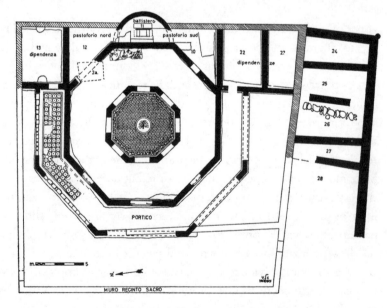

Fig. 11.5. Aerial view of an
ancient synagogue and a
contemporary church built
above an ancient ruin from the
fifth century C.E. at Capernaum (Photo courtesy of Todd
Bolen/BiblePlaces.com)

Fig. 11.6. Plan of a fifth-
century octagonal church at
Capernaum built above the
domus ecclesiae (Courtesy of
the Franciscan Printing Press,
Jerusalem)

Judaism and Christianity also expressed their vitality through a remarkable level of literary output. Sepphoris and Tiberias were particularly important hosts to influential groups of scholars, but cities outside Galilee like Caesarea Maritima and Lod were also hubs of rabbinic thought. The processes of gathering, synthesizing, and editing oral traditions into written texts that had been witnessed earlier in the compilation of the Mishnah continued. In the late third and the early fourth century, Galilean rabbis collected traditions that were not included in the Mishnah but were thought nonetheless to have emanated from early rabbis, organizing them into a collection known as the Tosefta (literally, "the supplement") that was designed to illuminate the topics discussed in the Mishnah. An even more influential companion to the Mishnah took shape at the end of the fourth century c.e.: the Talmud of the Land of Israel, also called the Yerushalmi or Jerusalem Talmud. In a sense, this monumental text is misnamed, for the rabbis who compiled it were largely based in Galilee, not Jerusalem. They drew mostly from traditions associated with the rabbis of Palestine, but the inclusion of materials from rabbis in Babylonia demonstrates that the two rabbinic communities were each aware of discussions occurring in the other. The Talmud of the Land of Israel anticipated by approximately a century the emergence of the Talmud Bavli, or Babylonian Talmud, from rabbis to the east. The two Talmuds would prove enormously influential for subsequent rabbinic Judaism. Other forms of Jewish literary activity also flourished. Some of the Targumim, translations of biblical books from Hebrew to the more widely spoken Aramaic, had appeared in the Roman period, but their editing continued in the Byzantine era. Midrashim, interpretive works focusing on particular biblical books, continued to be produced, reflecting the teaching found in synagogues, and *piyyutim,* poems designed for liturgical use, were crafted.[6]

The Christian texts produced in Byzantine Palestine did not prove as foundational for the Christian tradition as did the rabbinic texts for Judaism, but they were important nonetheless. Eusebius's career, for example, extended into the early decades of the Byzantine period. Serving as bishop of Caesarea Maritima, he was aware of the importance of the rabbinic community in his city, and his writings show that he was sometimes in touch with Jewish scholars. As the canon of the New Testament became more fixed, scholars like Eusebius pro-

Fig. 11.7. Interior of the Byzantine Church of the Nativity,
Bethlehem (Photo courtesy
of Todd Bolen/BiblePlaces.
com)

Fig. 11.7. Interior of the Byzantine Church of the Nativity,
Bethlehem (Photo courtesy
of Todd Bolen/BiblePlaces.
com)

duced aids to help biblical interpreters. The Eusebian canons reflect
the bishop's division of the four Gospels into single-story units; biblical manuscripts would preserve them for centuries. His *Onomasticon*
was a gazetteer of places mentioned in the Bible, offering topographi-
cal and historical information about each of them. Perhaps the best
known of his works are *Church History* and *The Life of Constantine,* two
of the most important sources for reconstructing the early centuries of
Christian history. Another especially influential Christian scholar of
the Holy Land was Jerome, who spent the last thirty-five years or so
of his life in a monastery in Bethlehem (fig. 11.7). He produced numerous commentaries, letters, and other works, but it was his translation of the Bible into Latin that had the most significant impact.
Known as the Vulgate, his translation would serve as the authoritative
version of the Bible for what became known as the Roman Catholic
Church. Other important Christian writers included Cyril of Jerusalem, Procopius of Gaza, John Malalas, and Cyril of Scythopolis.[7]

As for the pagan cults, they yielded to the imperial sponsorship
of Christianity, although their demise was a slow one. Over time, most
temples were simply shut down or abandoned. Worship at the cultic
sites at Banias, for example, seems to have largely ceased around the

end of the fourth century, and the site of the old temple of Augustus and Roma at Caesarea Maritima served as the platform for a new octagonal church. A few temples were destroyed, such as the one razed to allow the construction of the Church of the Holy Sepulcher and the shrine to Marnas at Gaza, which was replaced by a church honoring Empress Eudocia at the beginning of the fifth century. Architectural fragments from derelict temples often found their way into churches and other buildings as spolia, tangibly reflecting the adaptation of the cultural elements of the past in a new era.[8]

By the time of the Persian invasion in 614, paganism seems to have largely faded away, completing the process set in motion three hundred years earlier by Constantine (fig. 11.8). Byzantine forces were able to rout the Persians in 628, but they were unable to withstand the Arab armies that approached soon thereafter. Jerusalem surrendered to Arab forces in 638, and Caesarea Maritima, the last holdout of the Byzantines, fell just a few years later. Thus began yet another transformation of the region's material culture and the imposition once again of a new framework of sacred geography upon the ancient landscape.

Fig. 11.8. Bust of Constantine in marble, from the Consistory Palace in Rome (Photo courtesy of Dennis E. Groh, ASOR Archive)

Abbreviations

Ant.	Josephus, *Jewish Antiquities*
BA	*Biblical Archaeologist*
BAR	*Biblical Archaeology Review*
BASOR	*Bulletin of the American Schools of Oriental Research*
IEJ	*Israel Exploration Quarterly*
INJ	*Israel Numismatic Journal*
JBL	*Journal of Biblical Literature*
JJS	*Journal of Jewish Studies*
JSJ	*Journal for the Study of Judaism in the Persian, Hellenistic, and Roman Periods*
Life	Josephus, *The Life*
NEA	*Near Eastern Archaeology*
NEAEHL	Ephraim Stern et al., eds., *The New Encyclopedia of Archaeological Excavations in the Holy Land,* vols. 1–4 (Jerusalem: The Israel Exploration Society and Carta; New York: Simon and Schuster, 1993), vol. 5 (Jerusalem: The Israel Exploration Society; Washington, D.C.: Biblical Archaeology Society, 2008)
NTS	*New Testament Studies*
OEANE	Eric M. Meyers, ed., *The Oxford Encyclopedia of Archaeology in the Near East,* 5 vols. (New York: Oxford University Press, 1997)
PEQ	*Palestine Exploration Quarterly*
QDAP	*Quarterly of the Department of the Antiquities in Palestine*
TA	*Tel Aviv*
War	Josephus, *The Jewish War*
ZDPV	*Zeitschrift des Deutschen Palästina-Vereins*
ZPE	*Zeitschrift für Papyrologie und Epigraphik*

In citing biblical, rabbinic, and other ancient sources, we have generally used abbreviations and formatting instructions in Patrick H. Alexander et al., eds., *The SBL Handbook of Style for Ancient Near Eastern, Biblical, and Early Christian Studies* (Peabody, Mass.: Hendrickson, 1999). Quotations from the Bible generally use the New Revised Standard Version, although in some cases the translations are our own.

Notes

Chapter 1. The Persian Period and the Transition to Hellenism

1. Oded Lipschits reviews this data and offers his own position in his most recent article, "Persian Period Finds." Ronny Reich in his assessment of the extent of Persian-period remains in Jerusalem puts it this way: "The archaeological record, in any case, shows a limited settlement during this period, crowded on the City of David Hill only. . . . The small size of the settlement in Jerusalem continued to give the character of a small town, and perhaps even less than that" (*Excavating the City of David,* 321).

2. J. P. Weinberg was responsible for the high estimate after publication of his influential article, "Demographische Notizen." Charles Carter's monograph in 1999 began a period of reassessment and lower estimates for the city and province (*Emergence of Yehud in the Persian Period,* 1999).

3. Lipschits, "Persian Period Finds," 3.

4. Finkelstein, "Jerusalem in the Persian (and Early Hellenistic) Period," 501–7.

5. Finkelstein, "The Territorial Extent and Demography of Yehud/Judea," 54.

6. Lipschits, "Persian Period Finds," 20. Although Lipschits's figures on all of the province of Yehud are not yet available, it is fair to say they would be considerably higher than Finkelstein's.

7. Albright, *Archaeology of Palestine,* 143.

8. Stern, *Material Culture of the Land of the Bible in the Persian Period,* 232.

9. C. L. Meyers and E. M. Meyers, "Persian Period at Sepphoris," 141.

10. Stern, *Dor: Ruler of the Seas,* 157–64, 201ff.

11. Ball, *Rome in the East,* 248–55.

12. For a comprehensive overview of the material culture of this period, see Betlyon, "A People Transformed," and the spread within that article on Attic pottery by S. Rebecca Martin on 24–25.

13. Gitler, "Coins."

14. For an older but mostly reliable treatment of this corpus see Meshorer, *Ancient Jewish Coinage,* vol. 1, 13–34, and Hendin, *Guide to Biblical Coins,* 113–15.

15. We should not confuse the Attic standard with the weight of Persian-period Yehud coins, which varied with the image on them. For example, silver coins with the Athenian owl on them weighed 0.48 grams and those with the Persian king on them 0.26 grams. These weights correspond to a *gerah* or half-gerah (one gerah = 0.475

grams), 12 of which equal the half-shekel that was used to pay the temple tax (Hendin, *Biblical Coins,* 115–16).

16. E. Meyers, "Shelomit Seal." Unfortunately this corpus of seals was purchased on the open market and hence technically is unprovenanced. No scholar to the best of our knowledge has questioned their authenticity to date.

17. Avigad, *Bullae and Seals.*

18. Oded Lipschits and David Vanderhooft's monograph on the subject, *Yehud Stamp Impressions: A Corpus of Inscribed Stamp Impressions from the Persian and Hellenistic Periods in Judah,* appeared recently in 2011 from Eisenbrauns, but also see their article "A New Typology of Yehud Stamp Impressions," where they lay out a typology for understanding seventeen different subtypes from the Persian to the early Hellenistic periods. Hillel Geva presents the data from Jerusalem and dates the paleo-Hebrew examples to the beginning of the Hasmonean period in "Chronological Reevaluation of Yehud Stamp Impressions."

19. See Lipschits, Gadot, Arubas, and Oeming, "Ramat Rahel and Its Secrets" and "Palace and Village, Paradise and Oblivion."

20. Stern, "Persian Empire and the Political and Social History of Palestine," 70–87, especially 76, and Barag, "Effects of the Tennes Rebellion."

21. Cross, Jr., "Papyri and Their Historical Implications." Wright had proposed that Shechem was destroyed at this time; Stern disagrees and says there is no sign of it (*Archaeology of the Land of the Bible,* 424–28).

22. Bialik and Ravnitsky, *Book of Legends,* 166–68.

23. Rainey and Notley, *Sacred Bridge,* 298.

24. Stern and Magen, "Archaeological Evidence."

25. Campbell, "Shechem," and Avigad, "Samaria," 1306–7.

Chapter 2. The Advent of Hellenism Under the Greek Kingdoms and the Hasmoneans

1. Green and Lattimore, *Complete Greek Tragedies,* 80.

2. Gruen, *Heritage and Hellenism,* xiv.

3. Zangenberg and Van De Zande, "Urbanization," 166.

4. Tal, *Archaeology of Hellenistic Palestine,* 15–38, especially charts on pages 29 and 34.

5. For a convenient and concise summary of their contents and their relevance to Jewish affairs see Grabbe, *Judaic Religion in the Second Temple Period,* 39–40.

6. Zenon papyrus translation courtesy of the Duke University Databank of Documentary Papyri, series P.Col., vol. 4, 66, Letter of a Non-Greek Complaining About Wages and Contemptuous Treatment (http://papyri.info/ddbdp/p.col;4;66).

7. Anything consumed in connection with pagan worship was forbidden to Jews, and because wine was so frequently associated with idolatrous practice a strict prohibition against Gentile wine was enacted in rabbinic times, though its date of origin is assigned to Hellenistic times and the Men of the Great Assembly (*b. Shabbat* 17b).

8. An excellent survey of the Hellenistic period, slightly out of date but still very useful, may be found in Berlin, "Between Large Forces."

9. C. Meyers and E. Meyers, *Haggai, Zechariah,* 340–43, especially chart 13 on 342.

10. Mazar, "The Tobiads," 141.

11. Zayadine, "Iraq el-Emir"; Berlin, "Archaeological Sources for the History of Palestine," 12.

12. For a brief summary of the Septuagint and its significance see Grabbe, *Judaic Religion in the Second Temple Period,* 49–50. It should be noted also that the Septuagint text type is well represented at Khirbet Qumran, where the Dead Seas Scrolls were recovered. In some examples the Greek version found represents not only a different text type from the Masoretic text but an altogether different version, as is the case with Jeremiah, Job, and Proverbs.

13. For a more recent discussion of the Septuagint, see Rajak, *Translation and Survival.*

14. The fragmentary copy of the Hebrew of Ben Sira was found at Masada in 1964 and may be dated to the pre-Herodian or middle to late Hasmonean period (Yadin, *Ben Sira Scroll*).

15. Meshorer, *Ancient Jewish Coinage,* volume 1, 14–34.

16. Geraty, "Khirbet el-Kom Bilingual Ostracon."

17. An older, outdated treatment of this subject is a Ph.D. dissertation by James Christoph, "The Yehud Stamped Jar Handle Corpus," Duke University, 1993. More recent works are Lipschits and Vanderhooft, "Yehud Stamp Impressions in the Fourth Century," 75–94, and their similar but more up-to-date treatment, "New Typology of the Yehud Stamp Impressions." These studies anticipate Lipschits and Vanderhooft's 2011 monograph, which appeared too late to be consulted.

18. Harrison, "Hellenization in Syria-Palestine." Even if we date Ecclesiastes to the earlier Persian period it would not mean that the author could not have been influenced by Greek ideas, since we have already established the case for considerable Greek influence in that period.

19. Meyers, "Jewish Culture in Greco-Roman Palestine," 137–43, and Collins, *Apocalyptic Vision of the Book of Daniel,* 198–210.

20. McCane, *Roll Back the Stone,* 8–12.

21. Cotton and Wörrle, "Seleukos IV to Heliodoros."

22. Herbert and Berlin, "New Administrative Center."

23. Meshorer, *Treasury of Jewish Coins,* 25; Herman, "Coins of the Itureans."

24. See the discussions of competing scholarly positions in Collins, "Sectarian Communities in the Dead Sea Scrolls," and E. Meyers, "Khirbet Qumran and Its Environs."

25. On the swift expansion of the territory and population of the Hasmoneans, see Finkelstein, "Territorial Extent and Demography of Yehud." On archaeological evidence for the Hasmonean conquests, see Berlin, "Hellenistic Period" and "Between Large Forces."

26. Reich, "Archaeological Evidence of the Jewish Population"; Reich, "'Boundary of Gezer' Inscriptions Again."

27. Frey, *Corpus Inscriptionum Iudaicarum,* vol. 2, no. 1184.

28. The verse in the Torah that is the source of such a practice is Lev 11:36, which refers to a naturally gathered body of water. The Septuagint, however, understands this term as a discreet item.

29. Lawrence, *Washing in Water.*

30. Zissu and Amit, "Common Judaism, Common Purity," 49. A similar pattern may be found in Galilee.

31. The oldest ritual baths found in Galilee cannot be definitively dated to earlier than 100 B.C.E.

32. Stern, *Dor: Ruler of the Seas,* 211–13; Gera, "Tryphon's Sling Bullet."

33. Sivan and Solar, "Excavations in the Jerusalem Citadel."

34. Berlin, "Between Large Forces," 28–31.

35. Magen, Misgav, and Tsfania, *Mount Gerizim Excavations,* vol. 1, 12.

36. Avigad, "Samaria (City)."

37. Berlin, "Between Large Forces," 28–31.

38. Meshorer, *Nabatean Coins,* 86–87.

39. Smith and McNicoll, "The 1982 and 1983 Seasons at Pella," esp. 29.

40. Berlin, "Between Large Forces," 36–41.

41. Kaplan and Ritter-Kaplan, "Tel Aviv."

42. See discussions and citations in Chancey, *Myth of a Gentile Galilee,* 41–47; Chancey, "Archaeology, Ethnicity, and First-Century C.E. Galilee"; and Reed, *Archaeology and the Galilean Jesus,* 39–43.

43. Syon, "Coins from the Excavations at Khirbet esh-Shuhara."

44. Segal and Naor, "Shaar Ha'amaqim"; Adan-Bayewitz and Aviam, "Iotapata"; Shatzman, *Armies of the Hasmoneans and Herods,* 86–87.

45. Frankel, Getzov, Aviam, and Degani, *Settlement Dynamics and Regional Diversity,* 65.

46. Frankel and Ventura, "Mispe Yamim Bronzes"; Herzog, "Beersheba."

47. Berlin, "Archaeology of Ritual."

48. Herbert et al., *Tel Anafa I;* Berlin, "Between Large Forces," 40.

49. Graf, "The Nabateans"; Negev, "Negev"; Cohen, "Negev"; and Oren, "Sinai."

50. Berlin, "Jewish Life Before the Revolt."

51. Wightman, *Walls of Jerusalem,* 85–87, 107–9; Levine, *Jerusalem,* 106–13.

52. Levine, *Jerusalem,* 106–13.

53. Levine, *Jerusalem,* 111; Geva, "Estimating Jerusalem's Population"; Finkelstein, "Territorial Extent and Demography of Yehud."

54. Berlin, "Power and Its Afterlife"; Hachlili, *Jewish Funerary Customs;* Fine, *Art and Judaism,* 60–65.

55. Netzer, *Palaces of the Hasmoneans and Herod.*

56. Rappaport, "Numismatics"; Berlin, "Between Large Forces," 26; Meshorer, *Nabatean Coins;* Herman, "Coins of the Itureans."

57. On the topics addressed in the following discussion of Hasmonean coinage, see Meshorer, *Treasury of Jewish Coins,* 23–59.

58. Meshorer, *Nabatean Coins;* Hanson, *Tyrian Influence.*

59. E. Meyers, "Jewish Art in the Greco-Roman Period."

60. Chancey, "Temple Tax."

61. See most notably Pixner, "History of the 'Essene Gate' Area."

62. Capper, "Essene Community Houses and Jesus' Early Community."

63. Zissu and Amit, "Common Judaism, Common Purity." 49.

64. Adler, "Ritual Baths Adjacent to Tombs," 57–60, 73.

65. Zissu and Amit, "Common Judaism, Common Purity," 51.

66. Ibid., 52.

67. Ibid., 54 and notes.

68. Sanders, *Judaism: Practice and Belief;* Udoh, Heschel, Chancey, and Tatum, *New Views of First-Century Jewish and Christian Self-Definition;* McCready and Reinhartz, *Common Judaism;* and Miller, "Stepped Pools, Stone Vessels."

Chapter 3. Herod the Great and the Introduction of Roman Architecture

1. On the career of Herod the Great, see Richardson, *Herod,* and Rocca, *Herod's Judaea;* on his building projects, see Netzer, *Architecture of Herod;* Roller, *Building Program of Herod;* Lichtenberger, *Die Baupolitik Herodes;* Lichtenberger, "Herod and Rome"; Richardson, *Herod,* 174–215; and the summary in Chancey, *Greco-Roman Culture,* 73–82.

2. Roller, *Building Program of Herod,* 71.

3. On Roman construction techniques such as opus reticulatum and opus sectile as well as bath technology, see Adam, *Roman Building.* On Herod's wall paintings, see Fittschen, "Wall Decorations in Herod's Kingdom."

4. On Antipas, see Chancey, "Disputed Issues."

5. Richardson, *Herod,* 236–37; Fabian E. Udoh, *To Caesar What Is Caesar's,* 180–206.

6. Udoh, *To Caesar What Is Caesar's,* 279–85, attributes this tendency to the influence of Heuver, *Teachings of Jesus Concerning Wealth.* Heuver was followed in this respect by Grant, *Economic Background of the Gospels,* and others.

7. The description of the temple draws on the following: Bahat, "Herodian Temple"; Bahat, "Architectural Origins of Herod's Temple Mount"; Richardson, *Building Jewish in the Roman East,* 253–98; Levine, *Jerusalem,* 219–43; Ritmeyer, *Quest;* Netzer, *Architecture of Herod,* 137–78; Sanders, *Judaism,* 47–72.

8. "Building the Western Wall: Herod Began It but Didn't Finish It," Israel Antiquities Authority Press Release, December 2011 (www.antiquities.org.il).

9. Estimated measurements of Bahat, "Herodian Temple," 43.

10. Bahat provides the estimate of 600 tons ("Herodian Temple," 46); Ritmeyer suggests 175 tons (*Quest,* 32).

11. Mazar, "Herodian Jerusalem." The inscription from this trumpeting station is discussed in Chapter 9.

12. Fischer, *Marble Studies,* 40–43.

13. Segal, "Penalty of the Warning Inscription."

14. Richardson, *Building Jewish,* 295.

15. Frey, *Corpus Inscriptionum Judaicarum,* vol. 2, 1256.

16. Meshorer, *Treasury of Jewish Coins,* 143–45.

17. Richardson, *Building Jewish,* 271–98.

18. Ball, *Rome in the Middle East,* 318.

19. McCane, "Simply Irresistible."

20. Ibid.

21. On the ambiguity of the terminology, see Humphrey, " 'Amphitheatrical' Hippo-Stadia."

22. A recent suggestion points to the so-called Sultan's Pool, an area where outdoor concerts are now held west of the Jaffa Gate and east of the modern King David Hotel (Kloner and Weinstein, "Hippo-Stadium/Amphitheater").

23. Udoh, "Jewish Antiquities XV.205, 207–8."

24. Reich and Billig, "Group of Theater Seats"; but see the reservations expressed in Patrich, "Herod's Theatre in Jerusalem" and Lichtenberger, "Jesus and the Theater."

25. Levine, *Jerusalem,* 196–201.

26. Syntheses of finds at Caesarea Maritima are provided by Roller, *Building Program of Herod,* 133–44; Netzer, *Architecture of Herod,* 94–118; and Richardson, *City and Sanctuary,* 104–28. The literature on the site is enormous. For thorough bibliographic information, see the multiple articles under the general heading "Caesarea," in *NEAEHL* 5: 1656–84, and the earlier entry "Caesarea" in *NEAEHL* 1: 270–91.

27. Measurements from Netzer, *Architecture of Herod,* 103–5.

28. Measurements from ibid., 106–12.

29. Roller, *Building Program of Herod,* 139.

30. Oleson and Branton, "Technology of King Herod's Harbour"; measurement of the block provided in Holum, Hohlfelder, Bull, and Raban, *King Herod's Dream,* 101.

31. Roller, *Building Program of Herod,* 209–12; Netzer, *Architecture of Herod,* 81–93.

32. On Herod's three temples to the emperor, see Bernett, *Der Kaiserkult in Judäa,* 52–146.

33. On a Banias location, see Berlin, "Where Was Herod's Temple to Augustus?"; for Omrit, see Overman, Olive, and Nelson, "Discovering Herod's Shrine to Augustus."

34. On the Tomb of the Patriarchs and the Mamre structure, see Netzer, *Architecture of Herod,* 228–32, and Roller, *Building Program of Herod,* 162–64, 186–87. On Tel Shosh as Gaba, see Siegelmann, "The Identification of Gaba Hippeon."

35. Netzer, *Palaces of the Hasmoneans and Herod,* 68–78; Netzer, *Architecture of Herod,* 202–17; Roller, *Building Program of Herod,* 128–213.

36. Netzer, *Palaces of the Hasmoneans and Herod,* 13–67; Netzer, *Architecture of Herod,* 42–80; Roller, *Building Program of Herod,* 171–74.

37. Roller, *Building Program of Herod,* 164–68; Netzer, *Palaces of the Hasmoneans and Herod,* 98–116, and *Architecture of Herod,* 179–201. On the sarcophagus and related discoveries, see *Architecture of Herod,* ix–xiv.

38. Roller, *Building Program of Herod,* 187–90; Netzer, *Palaces of the Hasmoneans and Herod,* 79–97, and *Architecture of Herod,* 17–41. In *Back to Masada,* Amnon Ben-Tor offers a synthesis of discoveries since the publication of Yigael Yadin's classic *Masada: Herod's Fortress and the Zealots' Last Stand.*

39. Meshorer, *Treasury of Jewish Coins,* 61–78.

40. Magen, *Stone Vessel Industry;* Miller, "Stepped Pools, Stone Vessels"; Gal, "Stone-Vessel Manufacturing Site"; Oshri, "Bet Lehem of Galilee."

41. Hachlili, *Jewish Funerary Customs;* Hachlili, "Burial Practices"; Rahmani, *Catalogue of Jewish Ossuaries,* 53–55; Fine, "Note on Ossuary Burial"; McCane, *Roll Back the Stone,* 39–47.

42. Rahmani, *Catalogue of Jewish Ossuaries.*

Chapter 4. Khirbet Qumran and the Dead Sea Scrolls

1. Magness, "Qumran," 1126.

2. De Vaux, *Archaeology and the Dead Sea Scrolls,* first published in French in 1961 and with revisions in a first English translation in 1972.

3. Magness, "Qumran," 1126; de Vaux, *Archaeology and the Dead Sea Scrolls,* 1–3.

4. Magness, "Qumran"; de Vaux, *Archaeology and the Dead Sea Scrolls,* 3–5.

5. Magness, "Qumran," 1127–28; de Vaux, *Archaeology and the Dead Sea Scrolls,* 5–24.

6. Magness, "Qumran," 1128–29; de Vaux, *Archaeology and the Dead Sea Scrolls,* 24–41.

7. De Vaux, *Archaeology and the Dead Sea Scrolls,* 102–6, 111–38; Kugler, "Dead Sea Scrolls," 522.

8. Kugler, "Dead Sea Scrolls," 522.

9. As a general introduction to the history of the Dead Sea Scrolls see Fields, *The Dead Sea Scrolls.*

10. Meyers, "Khirbet Qumran and Its Environs"; Magness, *Archaeology of Qumran,* 73–89, 153–54.

11. Magness, *Archaeology of Qumran,* 75–76.

12. Ibid., 13.

13. Meyers, "Khirbet Qumran," 22.

14. Taylor, "Classical Sources on the Essenes," 183–84.

15. Collins and Lim, "Introduction," 5.

16. Collins, *Beyond the Qumran Community,* 208–11.

17. Golb, "Who Hid the Dead Sea Scrolls?"

18. Magen and Peleg, "Back to Qumran," 79–84, 99–101.

19. Yellin and Broshi, "Pottery of Qumran and Ein Ghuweir."

20. Magen and Peleg maintain that only a few of the ritual baths were used for purification purposes ("Back to Qumran").

21. Donceel and Donceel-Voûte, "Archaeology of Khirbet Qumran."

22. Broshi and Eshel, "Qumran and the Dead Sea Scrolls," 166.

23. Magness, *Archaeology of Qumran,* 37–38.

24. Crown and Cansdale, "Qumran—Was It an Essene Settlement?"

25. Broshi, "Was Qumran a Crossroads?" 273–76.

26. Zangenberg, "Opening Up Our View," 174.

27. Hirschfeld, *Qumran in Context.*

28. Ibid., 230–40.

29. Ibid., 242.

30. Ibid., 243.

31. Humbert, "Some Remarks."

32. Ibid., 19.

33. Zangenberg, "Opening Up Our View."

34. Schofield, "Wilderness."

35. Fields, *The Dead Sea Scrolls,* 153, note 31.

36. Humbert, "Some Remarks," 36-39; Magness, *Archaeology of Qumran,* 66.

37. Magness, *Archaeology of Qumran,* 67.

38. Magness, *Archaeology of Qumran,* 68; Meyers, "Khirbet Qumran and Its Environs," 30-31.

39. Taylor, "Khirbet Qumran in Period III," 38-41.

40. De Vaux, *Archaeology and the Dead Sea Scrolls,* 38-41.

41. Taylor, "Khirbet Qumran in Period III," 146.

42. Ibid., 145.

43. Magness, *Archaeology of Qumran,* 66.

44. Broshi, "Qumran: Archaeology," 734. The normal means of calculation of population is based on 250 persons per hectare (1,000 square meters). Taking into account the caves for living space along with the small size of the settlement the suggested range is 150-200 souls. On population estimates for this period see Broshi, "Population of Western Palestine."

45. Hirschfeld, *Qumran in Context,* 65.

46. Magness, *Archaeology of Qumran,* 122-26.

47. Hirschfeld, *Qumran in Context,* 104.

48. Humbert, "Some Remarks," 38.

49. Reich, "Miqwa'ot at Khirbet Qumran," 728-31.

50. Wood, "To Dip or Sprinkle?"

51. Reich, "Miqwa'ot at Khirbet Qumran," 728-31.

52. Magness, *Archaeology of Qumran,* 127-29.

53. Meyers, "Khirbet Qumran and Its Environs," 33-34.

54. Branham, "Hedging the Holy at Qumran."

55. Ibid., 131.

56. Hachlili, "Qumran Cemetery Reassessed," 71.

57. Ibid., 67-70.

58. Ibid., 73.

59. Meyers, "Khirbet Qumran and Its Environs," 24-29.

60. This point is made several times in Fields, *The Dead Sea Scrolls.*

61. Bar-Nathan, "Qumran and the Hasmonean and Herodian Winter Palaces."

62. Magness, "Why Scroll Jars?"

63. See Schiffman, "Miqsat Ma'asei Ha-Torah" and the bibliography there.

64. This is one of the major conclusions drawn from an exhaustive study of the manuscripts of the so-called Manual of Discipline, or Community Rule, by Alison Schofield in *From Qumran to the Yahad,* 188-90.

65. Hultgren, *From the Damascus Covenant,* 318.

66. VanderKam, *Dead Sea Scrolls Today,* 50.

Chapter 5. From Herod to the Great Revolt

1. For historical overviews of the period, see Smallwood, *Jews Under Roman Rule,* 144–200, 256–92; Grabbe, *Judaism from Cyrus to Hadrian,* vol. 2, 383–445; Schäfer, *History of the Jews,* 101–20.

2. Richardson, *Herod,* 33–41.

3. Hizmi, "Beiyudat, Khirbet e-" and "Archelaus Builds Archelais."

4. On the dating of the renovations of the third palace, see Netzer, "Jericho," especially 690.

5. Meshorer, *Treasury of Jewish Coins,* 78–81.

6. Jensen, *Herod Antipas in Galilee.*

7. Nagy, C. Meyers, E. Meyers, and Weiss, *Sepphoris in Galilee.* On a first-century date for the basilical building, see Strange, "Eastern Basilical Building." The extensive Hebrew University excavations in the lower eastern sector of the city, however, tend to support a dating to the early second century or even later for expansion to that area.

8. Reed, *Archaeology and the Galilean Jesus,* 80.

9. Meshorer, *Treasury of Jewish Coins,* 81–82.

10. Jensen, *Herod Antipas,* 135–49; on the possible stadium, see Stepansky, Hirschfeld, and Gutfeld, "Tiberias."

11. Hendin, "New Coin Type of Herod Antipas"; Meshorer, *Treasury of Jewish Coins,* 81–85.

12. Herzog, II, *Jesus, Justice, and the Reign of God,* 90–108; Horsley, *Galilee: History, Politics, People,* 202–21; Crossan, *Birth of Christianity,* 215–23; Crossan and Reed, *Excavating Jesus,* 54–70. Reed offers a more cautious approach in "Instability in Jesus' Galilee."

13. Jensen, *Herod Antipas,* makes these points persuasively. See also Fiensy, "Ancient Economy and the New Testament," and Chancey, "Disputed Issues."

14. Chancey, *Greco-Roman Culture,* 221–29.

15. Meshorer, *City-Coins of Eretz-Israel,* 68–69, and "Coins of Caesarea Paneas."

16. Wilson, *Caesarea Philippi,* 18–23.

17. See, for example, Green, "Honorific Naming of Bethsaida-Julias."

18. The essays in Arav and Freund, *Bethsaida,* vol. 2, identify et-Tell as Bethsaida and the building as an imperial temple. R. Steven Notley contests the site identification in "Et-Tell Is Not Bethsaida"; cf. Rainey and Notley, *Sacred Bridge.* Notley and Arav respond to each other's arguments in a 2011 issue of *NEA;* see Arav, "Bethsaida: A Response," Notley, "Reply to Arav," and Arav, "A Reponse to Notley's Reply." Chancey questions the interpretation of the building as an imperial temple in *Greco-Roman Culture,* 90–94.

19. Meshorer, *Treasury of Jewish Coins,* 85–90.

20. On Gamla, see Gutman, "Gamala." A more detailed discussion is found in Chapter 6.

21. Kokkinos, *Herodian Dynasty,* 271–304.

22. Kathleen Kenyon, L. H. Vincent, G. J. Wightman, and others argued for the smaller city; E. L. Sukenik, L. A. Mayer, and others for the larger. For reviews of the

arguments, see Avigad and Geva, "Jerusalem: The Second Temple Period," especially 744–46; Levine, *Jerusalem*, 314–18; and Wightman, *Walls of Jerusalem*, 159 81.

23. Patrich, "Caesarea."

24. Hizmi, "Archelaus Builds Archelais."

25. Meshorer, *Treasury of Jewish Coins*, 90–102.

26. Qedar, "Two Lead Weights."

27. Kokkinos, *Herodian Dynasty*, 317–41.

28. Wilson, *Caesarea Philippi*, 36–37; Wilson and Tzaferis, "Banias Dig Reveals King's Palace."

29. Meshorer, *Treasury of Jewish Coins*, 102–14.

30. Smallwood, *Jews Under Roman Rule*, 144–80.

31. Chancey, *Greco-Roman Culture*, 43–70.

32. Meshorer, *Treasury of Jewish Coins*, 167–76.

33. Porath, "Caesarea"; Patrich, "Caesarea."

34. Lehmann and Holum, *Greek and Latin Inscriptions of Caesarea Maritima*, 67–70; Taylor, "Tiberius' Refusals of Divine Honors."

35. Reich offers the estimate of "a few tens of thousands" in *Excavating the City of David*, 332; cf. 329. Levine discusses the issue at length and provides the 100,000 figure in *Jerusalem*, 340–43.

36. Reich and Billig, "Jerusalem," especially 1809–10; Levine, *Jerusalem*, 319–26.

37. Reich and Billig, "Jerusalem," 1807–8; Reich, *Excavating the City of David*, 330–31.

38. Levine, *Jerusalem*, 326–35; Berlin, "Jewish Life Before the Revolt." On the pig, see Fine, *Art and Judaism*, 78; on the bird, see Avigad and Geva, "Jerusalem," 735.

39. Geva, *Jewish Quarter Excavations in the Old City*, 120.

40. Berlin, "Jewish Life Before the Revolt."

41. Despite the tomb's traditional association with Herod's family, it is unlikely the king was buried there, given Josephus's report of his burial at Herodium (*War* 1.667–73; *Ant.* 17.195–99).

42. Berlin, "Power and Its Afterlife"; Hachlili, *Jewish Funerary Customs*, 235–73.

43. Berlin, "Romanization and Anti-Romanization," and "Jewish Life Before the Revolt."

44. Adan-Bayewitz, Asaro, Wieder, and Giauque, "Preferential Distribution of Lamps"; cf. Berlin, "Jewish Life Before the Revolt."

45. Magen, *Stone Vessel Industry;* Magen, *"Purity Broke Out in Israel";* Chancey, "Stone Vessels."

46. Galor, "Stepped Water Installations"; Lawrence, *Washing in Water;* McCane, "Miqva'ot." David Amit puts the number of ritual baths in Israel at over 750 (personal communiqué from David Amit to Eric M. Meyers, 2009).

47. Aviam and Syon, "Jewish Ossilegium in Galilee"; Rahmani, *Catalogue of Jewish Ossuaries*, 21–23. On the Agrippina inscription, see Rahmani, *Catalogue of Jewish Ossuaries,* no. 789.

48. E. Meyers, "Sanders's 'Common Judaism' and the Common Judaism of Material Culture." On the difficulty of associating particular artifacts with particular sects

or of identifying sectarian distinctions in practices, see Chancey, "Archaeology, Ethnicity, and First-Century C.E. Galilee."

Chapter 6. The Great Revolt and the Bar Kokhba Rebellion

1. For a critical assessment of Josephus's writings in regard to the politics of this era see Schwartz, *Josephus and Judaean Politics*. For a more recent treatment see Mason, *Flavius Josephus: Translation and Commentary*, vol. 1b, *Judean Wars 2*, and *Flavius Josephus: Translation and Commentary*, vol. 9, *Life of Josephus*.

2. Another critical assessment of Josephus is by Tessa Rajak, *The Historian and His Society*. Among many things she questions is his self-identification as a priest (14–21).

3. Rodgers, "Monarchy vs. Priesthood," 182–83.

4. Some of these matters are examined in E. Meyers, "Sepphoris: City of Peace."

5. Rappaport, "The Great Revolt," 9–10.

6. Horsley, "Power Vacuum and Power Struggle," 89.

7. Shahar, "Comparable Elements Between the Galilee and Judea," 32.

8. Meyers, "Sepphoris: City of Peace," 114–16. This article goes over in detail the reasons for Sepphoris's changing attitude at least as reflected in Josephus, but these arguments are too detailed to repeat here.

9. Meshorer, *City-Coins of Eretz-Israel*, 68.

10. Aviam, "First Century Jewish Galilee," 16–17.

11. See also Aviam, "Archaeology of the Battle of Yodefat."

12. Ibid., 110.

13. On this point see Bauckham, "Josephus' Account of the Temple."

14. Aviam, "Archaeology of the Battle of Yodefat," 112–15.

15. Ibid., 118.

16. Ibid., 119.

17. See also Chancey, "Jotapata." A similar story or legend predicting Vespasian's emperorship is recorded in the Babylonian Talmud (*b. Gittin* 56) and is a prophecy attributed to the great rabbi Yochanan ben Zakkai.

18. See especially on this point Cohen, "Masada."

19. Syon, "'City of Refuge,'" 63.

20. Ibid., 55.

21. Ibid., 64–65.

22. Atkinson, "Gamla," 658.

23. Syon, "'City of Refuge,'" 58–59.

24. Syon, "Coins from Gamla," and Syon, "'City of Refuge,'" 64; translation of Josephus is by Syon.

25. Berlin, *Gamla I*.

26. We fully intend that the term "Zealots" be used in a general way, meaning "extremist" or "revolutionary," embracing other groups of extremists such as the Sicarii.

27. Geva, *Jewish Quarter Excavations in the Old City*, 68.

28. Mazar, "Archaeological Excavations Near the Temple Mount," 35.

29. See Cotton et al., *Corpus Inscriptionum Iudaeae/Palaestinae*, vol. 1, part 1, 49, no. 5.

30. Geva, *Jewish Quarter Excavations in the Old City*, 67–68.

31. Avigad, *Discovering Jerusalem*, 125.

32. Ibid., 129–30, figure 124; Reich, "Stone Scale Weights," 350–51.

33. Schwartz, "Bar Qatros and the Priestly Families of Jerusalem."

34. Geva, *Jewish Quarter Excavations in the Old City*, 316.

35. Priests were required to maintain a high level of ritual purity since they interacted with the Temple so much. In addition to ritual bathing they utilized stone vessels used for strong liquids, washing the hands and feet, and for serving food. That is not to say other pious elements of Jewish society from the late Second Temple period onward did not also use such vessels. See Magen, *Stone Vessel Industry*.

36. *Aboth de Rabbi Nathan*, ch. 4; cf. *b. Gittin* 50a-b.

37. Ben-Tor, *Back to Masada*, 148–207.

38. Ibid., 73–75.

39. Ibid., 75–88.

40. Ibid., 237–40.

41. Ibid., 238.

42. Ibid., 254; Atkinson, "Masada," 921.

43. Shaye J. D. Cohen ("Masada") has stated the feelings of many when he expresses sincere doubt about the story of mass suicide, which is not supported by the material evidence either. Joseph Zias ("Whose Bones?") has questioned whether any bones on the site can be identified with any of the Zealots, and the few that have been recovered may be identified with later residents at the site. Ronny Reich in respect to the destruction of Jerusalem has suggested that the Tenth Legion collected the bodies and burned them (*Excavating the City of David*, 334). This could have been the situation at Gamla as well.

44. Yadin, *Masada*, 201. In the final publication twelve ostraca are listed; see Ben-Tor, *Back to Masada*, 157–59.

45. Yadin, *Masada*.

46. Ben-Yehudah, *Masada Myth* and *Sacrificing Truth*. The most recent criticism of Ben-Yehudah has been by Amnon Ben-Tor in *Back to Masada*.

47. Alsop, "The Masada Complex."

48. A stinging rebuttal of Ben-Yehudah's views appears in the summary volume of the Masada excavations by Amnon Ben-Tor, *Back to Masada*, 269–309.

49. Magness, "In the Footsteps of the Tenth Roman Legion."

50. Schäfer, *History of the Jews*, 131 and notes.

51. Levine, *Ancient Synagogue*, 496–97. See also Grey, *Jewish Priests and the Social History*.

52. Schäfer, *History of the Jews*, 138, with full translation of the rabbinic text on pp. 137–38.

53. Schürer, *History of the Jewish People*, vol. 1, 529–34. See also Ben Zeev, "Diaspora Uprisings," 539, and Ben Zeev, *Diaspora Judaism in Turmoil*.

54. Schürer, *History of the Jewish People*, 530 and note 74.

55. Ibid., 530–51.

56. Ibid., 531, note 76.

57. Schäfer, *History of the Jews,* 131–42.

58. Yadin, *Bar-Kokhba,* 18–19, and list of sources on 255ff. The major rabbinic source is *Midrash Rabbah Lamentations* (London: Soncino Press, 1939), 157–61. See also *b. Gittin* 57–58.

59. Wise, "Bar Kochba Letters."

60. Eshel, "Bar Kokhba Revolt," 424.

61. Eshel, "Bar Kochba Caves."

62. Leviticus 19:19 and Deuteronomy 22:5, 9–11. See also Yadin, *Bar-Kokhba,* 66 ff. and his full report in *Finds from the Bar-Kokhba Period,* especially 170.

63. Yadin, *Bar-Kokhba,* 69.

64. Wise, "Bar Kochba Letters."

65. A document from the Nahal Seelim (XHev/Se 30) begins with this sentence: "To Simeon ben Kosiba, from Simeon ben Mattabyah; Greetings, beloved father . . ." (Wise, "Bar Kochba Letters," 419).

Chapter 7. The Emergence of Christianity

1. Reich and Billig, "Jerusalem," 1807–8.

2. Lehmann and Holum, *Greek and Latin Inscriptions of Caesarea Maritima,* 67–70.

3. Steffy and Wachsmann, "Migdal Boat Mosaic."

4. Wachsmann, *Excavations of an Ancient Boat;* on Mark 4, see Wachsmann, "Literary Sources on Kinneret Seafaring."

5. Reed, "Stone Vessels and Gospel Texts."

6. Naveh, "Ossuary Inscriptions from Givat ha-Mivtar"; Haas, "Anthropological Observations on the Skeletal Remains"; Tzaferis, "Crucifixion: The Archaeological Evidence." The analyses of the skeletal remains in the preceding articles should be read in light of the reassessment of Zias and Sekeles in "The Crucified Man from Giv'at ha-Mivtar."

7. Hachlili, *Jewish Funerary Customs,* 64, but cf. the reservations of Kloner, "Did a Rolling Stone Close Jesus' Tomb?"

8. For a representative overview of the geographic parameters of Jesus' activity, see Theissen and Merz, *Historical Jesus.*

9. For various options, see Freyne, *Galilee, Jesus, and the Gospels,* 139–43; Reed, *Archaeology and the Galilean Jesus,* 100–108; Bösen, *Galiläa,* 69–75.

10. Horbury, "Beginnings of Christianity."

11. Paget, "Jewish Christianity."

12. Irshai, "From Oblivion to Fame"; Ascough, "Christianity in Caesarea Maritima."

13. Eusebius, *Church History* 5.22, 5.23, 6.19.17, 6.27, 7.5.1, 7.14, 7.32.21, 7.32.24.

14. Hunt, *Holy Land Pilgrimage,* 28–49.

15. Drijvers, *Helena Augusta.*

16. Quote from Broshi, "Evidence of Earliest Christian Pilgrimage," where Broshi also discusses Benoit's reading. See also Broshi and Barkay, "Excavations in the Chapel of St. Vartan."

17. Gibson and Taylor, *Beneath the Church of the Holy Sepulchre,* 25–48.

18. Limor provides a historical overview of the development of pilgrimage sites in " 'Holy Journey.' "

19. Barkay, "The Garden Tomb."

20. Strange offers an excellent review of literature on this issue in "Archaeological Evidence of Jewish Believers?"

21. Bagatti and Milik, *Gli Scavi del 'Dominus Flevit,'* vol. 1.

22. Clermont-Ganneau, "Epigraphes hébraiques et grecques."

23. Sukenik, "Earliest Records of Christianity."

24. Strange, "Archaeological Evidence of Jewish Believers?"

25. See the literature cited in Marcus, "*Birkat Ha-Minim* Revisited," and Kimelman, "Identifying Jews and Christians," both of which are sympathetic to the identification of *minim* as Jewish Christians.

26. Bagatti, *Excavations in Nazareth,* vol. 1, 27–218.

27. Bagatti, *Excavations in Nazareth,* vol. 1, 100–102; cf. Taylor, *Christians and the Holy Places,* 243.

28. Bagatti, *Excavations in Nazareth,* 210, figure 172; Meyers and Strange date the coin to Constantine in *Archaeology,* 131.

29. Bagatti, *Excavations in Nazareth,* 156–58; for "Christ, Mary," see Meyers and Strange, *Archaeology,* 133–34.

30. Taylor, *Christians and the Holy Places,* 258.

31. Bagatti, *Excavations in Nazareth,* 123 no. 3, 127–29.

32. Ibid., 120–31, 228–32.

33. Taylor, *Christians and the Holy Places,* 244–52; cf. Strange, "Archaeological Evidence of Jewish Believers?" 725–26.

34. Taylor's critique of Bagatti's interpretation is devastating (*Christians and the Holy Places,* 258–64); cf. Strange's more reserved assessment in "Archaeological Evidence of Jewish Believers?" 727.

35. Wilkinson, trans., *Egeria's Travels,* 194.

36. Corbo, *House of St. Peter at Capharaum;* Loffreda, *Recovering Capharnaum,* 50–66; Testa, *Graffiti della Casa di S. Pietro.* Strange and Shanks provide an accessible overview of some of the issues in "Has the House Where Jesus Stayed in Capernaum Been Found?"

37. Taylor, *Christians and the Holy Places,* 273–84.

38. Testa, *Graffiti della Casa di S. Pietro;* Strange, "Capernaum and Herodium Publications," and "Capernaum and Herodium Publications, Part 2"; Strange, "Archaeological Evidence of Jewish Believers?" 730; Taylor, *Christians and the Holy Places,* 284–85.

39. On the use of the term "domus ecclesiae" in this way, see White, *Building God's House in the Roman World.* White differentiates the *domus ecclesiae* from another type of renovated structure that he dubs the *aula ecclesiae,* or "hall of the church," a larger meeting hall.

40. Chrysostom, *Homilies Against the Jews* 1.3, 5; Origen, *Contra Celsum* 4.31.

41. Marcus, "*Birkat Ha-Minim* Revisited"; Kimelman, "Identifying Jews and Christians," 308.

42. Shanks and Witherington, *Brother of Jesus.*

43. On the evolution of the controversy and the critiques, see Byrne and McNary-Zak, *Resurrecting the Brother of Jesus*, especially McCane, "Bones of James Unpacked," which points out the published models for the inscription on 27.

44. Shanks and Witherington, *Brother of Jesus*, 54–63.

45. Ibid., 62–63.

46. Ibid., 58–59.

47. McCane underscores the logical tendentiousness of many of the proposed statistical arguments in "Bones of James Unpacked."

48. Dahari et al., *Final Report of the Examining Committees*, reprinted in Shanks and Witherington, *Brother of Jesus*, 227–37; Paul V. M. Flesher, "The Ossuary of James the Brother of Jesus: From Trial to Truth?" (March 2012), *The Bible and Interpretation* (www .bibleinterp.com).

49. Jacobovici and Pellegrino, *Jesus Family Tomb;* Tabor, *Jesus Dynasty.* For the reading of *Mariame kai Mara,* see Pfann, "Mary Magdalene Has Left the Room." Pfann is a critic of the Jacobovici and Tabor theses.

50. See the articles collected in "Forum: The Talpiot 'Jesus' Family Tomb," *NEA* 69:3–4 (2006): 116–37.

51. Rollston, "Inscribed Ossuaries."

52. Ilan, "Notes on the Distribution of Jewish Women's Names."

53. Tepper and Di Segni, *Christian Prayer Hall;* for an early response, see Adams, "Ancient Church at Megiddo."

Chapter 8. Early Judaism and the Rise of the Synagogue

1. Levine, *Ancient Synagogue,* 21.

2. Runesson, "Persian Imperial Politics," 63.

3. Levine, *Ancient Synagogue,* 19–41, and Binder, *Into the Temple Courts,* 204–26.

4. Runesson, "Persian Imperial Politics," 70, 80–81. This view is also adopted by Richardson, *Building Jewish,* 111–13, who calls them *collegia.*

5. Runesson, "Persian Imperial Politics," 71.

6. Strange, "Ancient Texts, Archaeology as Text," especially 28.

7. Ibid., 72.

8. Richardson, *Building Jewish,* 115–16. See also Levine, *Ancient Synagogue,* 75–82.

9. Richardson, *Building Jewish,* 116.

10. *T. Sukkah* 4:6, *y. Sukkah* 5, I, 555 a-b, and *b. Sukkah* 51 b. The text is translated and commented on in Levine, *Ancient Synagogue,* 84.

11. Levine, *Ancient Synagogue,* 85, 242–49.

12. Ibid., 100–105. See also Trümper, "Oldest Original Synagogue Building."

13. White, "Delos Synagogue Revisited"; Levine, *Ancient Synagogue,* 100.

14. Levine, *Ancient Synagogue,* 101; Kraabel, "Diaspora Synagogue," 491.

15. Bruneau, "Les Israelites de Délos et la juiverie délienne."

16. Kraabel, "New Evidence for the Samaritan Diaspora."

17. Plassart, "La synagogue juive de Délos."

18. Kraabel, "Diaspora Synagogue," 498–99; Squarciapino, "Synagogue at Ostia," 25; and Levine, *Ancient Synagogue,* 97–99.

19. Runesson, "Monumental Synagogue from the First Century"; Levine, *Ancient Synagogue,* 97.

20. Mitternacht, "Current Views on Jews and the Synagogue." L. Michael White, though he admits that there is an earlier stage of the synagogue, has largely focused on other parts of Ostia in his recent work there, but see his comments in *Building God's House,* 69.

21. The inscription is found in Frey, *Corpus Inscriptionem Judaicarum,* vol. 2, 1404, and is revised and quoted in Kloppenborg Verbin, "Dating Theodotus (CIJ 1404)," and Richardson, *Building Jewish,* 128. This translation is a blend of all of these and is informed also by the translation and brief commentary in Cotton et al., *Corpus Inscriptionem Judaeae/Palaestinae,* vol. 1, part 1, 53–56.

22. Levine, *Ancient Synagogue,* 55.

23. Reich, "Synagogue and the *Miqveh* in Eretz-Israel," especially 291–92.

24. Levine, *Ancient Synagogue,* 42–50 and notes 4–7 on pages 43–44. On Jesus' avoidance of cities and the issues involved in determining why, for instance, Sepphoris is never mentioned in the New Testament, see Jonathan Reed, *Archaeology and the Galilean Jesus,* 100–114.

25. Chancey, *Myth of a Gentile Galilee,* 174–75.

26. Ibid., 104–5.

27. Loffreda, "Capernaum"; Strange and Shanks, "Synagogue Where Jesus Preached Found."

28. See provisionally http://www.antiquities.org.il/article and other blog spots. R. Steven Notley spoke on this remarkable discovery at a conference on Talmudic archaeology at Yeshiva University on March 28, 2011, describing the synagogue as the most "elegant of all the early synagogues dated to the Second Temple period" and comparing the frescoes and mosaics to the priestly houses at Jerusalem and the Herodian royal box at Herodium in the theater. He had no suggestion as to the purpose of the pedestal with menorah on the side, but in conversation agreed that it seemed to be for a base of a table of sorts. As for the dates he proposed 50 B.C.E. to ca. 100 C.E. and destruction or abandonment by natural causes.

29. For the ceramist the kinds of lamps depicted on the pedestal date to the late Hellenistic period and are known as "Maccabean lamps." This would possibly move the date of this piece at least to a bit earlier time. If the pedestal and building are of the same date then 50 B.C.E. is not out of the question. Shanks calls the pedestal a "Torah Table" in his recent article, "New Synagogue Excavations in Israel and Beyond," and writes in the caption to a photo of it: "The stone may have served as a table on which the Torah scrolls were rolled out."

30. Avigad, *Discovering Jerusalem,* 148. The coins of Mattathias Antigonus also bear the symbol of the menorah. The other examples from this period include several depictions on ossuaries, a graffito from Jason's Tomb in Jerusalem, a sundial found in the Jewish Quarter in a priestly home, and some terra-cotta lamps. Rahmani discusses these in *Catalogue of Jewish Ossuaries,* 51–52 and notes. He asserts that menorot at this early date are all associated with priestly names and thus would probably identify the synagogue at Magdala as such.

31. Gutman, "Synagogue at Gamla," 30–34; Maoz, "Synagogue of Gamla and the Typology"; Gutman, "Gamala"; and Levine, *Ancient Synagogue,* 51–52.

32. Levine, *Ancient Synagogue,* 51, fig. 4.

33. Maoz, "Synagogue at Gamla," 39.

34. Yadin, "Synagogue at Masada."

35. Foerster, "Synagogues at Masada and Herodium."

36. Ibid., 29, and see *t. Megillah* 3:22, "One should only place the entrance to synagogues in the East, for we find that in the Temple the entrance faced east."

37. Levine, *Ancient Synagogue,* 65–66. He also discusses the site in "The First-Century Synagogue: Critical Reassessments," 84–86. See the full report on the site by Magen, Zionit, and Sirkis, "Kiryat Sefer."

38. See for the time being Onn, Wexler-Bdolah, Rapuanno, and Kanias, "Khirbet Umm el-Umdan," and Levine, "The First-Century Synagogue," 86–87.

39. Updated information may be found at the Israel Antiquities Authority Web site, as in the case of Magdala above, http://www.antiquities.org.il/article. But see also Levine, "The First-Century Synagogue," 86.

40. Levine, "First-Century Synagogue," 87.

41. Netzer, "Synagogue from the Hasmonean Period."

42. Levine, *Ancient Synagogue,* 68.

43. Levine, "First-Century Synagogue," 89.

44. Levine, "Synagogues," 1262.

45. On these and related matters see Kee, "Defining the First-Century C.E. Synagogue."

46. The subject of the paucity of physical remains of synagogues after 70 C.E. is treated in E. Meyers, "Problem of the Scarcity of Synagogues."

47. Levine, *Ancient Synagogue,* 169.

48. Ibid., 177–93.

49. See Schwartz, *Imperialism and Jewish Society,* 103–4.

50. E. Meyers and C. Meyers, *Excavations at Ancient Nabratein,* 34–44. On the point of sacred orientation toward the Torah Shrine and Jerusalem see also Fine, *This Holy Place,* 105–12.

51. Zissu and Ganor, "Horvat 'Ethri."

52. See Levine's cautionary remarks in "The First-Century Synagogue," 89.

53. Levine, *Ancient Synagogue,* 169.

54. Epiphanius in *Panarion* 30.12 mentions the building of a Hadrianeum in Tiberias, which may be a possible reference to an event in connection with the rabbinic hints at the destruction of a synagogue at this time there; Levine, *Ancient Synagogue,* 170. The destruction of the synagogue(s) in Alexandria is doubtless a reflection of the revolt of 115–117 C.E., which has left echoes in the Jerusalem Talmud (*y. Sukkah* 5,1, 55b).

55. See for example the following mishnayot: *Ber.* 7:3; *Ter.* 1:10; *Bik.* 1:4; *Shab.* 16:22; *Pes.* 10:8; *Taanait* 2:4, 3:4; *Rosh HaShanah* 2:7; *Yoma* 3:18; *Suk.* 2:10, 4:5, 4:6; *Meg.* 2:3, 5, 12, 13, 14, 16, 17, 18, 3:12, 21, 22; *Sotah* 6:3; *Baba Qamma* 11:3; *Baba Metzia* 11:23; *Ohalot.* 4:2; *Neg.* 6:3, 7:11; *Tehar.* 8:10, and parallel and other passages in the Tosefta. See also Fine, *This Holy Place,* 35–94.

56. See their Web site for illustrations: www.nazarethvillage.com.

57. See E. Meyers, Kraabel, and Strange, *Ancient Synagogue Excavations at Khirbet Shema,* 39–45.

58. Levine, *Ancient Synagogue,* 179–81, and Fine, *This Holy Place,* 105–11.

59. E. Meyers and C. Meyers, *Excavations at Ancient Nabratein,* 35–78, and E. Meyers, "Ancient Synagogues: An Archaeological Introduction."

60. Chen, "Ancient Synagogue at Nabratein."

61. E. Meyers and C. Meyers, *Excavations at Ancient Nabratein,* 75, figure 25.

62. E. Meyers, "Torah Shrine in the Ancient Synagogue," especially 206–7 and notes 44–46.

63. See E. Meyers, "Dating of the Gush Halav Synagogue: Response to Jodi Magness." These arguments are very technical and mainly focus on ceramic typology, stratigraphy, and numismatic matters.

64. See Fine, *Art and Judaism.*

65. Leibner, "Khirbet Wadi Hamam."

66. Talgam and Weiss, *Mosaics of the House of Dionysos,* 125–31.

67. Hachlili, *Ancient Mosaic Pavements,* 35–56, which considers the theme of the zodiac in Byzantine Jewish art as well as many others. See also Hachlili, "Synagogues in the Land of Israel."

68. Meshorer, "Sepphoris and Rome," 170.

69. Ibid., 169–70.

70. Hachlili, "Art and Architecture," 113–15, though there she hints that the tendency to decorative art may have already started in the third century.

71. Hachlili, *Ancient Mosaic Pavements,* 241–42.

72. The cross, for example, does not become a Christian symbol till after Constantine; Snyder, *Ante Pacem,* 26–9. The interested reader and in particular students of this period are advised to follow these matters in the appropriate places on the Internet and printed journals. Given the fact that so much work is now in progress there will of necessity be a considerable time lag in publication.

73. Regev, "Non-Priestly Purity."

74. A personal communiqué from David Amit, in 2009, estimated the number to be 750. His colleague and collaborator, Yonatan Adler, recently raised that number to 850 (see below note 85).

75. Haber, "Common Judaism," quote from 65.

76. Kloppenborg Verbin, "Dating Theodotus."

77. Haber, "Common Judaism," 68, note 36.

78. Haber, "Common Judaism," 69; E. Meyers and C. Meyers, *Excavations at Ancient Nabratein,* 144–49.

79. Regev, "Pure Individualism," 187.

80. Ibid., 191.

81. Although the final report on these ritual baths is still unpublished, some of this information is available in E. Meyers, "Aspects of Everyday Life in Roman Palestine," 211–20, and Zissu and Amit, "Common Judaism, Common Purity," 238, note 8, which points to the continuation of ritual baths long into the rabbinic period,

or late Roman and Byzantine periods, as well as the continuation of stone vessels for purity. See also Weiss, *Sepphoris Synagogue,* 310 and notes 149–51. Weiss says quite clearly that stone vessels remained in use well into the Byzantine period and cites evidence at other sites to support it. He also has an unpublished report on this subject that he has shared with me and has an M.A. student doing a thesis on the subject. This is also the subject of the essay by Amit and Adler, "Observance of Ritual Purity After 70 C.E." The authors, however, want to see this as a reflection on the high concentration of priestly families at the site, 137, a suggestion about which we have some reservations. On this debate see Stuart Miller, "Some Observations on Stone Vessel Finds," who says they may also indicate the practice of commoners.

82. Adler's paper on this subject delivered at Yeshiva University on March 28, 2011, taken from his unpublished Ph.D. dissertation on the subject, asserted that the only other sites with *miqvaot* after 135 C.E. in the country are Sepphoris, Beth Shearim, and Susiyeh in Judea on the fringes of the desert. The total number of ritual baths now positively identified in the Land of Israel is 850, although when Reich did his initial research for his dissertation in 1990 there were only 300 known. In charts of sites with stone vessels he numbers 251 in all, north and south, with the main concentration of sites in the south.

83. See E. Meyers, "Sanders's Common Judaism and the Common Judaism of Material Culture"; Zangenberg, "Common Judaism and the Multidimensional Character."

84. Adan-Bayewitz, Asaro, Wieder, and Giauque, "Preferential Distribution of Lamps," 37, 77–78.

85. Ibid., 73–77.

Chapter 9. The Archaeology of Paganism

1. Rives, *Religion in the Roman Empire.*
2. Oren Tal discusses some of the pertinent evidence in *Archaeology of Hellenistic Palestine,* 71–90.
3. Gitler and Tal, *Coinage of Philistia.*
4. Stern, "Zafit, Tel"; Stager, "Ashkelon," especially 109.
5. Betlyon, "A People Transformed," especially 50.
6. Fuks, "Mediterranean Pantheon"; Kadman, *Coins of Akko.*
7. Lupo, "New Look at Three Inscriptions."
8. The inscriptions mentioned in this paragraph are drawn respectively from Biran, "To the God Who Is in Dan"; Crowfoot, Crowfoot, and Kenyon, *Objects from Samaria,* 37, no. 13; Avi-Yonah, "Syrian Gods at Ptolemais-Accho"; and Landau, "Greek Inscription from Acre."
9. *Supplementum epigraphicum graecum* 8, part 1 (1937), no. 33.
10. Lupo, "New Look."
11. Ariel and Naveh, "Selected Inscribed Sealings from Kedesh"; Herbert and Berlin, "New Administrative Center."

12. Herzog, "Beersheba: Tel Beersheba," and "Beersheba."

13. Ussishkin, "Lachish."

14. Dar, *Settlements and Cult Sites on Mount Hermon.*

15. Hoffmann, "Hellenistic Gadara," especially 395–96; Weber, "Gadara and the Galilee," especially 461–63.

16. Stern, "Dor"; Stewart and Martin, "Hellenistic Discoveries at Tel Dor"; Segal and Eisenberg, "Sussita-Hippos of the Decapolis."

17. Frankel and Ventura, "Mispe Yamim Bronzes"; Frankel, "Mizpe Yammim, Mount."

18. The number of statues and figurines is still relatively limited, however, and their interpretation is complicated by the difficulty of distinguishing Hellenistic statuary from later Roman imitations. On this point, see Fischer and Tal, "Architectural Decoration in Ancient Israel in Hellenistic Times." One wonders about this possibility in regard to the early Hellenistic date of a statue offered in Iliffe, "Nude Terra-Cotta Statuette of Aphrodite."

19. Stern, *Dor: Ruler of the Seas,* 246–49; Stern, "Dor"; Stern, "Goddesses and Cults at Tel Dor."

20. Fischer, "Yavneh-Yam."

21. Aviam, "Hellenistic Fortifications in the 'Hinterland,'" especially 28–29.

22. Herbert, "Tel Anafa, 1980"; Weinberg, "Tel Anafa: The Second Season"; Weinberg, "Tel Anafa: The Hellenistic Town."

23. Erlich and Kloner, *Maresha Excavations Final Report II: Hellenistic Terracotta Figurines;* Stern, Osband, Alpert, and Sagiv, "Maresha, Subterranean Complex"; Kloner, "Maresha (Marisa)," in *NEAEHL* 1 and 5; for the inscription to Apollo, see Kloner, *Maresha Excavations Final Report I: Subterranean Complexes,* 9–10.

24. MacMullen, "Epigraphic Habit."

25. For virtually all of the sites mentioned in this chapter and many others, see the impressively comprehensive study of Belayche in *Iudaea-Palaestina: The Pagan Cults.*

26. Welles, "Inscriptions," no. 15.

27. Meshorer, *City-Coins.*

28. Arav, "Hermon, Mount"; Dar, *Settlements and Cult Sites,* 65–69; Fischer, Ovadiah, and Roll, "Epigraphic Finds from the Roman Temple"; Fischer, Ovadiah, and Roll, "Inscribed Altar from the Roman Temple"; Fischer, Ovadiah, and Roll, "Roman Temple at Kedesh."

29. Healey, *Religion of the Nabateans;* Graf, "Nabateans"; Bartlett, "Nabataean Religion"; Negev, "Temple of Obodas"; Meshorer, *Nabataean Coins;* Schmitt-Korte, "Nabataean Coinage—Part II"; Spijkerman, *Coins of the Decapolis and Provincia Arabia,* 60–61 nos. 1–3.

30. Stager, "Ashkelon"; Fuks, "Mediterranean Pantheon."

31. Meshorer, *City-Coins.*

32. Ball, *Rome in the East,* 188–91, 325–29.

33. Belayche, *Iudaea-Palaestina: The Pagan Cults,* 64; Magness, "Cults of Isis and Kore at Samaria-Sebaste."

34. Aliquot, "Sanctuaries and Villages on Mt Hermon."

35. For the coins, see Meshorer, *City-Coins;* for figurines from Dor, Stern, *Dor: Ruler of the Seas,* 246–49; for Khisfin, Gregg and Urman, *Jews, Pagans, and Christians,* 75; for Jerash, Welles, "Inscriptions," 383 no. 17.

36. Welles, "Inscriptions," no. 2; *Supplementum epigraphicum graecum* 20.546; Meshorer, *City-Coins,* 75; Lehmann and Holum, *Greek and Latin Inscriptions of Caesarea Maritima,* 121 no. 124.

37. Belayche, *Iudaea-Palaestina: The Pagan Cults,* 108–70; Avigad and Geva, "Jerusalem," 758–67; Meshorer, *Coinage of Aelia Capitolina.*

38. For the Tel Shalem statue, see Foerster, "Cuirassed Bronze Statue of Hadrian"; for the Legio altar and the DM inscriptions, see Avi-Yonah, "Newly Discovered Latin and Greek Inscriptions," nos. 4, 5, and 7.

39. Bernett, *Der Kaiserkult in Judäa.*

40. Welles, "Inscriptions," nos. 2–4.

41. Fischer, Ovadiah, and Roll, "Inscribed Altar"; Dar and Kokkinos, "Greek Inscriptions from Senaim," no. 2; Di Segni, "New Toponym in Southern Samaria."

42. Meshorer, *Treasury of Jewish Coins;* on the coins depicting Nero's relatives, see Bernett, "Roman Imperial Cult in the Galilee," especially 352–53.

43. Graf, "Roman Festivals in Syria Palaestina"; see also Jacobs, "Pagane Temple in Palästina-rabbinische Aussagen."

44. Hachlili and Killebrew, "Horbat Qazion"; Aviam, "Borders Between Jews and Gentiles," 17.

45. This and subsequent paragraphs draw on Donaldson, *Religious Rivalries and the Struggle for Success;* Gersht, "Representation of Deities and the Cults of Caesarea"; Lehmann and Holum, *Greek and Latin Inscriptions of Caesarea Maritima,* 118–24.

46. Meshorer, *Treasury of Jewish Coins,* 99–102; Meshorer, *City-Coins,* 20–21.

47. Belayche discusses the intaglios in *Iudaea-Palaestina: The Pagan Cults,* 186. For the inscriptions, see Lehmann and Holum, *Greek and Latin Inscriptions of Caesarea Maritima,* 118–24. For the Mount Carmel inscription, see Avi-Yonah, "Mount Carmel and the God of Baalbak."

48. Wilson, *Caesarea Philippi;* Berlin, "Archaeology of Ritual"; Friedland, "Graeco-Roman Sculpture in the Levant"; Tzaferis, "Cults and Deities Worshipped at Caesarea Philippi-Banias."

49. Berlin, "Archaeology of Ritual."

Chapter 10. The Growth of Greco-Roman Culture and the Case of Sepphoris

1. *Ant.* 19.356–66, 20.122, 20.176; *War* 2.236. For references to the locations of Roman garrisons, see Schürer, *History,* 1: 365.

2. Chancey, *Greco-Roman Culture,* 61–69.

3. Isaac, *Limits of Empire,* 107–13; Millar, *Roman Near East,* 108–9.

4. For these and other examples, see Meshorer, *City-Coins.*

5. Harl, *Civic Coins and Civic Politics;* Meshorer, *City-Coins.*

6. MacMullen, "Epigraphic Habit."

7. See, for example, Lehmann and Holum, *Greek and Latin Inscriptions of Caesarea Maritima.*

8. Van der Worst, "Inscriptions."

9. Schwabe and Lifshitz, *Beth Shearim,* vol. 2; Avigad, *Beth Shearim,* vol. 3.

10. Cotton, "Guardianship of Jesus Son of Babatha."

11. Segal, *From Function to Monument;* Ball, *Rome in the East;* Chancey, *Greco-Roman Culture.*

12. Segal, *Theatres in Roman Palestine;* Weiss, "Adopting a Novelty"; Sperber, *City in Roman Palestine,* 58–91.

13. MacMullen, "Roman Imperial Building in the Provinces"; Pollard, *Soldiers, Cities, and Civilians,* 242–50.

14. Lehmann and Holum, *Greek and Latin Inscriptions of Caesarea Maritima,* 12–14, 71–77, no. 45–54.

15. Welles, "Inscriptions," 399 no. 52.

16. *B. Shab.* 33b.

17. Lehmann and Holum, *Greek and Latin Inscriptions of Caesarea Maritima.*

18. Mazor, "Beth-Shean"; and Arubas, Foerster, and Tsafrir, "Beth-Shean."

19. Magen, "Shechem: Neapolis."

20. Avigad, "Samaria (City)."

21. The most recent and comprehensive treatment of this great mosaic is in Piccirillo and Alliata, *Madaba Map Centenary.*

22. For a recent broad overview of developments in Jerusalem, see "Jerusalem," *NEAEHL* 5: 1801–37.

23. Batey, *Jesus and the Forgotten City,* illustrated by J. Robert Teringo. The book created a furor in some circles, especially its illustrations, which presented Jews in an inaccurate and sometimes unflattering light: walking near the theater wrapped in prayer shawls and phylacteries, bearded and dark in contrast to fair, clean-cut Gentiles, their noses long to the point of caricature. The illustrations were originally intended for *National Geographic Magazine* but were rejected by it after protests from excavators and other scholars.

24. Weiss, "Sepphoris."

25. Antoninus was such a common name among Roman emperors that the older literature identified this Antoninus as the contemporary of Rabbi Judah with whom many of the rabbinic legends deal. Alexander Guttman has convincingly demonstrated that the emperor whom Rabbi Judah befriended and about whom the rabbinic legends speaks was Caracalla (198–217 C.E.), suggesting that Rabbi Judah died in 222 C.E. See Guttman's "Patriarch Judah I."

26. Weiss, "Buildings for Entertainment."

27. Weiss, "Artistic Trends," especially 167–71.

28. Weiss, "Notes and News: Sepphoris (Sippori), 2009."

29. See the catalogue, Nagy, E. Meyers, C. Meyers, and Weiss, *Sepphoris in Galilee.*

30. A full report on the Dionysos mansion may be found in Talgam and Weiss, *Mosaics of the House of Dionysos.* For a discussion of this date see 27–29 and Marva Balouka's discussion of pottery on 35–45.

31. Most books would end the Roman period in ancient Palestine around the time of Constantine's victory, circa 312 C.E. By suggesting a later date and attaching it to the great earthquake of 363 C.E., we are merely conveying a sense that in material culture a very strong sense of continuity may be observed at Sepphoris and many other sites in the Holy Land at midcentury and that major changes can be observed in pottery and other forms of material culture from that time forward.

32. Pictures of the entire floor appear in Talgam and Weiss, *Mosaics of the House of Dionysos.*

33. Talgam and Weiss, *Mosaics of the House of Dionysos,* 127–32.

34. Weiss has said in a recent conversation that he would not support that view any longer. Since what he says in print is what is available to the public we leave it, especially since many would agree with that position. We have suggested that the mansion might have served as an inn and meeting place for the municipal council.

35. E. Meyers and C. Meyers, "Sepphoris," and Meshorer, *City-Coins,* 37. In reexamining the coins discovered at the dig, the numismatists Donald Ariel and Dave Hendin have identified a badly worn exemplar of the commemorative medallion or coin, the first one ever found at the site. Although this does not prove anything about who lived in a particular location it lends further credence to the Talmudic legends that ascribed great meaning to the rabbi's friendship with Caracalla—called Antoninus in the sources. See *b. Avodah Zarah* 10a, b, and *Baba Metziah* 85a.

36. Meshorer, "Sepphoris and Rome," 170, note 42, where he cites *y. Peah, 16a.* Stuart Miller has discussed this issue in two long footnotes in "Those Cantakerous Sepphoreans Revisited," 555–56, notes 57 and 58, where he does not accept Meshorer's reading of the legend and offers that the Greek word "holy" refers to the Roman Senate and not the boule of Sepphoris.

37. Stern, "Babylonian Talmud, *Avodah Zarah* 16a."

38. Stern, "Rabbi and the Origins of the Patriarchate."

39. A corpus of these lamps is being prepared for publication by Eric Lapp. Meanwhile see his comments in Nagy, E. Meyers, C. Meyers, and Weiss, *Sepphoris in Galilee,* 218–24.

40. E. Meyers, "Ceramic Incense Shovels from Sepphoris."

41. Some of this is gathered in a provisional way in E. Meyers, "Problems of Gendered Space in Syro-Palestinian Domestic Architecture," 44–66.

42. Bland, *Artless Jew,* 3–12.

43. E. Meyers, "Jewish Culture in Greco-Roman Palestine," 135, and Schwartz, *Imperialism and Jewish Society,* 167–72, for a full discussion of this text.

44. Fine, *Art and Judaism,* 112.

45. Avigad and Mazar, "Beth Shearim."

46. Ibid., 242.

47. Fine, *Art and Judaism,* 87.

48. There is general agreement about the dating of the Talmud of the Land of Israel to the late fourth century. The details of its editing are not entirely clear, however, but its Galilean character and setting are. For a discussion of this see Leibner, "Settlement Patterns in Eastern Galilee."

49. For the best collection of the restrictive laws limiting Jewish participation in public life, see Linder, *Jews in Imperial Legislation.*

Chapter 11. After Constantine

1. Parker, "Byzantine Period"; Wilken, *Land Called Holy.*

2. Limor and Stroumsa, *Christians and Christianity in the Holy Land,* especially Patrich, "Early Christian Churches," and Hirschfeld, "Monasteries of Palestine"; Avi-Yonah, Cohen, and Ovadiah, "Churches"; Cohen, "Monasteries."

3. Levine, *Ancient Synagogue.*

4. Dothan, *Hammath Tiberias.*

5. Aviam, *Jews, Pagans, and Christians in the Galilee.*

6. Fonrobert and Jaffee, *Cambridge Companion to the Talmud and Rabbinic Judaism;* Katz, *Cambridge History of Judaism,* vol. 4.

7. Markschies, "Intellectuals and Church Fathers in the Third and Fourth Centuries."

8. Sivan, *Palestine in Late Antiquity.*

Bibliography

Adam, Jean-Pierre. *Roman Building: Materials and Techniques.* Trans. Anthony Mathew. Bloomington: Indiana University Press, 1994.

Adams, Edward. "The Ancient Church at Megiddo: The Discovery and an Assessment of Its Significance." *The Expository Times* 120:2 (2008): 62–69.

Adan-Bayewitz, David, Frank Asaro, Moshe Wieder, and Robert D. Giauque. "Preferential Distribution of Lamps from the Jerusalem Area in the Late Second Temple Period (Late First Century B.C.E.–70 C.E.)." *BASOR* 350 (2008): 37–85.

Adan-Bayewitz, David, and Mordechai Aviam. "Iotapata, Josephus, and the Siege of 67: Preliminary Report on the 1992–1994 Seasons." *Journal of Roman Archaeology* 10 (1997): 131–65.

Adler, Yonatan. "Ritual Baths Adjacent to Tombs: An Analysis of the Archaeological Evidence in Light of Halakhic Sources." *JSJ* 40 (2009): 57–60, 73.

Aharoni, Yohanan. "Excavations at Tel Beer-Sheba: Preliminary Report of the Fifth and Sixth Seasons, 1973–1974." *TA* 2 (1975): 146–68.

Albright, W. F. *The Archaeology of Palestine.* Baltimore: Penguin, 1961.

Aliquot, Julien. "Sanctuaries and Villages on Mt Hermon During the Roman Period." In *The Variety of Local Religious Life in the Near East in the Hellenistic and Roman Periods,* ed. Ted Kaizer, 73–96. Leiden: Brill, 2008.

Alsop, Stewart. "The Masada Complex." *Newsweek* (July 12, 1971): 92.

Amit, David, and Yonatan Adler. "The Observance of Ritual Purity After 70 C.E.: Reevaluation of the Evidence in Light of Archeological Discoveries." In *"Follow the Wise" (B. Sanhedrin 32b): Studies in Jewish History and Culture in Honor of Lee I. Levine,* ed. Zeev Weiss, Oded Irshai, Jodi Magness, and Seth Schwartz, 121–43. Winona Lake, Ind.: Eisenbrauns, 2010.

Applebaum, Shimon, and Arthur Segal. "Gerasa." *NEAEHL* 2: 470–79.

Arav, Rami. "Bethsaida: A Response to Steven Notley." *NEA* 74:2 (2011): 92–100.

Arav, Rami. *Hellenistic Palestine: Settlement Patterns and City Planning, 337–31 B.C.E.* Oxford: BAR, 1989.

Arav, Rami. "A Response to Notley's Reply." *NEA* 74:2 (2011): 103–5.

Arav, Rami, and Richard A. Freund, eds. *Bethsaida: A City by the North Shore of the Sea of Galilee.* Vol. 2. Kirksville, Mo.: Truman State University Press, 1999.

Ariel, Donald T., and Joseph Naveh. "Selected Inscribed Sealings from Kedesh in the Upper Galilee." *BASOR* 329 (2003): 61–80.

Arubas, Benny, Gideon Foerster, and Yoram Tsafrir. "Beth-Shean: The Hellenistic to

Early Islamic Periods at the Foot of the Mound: The Hebrew University Excavations." *NEAEHL* 5: 1636–41.

Ascough, Richard S. "Christianity in Caesarea Maritima." In *Religious Rivalries and the Struggle for Success in Caesarea Maritima,* ed. Terence L. Donaldson, 153–79. Waterloo, Ont.: Wilfrid Laurier, 2000.

Atkinson, Kenneth. "Gamla." In *The Eerdmans Dictionary of Early Judaism,* ed. John J. Collins and Daniel C. Harlow, 657–58. Grand Rapids: Wm. B. Eerdmans, 2010.

Atrash, Walid. "Tiberias, The Roman Theater: Preliminary Report." *Hadashot Arkheologiyot: Excavations and Surveys in Israel* 122 (2010). http://www.hadashot-esi.org.il/index_eng.asp.

Avener, Uzi. "Ancient Cult Sites in the Negev and Sinai Deserts." *TA* 11 (1984): 115–31.

Aviam, Mordechai. "The Archaeology of the Battle of Yodefat." In Mordechai Aviam, *Jews, Pagans, and Christians in the Galilee,* 110–22. Rochester: University of Rochester Press, 2004.

Aviam, Mordechai. "Borders Between Jews and Gentiles in the Galilee." In *Jews, Pagans, and Christians in the Galilee,* 9–21. Rochester: University of Rochester Press, 2004.

Aviam, Mordechai. "First Century Jewish Galilee." In *Religion and Society in Roman Palestine: Old Questions, New Approaches,* ed. Douglas R. Edwards, 7–27. New York: Routledge, 2004.

Aviam, Mordechai. *Jews, Pagans, and Christians in the Galilee.* Rochester: University of Rochester Press, 2004.

Aviam, Mordechai. "Yodefat/Jotapata: The Archaeology of the First Battle." In *The First Jewish Revolt: Archaeology, History, and Ideology,* ed. Andrea M. Berlin and J. Andrew Overman, 121–33. London: Routledge, 2002.

Aviam, Mordechai, and Danny Syon. "Jewish Ossilegium in Galilee." In *What Athens Has to Do with Jerusalem,* ed. Leonard V. Rutgers, 151–85. Leuven: Peeters, 2002.

Avigad, Nahman. *Beth Shearim.* Vol. 3, *The Excavations, 1953–1958.* New Brunswick: Rutgers University Press, 1976.

Avigad, Nahman. *Bullae and Seals from a Post-exilic Judean Archive.* Jerusalem: Israel Exploration Society, 1976.

Avigad, Nahman. *Discovering Jerusalem.* Nashville: Thomas Nelson, 1983.

Avigad, Nahman. "Samaria (City)." *NEAEHL* 4: 1300–1310.

Avigad, Nahman, and Hillel Geva. "Jerusalem: The Second Temple Period." *NEAEHL* 2: 717–57.

Avigad, Nahman, and Benjamin Mazar. "Beth She'arim." *NEAEHL* 1: 236–48.

Avi-Yonah, Michael. "Mount Carmel and the God of Baalbak." *IEJ* 11 (1952): 118–24.

Avi-Yonah, Michael. "Newly-Discovered Latin and Greek Inscriptions." *QDAP* 12 (1946): 84–102.

Avi-Yonah, Michael. "Syrian Gods at Ptolemais-Accho." *IEJ* 9 (1959): 1–12.

Avi-Yonah, Michael, Rudolf Cohen, and Asher Ovadiah. "Churches: Early Churches." *NEAEHL* 1: 305–14.

Bagatti, Bellarmino. *The Church from the Circumcision: History and Archaeology of the Judaeo-Christians.* Trans. Eugene Hoade. Jerusalem: Franciscan Printing Press, 1971.

Bagatti, Bellarmino. *Excavations in Nazareth.* Vol. 1. Trans. E. Hoade. Jerusalem: Franciscan Printing Press, 1969.

Bagatti, Bellarmino, and J. T. Milik. *Gli Scavi del "Dominus Flevit": I: La necropoli del periodo romano.* Jerusalem: Franciscan Printing Press, 1958.

Bahat, Dan. "The Architectural Origins of Herod's Temple Mount." In *Herod and Augustus: Papers Presented at the IJS Conference, 21st–23rd June 2005,* ed. David M. Jacobson and Nikos Kokkinos, 235–45. Leiden: Brill, 2009.

Bahat, Dan. "The Herodian Temple." In *The Cambridge History of Judaism,* ed. William Horbury, W. D. Davies, and John Sturdy, 3: 38–58. Cambridge: Cambridge University Press, 1999.

Ball, Warwick. *Rome in the East: The Transformation of an Empire.* London: Routledge, 2001.

Barag, Dan. "The Effects of the Tennes Rebellion on Palestine." *BASOR* 183 (1966): 6–12.

Barag, Dan. "King Herod's Royal Castle at Samaria-Sebaste." *PEQ* 125 (1993): 3–18.

Bar-Nathan, Rachel. "Qumran and the Hasmonean and Herodian Winter Palaces of Jericho: The Implication of the Pottery Finds for Interpretation of the Settlement of Qumran." In *The Site of the Dead Sea Scrolls: Archeological Interpretations and Debates,* ed. Katharina Galor, Jean-Baptiste Humbert, and Jürgen Zangenberg, 263–80. Leiden: Brill, 2006.

Barstad, Hans. *The Myth of the Empty Land: A Study in the History and Archaeology of Judah During the "Exilic" Period.* Oslo: Scandinavian University Press, 1996.

Bartlett, John R. "Nabataean Religion." In *The World of the Nabataeans: Volume 2 of the International Conference The World of the Herods and the Nabataeans Held at the British Museum, 17–29 April 2001,* ed. Konstantinos D. Politis, 55–78. Franz Steiner Verlag, 2007.

Batey, Richard A. *Jesus and the Forgotten City: New Light on Sepphoris and the Urban World of Jesus.* Illustrated by J. Robert Teringo. Grand Rapids: Baker Book House, 1991.

Bauckham, Richard. "Josephus' Account of the Temple in *Contra Apionem* 2.102–109." In *Contra Apionem: Studies in Character and Context with a Latin Concordance to the Portion Missing in Greek,* ed. Louis H. Feldman and John R. Levinson, 339–47. Leiden: Brill, 1996.

Baumgarten, A. I. "Invented Traditions of the Maccabean Era." In *Geschichte, Tradition, Reflexion: Festschrift für Martin Hengel zum 70. Gebertstag,* ed. Hubert Cancik, Hermann Lichtenberger, and Peter Schäfer, 1: 197–210. Tübingen: J. C. B. Mohr (Paul Siebeck), 1996.

Belayche, Nicole. *Iudaea-Palaestina: The Pagan Cults in Roman Palestine, Second to Forth Century.* Tübingen: Mohr Siebeck, 2001.

Ben-Tor, Amnon. *Back to Masada.* Jerusalem: Israel Exploration Society, 2009.

Ben-Yehudah, Nachman. *The Masada Myth: Collective Memory and Mythmaking in Israel.* Madison: University of Wisconsin Press, 1995.

Ben-Yehudah, Nachman. *Sacrificing Truth: Archaeology and the Myth of Masada.* Amherst, N.Y.: Humanity Books, 2002.

Ben Zeev, Miriam Pucci. "Diaspora Uprisings." *The Eerdmans Dictionary of Early Juda-*

ism, ed. John. J. Collins and Daniel C. Harlow, 539–42. Grand Rapids: Wm. B. Eerdmans, 2010.

Ben Zeev, Miriam Pucci. *Diaspora Judaism in Turmoil, 116/117 c.e.: Ancient Sources and Modern Insights.* Leuven: Peeters, 2005.

Berlin, Andrea M. "The Archaeology of Ritual: The Sanctuary of Pan at Banias/Caesarea Philippi." *BASOR* 315 (1999): 27–45.

Berlin, Andrea M. "Between Large Forces: Palestine in the Hellenistic Period." *Biblical Archaeologist* 60:1 (1997): 2–51.

Berlin, Andrea M. "From Monarchy to Markets: The Phoenicians in Hellenistic Palestine." *BASOR* 306 (1997): 75–88.

Berlin, Andrea M. *Gamla I: The Pottery of the Second Temple Period.* Jerusalem: Israel Antiquities Authority, 2006.

Berlin, Andrea M. "The Hellenistic Period." In *Near Eastern Archaeology: A Reader,* ed. Suzanne Richard, 418–33. Winona Lake, Ind.: Eisenbrauns, 2003.

Berlin, Andrea M. "Jewish Life Before the Revolt: The Archaeological Evidence." *JSJ* 36:4 (2005): 417–70.

Berlin, Andrea M. "Power and Its Afterlife: Tombs in Hellenistic Palestine." *NEA* 65:2 (2002): 138–48.

Berlin, Andrea M. "Romanization and Anti-Romanization in Pre-Revolt Galilee." In *The First Jewish Revolt: Archaeology, History, and Ideology,* ed. Andrea M. Berlin and J. Andrew Overman, 57–73. London: Routledge, 2002.

Berlin, Andrea M. "Where Was Herod's Temple to Augustus? Banias Is Still the Best Candidate." *BAR* 29:5 (2003): 22–24.

Berlin, Andrea M., and J. Andrew Overman, eds. *The First Jewish Revolt: Archaeology, History, and Ideology.* London: Routledge, 2002.

Bernett, Monika. *Der Kaiserkult in Judäa unter den Herodiern und Römern: Untersuchungen zur politischen und religiösen Geschichte Judäas von 30 v. bis 66 n. Chr.* Tübingen: Mohr Siebeck, 2007.

Bernett, Monika. "Roman Imperial Cult in the Galilee: Structures, Functions, and Dynamics." In *Religion, Ethnicity, and Identity in Ancient Galilee,* ed. Jürgen Zangenberg, Harold W. Attridge, and Dale B. Martin, 337–56. Tübingen: Mohr Siebeck, 2007.

Betlyon, John W. "A People Transformed: Palestine in the Persian Period." *NEA* 68: 1–2 (2005): 4–58.

Betz, Otto. "The Essenes." In *The Cambridge History of Judaism,* ed. William Horbury, W. D. Davies, and John Sturdy, 3: 440–70. Cambridge: Cambridge University Press, 1999.

Bialik, Hayim Nahman, and Yehosua Hana Ravnitsky, eds. *The Book of Legends: Sefer Ha-Aggadah.* Trans. William G. Braude. New York: Schocken, 1992.

Binder, Donald D. *Into the Temple Courts: The Place of the Synagogues in the Second Temple Period.* Atlanta: Society of Biblical Literature Diss. Ser. 169, 1999.

Biran, Avraham. "Dan." *NEAEHL* 1: 323–32.

Biran, Avraham. "To the God Who Is in Dan." *In Temples and High Places in Biblical Times,* ed. Avraham Biran, 142–51. Jerusalem: Nelson Glueck School of Biblical Archaeology of Hebrew Union College–Jewish Institute of Religion, 1981.

Bland, Kalman P. *The Artless Jew: Medieval and Modern Affirmations and Denials of the Visual.* Princeton: Princeton University Press, 2000.

Bösen, Willibald. *Galiläa als Lebensraum und Wirkungsfeld Jesu.* Basel: Herder Freiburg, 1985.

Brandon, C., S. Kemp, and M. Grove. "Pozzolana, Lime, and Single-Mission Barges (Area K)." In *Caesarea Papers 2,* ed. K. G. Holum, A. Raban, and J. Patrich, 169–78. Portsmouth, R.I.: Journal of Roman Archaeology, 1999.

Branham, Joan. "Hedging the Holy at Qumran: Walls as Symbolic Devices." In *The Site of the Dead Sea Scrolls: Archaeological Interpretations and Debates,* ed. Katharina Galor, Jean-Baptiste Humbert, and Jürgen Zangenberg, 117–31. Leiden: Brill, 2006.

Bricault, Laurent. "Deities from Egypt on the Coins of the Southern Levant." *Israel Numismatic Research* 1 (2006): 123–36.

Broshi, Magen. "Essene Gate." In *Encyclopedia of the Dead Sea Scrolls,* ed. Lawrence Schiffman and James C. Vanderkam, 261–62. Oxford: Oxford University Press, 2000.

Broshi, Magen. "The Population of Western Palestine in the Roman-Byzantine Period." *BASOR* 236 (1979): 1–10.

Broshi, Magen. "Qumran: Archaeology." In *Encyclopedia of the Dead Sea Scrolls,* ed. Lawrence H. Schiffman and James C. Vanderkam, 733–39. Oxford: Oxford University Press, 2000.

Broshi, Magen. "Was Qumran a Crossroads?" *Revue de Qumran* 18 (1999): 273–76.

Broshi, Magen, and Hanan Eshel. "Qumran and the Dead Sea Scrolls: The Contention of Twelve Theories." In *Religion and Society in Roman Palestine,* ed. Douglas R. Edwards, 162–69. New York: Routledge, 2004.

Broshi, Magen, and Shimon Gibson. "Excavations Along the Western and Southern Walls of the Old City of Jerusalem." In *Ancient Jerusalem Revealed,* ed. Hillel Geva, 147–55. Jerusalem: Israel Exploration Society, 1994.

Bruneau, P. "Les Israelites de Délos et la juiverie délienne." *Bulletin de Correspondance Hellénique* 106 (1982): 465–504.

Byrne, Ryan, and Bernadette McNary-Zak, eds. *Resurrecting the Brother of Jesus: The James Ossuary Controversy and the Quest for Religious Relics.* Chapel Hill: University of North Carolina Press, 2009.

Campbell, Edward F. "Shechem." *NEAEHL* 4: 1353–54.

Capper, Brian J. "Essene Community Houses and Jesus' Early Community." In *Jesus and Archaeology,* ed. James H. Charlesworth, 472–502. Grand Rapids: Wm. B. Eerdmans, 2006.

Cargill, Robert R. *Qumran Through Real Time: A Virtual Reconstruction of Qumran and the Dead Sea Scrolls.* Piscataway, N.J.: Gorgias, 2009.

Carroll, Robert P. "The Myth of the Empty Land." *Semeia* 59 (1993): 79–93.

Carter, Charles E. *The Emergence of Yehud in the Persian Period: A Social and Demographic Study.* Sheffield: Sheffield Academic Press, 1999.

Chancey, Mark A. "Archaeology, Ethnicity, and First-Century C.E. Galilee: The Limits of Evidence." In *A Wandering Galilean: Essays in Honour of Sean Freyne,* ed. Zuleika Rodgers with Margaret Daly-Denton and Anne Fitzpatrick McKinley, 205–18. Leiden: E. J. Brill, 2009.

Chancey, Mark A. "The Cultural Milieu of Ancient Sepphoris." *NTS* 47:2 (2001): 127–45.

Chancey, Mark A. "Disputed Issues in the Study of Cities, Villages, and the Economy in Jesus' Galilee." In *The World of Jesus and the Early Church: Identity and Interpretation in Communities of Faith,* ed. Craig Evans, 53–68. Peabody, Mass.: Hendrikson, 2011.

Chancey, Mark A. *Greco-Roman Culture and the Galilee of Jesus.* Cambridge: Cambridge University Press, 2005.

Chancey, Mark A. "Jotapata." In *The Eerdmans Dictionary of Early Judaism,* ed. John J. Collins and Daniel C. Harlow, 842–43. Grand Rapids: Wm. B. Eerdmans, 2010.

Chancey, Mark A. *The Myth of a Gentile Galilee.* Cambridge: Cambridge University Press, 2002.

Chancey, Mark A. "Temple Tax." In *The Eerdmans Dictionary of Early Judaism,* ed. John J. Collins and Daniel C. Harlow, 1294. Grand Rapids: Wm. B. Eerdmans, 2010.

Chancey, Mark A., and Adam Porter. "The Archaeology of Roman Palestine." *NEA* 64 (2001): 164–203.

Charlesworth, James H., ed. *Jesus and Archaeology.* Grand Rapids: Wm. B. Eerdmans, 2006.

Chen, Doron. "The Ancient Synagogue at Nabratein: Design and Chronology." *PEQ* 119 (1987): 44–49.

Christoph, James. "The Yehud Stamped Jar Handle Corpus: Implications for the History of Postexilic Palestine." Ph.D. diss., Duke University, 1993.

Clermont-Ganneau, Charles. "Épigraphique hébraïques et grecques sur des ossuaires juifs inédits." *Revue archéologique,* 3rd ser., 1 (1883): 257–76.

Cohen, Rudolf. "Monasteries." *NEAEHL* 3: 1063–70.

Cohen, Rudolf. "Negev: Hellenistic, Roman, and Byzantine Sites." *NEAEHL* 3: 1135–45.

Cohen, Shaye J. D. *The Beginnings of Jewishness: Boundaries, Varieties, Uncertainties.* Berkeley: University of California Press, 1999.

Cohen, Shaye J. D. *From the Maccabees to the Mishnah.* Philadelphia: Westminster, 1986.

Cohen, Shaye J. D. "Literary Tradition, Archeological Remains, and the Credibility of Josephus." *JJS* 33 (1982): 385–405.

Collins, John J. *The Apocalyptic Vision of the Book of Daniel.* Missoula, Mont.: Scholars Press, 1977.

Collins, John J. *Beyond the Qumran Community: The Sectarian Movement of the Dead Sea Scrolls.* Grand Rapids: Wm. B. Eerdmans, 2010.

Collins, John J. "Sectarian Communities in the Dead Sea Scrolls." In *The Oxford Handbook of the Dead Sea Scrolls,* ed. Timothy H. Lim and John J. Collins, 151–72. Oxford: Oxford University Press, 2010.

Collins, John J., and Timothy H. Lim. "Introduction: Current Issues in Dead Sea Scroll Research." In *The Oxford Handbook of the Dead Sea Scrolls,* ed. Timothy H. Lim and John J. Collins, 1–20. Oxford: Oxford University Press, 2010.

Collins, John J., and Timothy H. Lim, eds. *The Oxford Handbook of the Dead Sea Scrolls.* Oxford: Oxford University Press, 2010.

Corbo, V. *Cafarnao I: Gli edifici della citta.* Jerusalem: Franciscan Press, 1975.

Corbo, V. *The House of St. Peter at Capharnaum.* Jerusalem: Franciscan Press, 1969.

Cotton, Hannah M. "The Guardianship of Jesus Son of Babatha: Roman and Local Law in the Province of Arabia." *Journal of Roman Studies* 83 (1993): 94–108.

Cotton, Hannah M., and K. Wörrle. "Seleukos IV to Heliodoros: A New Dossier of Royal Correspondence from Israel." *ZPE* 159 (2007): 191–205.

Cotton, Hannah M., et al., eds. *Corpus Inscriptionem Judaeae/Palaestinae.* Vol. 1, part 1. Berlin: De Gruyter 2010.

Cross, Jr., Frank Moore. "The Papyri and Their Historical Implications." In *Discoveries in the Wadi ed-Daliyeh,* ed. Paul W. Lapp and Nancy L. Lapp, 17–32. Cambridge: ASOR, 1974.

Crossan, John Dominic. *The Birth of Christianity.* San Francisco: HarperSanFrancisco, 1998.

Crossan, John Dominic, and Jonathan L. Reed. *Excavating Jesus: Beneath the Stones, Behind the Texts.* San Francisco: HarperSanFrancisco, 2002.

Crowfoot, J. W., G. M. Crowfoot, and Kathleen M. Kenyon. *The Objects from Samaria,* vol. 3 of *Samaria-Sebaste: Reports of the Work of the Joint Expedition in 1931–1933 and of the British Expedition in 1935.* London: Palestine Exploration Fund, 1957.

Crown, Alan D., and Lena Cansdale. "Qumran—Was It an Essene Settlement?" *BAR* 20:5 (1994): 24–37, 73–78.

Dar, Shimon. *Landscape and Pattern: An Archaeological Survey of Samaria 800 B.C.E.–636 C.E.* Oxford: BAR, 1986.

Dar, Shimon. *Settlements and Cult Sites on Mount Hermon, Israel: Ituraean Culture in the Hellenistic and Roman Periods.* Oxford: BAR 1993.

Dar, Shimon, and Nikos Kokkinos. "The Greek Inscriptions from Senaim on Mount Hermon." *PEQ* 124 (1992): 9–25.

Davies, W. D., and Louis Finkelstein, eds. *The Cambridge History of Judaism.* Vol. 2, *The Hellenistic Age.* Cambridge: Cambridge University Press, 1989.

de Vaux, Roland. *Archaeology and the Dead Sea Scrolls: The Schweich Lectures of the British Academy, 1959.* London: Oxford University Press, 1973.

Di Segni, Leah. "A New Toponym in Southern Samaria." *Liber Annuus* 44 (1994): 579–84.

Donaldson, Terence L., ed. *Religious Rivalries and the Struggle for Success in Caesarea Maritima.* Waterloo, Ont.: Wilfrid Laurier University Press, 2000.

Donceel, Robert, and Pauline Donceel-Voûte. "The Archaeology of Khirbet Qumran." In *Methods of Investigation of the Dead Sea Scrolls and Khirbet Qumran Site: Present Realities and Future Prospects,* ed. M. O. Wise, N. Golb, John J. Collins, and D. Pardee, 1–38. New York: New York Academy of Sciences, 1994.

Dothan, Moshe. "Ashdod." *NEAEHL* 1: 93–102.

Dothan, Moshe. *Hammath Tiberias: Early Synagogues and the Hellenistic and Roman Remains.* Jerusalem: Israel Exploration Society; Haifa: University of Haifa Department of Antiquities and Museums, 1983.

Drijvers, J. W. *Helena Augusta: The Mother of Constantine the Great and the Legend of Her Finding of the True Cross.* Leiden, 1992.

Elgavish, Joseph. "Shiqmona." *NEAEHL* 4: 1373–78.

Erlich, Adi. *The Art of Hellenistic Palestine.* Oxford: Archaeopress, 2009.

Erlich, Adi, and Amos Kloner. *Maresha Excavations Final Report II: Hellenistic Terracotta Figurines from the 1989–1996 Seasons.* Jerusalem: Israel Antiquities Authority, 2008.

Eshel, Hanan. "Bar Kokhba Caves." In *The Eerdmans Dictionary of Early Judaism,* ed. John J. Collins and Daniel C. Harlow, 417–18. Grand Rapids: Wm. B. Eerdmans, 2010.

Eshel, Hanan. "Bar Kokhba Letters." In *The Eerdmans Dictionary of Early Judaism,* ed. John J. Collins and Daniel C. Harlow, 418–21. Grand Rapids: Wm. B. Eerdmans, 2010.

Eshel, Hanan. "Bar Kokhba Revolt." In *The Eerdmans Dictionary of Early Judaism,* ed. John J. Collins and Daniel C. Harlow, 421–25. Grand Rapids: Wm. B. Eerdmans, 2010.

Evans, Craig A. *Jesus and the Ossuaries: What Jewish Burial Practices Reveal About the Beginning of Christianity.* Waco: Baylor University Press, 2003.

Fields, Weston W. *The Dead Sea Scrolls: A Full History.* Vol. 1, *1947–1960.* Leiden: Brill, 2009.

Fiensy, David A. "Ancient Economy and the New Testament." In *Understanding the Social World of the New Testament,* ed. Dietmar Neufeld and Richard E. DeMaris, 194–206. London: Routledge, 2010.

Fiensy, David A. *Jesus the Galilean: Soundings in a First Century Life.* Piscataway, N.J.: Gorgias, 2007.

Fine, Steven. *Art and Judaism in the Greco-Roman World: Toward a New Jewish Archaeology.* Cambridge: Cambridge University Press, 2005.

Fine, Steven. "A Note on Ossuary Burial and Resurrection of the Dead in First Century Jerusalem." *JJS* 51 (2000): 69–76.

Fine, Steven. *Sacred Realm: The Emergence of the Synagogue in the Ancient World.* New York: Oxford University Press, 1996.

Fine, Steven. *This Holy Place: On the Sanctity of the Synagogue During the Greco-Roman Period.* Notre Dame: University of Notre Dame Press, 1997.

Finegan, Jack. *The Archaeology of the New Testament: The Life of Jesus and the Beginning of the Early Church.* Rev. ed. Princeton: Princeton University Press, 1992.

Finkelstein, Israel. "Jerusalem in the Persian (and Early Hellenistic) Period and the Wall of Nehemiah." *Journal for the Study of the Old Testament* 32 (2008): 501–20.

Finkelstein, Israel. "The Territorial Extent and Demography of Yehud/Judea in the Persian and Early Hellenistic Periods." *Revue biblique* 117:1 (2010): 39–54.

Fischer, Moshe. *Marble Studies: Roman Palestine and the Marble Trade.* Konstanz: Universitätsverlag Konstanz, 1998.

Fischer, Moshe. "Yavneh-Yam." *NEAEHL* 5: 2073–75.

Fischer, Moshe, Asher Ovadiah, and Israel Roll. "The Epigraphic Finds from the Roman Temple at Kedesh in the Upper Galilee." *TA* 13 (1986): 60–66.

Fischer, Moshe, Asher Ovadiah, and Israel Roll. "An Inscribed Altar from the Roman Temple at Kadesh (Upper Galilee)." *ZPE* 49 (1982): 155–58.

Fischer, Moshe, Asher Ovadiah, and Israel Roll. "The Roman Temple at Kedesh, Upper Galilee: A Preliminary Study." *TA* 11 (1984): 146–72.

Fischer, Moshe, and O. Tal. "Architectural Decoration in Ancient Israel in Hellenistic Times: Some Aspects of Hellenization." *ZDPV* 119 (2003): 19–37.

Fittschen, Klaus. "Wall Decorations in Herod's Kingdom: Their Relationship with Wall Decorations in Greece and Italy." In *Judaea and the Greco-Roman World in the Time of Herod in the Light of Archaeological Evidence,* ed. Klaus Fittschen and Gideon Foerster, 139–62. Göttingen: Vendenhoeck and Ruprecht, 1996.

Foerster, G. "The Synagogues at Masada and Herodium." In *Ancient Synagogues Revealed,* ed. Lee I. Levine, 24–29. Jerusalem: Israel Exploration Society, 1981.

Fonrobert, Charlotte E., and Martin S. Jaffee, eds. *A Cambridge Companion to the Talmud and Rabbinic Judaism.* Cambridge: Cambridge University Press, 2007.

Frankel, Rafael. "Mizpe Yammim, Mount." *NEAEHL* 3: 1061–63.

Frankel, Rafael, Nimrod Getzov, Mordechai Aviam, and Avi Degani. *Settlement Dynamics and Regional Diversity in Ancient Upper Galilee: Archaeological Survey of Upper Galilee.* Jerusalem: Israel Antiquities Authority, 2001.

Frankel, Rafael, and Raphael Ventura. "The Mispe Yamim Bronzes." *BASOR* 311 (1998): 39–55.

Frey, Jean-Baptiste. *Corpus Inscriptionem Judaicarum.* 2 vols. Rome: Pontificio Istituto di Archeologica Cristiana, 1936–1952.

Freyne, Sean. *Galilee, Jesus, and the Gospels: Literary Approaches and Historical Investigations.* Philadelphia: Fortress, 1988.

Freyne, Sean. *Galilee from Alexander the Great to Hadrian: A Study of Second Temple Judaism.* Wilmington, Del.: Glazier, and Notre Dame: University of Notre Dame, 1980; reprint, Edinburgh: T & T Clark, 1998.

Freyne, Sean. *Galilee and Gospel: Collected Essays.* Tübingen: Mohr Siebeck, 2000.

Friedheim, Emmanuel. *Rabbinisme et paganisme en Palestine romaine: étude historique des Realia talmudiques (Ier–IVème siècles).* Leiden: Brill, 2006.

Friedland, Elise. "Graeco-Roman Sculpture in the Levant: The Marble from the Sanctuary of Pan at Caesarea Philippi (Banias)." In *The Roman and Byzantine Near East,* ed. J. H. Humphrey, 2: 7–22. Portsmouth, R.I.: Journal of Roman Archaeology, 1999.

Fuks, Gideon. "A Mediterranean Pantheon: Cults and Deities in Hellenistic and Roman Ashkelon." *Mediterranean Historical Review* 15:2 (2000): 27–48.

Gal, Zvi, ed. *Eretz Zafon: Studies in Galilean Archaeology.* Jerusalem: Israel Antiquities Authority, 2002.

Gal, Zvi. "A Stone-Vessel Manufacturing Site in the Lower Galilee." *Atiqot* 20 (1991): 179–80.

Galor, Katharina. "The Stepped Water Installations of the Sepphoris Acropolis." In *The Archaeology of Difference: Gender, Ethnicity, Class and the "Other" in Antiquity: Studies in Honor of Eric M. Meyers,* ed. Douglas R. Edwards and C. Thomas McCollough, 201–13. Boston: ASOR, 2007.

Galor, Katharina, Jean-Baptiste Humbert, and Jürgen Zangenberg, eds. *The Site of the Dead Sea Scrolls: Archeological Interpretations and Debates.* Leiden: Brill, 2006.

Gera, Dov. "Tryphon's Sling Bullet from Dor." In *Excavations at Dor: Final Report.* Vol. 1B, ed. Ephraim Stern et al., 491–96. Jerusalem: Israel Exploration Society, 1995.

Geraty, Lawrence T. "The Khirbet el-Kom Bilingual Ostracon." *BASOR* 220 (1975): 55–61.

Gersht, Rivka. "Representation of Deities and the Cults of Caesarea." In *Caesarea Maritima: A Retrospective After Two Millennia,* ed. Avner Raban and Kenneth G. Holum, 305–24. Leiden: E. J. Brill, 1996.

Geva, Hillel. "A Chronological Reevaluation of Yehud Stamp Impressions in Palaeo-Hebrew Script, Based on Finds from Excavations in the Jewish Quarter of the Old City of Jerusalem." *TA* 34 (2007): 92–103.

Geva, Hillel. "Estimating Jerusalem's Population in Antiquity: A Minimalist View." *Eretz Israel* 28 (2007): 50–65 (Hebrew).

Geva, Hillel. "Excavations at the Citadel of Jerusalem, 1976–1980." In *Ancient Jerusalem Revealed,* ed. Hillel Geva, 156–67. Jerusalem: Israel Exploration Society, 1994.

Geva, Hillel. "Jerusalem: The Roman Period." *NEAEHL* 2: 758–67.

Geva, Hillel. *Jewish Quarter Excavations in the Old City of Jerusalem Conducted by Nahman Avigad, 1969–1982.* Vol. 4, *The Burnt House of Area B and Other Studies, Final Report.* Jerusalem: Israel Exploration Society and Institute of Archaeology, Hebrew University, 2010.

Gibson, Shimon. "Is the Talpiot Tomb Really the Family Tomb of Jesus?" *NEA* 69: 3–4 (2006): 118–23.

Gibson, Shimon, and Joan E. Taylor. *Beneath the Church of the Holy Sepulchre Jerusalem: The Archaeology and Early History of Traditional Golgotha.* London: Palestine Exploration Fund, 1994.

Gitler, Haim. "Coins." In *The Eerdmans Dictionary of Early Judaism,* ed. John J. Collins and Daniel C. Harlow, 480. Grand Rapids: Wm. B. Eerdmans, 2010.

Gitler, Haim, and Oren Tal. *The Coinage of Philistia in the Fifth and Fourth Centuries B.C.: A Study of the Earliest Coins of Palestine.* Milan: Edizioni Ennerre, New York: Amphora Books, B & H Kreindler, 2006.

Golb, Norman. "Who Hid the Dead Sea Scrolls?" *BA* 48 (1985): 68–82.

Goodman, Martin. "Current Scholarship on the First Revolt." In *The First Jewish Revolt: Archaeology, History, and Ideology,* ed. Andrea M. Berlin and J. Andrew Overman, 15–24. London: Routledge, 2002.

Goodman, Martin. *The Ruling Class of Judaea: The Origins of the Jewish Revolt Against Rome, A.D. 66–70.* Cambridge: Cambridge University Press, 1987.

Grabbe, Lester L. *Judaic Religion in the Second Temple Period: Belief and Practice from the Exile to Yavneh.* London: Routledge, 2000.

Grabbe, Lester L. *Judaism from Cyrus to Hadrian.* 2 vols. Minneapolis: Fortress, 1992.

Graf, David. "The Nabateans." In *Near Eastern Archaeology: A Reader,* ed. Suzanne Richard, 134–39. Winona Lake, Ind.: Eisenbrauns, 2003.

Graf, Fritz. "Roman Festivals in Syria Palaestina." In *The Talmud Yerushalmi and Graeco-Roman Culture,* ed. Peter Schäfer, 3: 436–51. Tübingen: Mohr Siebeck, 2002.

Grant, Frederick C. *The Economic Background of the Gospels.* Oxford: Oxford University Press, 1926.

The Great Revolt in the Galilee. Haifa: Hecht Museum, 2008.

Green, David, and Richmond Lattimore, eds. *The Complete Greek Tragedies*. Chicago: University of Chicago Press, 1959–1960.

Gregg, Robert C., and Dan Urman. *Jews, Pagans, and Christians in the Golan Heights: Greek and Other Inscriptions of the Roman and Byzantine Eras*. Atlanta: Scholars Press, 1996.

Grey, Matthew J. "Jewish Priests and the Social History of Post-70 Palestine." Ph.D. diss., University of North Carolina at Chapel Hill, 2011.

Gruen, Eric S. *Heritage and Hellenism: The Reinvention of Jewish Tradition*. Berkeley: University of California Press, 1998.

Guri-Rimon, Ofra. "Preface." *The Great Revolt in the Galilee*, 5–7. Haifa: Hecht University Museum, 2008.

Gutman, S. "Gamala." *NEAEHL* 2: 460–62.

Gutman, S. "The Synagogue at Gamla." In *Ancient Synagogues Revealed*, ed. Lee I. Levine, 30–34. Jerusalem: Israel Exploration Society, 1981.

Guttman, A. "The Patriarch Judah I—His Birth and His Death." *Hebrew Union College Annual* 25 (1954): 239–61.

Haas, N. "Anthropological Observations on the Skeletal Remains from Giv'at ha-Mivtar." *IEJ* 20 (1970): 38–59.

Haber, Susan. "Common Judaism, Common Synagogue? Purity, Holiness, and Sacred Space at the Turn of the Common Era." In *Common Judaism: Explorations in Second-Temple Judaism*, ed. Wayne O. McCready and Adele Reinhartz, 63–77. Minneapolis: Fortress, 2008.

Hachlili, Rachel. *Ancient Jewish Art and Archaeology in the Land of Israel*. Leiden: E. J. Brill, 1988.

Hachlili, Rachel. *Ancient Mosaic Pavements: Themes, Issues, and Trends, Selected Studies*. Leiden: Brill, 2009.

Hachlili, Rachel. *Jewish Funerary Customs, Practices, and Rites in the Second Temple Period*. Leiden: Brill, 2005.

Hachlili, Rachel. "The Qumran Cemetery Reassessed." In *The Oxford Handbook of the Dead Sea Scrolls*, ed. Timothy H. Lim and John J. Collins, 46–78. Oxford: Oxford University Press, 2010.

Hachlili, Rachel, and Ann E. Killebrew. "Horbat Qazion." *Hadashot Arkheologiyot* 109 (1999): 6–7.

Halpern-Zylberstein, Marie-Christine. "The Archeology of Hellenistic Palestine." In *The Cambridge History of Judaism*, ed. W. D. Davies and Louis Finkelstein, 2: 1–34. Cambridge: Cambridge University Press, 1989.

Hanson, Richard S. *Tyrian Influence in the Upper Galilee*. Cambridge, Mass.: ASOR, 1980.

Harl, Kenneth W. *Civic Coins and Civic Politics in the Roman East A.D. 180–275*. Berkeley: University of California Press, 1987.

Harrison, Robert. "Hellenization in Syria-Palestine: The Case of Judea in the Third Century B.C.E." *BA* 57 (1994): 98–108.

Healey, John F. *The Religion of the Nabateans: A Conspectus*. Leiden: Brill, 2001.

Hendin, David. *Guide to Biblical Coins*. Fifth ed. Nyack, N.Y.: Amphora, 2010.

Hendin, David. "A New Coin Type of Herod Antipas." *INJ* 15 (2003–2006): 56–61.

Hengel, Martin. *Judaism and Hellenism: Studies in Their Encounter in Palestine During the Early Hellenistic Period.* Philadelphia: Fortress, 1974.

Herbert, Sharon C. "Tel Anafa, 1980." *Muse* 14 (1980): 24–30.

Herbert, Sharon C., and Andrea M. Berlin. "A New Administrative Center for Persian and Hellenistic Galilee: Preliminary Report of the University of Michigan/University of Minnesota Excavations at Kedesh." *BASOR* 329 (2003): 13–59.

Herbert, Sharon C., et al. *Tel Anafa I: Final Report on Ten Years of Excavation at a Hellenistic and Roman Settlement in Northern Israel.* Ann Arbor, Mich.: Journal of Roman Archaeology, 1994.

Herman, Daniel. "The Coins of the Itureans." *Israel Numismatic Research* 1 (2006): 51–72.

Herzog, William R., II. *Jesus, Justice, and the Reign of God.* Louisville: Westminster/John Knox, 2000.

Herzog, Ze'ev. "Beersheba: Tel Beersheba." *NEAEHL* 1: 167–73.

Heuver, Gerald D. *The Teachings of Jesus Concerning Wealth.* Chicago: Fleming H. Revell, 1903.

Hirschfeld, Yizhar. "The Monasteries of Palestine in the Byzantine Period." In *Christians and Christianity in the Holy Land,* ed. Ora Limor and Guy G. Stroumsa, 401–19. Turnhout: Brepols, 2006.

Hirschfeld, Yizhar. *Qumran in Context: Reassessing the Archaeological Evidence.* Peabody, Mass.: Hendrickson, 2004.

Hizmi, Hananya. "Archelaus Builds Archelais." *BAR* 34:4 (2008): 48–59, 78.

Hizmi, Hananya. "Beiyudat, Khirbet e-." *NEAEHL* 5: 1600–1602.

Hoffmann, Adolf. "Hellenistic Gadara." *Studies in the History and Archaeology of Jordan* 7 (2001): 391–97.

Hoglund, Kenneth G. *Achaemenid Imperial Administration in Syria-Palestine and the Missions of Ezra and Nehemiah.* Atlanta: Scholars Press, 1989.

Holum, Kenneth G., Robert L. Hohlfelder, Robert J. Bull, and Avner Raban. *King Herod's Dream: Caesarea on the Sea.* New York: W. W. Norton, 1988.

Horbury, William. "Beginnings of Christianity in the Holy Land." In *Christians and Christianity in the Holy Land: From the Origins to the Latin Kingdoms,* ed. Ora Limor and Guy G. Stroumsa, 7–89. Turnhout, Belgium: Brepols, 2006.

Horbury, William, W. D. Davies, and John Sturdy, eds. *The Cambridge History of Judaism.* Vol. 3, *The Early Roman Period.* Cambridge: Cambridge University Press, 1999.

Horsley, Richard A. *Galilee: History, Politics, People.* Valley Forge: Trinity, 1995.

Horsley, Richard A. "Power Vacuum and Power Struggle." In *The First Jewish Revolt: Archaeology, History, and Ideology,* ed. Andrea M. Berlin and J. Andrew Overman, 87–109. London: Routledge, 2002.

Hultgren, Stephen. *From the Damascus Covenant to the Covenant of the Community: Literary, Historical, and Theological Studies.* Leiden: Brill, 2007.

Humbert, Jean-Baptiste. "Some Remarks on the Archaeology of Qumran." In *Qumran, the Site of the Dead Sea Scrolls: Archaeological Interpretations and Debates: Proceedings of the Conference Held at Brown University, November 17–19,* ed. K. Galor, J.-B. Humbert, and J. Zangenberg, 19–39. Leiden: Brill, 2006.

Humphrey, John H. " 'Amphitheatrical' Hippo-Stadia." In *Caesarea Maritima: A Retro-*

spective After Two Millennia, ed. Avner Raban and Kenneth G. Holum, 121–29. Leiden: Brill, 1996.

Hunt, E. D. *Holy Land Pilgrimage in the Later Roman Empire, A.D. 312–460.* Oxford: Oxford University Press, 1982.

Ilan, Tal. *Lexicon of Jewish Names in Late Antiquity,* Part 1, *Palestine, 330 B.C.E.–200 C.E.* Tübingen: Mohr Siebeck, 2002.

Ilan, Tal. "Notes on the Distribution of Jewish Women's Names in Palestine in the Second Temple and Mishnaic Periods." *JJS* 40 (1989): 186–200.

Iliffe, J. H. "A Nude Terra-Cotta Statuette of Aphrodite." *QDAP* 3 (1934): 106–11.

Irshai, Oded. "From Oblivion to Fame: The History of the Palestinian Church (135–303 C.E.)." In *Christians and Christianity in the Holy Land: From the Origins to the Latin Kingdoms,* ed. Ora Limor and Guy G. Stroumsa, 91–139. Turnhout, Belgium: Brepols, 2006.

Isaac, Benjamin. *The Limits of Empire: The Roman Army in the East.* Rev. ed. Oxford: Clarendon Press, 1990.

Jacobovici, Simcha, and Charles Pellegrino. *The Jesus Family Tomb: The Discovery, the Investigation, and the Evidence That Could Change History.* San Francisco: HarperCollins, 2007.

Jacobs, Martin. "Pagane Temple in Palästina-rabbinische Aussagen im Vergleich mit archäologischen Funden." In *The Talmud Yerushalmi and Graeco-Roman Culture,* ed. Peter Schäfer and Catherine Hezser, eds., 2: 139–59. Tübingen: Mohr Siebeck, 2000.

Jacobson, David M., and Nikos Kokkinos, eds. *Herod and Augustus: Papers Presented at the IJS Conference, 21st–23rd June 2005.* Leiden: Brill, 2009.

Jensen, Morten Hørning. *Herod Antipas in Galilee.* Tübingen: Mohr Siebeck, 2006.

Kadman, Leo. *The Coins of Akko Ptolemais.* Tel Aviv: Schocken, 1961.

Kaplan, Jacob, and Haya Ritter-Kaplan. "Tel Aviv." *NEAEHL* 4: 1451–57.

Katz, Steven T., ed. *The Cambridge History of Judaism.* Vol. 4. Cambridge: Cambridge University Press, 2006.

Kee, Howard Clark. "Defining the First-Century C.E. Synagogue, Problems and Progress." In *Evolution of the Synagogue: Problems and Progress,* ed. Howard Clark Kee and Lynn Y. Cohick, 7–26. Harrisburg: Trinity International Press, 1999.

Kee, Howard Clark, and Lynn Y. Cohick, eds. *Evolution of the Synagogue: Problems and Progress.* Harrisburg: Trinity International Press, 1999.

Kimelman, Reuven. "Identifying Jews and Christians in Roman Syria-Palestine." In *Galilee Through the Centuries: Confluence of Cultures,* ed. Eric M. Meyers, 301–33. Winona Lake, Ind.: Eisenbrauns, 1999.

Kloner, Amos. "Maresha (Marisa)." *NEAEHL* 1: 948–57 and 5: 1918–25.

Kloner, Amos. *Maresha Excavations Final Report 1: Subterranean Complexes 21, 44, 70.* Jerusalem: Israel Antiquities Authority, 2003.

Kloner, Amos. "A Tomb with Inscribed Ossuaries in East Talpiyot, Jerusalem." *Atiqot* 29 (1996): 15–22.

Kloner, Amos, and Sherry Weinstein. "The Hippo-Stadium/Amphitheater in Jerusalem." In *"Follow the Wise" (B. Sanhedrin 32b): Studies in Jewish History and Culture in Honor of Lee I. Levine,* ed. Zeev Weiss, Oded Irshai, Jodi Magness, and Seth Schwartz, 163–76. Winona Lake, Ind.: Eisenbrauns, 2010.

Kloppenborg Verbin, John S. "Dating Theodotus (*CIJ* II 1410)." *JJS* 51 (2000): 243–80.

Knoppers, Gary N., and Lester L. Grabbe with Deirdre Fulton, eds. *Exile and Restoration Revisited: Essays on the Babylonian Periods in Memory of Peter R. Ackroyd.* London: T & T Clark, 2009.

Kraabel, A. T. "The Diaspora Synagogue: Archaeological and Epigraphic Evidence Since Sukenik." *Aufstieg und Niedergang der römischen Welt* II, 19.1, ed. H. Temporini and W. Haase, 477–510. Berlin: de Gruyter, 1979.

Kraabel, A. T. "New Evidence for the Samaritan Diaspora Has Been Found at Delos." *BA* 47 (1984): 44–46.

Kugler, Robert. "Dead Sea Scrolls." In *The Eerdmans Dictionary of Early Judaism,* ed. John J. Collins and Daniel C. Harlow, 520–24. Grand Rapids: Wm. B. Eerdmans, 2010.

Lawrence, Jonathan D. *Washing in Water: Trajectories of Ritual Bathing in the Hebrew Bible and Second Temple Literature.* Atlanta: Society of Biblical Literature, 2006.

Lehmann, Clayton Miles, and Kenneth G. Holum. *The Greek and Latin Inscriptions of Caesarea Maritima.* Vol. 5 of *The Joint Expedition to Caesarea Maritima Excavation Reports.* Boston: ASOR, 2000.

Leibner, Uzi. "Khirbet Wadi Hamam: A Roman Period Village and Synagogue in Galilee." *Qadmoniot* 43 (2010): 30–40 (Hebrew).

Leibner, Uzi. "Settlement Patterns in Eastern Galilee: Implications Regarding the Transformation of Rabbinic Culture in Late Antiquity." In *Jewish Identities in Antiquity: Studies in Memory of Menahem Stern,* ed. Lee I. Levine and Daniel R. Schwartz, 286–91. Tübingen: Mohr Siebeck, 2009.

Levine, Lee I. *The Ancient Synagogue: The First Thousand Years.* New Haven: Yale University Press, 2000.

Levine, Lee I., ed. *Ancient Synagogues Revealed.* Jerusalem: Israel Exploration Society, 1981.

Levine, Lee I. "The First-Century Synagogue: Critical Reassessments and Assessments of the Critical." In *Religion and Society in Roman Palestine: Old Questions, New Approaches,* ed. Douglas R. Edwards, 70–102. New York: Routledge, 2004.

Levine, Lee I. "Hasmonean Jerusalem: A Jewish City in a Hellenistic Orbit." *Judaism* 46:2 (1997): 140–46.

Levine, Lee I. *Jerusalem: Portrait of the City in the Second Temple Period (538 B.C.E.–70 C.E.).* Philadelphia: Jewish Publication Society, 2002.

Levine, Lee I. "The Nature and Origin of the Palestinian Synagogue Reconsidered." *JBL* 115:3 (1996): 424–48.

Levine, Lee I. "Synagogues." In *The Eerdmans Dictionary of Early Judaism,* ed. John J. Collins and Daniel C. Harlow, 1260–71. Grand Rapids: Wm. B. Eerdmans, 2010.

Lichtenberger, Achim. *Die Baupolitik Herodes des Großen.* Wiesbaden: Harrassowitz Verlag, 1999.

Lichtenberger, Achim. "Herod and Rome: Was Romanisation a Goal of the Building Policy of Herod?" In *Herod and Augustus: Papers Presented at the IJS Conference,*

21st–23rd June 2005, ed. David M. Jacobson and Nikos Kokkinos, 43–62. Leiden: Brill, 2009.

Lichtenberger, Achim. "Jesus and the Theater in Jerusalem." In *Jesus and Archaeology,* ed. James H. Charlesworth, 283–99. Grand Rapids: Wm. B. Eerdmans, 2006.

Limor, Ora, and Guy G. Stroumsa, eds. *Christians and Christianity in the Holy Land: From the Origins to the Latin Kingdoms.* Turnhout, Belgium: Brepols, 2006.

Linder, Amnon. *The Jews in Imperial Legislation.* Detroit: Wayne State University Press; Jerusalem: Israel Academy of Science and Humanities, 1987.

Lipschits, Oded. *The Fall and Rise of Jerusalem.* Winona Lake, Ind.: Eisenbrauns, 2005.

Lipschits, Oded. "Persian Period Finds from Jerusalem: Facts and Interpretations." *Journal of Hebrew Scriptures* 9 (2009): 2–30.

Lipschits, Oded, Yuval Gadot, Benjamin Arubas, and Manfred Oeming. "Palace and Village, Paradise and Oblivion: Unraveling the Riddles of Ramat Rahel." *NEA* 74 (2011): 2–49.

Lipschits, Oded, Yuval Gadot, Benjamin Arubas, and Manfred Oeming. "Ramat Rahel and Its Secrets." *Qadmoniot* 42 (2009): 58–77 (Hebrew).

Lipschits, Oded, Gary N. Knoppers, and Rainer Albertz, eds. *Judah and the Judeans in the Fourth Century B.C.E.* Winona Lake, Ind.: Eisenbrauns, 2007.

Lipschits, Oded, and Manfred Oeming, eds. *Judah and the Judeans in the Persian Period.* Winona Lake, Ind.: Eisenbrauns, 2006.

Lipschits, Oded, and David Vanderhooft. "A New Typology of the Yehud Stamp Impressions." *TA* 34 (2007): 12–37.

Lipschits, Oded, and David Vanderhooft. *Yehud Stamp Impressions: A Corpus of Inscribed Stamp Impressions from the Persian and Hellenistic Periods in Judah.* Winona Lake, Ind.: Eisenbrauns, 2011.

Lipschits, Oded, and David Vanderhooft. "Yehud Stamp Impressions in the Fourth Century B.C.E.: A Time of Administrative Consolidation." In *Judah and the Judeans in the Fourth Century B.C.E.,* ed. Oded Lipschits, Gary N. Knoppers, and Rainer Albertz, 75–94. Winona Lake, Ind.: Eisenbrauns, 2007.

Lupo, Eran. "A New Look at Three Inscriptions from Jaffa, Jerusalem, and Gaza." *Scripta Classica Israelica* 22 (2003): 193–202.

McCane, Byron R. "Miqva'ot." In *The Eerdmans Dictionary of Early Judaism,* ed. John J. Collins and Daniel C. Harlow, 954–56. Grand Rapids: Wm. B. Eerdmans, 2010.

McCane, Byron R. *Roll Back the Stone: Death and Burial in the World of Jesus.* Harrisburg: Trinity Press International, 2003.

McCane, Byron R. "Simply Irresistible: Augustus, Herod, and the Empire." *JBL* 127:4 (2008): 725–35.

McCready, Wayne O., and Adele Reinhartz, eds. *Common Judaism: Explorations in Second-Temple Judaism.* Minneapolis: Fortress, 2008.

MacMullen, Ramsay. "The Epigraphic Habit in the Roman Empire." *American Journal of Philology* 103 (1982): 233–46.

McNicoll, A. W., et al. *Pella in Jordan 2: The Second Interim Report of the Joint University of Sydney and College of Wooster Excavations at Pella, 1982–1985.* Sydney: Meditarch, 1992.

Magen, Itzhak. "Shechem: Neapolis." *NEAEHL* 4: 1354–59.

Magen, Yitzhak. *Purity Broke Out in Israel.* The Reuben and Edith Hecht Museum, University of Haifa, 1994.

Magen, Yitzhak. *The Stone Vessel Industry in the Second Temple Period: Excavations at Hizma and the Jerusalem Temple Mount.* Jerusalem: Israel Exploration Society, Israel Antiquities Authority.

Magen, Yitzhak, Haggai Misgav, and Levana Tsfania. *Mount Gerizim Excavations.* Vol. 1, *The Aramaic, Hebrew, and Samaritan Inscriptions.* Jerusalem: Israel Antiquities Authority, 2004.

Magen, Yitzhak, Y. Zionit, and E. Sirkis. "Kiryat Sefer: A Jewish Village and Synagogue." *Qadmoniot* 33 (1999): 25–32 (Hebrew).

Magen, Yizhaq, and Yuval Peleg. "Back to Qumran: Ten Years of Excavation and Research, 1993–2004." In *Qumran, the Site of the Dead Sea Scrolls: Archaeological Interpretations and Debates: Proceedings of the Conference Held at Brown University, November 17–19,* ed. Katharina Galor, Jean-Baptiste Humbert, and Jürgen Zangenberg, 55–113. Leiden: Brill, 2006.

Magness, Jodi. *The Archaeology of Qumran and the Dead Sea Scrolls.* Grand Rapids: Wm. B. Eerdmans, 2002.

Magness, Jodi. "In the Footsteps of the Tenth Roman Legion." In *The First Jewish Revolt: Archaeology, History, and Ideology,* ed. Andrea M. Berlin and J. Andrew Overman, 189–212. London: Routledge, 2002.

Magness, Jodi. "The Question of the Synagogue: The Problem of Typology." In *Judaism in Late Antiquity.* Part 3, *Where We Stand: Issues and Debates in Ancient Judaism.* Vol. 4, *The Special Problem of the Synagogue,* ed. Alan J. Avery-Peck and Jacob Neusner, 1–48. Leiden: Brill, 2001.

Magness, Jodi. "Qumran." In *The Eerdmans Dictionary of Early Judaism,* ed. John J. Collins and Daniel C. Harlow, 1126–31. Grand Rapids: Wm. B. Eerdmans, 2010.

Magness, Jodi. "Why Scroll Jars?" In *Religion and Society in Roman Palestine: Old Questions, New Approaches,* ed. Douglas R. Edwards, 170–87. New York: Routledge, 2004.

Mancini, Ignazio. *Archaeological Discoveries Relative to the Judaeao-Christians: Historical Survey.* Jerusalem: Franciscan Press, 1970.

Ma'oz, Z. "The Synagogue of Gamla and the Typology of Second-Temple Synagogues." In *Ancient Synagogues Revealed,* ed. Lee I. Levine, 35–41. Jerusalem: Israel Exploration Society, 1981.

Marcus, Joel. "*Birkat Ha-Minim* Revisited." *NTS* 55:4 (2009): 523–51.

Markschies, Christoph. "Intellectuals and Church Fathers in the Third and Fourth Centuries." In *Christians and Christianity in the Holy Land,* ed. Ora Limor and Guy G. Stroumsa, 239–56. Turnhout: Brepols, 2006.

Mason, Steve. *Flavius Josephus: Translation and Commentary.* Vol. 9, *Life of Josephus.* Leiden: Brill, 2001.

Mason, Steve. *Flavius Josephus: Translation and Commentary.* Vol. 1B, *Judean War 2.* Leiden: Brill, 2008.

Mazar, Amihai. *Archaeology of the Land of the Bible.* Vol. 1, *10,000–586 B.C.E.* New York: Doubleday, 1990.

Mazar, Amihai. "Beth-Shean from the Late Bronze Age IIB to the Medieval Period."

In *Excavations at Tel Beth-Shean, 1989–1996,* ed. A. Mazar and R. Muillins, 26–47. Jerusalem: Israel Exploration Society, 2007.

Mazar, Benjamin. "The Archaeological Excavations near the Temple Mount." In *Jerusalem Revealed: Archaeology in the Holy City, 1968–1974,* ed. Yigael Yadin, 25–40. Jerusalem: Israel Exploration Society, 1975.

Mazar, Benjamin. "Herodian Jerusalem in the Light of the Excavations South and Southwest of the Temple Mount." *IEJ* 28 (1978): 230–37.

Mazar, Benjamin. "The Tobiads." *IEJ* 7 (1957): 137–45.

Mazar, Benjamin, et al. "Jerusalem: The Early Periods and the First Temple Periods." *NEAEHL* 2: 698–804.

Mazar, Eilat, et al. "Jerusalem." *NEAEHL* 5: 1801–37.

Mazor, Gabi. "Beth-Shean: The Hellenistic to Early Islamic Periods: The Israel Antiquities Authority Excavations." *NEAEHL* 5: 1623–36.

Meshorer, Ya'akov. *Ancient Jewish Coinage.* Vol. 1, *Persian Period Through Hasmonaeans.* Dix Hill, N.Y.: Amphora, 1982.

Meshorer, Ya'akov. *City-Coins of Eretz-Israel and the Decapolis in the Roman Period.* Jerusalem: The Israel Museum, 1985.

Meshorer, Ya'akov. "The Coins of Caesarea Paneas." *INJ* 8 (1984–1985): 37–58.

Meshorer, Ya'akov. *Nabataean Coins.* Jerusalem: Institute of Archaeology, Hebrew University, 1975.

Meshorer, Ya'akov. *A Treasury of Jewish Coins.* Jerusalem: Yad Ben-Zvi Press, Nyack, N.Y.: Amphora, 2001.

Meshorer, Yaakov. *The Coinage of Aelia Capitolina.* Jerusalem: Israel Museum, 1989.

Meshorer, Yaakov. "The Coins of Dora." *INJ* 9 (1986–1987): 59–72.

Meshorer, Yaakov. "Sepphoris and Rome." In *Greek Numismatics and Archaeology: Essays in Honor of Margaret Thompson,* ed. O. Mørkholm and N. M. Waggoner, 159–71. Wetteren, Belgium: Cultura, 1979.

Meyers, Carol L., and Eric M. Meyers. *Haggai, Zechariah 1–8: Translation and Commentary.* Garden City, N.Y.: Doubleday, 1987.

Meyers, Carol L., and Eric M. Meyers. "The Persian Period at Sepphoris." *Eretz Israel* 29 (2009): 136–43.

Meyers, Carol L., and Eric M. Meyers. *Zechariah 9–14. Translation and Commentary.* Garden City, N.Y.: Doubleday, 1993.

Meyers, Eric M. "Ancient Synagogues: An Archaeological Introduction." In *Sacred Realm: The Emergence of the Synagogue in the Ancient World,* ed. Steven Fine, 3–21. New York: Oxford University Press, 1996.

Meyers, Eric M. "Aspects of Everyday Life in Roman Palestine with Special Reference to Private Domiciles and Public Baths." In *Jews in the Hellenistic and Roman Cities,* ed. John R. Bartlett, 211–20. London: Routledge, 2002.

Meyers, Eric M. "The Babylonian Exile Revisited: Demographics and the Emergence of the Canon of Scripture." In *Judaism and Crisis: Crisis as a Catalyst in Jewish Cultural History,* ed. Armin Lange, Diethard Roemheld, and Matthias Weigold, 61–73. Göttingen: Vandenhoeck and Ruprecht, 2011.

Meyers, Eric M. "The Ceramic Incense Shovels from Sepphoris: Another View." In

"I Will Speak Riddles of Ancient Times": Archaeological and Historical Studies in Honor of Amihai Mazar on the Occasion of His Sixtieth Birthday, ed. A. M. Maier and P. Miroschedji, 865–78. Winona Lake, Ind.: Eisenbrauns, 2006.

Meyers, Eric M. "The Dating of the Gush Halav Synagogue: Another Look at the Evidence." In *Judaism in Late Antiquity.* Part 3, *Where We Stand: Issues and Debates in Ancient Judaism.* Vol. 4, *The Special Problem of the Synagogue,* eds. Alan J. Avery-Peck and J. Neusner, 49–70. Leiden: Brill, 2001.

Meyers, Eric M. "Exile and Restoration in Light of Recent Archaeology and Demographic Studies." In *Exile and Restoration Revisited: Essays on the Babylonian and Persian Period in Memory of Peter R. Ackroyd,* ed. Gary N. Knoppers and Lester L. Grabbe with Deirdre Fulton, 166–74. London: T & T Clark, 2009.

Meyers, Eric. M. "From Myth to Apocalyptic: Dualism in the Hebrew Bible." In *Light Against Darkness: Dualism in Ancient Mediterranean Religion and the Contemporary World,* ed. Armin Lange, Eric M. Meyers, Bennie H. Reynolds, and Randall L. Styers, 92–106. Göttingen: Vandenhoeck and Ruprecht, 2011.

Meyers, Eric M., ed. *Galilee Through the Centuries: Confluence of Cultures.* Winona Lake, Ind.: Eisenbrauns, 1999.

Meyers, Eric M. "The Jesus Tomb Controversy: An Overview." *NEA* 69:3–4 (2006): 116–18.

Meyers, Eric M. "Jewish Art in the Greco-Roman Period: Were the Hasmonean and Herodian Eras Aniconic?" In *"Up to the Gates of Ekron": Essays on the Archaeology and History of the Eastern Mediterranean in Honor of Seymour Gitin,* ed. Sidnie White Crawford, 240–48. Jerusalem: W. F. Albright Institute of Archaeological Research and Israel Exploration Society, 2007.

Meyers, Eric M. "Jewish Culture in Greco-Roman Palestine." In *Cultures of the Jews,* ed. David Biale, 135–80. New York: Schocken, 2002.

Meyers, Eric M. "Khirbet Qumran and Its Environs." In *The Oxford Handbook of the Dead Sea Scrolls,* ed. Timothy H. Lim and John J. Collins, 21–45. Oxford: Oxford University Press, 2010.

Meyers, Eric M. "The Problem of the Scarcity of Synagogues from 70 to ca. 250 C.E.: The Case of Synagogue 1 at Nabratein (2nd–3rd Century C.E.)." In *"Follow the Wise" (B. Sanhedrin 32b): Studies in Jewish History and Culture in Honor of Lee I. Levine,* ed. Zeev Weiss, Oded Irshai, Jodi Magness, and Seth Schwartz, 433–46. Winona Lake, Ind.: Eisenbrauns, 2010.

Meyers, Eric M. "The Problems of Gendered Space in Syro-Palestinian Domestic Architecture: The Case of Roman-Period Galilee." In *Early Christian Families in Context: An Interdisciplinary Dialogue,* ed. David L. Balch and Carolyn Osiek, 44–66. Grand Rapids: Wm. B. Eerdmans, 2003.

Meyers, Eric M. "Sanders's 'Common Judaism' and the Common Judaism of Material Culture." In *Redefining First-Century Jewish and Christian Identities,* ed. Fabian E. Udoh, Susannah Heschel, Mark Chancey, and Gregory Tatum, 153–74. Notre Dame: University of Notre Dame Press, 2008.

Meyers, Eric M. "Sepphoris: City of Peace." In *The First Jewish Revolt: Archaeology, History, and Ideology,* ed. Andrea M. Berlin and J. Andrew Overman, 110–20. London: Routledge, 2002.

Meyers, Eric M. "The Shelomit Seal and Aspects of the Judean Restoration: Some Additional Observations." *Eretz Israel* 17 (1985): 33–38.

Meyers, Eric M. "The Torah Shrine in the Ancient Synagogue: Another Look at the Evidence." In *Jews, Christians, and Polytheists in the Ancient Synagogue,* ed. Steven Fine, 201–23. London: Routledge, 1999.

Meyers, Eric M., with S. Burt. "Exile and Return: From the Babylonian Destruction to the Beginnings of Hellenism." In *Ancient Israel: From Abraham to the Roman Destruction of the Temple,* ed. Hershel Shanks, 209–37. Third ed. Washington, D.C.: Biblical Archaeological Society, 2010.

Meyers, Eric M., A. Thomas Kraabel, and James F. Strange. *Ancient Synagogue Excavations at Khirbet Shema', Upper Galilee, Israel, 1970–1972.* Durham, N.C.: Duke University Press, 1976.

Meyers, Eric M., and Carol L. Meyers. *Excavations at Ancient Nabratein: Synagogue and Environs.* Winona Lake, Ind.: Eisenbrauns, 2009.

Meyers, Eric M., and Carol L. Meyers. "Response to Jodi Magness's Review of the Final Publication of Nabratein." *BASOR* 359 (2010): 67–76.

Meyers, Eric M., and Carol L. Meyers. "Sepphoris." *OEANE* 4: 527–36.

Meyers, Eric M., and James F. Strange. *Archaeology, The Rabbis, and Early Christianity.* Nashville: Abingdon, 1981.

Millar, Fergus. *The Roman Near East: 31 B.C.–337 C.E.* Cambridge: Harvard University Press, 1993.

Miller, Stuart S. "Some Observations on Stone Vessel Finds and Ritual Purity in Light of Talmudic Sources." In *Zeichen aus Text und Stein: Studien auf dem Weg zu einer Archäologie des Neunen Testamens,* ed. Stefan Alkier and Jürgen Zangenberg, 402–19. Tübingen: A. Francke Verlag, 2003.

Miller, Stuart S. "Stepped Pools, Stone Vessels, and Other Identity Markers of 'Complex Common Judaism.'" *JSJ* 41:2 (2010): 214–43.

Miller, Stuart S. "Those Cantankerous Sepphoreans Revisited." In *Ki Baruch Hu: Ancient Near Eastern, Biblical, and Judaic Studies in Honor of Baruch A. Levine,* ed. R. Chazan, W. W. Hallo, and L. H. Schiffman, 543–73. Winona Lake, Ind.: Eisenbrauns, 1999.

Mitternacht, Dieter. "Current Views on Jews and the Synagogue in Rome and Ostia." In *The Ancient Synagogue: From Its Origins Until 200 C.E.,* ed. Birger Olsson and Magnus Zetterholm, 521–71. Stockholm: Almqvist and Wiksell International, 2003.

Nagy, Rebecca Martin, Carol L. Meyers, Eric M. Meyers, and Zeev Weiss, eds. *Sepphoris in Galilee: Crosscurrents of Culture.* Raleigh: North Carolina Museum of Art, 1996.

Nakhai, Beth Alpert. "Beth-Zur." *OEANE* 1: 314.

Negev, Avraham. "Negev: The Persian to Byzantine Periods." *NEAEHL* 3: 1133–35.

Negev, Avraham. "Obodas the God." *IEJ* 36 (1986): 56–60.

Negev, Avraham. "The Temple of Obodas: Excavations at Oboda in July 1989." *IEJ* 41 (1991): 62–80.

Netzer, Ehud. *The Architecture of Herod the Great Builder,* paperback ed. Grand Rapids: Baker, 2008.

Netzer, Ehud. "The Augusteum at Samaria-Sebaste: A New Outlook." *Eretz Israel* 19 (1987): 97–105.

Netzer, Ehud. "Jericho: Telul Abu el-'Alayiq." *NEAEHL* 2: 682–91.

Netzer, Ehud. *The Palaces of the Hasmoneans and Herod the Great.* Jerusalem: Yad Ben-Zvi Press and Israel Exploration Society, 2001.

Netzer, Ehud. "A Synagogue from the Hasmonean Period Recently Exposed in the Western Plain of Jericho." *IEJ* 49 (1999): 203–21.

Nickelsburg, George W. E. *Ancient Judaism and Christian Origins: Diversity, Continuity, and Transformation.* Minneapolis: Fortress, 2003.

Notley, R. Steven. "Et-Tell Is *Not* Bethsaida." *NEA* 70:4 (2007): 220–30.

Notley, R. Steven. "Reply to Arav." *NEA* 74:2 (2011): 101–3.

Ofer, Avi. "Judea: Judean Hills Survey." *NEAEHL* 2: 815–16.

Oleson, John Peter, and Graham Branton. "The Technology of King Herod's Harbour." In *Caesarea Papers: Straton's Tower, Herod's Harbour, and Roman and Byzantine Caesarea,* ed. Robert Lindley Vann, 48–67. Ann Arbor, Mich.: Journal of Roman Archaeology, 1992.

Olsson, Birger, and Magnus Zetterholm, eds. *The Ancient Synagogue: From Its Origins Until 200 C.E.* Stockholm: Almqvist and Wiksell International, 2003.

Onn, A., S. Wexler-Bdolah, Y. Rapuanno, and T. Kanias. "Khirbet Umm el-'Umdan." *Hadashot Arkheologiyot: Excavations and Surveys in Israel* 14 (2002): 64–68. http://www.hadashot-esi.org.il/index_eng.asp.

Oren, Eliezer D. "Sinai." *OEANE* 5: 41–47.

Oren, Eliezer D. "Sinai: Northern Sinai." *NEAEHL* 4: 1386–96.

Oshri, Aviram. "Bet Lehem of Galilee." *Excavations and Surveys in Israel* 18 (1998): 29–30.

Ovadiah, Ruth, and Asher Ovadiah. *Hellenistic, Roman, and Early Byzantine Mosaic Pavements in Israel.* Rome: L'Erma di Bretschneider, 1987.

Overman, J. Andrew, Jack Olive, and Michael Nelson. "Discovering Herod's Shrine to Augustus." *BAR* 29:2 (2003): 40–49, 67–68.

Paget, J. Carleton. "Jewish Christianity." In *The Cambridge History of Judaism,* ed. W. Horbury, W. D. Davies, and John V. M. Sturdy, 3: 731–75. Cambridge: Cambridge University Press, 1999.

Parker, S. Thomas. "The Byzantine Period: An Empire's New Holy Land." *NEA* 62:3 (1999): 134–71.

Patrich, Joseph. "Caesarea." *NEAEHL* 5: 1673–80.

Patrich, Joseph. "Early Christian Churches in the Holy Land." In *Christians and Christianity in the Holy Land: From the Origins to the Latin Kingdoms,* ed. Ora Limor and Guy G. Stroumsa, 355–99. Turnhout, Belgium: Brepols, 2006.

Patrich, Joseph. "Herod's Theatre in Jerusalem: A New Proposal." *IEJ* 52 (2002): 231–39.

Patrich, Joseph, et al. "The Warehouse Complex and Governor's Palace (Areas KK, CC, and NN, May 1993–December 1995)." In *Caesarea Papers 2,* ed. Kenneth G. Holum, A. Raban, and J. Patrich, 70–108. Portsmouth, R.I.: Journal of Roman Archaeology, 1999.

Pfann, Stephen J. "Mary Magdalene Has Left the Room: A Suggested New Reading of Ossuary CJO 701." *NEA* 69:3–4 (2006): 130–31.

Piccirillo, M., and E. Alliata, eds. *The Madaba Map Centenary, 1897–1997: Travelling Through the Byzantine Period.* Jerusalem: Studium Biblicum Franciscanum, 1999.

Pixner, Bargil. "The History of the 'Essene Gate' Area." *ZDPV* 105 (1989): 96–104.

Plassart, A. "La synagogue juive de Délos." *Revue biblique* 23 (1914): 201–5.

Pollard, Nigel. *Soldiers, Cities, and Civilians in Roman Syria.* Ann Arbor: University of Michigan Press, 2000.

Porath, Yosef. "Caesarea: The Israel Antiquities Authority Excavations." *NEAEHL* 5: 1656–65.

Qedar, Shraga. "Two Lead Weights of Herod Antipas and Agrippa II and the Early History of Tiberias." *INJ* 9 (1986–1987): 29–35.

Raban, Avner. "Caesarea: Maritime Caesarea." *NEAEHL* 1: 286–91.

Rahmani, L. Y. *A Catalogue of Jewish Ossuaries in the Collection of the State of Israel.* Jerusalem: Israel Antiquities Authority, 1994.

Rainey, Anson F., and R. Steven Notley. *The Sacred Bridge: Carta's Atlas of the Biblical World.* Jerusalem: Carta, 2005.

Rajak, Tessa. *Josephus: The Historian and His Society.* 2nd ed. London: Duckworth, 2002.

Rajak, Tessa. "Jewish Millenarian Expectations." In *The First Jewish Revolt: Archaeology, History, and Ideology,* ed. Andrea M. Berlin and J. Andrew Overman, 164–88. London: Routledge, 2002.

Rappaport, Uriel. "The Great Revolt: An Overview." In *The Great Revolt in Galilee,* 9–13. Haifa: Hecht University Museum, 2008.

Rappaport, Uriel. "Numismatics." In *The Cambridge History of Judaism,* ed. W. D. Davies and Louis Finkelstein, 1: 2–59. Cambridge: Cambridge University Press, 1984.

Raynor, Joyce, and Ya'akov Meshorer with Richard S. Hanson. *The Coins of Ancient Meiron.* Winona Lake, Ind.: ASOR, Eisenbrauns, 1988.

Reed, Jonathan L. *Archaeology and the Galilean Jesus: A Re-Examination of the Evidence.* Harrisburg, Pa.: Trinity, 2002.

Reed, Jonathan L. "Instability in Jesus' Galilee: A Demographic Perspective." *JBL* 129:2 (2010): 343–65.

Regev, Eyal. "Non-Priestly Purity and Religious Aspects According to Historical and Archaeological Findings." In *Purity and Holiness: The Heritage of Leviticus,* ed. Marcel Poorthuis and Joshua Schwartz, 223–44. Leiden: Brill, 2008.

Reich, Ronny. "Archaeological Evidence of the Jewish Population at Hasmonean Gezer." *IEJ* 31 (1981): 48–52.

Reich, Ronny. "The 'Boundary of Gezer' Inscriptions Again." *IEJ* 40 (1990): 44–46.

Reich, Ronny. *Excavating the City of David: Where Jerusalem's History Began.* Jerusalem: Israel Exploration Society, 2011.

Reich, Ronny. "Miqwa'ot at Khirbet Qumran and the Jerusalem Connection." In *The Dead Sea Scrolls: Fifty Years After Their Discovery: Proceedings of the Jerusalem Congress, July 20–25, 1997,* ed. Lawrence H. Schiffman, Emanuel Tov, and James C. VanderKam, 728–31. Jerusalem: Israel Exploration Society, 2000.

Reich, Ronny. "Stone Scale Weights of the Late Second Temple Period from the Jewish Quarter." In *Jewish Quarter Excavations in the Old City of Jerusalem.* Vol. 3, *Area E and Other Studies, Final Report,* 329–88. Jerusalem: Israel Exploration Society and the Institute of Archaeology, Hebrew University, 2006.

Reich, Ronny. "The Synagogue and the *Miqveh* in Eretz-Israel in the Second–Temple,

Mishnaic, and Talmudic Periods." In *Ancient Synagogues: Historical Analyses and Archaeological Discovery,* ed. D. Urman and P. V. M. Flesher, 1: 289–97. Leiden: E. J. Brill, 1995.

Reich, Ronny, and Ya'akov Billig. "A Group of Theater Seats Discovered Near the South-Western Corner of the Temple Mount." *IEJ* 50:3–4 (2000): 175–84.

Reich, Ronny, and Yaakov Billig. "Jerusalem." *NEAEHL* 5: 1807–11.

Richardson, Peter. *Building Jewish in the Roman East.* Waco: Baylor University Press, 2004.

Richardson, Peter. *City and Sanctuary: Religion and Architecture in the Roman Near East.* London: SCM, 2002.

Richardson, Peter. *Herod: King of the Jews and Friend of the Romans.* Columbia: University of South Carolina Press, 1996.

Ritmeyer, Leen. *The Quest: Revealing the Temple Mount in Jerusalem.* Jerusalem: Carta, 2006.

Rives, James B. *Religion in the Roman Empire.* Malden, Mass.: Blackwell, 2007.

Rocca, Samuel. *Herod's Judaea: A Mediterranean State in the Classical World.* Tübingen: J. C. B. Mohr Siebeck, 2008.

Rodgers, Zuleika. "Monarchy vs. Priesthood: Josephus, Justus of Tiberias, and Agrippa." In *A Wandering Galilean: Essays in Honor of Sean Freyne,* ed. Zuleika Rodgers with Margaret Daly-Denton and Anne Fitzpatrick McKinley, 173–84. Leiden: Brill, 2009.

Roitman, Adolfo D. "From Dawn to Dusk Among the Qumran Sectarians." In *A Day at Qumran: The Dead Sea Sect and Its Scrolls,* ed. Adolfo D. Roitman, 19–22. Jerusalem: The Israel Museum, 1997.

Rollston, Christopher A. "Inscribed Ossuaries: Personal Names, Statistics, and Laboratory Tests." *NEA* 69:3–4 (2006): 125–29.

Runesson, Anders. "Persian Imperial Politics, the Beginnings of Public Torah Readings, and the Origin of the Synagogue." In *The Ancient Synagogue: From Its Origins until 200 C.E.,* eds. Birger Olsson and Magnus Zetterholm, 63–89. Stockholm: Almqvist and Wiksell International, 2003.

Safrai, Zeev. "The Gentile Cities of Judea: Between the Hasmonean Occupation and the Roman Liberation." In *Studies in Historical Geography and Biblical Historiography,* ed. Gerson Galil and Moshe Weinfeld, 63–90. Leiden: Brill, 2000.

Saldarini, Anthony J. "Good from Evil: The Rabbinic Response." In *The First Jewish Revolt: Archaeology, History, and Ideology,* ed. Andrea M. Berlin and J. Andrew Overman, 221–36. London: Routledge, 2002.

Sanders, E. P. "Jesus' Galilee." In *Fair Play: Diversity and Conflicts in Early Christianity,* ed. Ismo Dunderberg, Christopher Mark Tuckett, and Kari Syreeni, 3–41. Leiden: E. J. Brill, 2002.

Sanders, E. P. *Judaism: Practice and Belief, 63 B.C.E.–66 C.E.* London: SCM, and Philadelphia: Trinity, 1992.

Schäfer, Peter, ed. *The Bar Kokhba War Reconsidered.* Tübingen: Mohr Siebeck, 2003.

Schäfer, Peter. *The History of the Jews in Antiquity.* Luxembourg: Harwood Academic Publishers, 1995.

Schäfer, Peter, and Catherine Hezser, eds. *The Talmud Yerushalmi and Graeco-Roman Culture.* Vol. 2. Tübingen: Mohr Siebeck, 2000.

Scham, Sandra. "Trial by Statistics." *NEA* 69:3–4 (2006): 124–25.

Schaper, Joachim. "The Pharisees." In *The Cambridge History of Judaism,* ed. William Horbury, W. D. Davies, and John Sturdy, 3: 402–27. Cambridge: Cambridge University Press, 1999.

Schiffman, Lawrence H. "Miqsat Ma'asei Ha-Torah." In *Encyclopedia of the Dead Sea Scrolls,* ed. Lawrence H. Schiffman and James C. Vanderkam, 558–60. Oxford: Oxford University Press, 2000.

Schiffman, Lawrence H., and James C. Vanderkam, eds. *Encyclopedia of the Dead Sea Scrolls.* Oxford: Oxford University Press, 2000.

Schmitt-Korte, Karl. "Nabataean Coinage—Part II. New Coin Types and Variants." *Numismatic Chronicle* 150 (1990): 105–33.

Schofield, Alison. *From Qumran to the Yahad: A New Paradigm of Textual Development for The Community Rule.* Leiden: Brill, 2009.

Schofield, Alison. "Wilderness." In *The Eerdmans Dictionary of Early Judaism,* ed. John J. Collins and Daniel C. Harlow, 1293–94. Grand Rapids: Wm. B. Eerdmans, 2010.

Schürer, Emil. *The History of the Jewish People in the Age of Jesus Christ, 175 B.C.–A.D. 135,* new English version revised and edited by Geza Vermes and Fergus Millar. 3 vols. Edinburgh: T. & T. Clark, 1973.

Schwabe, Moshe, and Baruch Lifshitz, *Beth Shearim.* Vol. 2, *The Greek Inscriptions.* New Brunswick: Rutgers University Press, 1974.

Schwartz, Joshua J. "Archeology and the City." In Daniel Sperber, *The City in Roman Palestine,* 149–87. New York: Oxford University Press, 1998.

Schwartz, Joshua J. "Bar Qatros and the Priestly Families of Jerusalem." In *Jewish Quarter Excavations in the Old City of Jerusalem.* Vol. 3, *Area E and Other Studies, Final Report,* 308–19. Jerusalem: Israel Exploration Society and the Institute of Archaeology, Hebrew University, 2006.

Schwartz, Seth. *Imperialism and Jewish Society: 200 B.C.E. to 640 C.E.* Princeton: Princeton University Press, 2001.

Schwartz, Seth. *Josephus and Judaean Politics.* Leiden: Brill, 1990.

Segal, Arthur. *From Function to Monument.* Oxford: Oxbow Press, 1997.

Segal, Arthur. *Theatres in Roman Palestine and Province Arabia.* Leiden: E. J. Brill, 1995.

Segal, Arthur, and Michael Eisenberg. "Sussita-Hippos of the Decapolis: Town Planning and Architecture of a Roman-Byzantine City." *NEA* 70:2 (2007): 86–107.

Segal, Arthur, and Yehuda Naor. "Sha'ar Ha'amaqim." *NEAEHL* 4: 1339–40.

Segal, Peretz. "The Penalty of the Warning Inscription from the Temple of Jerusalem." *IEJ* 39 (1989): 79–84.

Shahar, Yuval. "Comparable Elements Between the Galilee and Judea in the Great Revolt." *The Great Revolt in the Galilee,* 29–37. Haifa: Hecht University Museum, 2008.

Shanks, Hershel. "New Synagogue Excavations in Israel and Beyond." *BAR* 37:4 (2011): 52–53.

Shanks, Hershel, and Ben Witherington, III. *The Brother of Jesus,* updated and expanded ed. San Francisco: HarperSanFrancisco, 2003.

Shatzman, Israel. *The Armies of the Hasmoneans and Herod.* Tübingen: J. C. B. Mohr (Paul Siebeck), 1991.

Siegelmann, Ayriel. "The Identification of Gaba Hippeon." *PEQ* 116 (1984–1985): 89–93.

Sivan, Hagith. *Palestine in Late Antiquity.* Oxford: Oxford University Press, 2008.

Sivan, Renée, and Giora Solar. "Excavations in the Jerusalem Citadel, 1980–1988." In *Ancient Jerusalem Revealed,* ed. Hillel Geva, 168–76. Jerusalem: Israel Exploration Society, 1994.

Smith, Robert H., and Anthony W. McNicoll. "The 1982 and 1983 Seasons at Pella of the Decapolis." *BASOR Supplement* 24 (1985): 21–50.

Snyder, Graydon F. *Ante Pacem: Archaeological Evidence of Church Life Before Constantine.* Atlanta: Mercer University Press, 1985.

Spijkerman, Augustus. *The Coins of the Decapolis and Provincia Arabia.* Jerusalem: Franciscan Printing Press, 1978.

Squarciapino, M. F. "The Synagogue at Ostia." *Archaeology* 16 (1963): 194–203.

Stager, Lawrence E. "Ashkelon." *NEAEHL* 1: 103–12.

Steffy, J. Richard, and Shelley Wachsmann. "The Migdal Boat Mosaic." In *The Excavations of an Ancient Boat in the Sea of Galilee (Lake Kinneret),* ed. Shelley Wachsmann. *Atiqot* 19 (1999): 115–18.

Stemberger, Günter. "The Sadducees—Their History and Doctrines." In *The Cambridge History of Judaism,* ed. William Horbury, W. D. Davies, and John Sturdy, 3: 428–43. Cambridge: Cambridge University Press, 1999.

Stepansky, Yosef, Yizhar Hirschfeld, and Oren Gutfeld. "Tiberias." *NEAEHL* 5: 2048–54.

Stern, Ephraim. *Archaeology of the Land of the Bible.* Vol. 2, *The Assyrian, Babylonian, and Persian Periods, 782–332 B.C.E.* New York: Doubleday, 2001.

Stern, Ephraim. "Dor." *NEAEHL* 5: 1695–1703.

Stern, Ephraim. *Dor: Ruler of the Seas.* Jerusalem: Israel Exploration Society, 1994.

Stern, Ephraim. "Goddesses and Cults at Tel Dor." In *Confronting the Past: Archaeological and Historical Essays on Ancient Israel in Honor of William G. Dever,* ed. Seymour Gitin, J. Edward Wright, J. P. Dessel, 177–80. Winona Lake, Ind.: Eisenbrauns, 2006.

Stern, Ephraim. "The Persian Empire and the Political and Social History of Palestine in the Persian Period." In *The Cambridge History of Judaism,* ed. W. D. Davies and Louis Finkelstein, 1: 70–87. Cambridge University Press, 1984.

Stern, Ephraim. "Zafit, Tel." *NEAEHL* 4: 1522–24.

Stern, Ephraim, and Yitzhak Magen. "Archaeological Evidence for the First Stage of the Samaritan Temple." *IEJ* 52 (2002): 49–57.

Stern, Ephraim, et al., eds. *Excavations at Dor: Final Report.* Vol. 1B. Jerusalem: Israel Exploration Society, 1995.

Stern, Sacha. "Babylonian Talmud, *Avodah Zarah* 16a: Paganism in Sepphoris—A Strange Baraita." Paper presented at Yeshiva University on March 28, 2011.

Stern, Sacha. "Rabbi and the Origins of the Patriarchate." *JJS* 54 (2003): 193–215.

Stewart, Andrew, and S. Rebecca Martin. "Hellenistic Discoveries at Tel Dor, Israel." *Hesperia* 72 (2003): 121–45.

Strange, James F. "Ancient Texts, Archaeology as Text, and the Problem of the First-Century Synagogue." In *Evolution of the Synagogue: Problems and Progress,* ed. Howard Clark Kee and Lynn H. Cohick, 27–45. Harrisburg: Trinity Press International, 1999.

Strange, James F. "Archaeological Evidence of Jewish Believers?" In *Jewish Believers in Jesus,* ed. Oskar Skarsaune and Reidar Hvalvik, 710–41. Peabody, Mass.: Hendrickson, 2007.

Strange, James F. "The Capernaum and Herodium Publications." *BASOR* 226 (1977): 65–73.

Strange, James F. "The Capernaum and Herodium Publications, Part 2." *BASOR* 233 (1979): 63–69.

Strange, James F., and Hershel Shanks. "Synagogue Where Jesus Preached Found at Capernaum." *BAR* 9 (1983): 24–31.

Sukenik, E. L. "The Earliest Records of Christianity." *American Journal of Archaeology* 51 (1947): 351–65.

Syon, Danny. " 'City of Refuge': The Archeological Evidence of the Revolt at Gamla." In *The Great Revolt in the Galilee,* 53–65. Haifa: Hecht University Museum, 2008.

Syon, Danny. "Coins from the Excavations at Khirbet esh-Shuhara." In *Eretz Zafon: Studies in Galilean Archaeology,* ed. Zvi Gal, 123–34. Jerusalem: Israel Antiquities Authority, 2002.

Syon, Danny. "The Coins from Gamla—an Interim Report." *INJ* 12 (1992–1993): 34–55.

Syon, Danny, and Zvi Yavor. "Gamala." *NEAEHL* 5: 1739–42.

Tabor, James D. *The Jesus Dynasty: The Hidden History of Jesus, His Royal Family, and the Birth of Christianity.* New York: Simon & Schuster, 2006.

Tabor, James D. "Testing a Hypothesis." *NEA* 69:3–4 (2006): 132–35.

Tal, Oren. *The Archaeology of Hellenistic Palestine Between Tradition and Renewal.* Jerusalem: The Bialik Institute, 2006 (Hebrew).

Talgam, Rina, and Zeev Weiss. *The Mosaics of the House of Dionysos at Sepphoris: Excavated by Eric M. Meyers, Ehud Netzer, and Carol L. Meyers.* Jerusalem: Institute of Archaeology, Hebrew University of Jerusalem, 2004.

Talmon, Shemaryahu. "Calendars and Mishmarot." In *Encyclopedia of the Dead Sea Scrolls,* ed. Lawrence Schiffman and James C. Vanderkam, 108–16. Oxford: Oxford University Press, 2000.

Taylor, Joan. *Christians and the Holy Places: The Myth of Jewish Christian Origins.* Oxford: Oxford University Press, 1993.

Taylor, Joan. "The Classical Sources on the Essenes and the Scrolls Communities." In *The Oxford Handbook of the Dead Sea Scrolls,* ed. Timothy H. Lim and John J. Collins, 173–99. Oxford: Oxford University Press, 2010.

Taylor, Joan. "Khirbet Qumran in Period III." In *Qumran, the Site of the Dead Sea Scrolls: Archaeological Interpretations and Debates; Proceedings of the Conference Held at Brown University, November 17–19,* ed. Katharina Galor, Jean-Baptiste Humbert, and Jürgen Zangenberg, 133–46. Leiden: Brill, 2006.

Taylor, L. R. "Tiberius' Refusals of Divine Honors." *Transactions of the American Philological Association* 60 (1929): 87–101.

Tepper, Yotam, and Leah Di Segni. *A Christian Prayer Hall of the Third Century C.E. at*

Kefar 'Othnay (Legio): Excavations at the Megiddo Prison 2005. Jerusalem: Israel Antiquities Authority, 2006.

Testa, E. *Cafarnao IV: I graffiti della casa de S. Pietro.* Jerusalem: Franciscan Printing Press, 1972.

Testa, Emmanuele. "Il Golgota, Porta della Quiete." In *Studia Hierosolymitana in Onore del P. B. Bagatti, I, Studie Archaeologici,* ed. Emmanuele Testa, Ignazio Mancini, Michele Piccirillo, 197–244. Jerusalem: Franciscan Printing Press, 1976.

Theissen, Gerd, and Annette Merz. *The Historical Jesus: A Comprehensive Guide.* Trans. John Bowden. Minneapolis: Fortress, 1998.

Trümper, Monica. "The Oldest Original Synagogue Building in the Diaspora: The Delos Synagogue Reconsidered." *Hesperia* 73 (2004): 513–98.

Tzaferis, Vassilios. "Crucifixion: The Archaeological Evidence." *BAR* 11:1 (1985): 44–53.

Tzaferis, Vassilios. "Cults and Deities Worshipped at Caesarea Philippi-Banias." In *Priests, Prophets, and Scribes,* ed. Eugene Ulrich et al., 190–204. Sheffield: Sheffield Academic Press, 1992.

Tzaferis, Vassilios, and Moshe Hartal. "Banias." *NEAEHL* 5: 1587–93.

Udoh, Fabian E. "*Jewish Antiquities* XV.205, 207–8 and 'The Great Plain.'" *PEQ* 134 (2002): 130–43.

Udoh, Fabian E. *To Caesar What Is Caesar's: Tribute, Taxes, and Imperial Administration in Early Roman Palestine, 63 B.C.E.–70 C.E.* Providence: Brown Judaic Studies, 2005.

Udoh, Fabian E., Susannah Heschel, Mark Chancey, and Gregory Tatum, eds. *New Views of First-Century Jewish and Christian Self-Definition.* Notre Dame: University of Notre Dame Press, 2008.

Ussishkin, David. "Lachish." *NEAEHL* 3: 897–911.

van der Horst, Pieter W. "Inscriptions." In *The Eerdmans Dictionary of Early Judaism,* ed. John J. Collins and Daniel C. Harlow, 763–66. Grand Rapids: Wm. B. Eerdmans, 2010.

Vanderkam, James C. *The Dead Sea Scrolls Today.* Grand Rapids: Wm. B. Eerdmans, 1994.

Weber, Thomas M. "Gadara and the Galilee." In *Religion, Ethnicity, and Identity in Ancient Galilee,* ed. Jürgen Zangenberg, Harold W. Attridge, and Dale B. Martin, 449–77. Tübingen: Mohr Siebeck, 2007.

Weinberg, J. P. "Demographische Notizen zur Geschichte der nachexilischen Gemeinde in Juda." *Klio* 54 (1972): 45–59.

Weinberg, Saul S. "Tel Anafa: The Hellenistic Town." *IEJ* 21 (1971): 86–109.

Weinberg, Saul S. "Tel Anafa: The Second Season." *Muse* 4 (1970): 15–24.

Weiss, Ze'ev. "Adopting a Novelty: The Jews and the Roman Games in Palestine." In *The Roman and Byzantine Near East.* Vol. 2, ed. J. H. Humphrey, 23–50. Portsmouth, R.I.: Journal of Roman Archaeology, 1999.

Weiss, Ze'ev. "Notes and News: Sepphoris (Sippori), 2009." *IEJ* 60 (2010): 98–107.

Weiss, Zeev. "Artistic Trends and Contact Between Jews and 'Others' in Late Antique Sepphoris: Recent Research." In *Religious Diversity in Late Antiquity,* ed. David M. Gwynn and Susanne Bangert, 167–88. Leiden: Brill, 2010.

Weiss, Zeev. "Buildings for Entertainment." In Daniel Sperber, *The City in Roman Palestine,* 77–91. New York: Oxford University Press, 1998.

Weiss, Zeev. "Sepphoris." *NEAEHL* 5: 2029–35.

Welles, C. B. "The Inscriptions." In *Gerasa: City of the Decapolis,* ed. Carl H. Kraeling, 355–496. New Haven, Conn.: American Schools of Oriental Research, 1938.

White, L. Michael. *Building God's House in the Roman World: Architectural Adaptation Among Pagans, Jews, and Christians.* Baltimore: The Johns Hopkins University Press, 1990.

White, L. Michael. "The Delos Synagogue Revisited: Recent Fieldwork in the Graeco-Roman Diaspora." *Harvard Theological Review* 80 (1987): 133–60.

Wightman, G. J. *The Walls of Jerusalem: From the Canaanites to the Mamluks.* Sydney: Meditarch, 1993.

Wilken, Robert Louis. *The Land Called Holy: Palestine in Christian History and Thought.* New Haven: Yale University Press, 1994.

Wilkinson, John, trans. *Egeria's Travels to the Holy Land.* Rev. ed. London: SPCK, 1981.

Wilson, John Francis. *Caesarea Philippi: Banias, the Lost City of Pan.* London: I. B. Tauris, 2004.

Wise, Michael O. "Bar Kokhba Letters." In *The Eerdmans Dictionary of Early Judaism,* ed. John J. Collins and Daniel C. Harlow, 415. Grand Rapids: Wm. B. Eerdmans, 2010.

Wood, Bryant G. "To Dip or Sprinkle? The Qumran Cisterns in Perspective." *BASOR* 256 (1984): 45–60.

Yadin, Yigael. *Bar-Kokhba: The Rediscovery of the Legendary Hero of the Last Jewish Revolt Against Imperial Rome.* London: Weidenfeld and Nicolson, 1971.

Yadin, Yigael. *The Ben Sira Scroll from Masada.* Jerusalem: The Israel Exploration Society and the Shrine of the Book, 1965.

Yadin, Yigael. *The Finds from the Bar-Kochba Period in the Cave of Letters.* Jerusalem: Israel Exploration Society, 1963.

Yadin, Yigael. *Masada: Herod's Fortress and Zealots' Last Stand.* London: Weidenfeld and Nicolson, 1966.

Yadin, Yigael. "The Synagogue at Masada." In *Ancient Synagogues Revealed,* ed. Lee I. Levine, 19–23. Jerusalem: Israel Exploration Society, 1981.

Yellin, Joseph, and Magen Broshi. "Pottery of Qumran and Ein Ghuweir: The First Chemical Exploration of Provenience." *BASOR* 321 (2001): 65–78.

Zangenberg, Jürgen. "Between Jerusalem and the Galilee: Samaria in the Time of Jesus." In *Jesus and Archaeology,* ed. James H. Charlesworth, 393–432. Grand Rapids: Wm. B. Eerdmans, 2006.

Zangenberg, Jürgen. "Common Judaism and the Multidimensional Character of Material Culture." In *Redefining First-Century Jewish and Christian Identities,* ed. Fabian E. Udoh, Susannah Heschel, Mark Chancey, and Gregory Tatum, 175–93. Notre Dame: University of Notre Dame Press, 2008.

Zangenberg, Jürgen. "Opening Up Our View: Khirbet Qumran in Regional Perspective." In *Religion and Society in Roman Palestine: Old Questions, New Approaches,* ed. Douglas R. Edwards, 170–87. New York: Routledge, 2004.

Zangenberg, Jürgen K., and Dianne Van De Zande. "Urbanization." In *The Oxford Handbook of Jewish Daily Life in Roman Palestine,* ed. Catherine Hezser, 165–88. Oxford: Oxford University Press, 2010.

Zayadine, Fawzi. "'Iraq el-Emir." *OEANE* 3: 177–81.

Zias, Joseph. "Whose Bones?" *BAR* 24:6 (1998): 40–45, 64–65.

Zissu, Boaz, and David Amit. "Common Judaism, Common Purity, and the Second Temple Period Judean Miqwa'ot (ritual immersion baths)." In *Common Judaism: Explorations in Second-Temple Judaism,* ed. Wayne O. McCready and Adele Reinhartz, 47–62. Minneapolis: Fortress, 2008.

Subject Index

Bes, 245

Bible, canonization of, 111–12, 204

bishops, 180

boule, 14, 145, 209, 232, 264, 277

burial practices, 25, 40–41, 79–80, 104–5, 137. *See also* ossuary

Burnt House, 133, 134, 148, 156–57

Byzantine Period, 189, 285, 319n31

Caiaphas, 130

Caligula, 255

Capitoline Triad, 254, 269

Caracalla, 277, 318n25, 319n35

Cassius Dio, 169

chi rho, 185, 186, 189

church (building), 187, 190–93, 285–87, 288, 289, 290, 293

Church of the Holy Sepulcher, 180–82, 183, 254, 285–86, 293

Church of the Nativity, 292

Church of Saint Joseph, 198

circus, 266, 268

city plan, 4, 63, 121, 250, 265

clothing, 171

coins

   as evidence of paganism, 241, 245, 246, 255

   Byzantine-period, 188, 286

   civic, 15, 17, 44–45, 46, 78, 99, 143, 144, 152, 167, 241, 245, 248, 249, 252, 253–54, 256, 257, 262, 264, 269, 277, 318n23, 319n35

   Hasmonean, 30, 33, 34, 35, 36, 37, 44–46, 121

   Herodian, 70, 77–78, 116–17, 119, 120, 121, 122, 123, 124, 125, 126, 128, 255, 256, 258

   Iturean, 30, 44

   Jewish Revolt, 59, 149, 151–52, 168

   Judea Capta, 128

   Nabatean, 44, 45

   procuratorial, 129

   Ptolemaic, 16, 21–22, 44

   Roman imperial, 262, 264

   Seleucid, 35

   of Yehud, 5–6, 21–22

colonies, Roman, 167, 262, 264, 268–69

columns, Greek, 19, 36, 40–41, 43, 57, 60, 64, 69, 70, 76, 213, 215, 243, 244, 249

"Common Judaism," 48, 49, 108–10, 138, 237–38

Community Rule (1QS), 92, 108, 234

Constantine, 180, 285, 293

Copper Scroll, 88, 89

cross, as symbol, 185–86, 189, 286–287

crucifixion, 176

Cybele, 245, 247

Damascus Document (CD), 92, 108

Dead Sea Scrolls, 30, 47, 83–84, 88–89, 105–6, 110–11

deities, syncretism of, 239–40

Demeter, 245, 257

Derketo, 248

Deuteronomy, 111

Diadochi, 14–15

Diocletian, 285

Dionysos, 249, 254, 257, 272, 274, 275–76, plates 14–16

Dioscuri, 241, 245, 248

Dome of the Rock, 53

domus ecclesiae, 190–94, 222, 310n39

Dushara (Dusares), 247, 248

Eastern Terra Sigillata, 36, 91, 107, 136

Ecce Homo arch, 269

Egeria, 182, 191

Egyptian influence, 21, 241, 242–43, 244, 245, 247, 248, 257

Egyptians, in Palestine, 7

epigraphic habit, 245, 264, 286

Eros, 245, plate 15

erubim, 31–32, 104

Essene Quarter, 97

Essenes, 47, 87–88, 92, 95, 96, 97, 99, 100, 164, 204

Esther, 111–12

ethrog, 59, 168, 187, 288

Eusebius, 180, 291–92

Fifth Syrian War, 25

figural representation in Jewish art, 41, 45, 77, 78, 123, 129, 133, 230, 232, 287

figurines, 35, 122, 241, 242, 243–45, 247, 252, 254, 257, 278, 316n18

fortress, 43–44, 71–76, 159. *See also* Antonia Fortress; Baris fortress

forum, 69, 268

"Four Seasons" (artistic motif), 288

Index of Place Names

Maps of the region are found on pages 29, 51, 115, 127, and 218

Index of Passages Cited